MANAGING
MEDIA WORK

MANAGING MEDIA WORK

Mark Deuze | editor

Indiana University
Leiden University

Los Angeles | London | New Delhi
Singapore | Washington DC

For information:

SAGE Publications, Inc.
2455 Teller Road
Thousand Oaks, California 91320
E-mail: order@sagepub.com

SAGE Publications Ltd.
1 Oliver's Yard
55 City Road
London EC1Y 1SP
United Kingdom

SAGE Publications India Pvt. Ltd.
B 1/I 1 Mohan Cooperative Industrial Area
Mathura Road, New Delhi 110 044
India

SAGE Publications Asia-Pacific Pte. Ltd.
33 Pekin Street #02-01
Far East Square
Singapore 048763

Printed in the United States of America

Library of Congress Cataloging-in-Publication Data

Deuze, Mark.
Managing media work / editor, Mark Deuze.
    p. cm.
Includes bibliographical references and index.
ISBN 978-1-4129-7124-9 (pbk.)
  1. Mass media—Management. I. Title.

P96.M34D47 2011
302.23068—dc22   2010013966

This book is printed on acid-free paper.

10   11   12   13   14   10   9   8   7   6   5   4   3   2   1

Acquisitions Editor:	Todd R. Armstrong
Editorial Assistant:	Nathan Davidson
Production Editor:	Libby Larson
Copy Editor:	Melinda Masson
Typesetter:	C&M Digitals (P) Ltd.
Proofreader:	Jenifer Kooiman
Indexer:	Sheila Bodell
Cover Designer:	Emily Merkley
Marketing Manager:	Helen Salmon

Contents _____

SECTION III: MEDIA PROFESSIONS

Key media professions are investigated in terms of the changing nature of work in these professions, focusing on concepts like portfolio work-lives, patchwork and boundaryless careers, re- and multiskilling, the learning economy and the learning organization, creative management, individualization of work, and the shift toward project- or team-based labor.

Preface _____

The *Managing Media Work* volume comprises work by 27 leading scholars in the fields of media management, media production, and media policy studies. Early in 2009 the various authors were asked to write original essays based on one key question: how they see their work contributing to a critical understanding of the management of media work. More specifically, it was suggested that this essay answer the question of what media managers (and media workers in general) should know about their work and how it could or should influence their work as they face increasingly complex issues regarding global, digital, and mobile media life (Deuze, 2011). The result is a distinctive book, offering a comprehensive view on the theory and practice of working in the media in the digital age; managing careers, projects, and companies in the media; and preparing for a life either in such industries or as a scholar of the media.

The idea for this book came from the research I did for *Media Work*, a book published by Polity Press (in 2007), which featured a review of the key issues facing and structuring the experiences of professionals working in journalism, advertising, marketing communications, public relations, computer and video game development, and film and television production. For that book my colleagues, students, and I interviewed over 600 media professionals in four countries (the United States, The Netherlands, South Africa, and New Zealand). I furthermore analyzed trade publications and Weblogs by media practitioners in these countries and studied the vast literature across disciplines as varied as economic geography, media studies, management and economics, organizational psychology, and cultural sociology where scholars talked with, discussed, or otherwise included media professionals and their production practices in research projects. When I finished chapters for *Media Work* on specific media professions, I asked experienced professionals working in such industries (whom I knew personally, generally having met them during the course of working on the book) to read the drafts and tell me whether they recognized the picture I was painting of their industry and their work style. One recurring element in all these interviews and e-mail discussions with people inside the creative industries was a general concern about management. As numerous people told me, "Sure, this is all pretty much on target, but who you should really be talking with is management."

In short, the problem of contemporary media work, as felt and experienced by its practitioners, is management. This does not just reflect what Zygmunt Bauman (2005) has called "a perpetual casus belli" (p. 55), as in the constant struggle between the cultural producer's craving of creative freedom and management's pressure to produce commercially viable and therefore market-oriented products. It is also not necessarily just a reflection of people complaining about those who govern their decisions, on whose livelihoods they depend. Given the increasingly global, networked, and unpredictable nature of the media industry, and the growing complexities of media work (determined in part by rapid technological developments), the challenge to the future of media work seems to be a uniquely managerial one. Yet this challenge all too often seems to go unmet by the people put in place as managers. Management is seen here not in traditional terms—as in designing business models, contemplating finance and accounting mechanisms, structuring strategic partnerships—but more in humanistic terms: the management of talent (both of yourself and others) and the management of your individual career in the media. This gives unique focus to the *Managing Media Work* volume and allows it to fill a gap in the current literature on media management and production.

Scholarship on the production side of media industries is relatively scarce (when considered next to content analysis and audience research) but growing as the prominence of media production in a worldwide "cultural economy" (du Gay & Pryke, 2002) increases, next to global concerns about the changing nature of (media) work. Next to this dearth of knowledge about what actually goes on inside various companies and organizations, the literature that is available tends to discuss the management of creative industries largely in the context of business structures, general economics, and unique high-profile cases (generally focusing on big-name corporations or exceptional firms). One of the most problematic results from this curious phenomenon is that students who enter media industries may understand the impact this industry has on audiences and politics (as these are the dominant areas of media and communication research and teaching), but generally they are not empowered to understand how and why the industry works the way it does or how contemporary worldwide social and technological changes and challenges—such as globalization, individualization, convergence, and fragmentation—affect the everyday managerial and creative practices throughout the industry.

By explaining, contextualizing, and thus understanding the changing nature of managing media work, this book not only hopes to prepare media students to become competent media practitioners; it also helps students become critically competent citizens in what Roger Silverstone (2007) has called the contemporary "mediapolis": society as a mediated public space where media underpin and overarch the experiences of everyday life. This is a society where meaningful distinctions between public and private life, work time and nonwork time, local and global, or lived and mediated reality are quickly fading. Furthermore, by focusing on the similarities of issues facing different professions and fields of cultural production, the volume acknowledges the likely boundaryless and portfolio career path of media and communication graduates, who will be moving from job to job, within and between converging multiple media organizations and networks. This reader will offer them a glimpse of their future and empower them to face it head-on.

The primary audience for this book consists of students in schools, departments, and programs in information science, journalism, advertising, games, film and television, and more broadly communication and media. The target reader is a student about to graduate or starting graduate school, looking toward either a career in media industries or a future as an academic studying the media production process. Some key educational markets include a growing number of creative industries and media management–related programs of study around the world. The book is also useful for general courses on media and society, media economics, or media and culture and can be of particular value to vocational programs seeking to add context and background to the training of media practitioners. The primary market for the book is, given the geographic location of the authors and examples used, international (based on their country of residence and national identity, the authors in this book represent 10 different nationalities).

The authors all offer overviews of their current and past work in the field of media management and production studies and offer theoretical insight and critical discussion, as well as practical advice for students and media professionals alike. The book will be of greatest value in courses where students are encouraged to design their career plans, develop business proposals, or otherwise engage in both individual and collective reflection on how they see their professional identity and social responsibility as media practitioners in the context of a rapidly evolving global cultural economy.

In conclusion, I sincerely hope this book will fill a void in the literature and inspire research questions and a renewed focus on (and respect for) the talent that makes up the creative industry workforce. This book completely relies on the brilliance of its contributors, all of whom are scholars whose work I came to admire in the course of my career. In fact, I originally put together the potential contributors by making a list of people I consider myself a fan of first. I am humbled by and deeply grateful for the enthusiasm, dedication, and inspiration of the authors featured in this volume.

Much thanks to the graduate students in my media work courses at Indiana University, who "road-tested" this volume and offered invaluable feedback. Furthermore, I'd like to thank Todd Armstrong and Nathan Davidson at SAGE for supporting this project.

As always, I look forward to hearing any comments you, the reader, undoubtedly have.

References

Bauman, Z. (2005). *Liquid life*. Cambridge, England: Polity Press.

Deuze, M. (2007). *Media work*. Cambridge, England: Polity Press.

Deuze, M. (2011). *Media life*. Cambridge, England: Polity Press.

du Gay, P., & Pryke, M. (Eds.). (2002). *Cultural economy: Cultural analysis and commercial life*. London, England: Sage.

Silverstone, R. (2007). *Media and morality: On the rise of the mediapolis*. Cambridge, England: Polity Press.

1 Managing Media Work

Mark Deuze and Brian Steward

People spend more time with media today than at any previous point in history. The number of media channels, forms, genres, devices, applications, and formats is proliferating—more media get produced every year. Yet at the same time, the news about the media as an industry is less than optimistic. Reports about massive layoffs in all the creative industries—most notably film and television entertainment, journalism, digital game development, and advertising—are paramount. This suggests a fascinating paradox: As people engage with media in an increasingly immersive, always-on, almost instantaneous and interconnected way, the very people whose livelihood and sense of professional identity depend on delivering content and experiences across such media seem to be at a loss on how to come up with survival strategies—in terms of business models, effective regulatory practices (for example regarding copyrights and universal access provisions), and perhaps most specifically the organization of entrepreneurial working conditions that would support and sustain the creative process needed to meet the demands of a global market saturated with media. In this book, different fields of study regarding the media as a creative industry are brought together to articulate a new theorization and practical implementation of strategic management in recognition of the changing ways in which people use media in their lives—living a life not *with* but rather *in* media.

This book and research project combines work and insights from specifically three strands of research and teaching on the media: management and organization, cultural policy and economics, and labor and work. The project can therefore be seen as an attempt to integrate theories of how media industries function in society, theories of how media professionals manage their individual careers and professional identity in this context, and case-based work on how media industries manage creativity and innovation. The assumption is that the combination of these perspectives will help articulate the gap (better yet: the bridge) between theory and practice in media management and work. Our approach to managing media work stems from a few key considerations about the field of media management:

- Media management tends to be underexplored and undertheorized (see especially the contribution of Bozena I. Mierzejewska for a critical articulation of this observation).

- Most media management research does not look across boundaries between media professions or academic disciplines (see, for example, chapters by Annet Aris, Geert Lovink and Ned Rossiter, and Tim Marjoribanks).

- The traditional tendency in much of the field has been to artificially maintain distinctions between management and creativity, which (with Chris Bilton) we find unhelpful.

- Media management should take an integrative, holistic approach—something advocated by many yet practiced by few.

Of crucial importance here is our conceptualization of media management as the management of companies as well as careers in the media. Particularly the latter part of this equation is largely absent from the literature in the field, as it tends to focus on either specific industries (journalism or Hollywood, for example), specific aspects of businesses within these industries (copyright enforcement, revenue models, product differentiation, concentration of ownership), or specific cases of company and firm projects (change management, work floor culture). We postulate that the addition of (individual or group) careers is of added value here for two key reasons: first, the ongoing casualization and individualization of labor and working conditions of professionals throughout the creative industries and, second, a motivation based on pedagogy. In a media-saturated world where cultural production and consumption dominate everyday life, it is not surprising schools, departments, programs, and courses in information science, (tele-) communication, journalism, and (digital) media studies attract more students every year. In fact, such departments are among the most popular units in contemporary higher education—whether it is in sub-Saharan Africa, Latin America, Southeast Asia, or Western Europe. The vast majority of undergraduate and graduate students majoring in these disciplines want to either work in media industries, manage media companies, or study and understand how the industry and its creative process work.

However, it proves to be difficult to adequately convey the complexity and dynamics of what it is like to work (anywhere) in the creative industries by a traditional pedagogical focus on the industry as the domain of corporations and companies. Such an institutional approach gets particularly enforced by relying on the literature (which, as we have argued, has generally omitted the individual from its consideration of media management) and by delegating "real world" experience to the realm of industry through the encouragement of internships and apprenticeships within such institutions. We do not claim that this approach is wrong or that it should be reversed. We argue, however, that theoretically the work that companies and firms do has increasingly less to do with the lived experience of working in the media, and that the models for media management and managing careers in the media need reconsideration. In this essay, we seek to integrate the work of the various authors in this book and the fields they reference into a coherent framework for studying (and, hopefully, practicing) media management and media work.

The Context of Managing Media Work

As a first step, we consider that what drives contemporary media management and media work in all the creative industries is a general shift in power away from professional content creators to users and owners (Annet Aris, Chris Bilton, Mark Deuze and Leopoldina Fortunati, Lucy Küng, Marina Vujnovic and Dean Kruckeberg). Control over storytelling (including the authority over what kind of stories are told and how they are told) and resources (needed to creatively and effectively convey these stories) gets whisked away from professionals and flows toward audiences and corporations, further emphasizing the hourglass structure of the industry (where a handful of corporations interact with hundreds of thousands of small firms and individuals on a global scale).

As more focus is placed on user-generated content and consumer engagement, and as corporate media owners gain control over their workforce (either by increasingly focusing on outsourcing production to loosely affiliated networks of professionals and firms or by abandoning production altogether in a bid to control the marketing and distribution of content produced elsewhere), those who professionally create content are left more or less powerless. In this way, work is being outsourced to both ends of the labor spectrum, leaving many media professionals alienated as exemplified by a constant and ongoing struggle for work and the loss of a direct sense of creative autonomy. A first key factor influencing our understanding of what goes on across the industry is therefore an overall precarity in media work.

Second, managing media work must be seen within the larger social architecture of which it is part. This means taking into consideration every factor contributing to the organization of media companies and careers: content, processes, people, technology, and all other variables—not in the least including the implicit and unconscious aspects of organizational life such as beliefs, values, and emotions that can have a tremendous influence on planning and behavior. Managing media work is necessarily made up of both material and immaterial factors, which must be considered in conjunction. In other words, a key approach to media management is focusing on the many resources (both human and nonhuman) that combine to form the source of all media action. By thinking in terms of such factors that make up the broad context within which media work takes place, we (following Liz McFall) emphasize both the distributed and the hybrid nature of media work. Media work does not simply involve the transfer of information (of books into treatments into screenplays into movies into franchises into . . .) but is instead involved in complex networks of information and understanding, including those of competition, markets, organization and structure, industry standards, technologies, and the evolving media environment (Susan Christopherson, Terry Flew, Tim Marjoribanks).

Arguably the most powerful of these influences or factors that are to be considered in media managerial strategy is the role of technology (Lucy Küng, Philip Napoli, Marina Vujnovic and Dean Kruckeberg). The plethora of technological innovations being developed and incorporated into society on a daily basis serve to supplement and undermine previous technologies. This shift presents media companies and individual professionals with the challenge of constant adaptation to the emergence of new technologies and the progressive abandonment of the old. In turn, the media as an industry (including its professionals) are at the forefront of supercharging the development of and demand for technological innovation. This is a fundamental stress point in any consideration of managing media work.

Similar to the process of adaptation to technological development is the challenge of adapting to the evolution of media content models. Business models are, like media technologies in general, always already remediated: When new models emerge, old models are supplemented and only rarely displaced. The broad shift in formulating business models that the media industries are experiencing is one from an emphasis on mass content to niche content and to participatory and user-generated content. Media products are becoming increasingly hybridized and are thus difficult to place into categories that can be isolated and therefore effectively managed. Overall, however, communication (between phases of the creative process, between elements of the global production network, and between technologies and practices, as well as between producers and consumers) is just as important of a function as content itself.

In relation to this increasing emphasis on niche-oriented and participatory media, the third influence on media strategy is the consumers' relationship with content. With technological advances facilitating the offering of niche products and an increased level of user participation, the industry-driven construction of audiences is progressing from a mass of static objects that simply accept and take in the media to active cocreators and people variously labeled by industry observers and scholars as "pro-ams," "amafessionals," "produsers," and "prosumers." Although this trend is supported by data showing a growing group of people (especially teenagers) actively sharing, cocreating, and up- and downloading content online, the audience seen as more or less passive consumers is just as much a product of industry rhetoric as the audience perceived as proactively cocreating media. Either way, this forces media managers and workers to rethink their processes and practices when making content and designing user experiences.

The contextual challenges that contribute to managing media work as discussed above are contributing to a different and much more unstable environment than in the past. Additionally, rising costs, declining revenue (especially from advertising), and increasing competition require companies and individuals to adapt to working with scarce resources. We suggest that this leads to an increased focus on idiosyncratic creativity as a necessity to rise above the many challenges and win the ongoing competition for market demand. In short, more creativity and innovation on both the firm and the individual level means more success and a greater competitive advantage (Pablo J. Boczkowski, Mark Deuze and Leopoldina Fortunati, Bozena I. Mierzejewska).

Understanding Media Management: The Macro Level

In order to accomplish an understanding of the management practices of media organizations and professionals, one necessary step is to consider media relationships at the macro, meso, and micro levels (Tim Marjoribanks). Managing media work can be viewed on these three levels as both separated and integrated.

At the macro level of media production industry regulations, technology, and competition are taken into consideration. The current major issue on the macro level of production is the shaping of new industries based on a New International Division of Cultural Labor (Toby Miller). In today's creative industries, all production is global, and all labor is local. The global movement of companies into emerging markets, deploying dynamic outsourcing and offshoring techniques, and stimulating runaway production (in all corners of the globe) benefits new locations by providing periods of increased local labor and jobs (Alisa Perren, Keith Randle). However, this is only sustained as long as the incentive to work in the given locale lasts. After a brief period of increased employment and productivity, the jobs and opportunities move on to the next place. This trend of increasingly "weightless" production affects job markets not only in Hollywood or the film industry (which indeed is suffering from the ongoing loss of employment in traditional key markets) but also in communities and media disciplines all over the globe that are hit by this cycle of accelerating global production networks.

At the macro level, we are seeing two seemingly contradictory trends. First, new small media firms are forming at unusually high rates (Charles H. Davis, Eric Harvey). This would suggest a cycle of self-renewal while also implying a strong entrepreneurial spirit in the industry, ensuring innovation and the generation of new media firms. Second, we are witnessing high levels of ownership concentration. At the same time, creative industries have come to rely on the "Hollywood model" as a way to organize their work flow and creative processes (Susan Christopherson). This vertical disintegration also involves

outsourcing and downsizing and has led to large pools of media workers leading precarious lifestyles. These workers, hired on short-term or no-term contracts, can never quite be sure where their next paychecks are coming from.
While some workers enjoy the freedom and sense of self-reliance this affords,
others find the insecurity stifling, which leads to a high rate of burnout
(Rosalind Gill, Aphra Kerr).

At the same time, in an effort to become known as creative cities, both
local- and state-level governments will pass tax incentives to attract media
companies. In a sort of policy hopscotch, local, regional, and national governments compete with one another to put together the most attractive package. What the cities and regions involved tend to have in common is a
crumbling industrial base they are scrambling to replace with the youthful
energy and dynamic spending patterns that are expected of the creative industries, yet when the next-best deal comes along, media companies will follow.
What they often leave in their wake is a new generation of media workers
seduced into a precarious lifestyle by the lure of media life.[1]

Understanding Media Management: The Meso Level

The meso level of managing media work considers the methods, culture,
strategies, and policies that shape media production. Of particular concern
on this level is the organizational management technique incorporated by
(professionals working in or for) media companies. In a time of increasing
precariousness across the creative industries, Rupert Murdoch's News
Corporation has managed to rise above most effects, making for an interesting target of observation. In looking at the style that has enabled this corporation to prevail in a time of failure, one will find a hands-off approach
to management in which there is little communication between separate fac-
tions (Tim Marjoribanks). This is indicative of the flexible and individualized trend that has become popular on the meso level of production, where
large corporations are considered not as a whole but as the wide variety of
small cells of which they are composed. An analogy to the loose organization of terrorist cells (that can suddenly spring into action but lay dormant
for large swaths of time) is somewhat appropriate for considering the mean-
dering networks of small companies competing around the world for projectized work, generally financed through large corporate parents or holding
firms (Aphra Kerr, Sean Nixon, Alisa Perren).

At the meso level, content has taken on a new identity. If, in the past, content was considered king, now it is safe to say content is *kings* (Annet Aris).
We live in an age of remix and remixability, where consumers in this convergence culture are no longer considered to be "just" consumers. Content today
takes on a wide variety of shapes and sizes, none of which look much like

those of the old days of linear value chains premised on the creation of specific content for specific channels using specific formats, as content is now:

- Content à la carte (made on demand, for niches or even individuals, customizable and editable).

- Content everywhere (adapted for multiple formats, distributed across many channels).

- Content for free (where content is an excuse for the commoditization of experiences).

- User-generated content (including practices of open-sourcing and crowdsourcing, and a decentering of content cocreation via online social networks).

- Global content (as content gets localized around the world).

- Content about content (the fastest-growing sector of content creation, including any and all advertising, marketing communications, and promotions, importantly including the notion of self-branding of media companies, work groups, and individuals largely through spec work).

One key focus in the field of media management must be the interdependency between the creative and managerial roles within media industries (Chris Bilton). In recent history, many changes have led to the devaluing of content as the core asset of or unique selling point for the creative industries. Technological, economic, social, and cultural changes have, instead, facilitated a rapid rise of a rather weightless global market based on access to more or less unique services and experiences—a shift from a "things to own" to a "things to do" economy. The relation of this trend to that of the evolving association between management and creativity is that the traditional (and often preferred) model of creative production—where individual artists are seen to create distinct, one-of-a-kind works—seems to be waning. Instead, a more complex model is developing in which individual creativity must be incorporated and embedded into large-scale networked production of all kinds of assets and deliverables, including but most definitely not limited to content. This growing bond between creativity and management as caused by a gradual devaluing of cultural content can be attributed to several trends.

The first of these trends is a shift in the function of media in society. In today's culture, more attention is focused on the delivery of the content than on the raw content itself. In a media economy where more and more focus is placed on conversation and cocreation, as opposed to simple consumption, media users are seen as more interested in the experiences and services that they can gain than the content itself. This general shift in media use has served to devalue the process of content creation (Annet Aris, Mark Deuze and Leopoldina Fortunati).

A second trend contributing to the devaluing of central content is the recent reemphasis on craft as an integral part of production (Chris Bilton, Toby Miller). The increased complexity of production due to technological advancements and global production networks has led to a newly developed labor force of craftspeople and those with highly specialized work skills, distributed all over the world (yet concentrated in specific regions). While the artists create the ideas, it requires another substantial workforce to craft the raw content into final, marketable products and experiences.

A third important trend is a change in society's outlook on media products. Regarding products previously viewed as unique and individual pieces of art, there is now a growing awareness of the role of consumers in shaping and cocreating value-added content. As mentioned before, this makes a consideration of the user as competitor-colleague central to the analysis and practice of managing media work.

Understanding Media Management: The Micro Level

The micro is the smallest level of managing media work, on which we consider the interactions and relationships that make up a company as a generally loosely integrated collective of collaborating individuals, or an individual's approach to her career. A key insight here relates to the construction of professional identity for media workers. Traditionally, and following from the primacy of content as an individual artist's providence, this has been the identity of a "soloist" (Annet Aris). However, in an age of remix and convergence culture and cross-media and multiplatform integration, bringing together the work of others in a meaningful and creative way seems not just a valuable but an increasingly crucial skill (Chris Hackley and Amy Tiwsakul, Jane B. Singer). In other words, capitalizing on the hybrid nature of contemporary cultural production— by synthesizing the work of colleagues, consumers, and companies—can be considered the foundation of a new sense of professional identity.

Media workers and managers today have moved away from the old notion of value chains and toward a more flexible, overlapping set of skills and competences, where individuals can no longer afford to concentrate on their own silo (Chris Bilton). Today's media worker, to survive, has to have a working knowledge of more than her immediate duties. To function effectively within a value network, she must also understand the roles of those around her and how they fit together. These are the types of skills that most likely will pay off when the value networks mature and move on (generally grounding in "know-who" rather than "know-how" types of considerations) to the next projectized enterprise. The paradox here is that while such advice seems empowering, it at the same time inevitably leads to greater precarity in the lives of the professionals involved.

Considering the changing nature of content on the meso level of media management and the devaluation of content creation as a core corporate practice on the macro level, one may wonder what remains to be done at the micro level of media work for the individual professional or tiny firm to survive. We assume a shift in professional identity formation from content creation as a soloist to the remixed performance of a superstar DJ (Annet Aris, Chris Bilton). The unique talent of the DJ is the creation of what can be described as meta-ideas: ideas that support the production and transmission of other ideas. By finding, editing, and remixing multiple strands of information and ideas, the DJ provides a platform for creativity and innovation crucial to survival in today's convergent industry and marketplace. Second, the DJ is a superstar largely based on her performance—both "live" as at work (on stage) and in between projects (shows, concerts) in the maintenance of a cult of personality by regularly updating (and upgrading) her image through, for example, online social networks and personal Web sites (Charles H. Davis, Chris Hackley and Amy Tiwsakul, Alisa Perren, Jane B. Singer). This manufacturing and performing of superstardom—of an *authentic talent*—is, in other words, not only telling a story about (and perhaps showing) being good at something. It is also about carefully cultivating and producing that image of being good.

Discussion and Conclusion

At the present time, research of the media industry in all its facets as discussed above tends to make four mistakes in its assessments, which we package in the following four statements:

- Opportunities for talent, excellence, success, and new sources of revenue automatically increase due to everything that is happening.

- Everything we hold dear about the nature of creative work and the identity of the artist is going down the drain.

- We are witnessing a time of epic transformation.

- Things change only gradually, if at all.

Rather than stepping into these traps, we advocate a more nuanced and grounded approach by looking across boundaries and disciplines, attempting to integrate new perspectives into today's style of managing media work. To better understand organizational practice, we look at the forces shaping today's media landscape—which necessarily include the political economy of new media, the individual and networked sources of creativity and innovation, and the enabling role of policymakers on the local, national, and international level (Terry Flew, Toby Miller, Philip Napoli).

An important question when considering the current practice and future of managing media work is why we still talk about firms, companies, and organizations in an era that seems to celebrate looseness and noncommitment (Geert Lovink and Ned Rossiter). The framing of this question suggests the answer lies in looking at media management differently—which is what we have aimed for in this admittedly brief, less than comprehensive, introductory essay. The recent history of managing media work suggests that media firms and scholars have gone through three phases of asking questions about the future of the media industry (questions and answers that, of course, exist side by side, do not replace what came before, and can even occur more or less simultaneously within the same corporation or holding company):

- How can we create and maintain the perfect digital or multimedia corporation of the (near) future?

- How can we effectively separate the mature business of offline production and the emerging business of online?

- How can we carefully build integrated functionalities, knowledge-sharing practices, and creative synergies across media companies and between media professionals (whom we employ or subcontract to)?

We suggest a new focus for media management research and teaching, considering what may be the new networks emerging throughout the creative industries, not necessarily tied to specific companies, products, or places, that define new and evolving constellations of skill sets, practices, and beliefs that could provide a road map through the morass of the contemporary creative industries. Added to that, we suggest that this focus include an emphasis on the role of the individual in negotiating these waters: as a soloist, a superstar DJ, a global networker, a form of self-programmable labor, and a critical student of her own role and professional identity.

Our essay has as its goal to outline the framework for this particular search. As it is also an indirect critique of the existing literature in the field of management and organization studies, we hope to inspire a more comprehensive approach to the study of managing media work. In other words, this essay is intended as a meta-idea.

Note

1. The precarity of working in the media internationally is something the first author of this piece explored in his book *Media Work*, published in 2007 by Polity Press.

SECTION I

Management and the Creative Industries

2 Media Management in Theory and Practice

Bozena I. Mierzejewska

In the field of mass communication, the term *theory* is often loosely defined. Paradigms, conceptual frameworks, models, normative theories, and, of course, actual theories are all frequently referred to as "theory," although they represent very different constructs. As traditionally defined in science, a theory is a systematically related set of statements about the causes or relationships underlying observable phenomena (Rudner, 1966). Theories are developed by abstracting from observation and are confirmed through repeated experiments designed to test hypotheses related to a theory. The result is often the development of law-like generalizations about underlying causes and relationships. The purpose of a theory is to increase scientific understanding through a systemized structure capable of both explaining and predicting phenomena (Hunt, 1991).

Accepted theories become a part of our understanding and are the basis for further explorations of less understood areas. Being a statement of cause and effect, they help us predict with a certain degree of confidence future consequences of our current actions. Sound theories also help describe what is happening and why; hence they are valuable tools for data interpretation. For all of their usefulness, theories do have limitations: First, they are focused and very specific, and therefore they cannot give full explanations of all factors involved. This very characteristic usually results in deterministic explanations. Second, they tend to be based on narrow, unrealistic assumptions. Theories aim to develop models used for predictions of future behavior and consequences, but they need to deal with complications of the unpredictability of individual humans and social groups.

Although most of the theories and conceptual frameworks from which media management research draws are based in organizational studies, the field of media management is distinctive in a number of ways. First, media organizations produce information products rather than tangible products, and the underlying economic characteristics of information products differ from those of other types of tangible goods in critical ways. These fundamental economic characteristics are related to crucial differences in demand, production, market, and distribution conditions, creating a very different management environment than what is found in many other industries. Most important, media products have extremely high social externality value because of the central role information and media content plays in economic, political, and social processes. Because media are one of the critical infrastructure industries in society, media management practices have implications far beyond the purely economic concerns of corporate investors. Thus, while media management research shares with organizational studies a concern with financial outcomes, the field extends its focus to include study of the effects of organizational management on media content and society. This very feature distinguishes the field of media management from the field of organizational studies. Indeed, Ferguson (1997) argued that until media management scholars develop distinctive theories that go beyond economics and applied management, it will be difficult to argue that media management is a domain of inquiry separate from either mass communication or organizational studies.

Even though media management aims to build a bridge between the general management theory and the specificities of the media industry, the field is far from being clearly defined or cohesive (Küng, 2007). Additionally it is underexplored and undertheorized. The subject of media management has been approached from media-related disciplines that are not necessarily anchored in the study of organizations such as media economics, political economy, journalism, and communications (Mierzejewska & Hollifield, 2006). This implies that the range of theories used in media management research is equally diverse. The remaining pages of this chapter will discuss main theoretical approaches used in the media management scholarship.

Theories Used in Media Management Research___

Strategic Management Theory

Strategic management has been the most widely used theoretical or conceptual framework in media management studies to date. Numerous case studies and analyses have been conducted in an effort to understand why some media firms outperform others, which is the primary focus of strategic management research. Those studies have addressed such issues as explaining the strategy of media market concentration (Albarran, 2002; Compaine & Gomery, 2000), adapting to changing market conditions (Greco, 1999; Picard, 2004),[1] and exploring strategic options for companies operating in various markets and regulatory settings (Gershon, 2000; Hoskins, Finn, & McFadyen, 1994).[2]

Two conceptual frameworks for studying strategic management are recognized as dominant (Chan-Olmsted, 2003a). The first builds on industrial-organization concepts and what has come to be known as the structure-conduct-performance (SCP) framework. The SCP approach focuses on the structure of industries and the linkage between an industry's structure and organizational performance and conduct. According to the SCP framework, the "structure" of an industry (e.g., number, size, and location of firms) affects how firms behave (or their individual or collective "conduct"). In turn, the industry's "performance" is related to the conduct of firms.

For media management scholars, "performance" stands for both economic performance—the traditional measure in organizational studies—and social responsibilities that media need to fulfill for the betterment of a democratic society (Fu, 2003). Studies that have applied the SCP paradigm to the media industry are numerous (Ramstad, 1997; Wirth & Bloch, 1995; Young, 2000).

The second strain of strategic management research, known as the resource-based view (RBV), builds on the assumption that each firm is a collection of unique resources that enable it to conceive and implement strategies. RBV strategies suggest that firms should discover those assets and skills that are unique to their organizations and cannot be imitated, thus protecting the organization with knowledge barriers (Barney & Hesterly, 1996). This approach is especially important and meaningful in the media industry due to the unique economic characteristics of information products (Chan-Olmsted, 2003b). In a content analysis of media strategy research, Chan-Olmsted (2003a) identified an even split between the SCP and RBV approaches in strategic management research on media companies.

A third important approach to studying strategic management that has emerged in the media management field is based on ecological niche theory from the biological sciences (Dimmick, 2003). Niche theory posits that industries occupy market niches just as biological species occupy ecological niches. The theory has proved valuable in examining competition among media corporations for scarce resources such as advertisers and audiences. It also helps explain how sectors of the media industry adapt to new competition such as that from the Internet or other new media and technologies.

Although the SCP and RBV approaches and niche theory represent the most frequently used theoretical approaches to studying strategic management, the study of strategy covers a wide range of other topics. Market-entry strategy, branding, joint-venture management, and new-product development are only a few of the more specific topics that can be conceptualized and studied as elements of strategic management. As research on the strategic management of media companies continues, the field may succeed in developing strategic theories specific to the media industry that take into account the special economic, social, and regulatory environments in which media industries and organizations operate.

Structural Theories

The primary approach in organizational studies to the study of issues of organizational structure has been the structural contingency theory. Structural contingency theories describe the relationships between organizational structures and performance outcomes. Grounded in assumptions of economic rationality, structural contingency theory argues that organizations will adopt structures that maximize efficiency and optimize financial performance according to the specific contingencies that exist within the organization's market environment (Donaldson, 1996). Consequently, there is no single organizational structure that will be equally effective for all companies.

Within media management research, structural contingency theory in its classic form has been little used. This may change in the future as the structures of media organizations grow increasingly complex through media consolidation and as variances in performance across seemingly similar media corporations become more evident. But if media scholars have invested little effort in exploring the effects of organizational structures on economic performance, they have, instead, developed a related but unique stream of research. That research concerns the effects of media ownership structures on media content and organizational priorities. This research stream first emerged in the 1970s in response to consolidation in the newspaper industry and today continues to be a major focus of research. It concentrates mainly on the effects of newspaper chain ownership on media content as compared to independent ownership. The types of effects on content that have been studied have included endorsements of political candidates, editorial positions on current issues, hard news and feature news coverage, and coverage of conflict and controversy in the community (Busterna & Hansen, 1990; Glasser, Allen, & Blanks, 1989). Although there have been some contradictory findings, most studies have concluded that ownership structures do affect content, although the mechanism by which that influence occurs continues to be debated.

More recently, the focus of media management research on ownership structures has shifted from comparing the effects of chain and independent ownership to comparing the effects of public and private ownership (Lacy & Blanchard, 2003; Picard & van Weezel, 2008). This research suggests pressure from financial markets to maximize investor returns is reducing the resources publicly owned media corporations invest in newsrooms and content production. That, in turn, is presumed to reduce the quality of the news and entertainment products those companies produce, although the connection between reduced newsroom resources and reduced content quality has not yet been fully established.

Finally, another related area of research concerning the impact of media ownership structures focuses on the effects of such structures on news managers' professional values and priorities, which are assumed to shape news decisions and the organizational resources invested in news coverage (Fedler & Pennington, 2003).

Important to note is that the majority of research on the effects of ownership structures on media content has focused on newspaper content. Relatively few structural studies have examined broadcast content. This, no doubt, has much to do with the affordability and accessibility of newspaper content as a subject of analysis compared to television and radio content. However, in the face of the rapid consolidation in the electronic sectors of the media industry since 1996, the increase in television and radio duopolies, and the development and diffusion of central casting models among broadcasters, there is a clear need to expand the samples used in media structure content research to include broadcast organizations.

Transnational Media Management Theory

In the past two decades, the rapid movement of media companies into the global markets has spurred a corresponding surge in research on transnational media management and economics (see also Tim Marjoribanks, in this volume). The topic has attracted interest for a number of reasons. There are many unanswered questions about how the kinds of consolidation and diversification involved in the global expansion affect corporate financial returns; how globalization impacts the content and quality of news, films, and other media products produced for a corporation's home market; how media management structures and practices shape the products and content produced for audiences in foreign markets; and, subsequently, how that content then impacts the politics, economics, cultures, and public interest in the countries that receive it.

One of the challenges of transnational media management research is developing theoretical or conceptual frameworks through which the phenomenon can be studied. Because transnational management includes so many different management topics, there is no single theoretical base for approaching research. This problem is characteristic of international business research in general (Parker, 1996). Indeed, perhaps the only unifying conceptual element in transnational organizational research is the assumption that having operations in multiple national markets will affect organizations or organizational outcomes in some way.

Research has tended to cluster around issues of organizational structure, strategy, and policy (Gershon, 2000). Relatively few studies have addressed specific issues of functional management such as finance, cross-cultural personnel management, leadership, product development, and operational coordination (Altmeppen, Lantzsch, & Will, 2007; Hoskins & McFadyen, 1993; Wasko, 1998). And few scholars have yet ventured into studies of human agency in transnational media management such as how leadership, social networks, and decisions influence global media expansion, product development, and outcomes. The use of such a variety of conceptual and theoretical frameworks has created a rich and wide-ranging view of transnational media management issues. However, it also has created a smorgasbord of only marginally related findings that offer little in-depth understanding of any particular issue or phenomenon. Far more systematic, programmatic research in specific areas of organizational structure, strategy, function, and leadership will be necessary before the field can claim to have a true understanding of the management issues and challenges facing transnational media corporations and their host countries.

Organizational Culture Theory

Culture is a powerful force within organizations. Organizational culture shapes decisions, determines priorities, influences behaviors, and impacts outcomes (Schein, 1992). It can be a source of organizational strength or a factor in organizational weakness. In media management, organizational culture became a topic of widespread research interest in the late 1990s and the early 21st century at least in part because journalists and financial analysts blamed organizational culture clashes for many of the problems that developed in major media corporations during that period (Ahrens, 2004; Klein, 2002; Landler & Kirkpatrick, 2002).

The concept of organizational culture has its roots in anthropology. Although the term *culture* has been defined in many ways, most definitions recognize that culture is historically and socially constructed; includes shared practices, knowledge, and values that experienced members of a group transmit to newcomers through socialization; and is used to shape a group's processes, material output, and ability to survive (Bloor & Dawson, 1994).

Organizational cultures are the product of a number of influences including the national culture within which the organization operates, the long-term influence of the organization's founder or early dominant leaders as well as its current leadership, and the organization's operating environment. The company's primary line of business, the technologies of production it employs, and the market environment in which it competes are components of the operating environment. Thus, in the media industry, companies operating in the same industry sector, such as television stations, would be expected to share some characteristics of organizational culture because of the similarities in their products, markets, and technologies, while they would be expected to differ culturally from newspapers and radio stations for the same reasons.

Within most media organizations, there also exist multiple professional and occupational subcultures. Professional cultures unite individuals within the same occupation, even though they work for different organizations (Toren, 1969). The presence and mix of professional subcultures within an organization influence the culture of the overall organization, while the interaction between competing occupational subcultures within the company influences organizational behavior and climate. Research suggests that conflict between organizational and professional cultures is common. In general, organizational cultures are viewed by professionals as impinging upon professional norms, freedom of action, and commitment to service of the public interest. Similar tensions occur between coexisting occupational subcultures within an organization.

Examination of media management research suggests that the application of organizational culture theory as a base for studying media organizations and management practices is relatively new, and the number of media management studies clearly grounded in culture theory remains small. An important example of these studies is an examination of the influence of corporate culture on the ability of news organizations to adapt to changing market conditions (Küng, 2000; see also her chapter in this volume).

In subsequent years, the underlying constructs of organizational and professional culture theory have infiltrated a wide range of media studies such as news construction, gatekeeping, ownership effects, and organizational innovation. News construction research is the study of how variables such as newsroom structures, news routines, the demographic profile of journalists, and journalists' relationships with sources affect the selection and framing of news stories. Within the news construction research tradition, research on news routines examines the processes journalists use in their work and the way those routines—or professional cultural norms—influence story and source selection (Hirsch, 1977). Another related area of study has been how the technologies of media production, a factor in organizational culture, influence the professional norms of news routines (Abbott & Brassfield, 1989; Killebrew, 2003).

Technology and Innovation

The management of innovation has been identified as one of the most critical areas of research for the field of media management and economics. This assertion was supported by a surge in published research on the management of technology and innovation in media organizations, which began around 2000 (Mierzejewska & Hollifield, 2006). Moreover, technological change is an inevitable and underlying force of progress in media industries. Volume and velocity of those changes pose a great challenge to all media sectors (Küng, 2007). This research focus on technology and innovation reflects the fact that the media are one of a handful of industries facing the emergence of potentially "disruptive" technologies. Disruptive technologies are defined as "science-based innovations that have the potential to create a new industry or transform an existing one" (Day & Schoemaker, 2000, p. 2).

The Internet, interactive television devices, and e-books are examples of the types of communication technologies that, when they emerge, have the potential to significantly disrupt the underlying business models of existing sectors of the media industry. Understanding the development, adoption, and economic and social impacts of new technologies on the media industry and its products is important to a wide range of stakeholders: media managers and professionals, economists, investors, policymakers, and consumers. Consequently, there is a need for programmatic research on technologies and innovations in media that will contribute to the development of innovation management theory.

The notion of "innovation" is defined as a subset of technology, but also technology is a subset of the broader construct of organizational change (Dougherty, 2006). By conceptualizing technology as "disruptive" and "nondisruptive" it is argued that organizations approach technology adoption and innovation management differently depending on the disruptive or nondisruptive potential of the technology or innovation in question (Christensen & Overdorf, 2000). The strategic importance of managing innovations and, closely related to them, creativity and creative processes is discussed in subsequent chapters of this book.

As yet, no consensus has developed among scholars regarding how media technologies are to be defined or classified, and such consensus is likely to be difficult, if not impossible, to develop in the future. The absence of consistent classification schemes almost certainly will hinder the development of theory in the study of media technologies. These definitional challenges notwithstanding, most research on technology and innovation in organizations is grounded in some underlying assumption about the nature of the technology and its role in the organization. Some of the more commonly used conceptual frameworks used to study technology and innovations in media organizations include the following:

- **New product development theory.** This approach sees new products, technologies, and innovations as a strategic weapon. The importance attached to new-product development reflects the fact that an organization's ability to innovate successfully has been linked to financial performance. Within the media management and mass communication literature, there has been relatively little examination of new-product development processes. Franke and Schreier (2002) studied how the Internet could be used as a new-product development tool for producers in all kinds of industries, and Saksena and Hollifield (2002) examined the internal organizational structures that U.S. newspapers had used to develop online editions as a new product. However, in general, organizational approaches to new-product development in the media industry have been a neglected area of research.

- **Diffusion theory.** Another conceptual approach to research on new media products is the use of diffusion theory, which is also known as *adoption of innovations* research. Diffusion theory is probably most frequently used to understand consumer behavior in response to new media technologies. The theory holds that the successful diffusion of innovations occurs according to a predictable pattern that moves from the "change agent," who introduces the innovation, to the "laggards," who refuse to accept it (Rogers, 1995). Demographic factors such as age, education, and income have been found to be at least somewhat related to consumers' willingness to adopt innovations. Diffusion theory helps explain a number of factors in new-product development, including success, failure, and pricing. In media management and economics research, diffusion theory has been used to examine consumer behavior in relationship to a large number of new media products and technologies, including DVD technology (Sedman, 1998), digital cable (Kang, 2002), digital broadcast television (Atkin, Neuendorf, & Jeffres, 2003), high-definition television (Pashupati & Kendrick, 2008), and the Internet (Hollifield & Donnermeyer, 2003). However, relatively few media management scholars have used diffusion theory to look at organizational adoption issues within media companies (Lawson-Borders, 2003).

- **Effects of adoption on organizations and employees.** Although few media management scholars have examined the processes of organizational technology adoption, quite a few have studied the effects of organizational technology adoption on media work processes and media professionals (Achtenhagen & Raviola, 2009). This research, although limited in scope, suggests that the introduction of new media production technologies decreases job satisfaction in the short term, changes job roles, forces media professionals to learn new skills, increases production time, and decreases the time spent developing content. However, the studies also suggest that the negative effects of new technologies dissipate over time.

- **Uses and gratifications.** This is a framework through which consumer behavior in regard to new media products and services has been examined. The *uses and gratifications* approach looks at the ways consumers use media and the utilities they receive from that use. Uses and gratifications is a conceptual framework rather than a theory, and generally it is used to describe and classify audience behavior rather than to predict it. Lacy and Simon (1993) identified five basic uses or gratifications that people receive from consuming media products: surveillance of the environment, decision making, entertainment and diversion, social cultural interaction, and self-understanding. Although uses and gratifications has been widely used to understand other aspects of media-use behavior, it has been less frequently applied as a framework for understanding consumers' use of new media technologies and products (Rao, 2001; Yi & Sung, 2007).

Leadership Theory

The topic of leadership is the most neglected area of research and theory development in the field of media management (Mierzejewska & Hollifield, 2006). This is not to say that leadership is considered unimportant. Much of what is written by journalists is about the role that one or more media executives have played in controlling and managing media companies.

But despite assumptions about the relationship between leadership and media organizations' behavior and performance, there has been very little systematic research by media management scholars on leadership behavior and effects. Although the subject is generally well covered by media management textbooks (Albarran, 2002; Küng, 2008; Redmond & Trager, 2004; Wicks, Sylvie, Hollifield, Lacy, & Sohn, 2004), the number of scholarly studies of media leadership that have used primary data and have been published in media management journals has been surprisingly small.

Within organizational studies, leadership incorporates a fairly wide array of topics, all of which are focused on issues of human behavior. These issues include leadership traits and styles, follower traits and styles, leadership contingencies and situations, decision-making styles, communication styles, motivation and job satisfaction, the acquisition and use of power within organizations, and managing change, to name just a few. Most theories of leadership and associated subjects are based in psychological theory.

In the media management literature, only a handful of studies have directly or indirectly examined leadership issues. These have looked at such topics as the relationship between leadership and change (Küng, 2000; Perez-Latre & Sanchez-Tabernero, 2003), organizational problems (Sylvie, 2003), and organizational values and priorities (Demers, 1996).

Motivation is another area of leadership research that has been largely ignored by media management scholars. The single area of motivation that has been seriously examined in the field is job satisfaction among journalists. The research shows that among journalists, the factors that contribute to job satisfaction vary by age and industry sector (Pollard, 1995). However, journalists are generally more satisfied when they believe they are producing a high-quality news product that keeps the public informed (Weaver & Wilhoit, 1991) and when they have good relationships with management, job autonomy (Bergen & Weaver, 1988), and higher social status (Demers, 1996). In other words, journalists tend to be intrinsically motivated and focus more on professional values than organizational values (see also Mark Deuze and Leopoldina Fortunati, in this volume).

An area of leadership research that began attracting attention from media scholars early in the 21st century is change management. In a changing economic, regulatory, and technical environment, change has become almost the only constant in the organizational environment of media companies. Indeed, many economists and organizational scholars believe that only organizations that are able to constantly change and adapt will succeed in the 21st century.

A handful of scholars have studied change management in the media, usually focusing on the effects of change on newsrooms and journalists (Killebrew, 2003; Perez-Latre & Sanchez-Tabernero, 2003). Generally, these studies have found that change is disruptive. However, the research generally also indicates that leadership plays a central role in shaping change-management outcomes.

Given the prevalence of change in the media industry, there clearly is a need for more research on change management, job satisfaction, and motivation issues. Additionally, there is a need to expand these research streams beyond journalists and newsrooms to examine how change and motivation issues are affecting media professionals and media performance in other sectors of the media industry. Other aspects of leadership such as power, decision making, and communication have, as yet, attracted little attention from media management researchers. Research on these topics would contribute immensely to understanding the factors of human agency that shape media content and organizational performance.

Emerging Challenges in
Media Management Practice

With the exponential growth of media products and their ever-increasing impact on our life and cultural practices, media employees operate in new conditions (Deuze, 2007). Getting noticed by an audience bombarded with an abundance of choice and getting paid for the content the company is producing are the two main challenges that media companies are facing. The general business model of traditional media businesses is to generate revenue from advertisers by "selling" audiences and at the same time sell their products to those audiences. This so-called dual-product marketplace influences the content strategy, for example by providing products appealing to the largest number of customers and giving a disproportionate amount of attention to groups that are most attractive to advertisers (Picard, 2002).

With the arrival of "new media" the old business model is being undermined. Nearly all sectors of the media have developed a range of responses to threats and opportunities offered by those new developments. Scholars as well as media practitioners have just started to address those issues in a systematic way, bringing up new hypotheses and starting to build new "theories." One such new area concentrates on new media consumption patterns in the era of digitalized products. As Napoli (2003) observed, the increasing wealth of specialized content available to media consumers is a result of the proliferation of distribution platforms, as well as content within those platforms. Media consumption is being fragmented and spread across media platforms, which contributes to the emergence of new patterns of media audience behavior. Such fragmentation makes the measurements and estimations of target audiences "sold" to advertisers increasingly difficult. Building up digital businesses implies using a whole new set of rules and competing with new entrants who are already fully geared to the digital world.

There is a widespread agreement that the digitalization of media products and the rise of new channels of distribution are fundamentally altering media purchase decisions. "Long tail" (Anderson, 2006) theory predicts that the proliferation of online channels will make consumption more heterogeneous and shift media consumption away from "hits" to a much larger number of lower-selling niche products. It contrasts with what has so far been a dominant view on the distribution of attention. Dubbed as the "theory of superstars" introduced in the 1980s (Rosen, 1981), it argues that people tend to converge on the same hit content regardless of the breadth and depth of niche content available. Because consumers prefer to watch the most talented performers and technology allows these performers to be everywhere at once, a few superstars will come to dominate the marketplace, resulting in winner-take-all outcomes.

The "long tail" hypothesis is subject to heated debates, with the empirical evidence rejecting it (Elberse, 2008; Page & Garland, 2009) and e-business enthusiasts believing the future of the niche markets. Consensus on the "correct" view about the nature of media consumption in the digital age is still to be reached, but the outcome of it might be critical for strategies and functioning of media companies.

Transition from theorizing and analytic reasoning to a practical, normative suggestion is not a straightforward act. Contingency factors present in every situation and company make such generalizations nearly impossible. Additionally since the core of media management research and theorizing originates in many disciplines, which are not applied science, this transition becomes even more challenging. Unfortunately media management scholarship and its findings are not yet closely connected to practice. As Hollifield (2008) reports about weak links between academia and media business practice, it is also evident that partially the reason for this distance lies in lack of applied problem-based research and knowledge transfer to industry.

Summary and Outlook

This chapter presents a selection of dominant theories used in media management research. As the media sector experiences unprecedented transition, many paradigms and assumptions may suffer erosion. Media management and economics as a subfield of the mass communication field is, by any measure, young. Moreover, as a specialized area within a much larger discipline, media management is the focus of only a small group of scholars when compared to mass communication as a whole or to organizational studies. Nevertheless, it has made remarkable progress in the development of theory in several areas. The strategic management of media companies has drawn the most consistent attention from scholars, resulting in the development of a strong body of research on the structures of media markets and the strategic management of the resources that media companies control. Although much of the research has been less systematic than necessary for theory development, Dimmick's (2003) work on media market niches is just one example of theoretical development in the area of strategic management that has contributed significantly to understanding the behavior of media companies.

Another area in which media management scholars have made a unique contribution to theory development is the implications and effects of organizational and corporate structures on media content. These are not the only areas, of course, in which media management research has contributed to theory development. However, the analysis of media management literature shows that one of the weaknesses of the field is that research tends to be fragmented, unsystematic, and nonprogrammatic. The development of media management theory is in need of careful reevaluation of the theoretical foundations on which most research in the field has been built. While many of the management theories drawn from organizational science naturally have proven valuable in the study of media companies, the theories were developed primarily through the study of manufacturing and service industries—industries in which the fundamental economic characteristics and production processes differ from those of the media industry in crucial ways. As a result, many organizational theories—such as those in the areas of strategic management, structural contingency, and leadership—may not be completely transferable to media firms. Media management researchers should treat at least some organizational theories tentatively until they have been systematically reexamined in the media industry. More research that uses "normal" industries as a control group also might be valuable for the purpose of theory development. Identifying differences between information industries and consumer-product and service industries may help shed light on the management of media companies. This, in turn, should help strengthen both the predictive and the prescriptive value of media management theory and research.

Media management almost certainly will continue to grow as a research specialty in coming decades. As media consolidation continues, there will be an increased demand for a better understanding of the relationships among media management, economics, content, and society. Additionally, as the competitive environment within the media industry changes in the face of new technologies, regulations, and market conditions, the industry itself will be seeking insights into effective management practices.

The examination of the current state of media management shows that the most glaring omission in the field is in research on media organizational leadership and employee motivation. Clearly, this gap must be addressed. This area of study will be particularly important given the rapid changes overtaking the media industry and the industry's heavy reliance on human capital in the creative processes of production. Among the critical research issues about media leadership that need to be addressed are the relationship between leadership and the ability of media companies to thrive in rapidly changing market environments; the effective management of change, creativity, innovation, and professional cultures; and the impact of media executives and their personal values on the content produced by their corporations. In particular, more attention needs to be given to understanding professional values, idiosyncrasies of talent, and people management issues like hiring and retention policies (see also Pablo J. Boczkowski, in this volume).

Finally, media management scholars must continue to extend research on the outcomes of management decisions and behaviors beyond financial performance and organizational efficiency measures to include the quality of media content and social externalities. Given the media industry's role as a central infrastructure in global communication, political, and economic systems, it is simply inadequate for media management scholars to adopt the traditional approach in organizational studies of measuring company and industry performance primarily in terms of financial and competitive outcomes. To develop theory that effectively predicts and explains the likely effects of media management decisions and behaviors on media content and, by extension, society may well prove to be the central conceptual challenge facing the field. But if the decisions of media executives and the behavior of media organizations matter enough to generate specialized study, then certainly understanding the full impact of those decisions both within and beyond the industry must be a central focus of media management research.

References

Abbott, E. A., & Brassfield, L. T. (1989). Comparing decisions on releases by television and newspaper gatekeepers. *Journalism Quarterly, 66,* 853–856.

Achtenhagen, L., & Raviola, E. (2009). Balancing tensions during convergence: Duality management in a newspaper company. *International Journal on Media Management, 11*(1), 32–41.

Ahrens, F. (2004, February 13). But would it work? Other media mergers provide lessons for Comcast-Disney. *The Washington Post,* p. E1.

Albarran, A. (1998). Media economics: Research paradigms, issues, and contributions to mass communication theory. *Mass Communication and Society, 1*(3/4), 117–129.

Albarran, A. B. (2002). *Management of electronic media* (2nd ed.). Belmont, CA: Wadsworth.

Altmeppen, K.-D., Lantzsch, K., & Will, A. (2007). Flowing networks in the entertainment business: Organizing international TV format trade. *International Journal on Media Management, 9*(3), 94–104.

Anderson, C. (2006). *The long tail: Why the future of business is selling less of more.* New York, NY: Hyperion.

Atkin, D. J., Neuendorf, K., & Jeffres, L. W. (2003). Predictors of audience interest in adopting digital television. *Journal of Media Economics, 16*(3), 159–173.

Barney, J. B., & Hesterly, W. (1996). Organizational economics: Understanding the relationship between organizations and economic analysis. In S. R. Clegg, C. Hardy, & W. R. Nord (Eds.), *Handbook of organization studies* (pp. 115–147). London, England: Sage.

Bergen, L. A., & Weaver, D. (1988). Job satisfaction of daily newspaper journalists and organization size. *Newspaper Research Journal, 9*(Winter), 1–13.

Bloor, G., & Dawson, P. (1994). Understanding professional culture in organizational context. *Organization Studies, 15*(2), 275–295.

Busterna, J. C., & Hansen, K. A. (1990). Presidential endorsement patterns by chain-owned newspapers, 1976–84. *Journalism Quarterly, 67,* 286–294.

Chan-Olmsted, S. M. (2003a). Fundamental issues and trends in media strategy research. *Journal of Media Economics & Culture, 1*(1), 9–37.

Chan-Olmsted, S. M. (2003b). Theorizing the strategic architecture of a broadband television industry. *Journal of Media Economics, 16*(1), 3–21.

Christensen, C. M., & Overdorf, M. (2000). Meeting the challenge of disruptive innovation. *Harvard Business Review,* March/April, 67–76.

Christensen, C. M., & Raynor, M. E. (2003). Why hard-nosed executives should care about management theory. *Harvard Business Review,* September, 67–74.

Compaine, B. M., & Gomery, D. (2000). *Who owns the media? Competition and concentration in the mass media industry.* Mahwah, NJ: Erlbaum.

Day, G. S., & Schoemaker, P. J. H. (2000). *Wharton on managing emerging technologies.* New York, NY: Wiley.

Demers, D. P. (1996). Corporate newspaper structure, profits, and organizational goals. *Journal of Media Economics, 9*(2), 1–24.

Dennis, E. A., & Ash, J. (2001). Toward a taxonomy of new media: Management views of an evolving industry. *International Journal of Media Management, 3*(1), 26–32.

Deuze, M. (2007). *Media work.* Cambridge, England: Polity.

Dimmick, J. W. (2003). *Media competition and coexistence: The theory of the niche.* Mahwah, NJ: Erlbaum.

Donaldson, L. (1996). The normal science of structural contingency theory. In S. R. Clegg, C. Hardy, & W. R. Nord (Eds.), *Handbook of organizational studies* (pp. 57–76). London, England: Sage.

Dupagne, M. (1992). Factors influencing the international syndication marketplace in the 1990s. *Journal of Media Economics, 5*(3), 3–30.

Dougherty, D. (2006). Organizing for innovation for 21st century. In S. R. Clegg, C. Hardy, T. B. Lawrence, & W. R. Nord (Eds.), *The Sage handbook of organization studies* (pp. 598–617). London, England: Sage.

Elberse, A. (2008). Should you invest in the long tail? *Harvard Business Review,* July/August, 88–96.

Ettema, J. S. (1982). The organizational context of creativity. In J. S. Ettema & D. C. Whitney (Eds.), *Individuals in mass media organizations: Creativity and constraint* (pp. 91–106). Beverly Hills, CA: Sage.

Fedler, F., & Pennington, R. (2003). Employee-owned dailies: The triumph of economic self-interest over journalistic ideals. *International Journal on Media Management, 5*(4), 262–274.

Ferguson, D. A. (1997). The domain of inquiry for media management researchers. In C. Warner (Ed.), *Media management review* (pp. 177–184). Mahwah, NJ: Erlbaum.

Franke, N., & Schreier, M. (2002). Entrepreneurial opportunities with toolkits for user innovation and design. *International Journal of Media Management, 4*(4), 225–234.

Fu, W. (2003). Applying the structure-conduct-performance framework in the media industry analysis. *International Journal of Media Management, 5*(4), 275–284.

Gade, P. (2002). Managing change: Editors' attitudes towards integrated marketing, journalism. *Newspaper Research Journal, 23*(2/3), 148–152.

Gade, P., & Perry, E. L. (2003). Changing the newsroom culture: A four-year case study of organizational development at the *St. Louis Post-Dispatch. Journalism & Mass Communication Quarterly, 80,* 327–347.

Gershon, R. A. (1997). *The transnational media corporation: Global messages and free market competition.* Mahwah, NJ: Erlbaum.

Gershon, R. A. (2000). The transnational media corporation: Environmental scanning and strategy formulation. *Journal of Media Economics, 13*(2), 81–101.

Glasser, T., Allen, D., & Blanks, E. (1989). The influence of chain ownership on news play: A case study. *Journalism Quarterly, 66,* 605–614.

Greco, A. (1999). The impact of horizontal mergers and acquisitions on corporate concentration in the U.S. book publishing industry, 1989–1994. *Journal of Media Economics, 12*(3), 165–180.

Hirsch, P. M. (1977). Occupational, organizational and institutional models in mass media research: Toward an integrated framework. In P. M. Hirsch, P. V. Miller, & F. G. Kline (Eds.), *Strategies for communication research* (pp. 13–42). Beverly Hills: CA: Sage.

Hollifield, C. A. (1999). The effects of foreign ownership on media content: Thomson's U.S. newspapers' coverage of the Quebec independence vote. *Newspaper Research Journal, 20*(1), 65–82.

Hollifield, C. A. (2001). Crossing borders: Media management research in a global media environment. *Journal of Media Economics, 14*(3), 133–146.

Hollifield, C. A. (2008). Invisible on the frontlines of the media revolution. *International Journal on Media Management, 10*(4), 179–183.

Hollifield, C. A., & Donnermeyer, J. F. (2003). Creating demand: Influencing information technology diffusion in rural communities. *Government Information Quarterly, 20*(2), 135–150.

Hoskins, C., Finn, A., & McFadyen, S. (1994). Marketing management and competitive strategy in the cultural industries. *Canadian Journal of Communication, 19*(3/4), 269–296.

Hoskins, C., & McFadyen, S. (1993). Canadian participation in international co-productions and co-ventures in television programming. *Canadian Journal of Communication, 18*(2), 219–236.

Hunt, S. D. (1991). *Modern marketing theory: Critical issues in the philosophy of marketing science.* Cincinnati, OH: South-Western.

Kang, M. H. (2002). Digital cable: Exploring factors associated with early adoption. *Journal of Media Economics, 15*(3), 193–208.

Killebrew, K. C. (2003). Culture, creativity and convergence: Managing journalists in a changing information workplace. *International Journal of Media Management, 5*(1), 39–46.

Klein, A. (2002, October 21). A merger taken AO-ill: Financials, culture, ideology divide Time Warner and its new-media partner. *The Washington Post,* p. E01.

Küng, L. (2000). Exploring the link between culture and strategy in media organizations: The cases of the BBC and CNN. *International Journal of Media Management, 2*(2), 100–109.

Küng, L. (2007). Does media management matter? Establishing the scope, rationale, and future research agenda for the discipline. *Journal of Media Business Studies, 4*(1), 21–39.

Küng, L. (2008). *Strategic management in the media: Theory to practice.* London, England: Sage.

Lacy, S., & Blanchard, A. (2003). The impact of public ownership, profits, and competition on number of newsroom employees and starting salaries at mid-sized daily newspapers. *Journalism & Mass Communication Quarterly, 80,* 949–968.

Lacy, S., & Simon, T. F. (1993). *The economics and regulation of United States newspapers.* Norwood, NJ: Ablex.

Landler, M., & Kirkpatrick, D. D. (2002, July 29). Bertelsmann's chief is fired after clash with ownership. *The New York Times,* p. 1A.

Lasorsa, D. L., & Reese, S. D. (1990). News source use in the crash of 1987: A study of four national media. *Journalism Quarterly, 67*(1), 60–71.

Lawson-Borders, G. (2003). Integrating new media and old media: Seven observations of convergence as a strategy for best practices in media organizations. *International Journal of Media Management, 5*(2), 91–99.

Mierzejewska, B., & Hollifield C. A. (2006). Theoretical approaches in media management research. In A. Albarran, S. Chan-Olmsted, & M. O. Wirth (Eds.), *Handbook of media management and economics* (pp. 37–65). Mahwah, NJ: Erlbaum.

Napoli, P. (2003). *Audience economics: Media institutions and the audience marketplace.* New York, NY: Columbia University Press.

Page, W., & Garland, E. (2009). The long tail of P2P. *Economic Insight—PRS for Music, 14.*

Parker, B. (1996). Evolution and revolution: From international business to globalization. In S. R. Clegg, C. Hardy, & W. R. Nord (Eds.), *Handbook of organization studies* (pp. 484–506). London, England: Sage.

Pashupati, K., & Kendrick, A. (2008). Advertising practitioner perceptions of HDTV advertising: A diffusion of innovations perspective. *International Journal on Media Management, 10*(4), 158–178.

Peer, L., & Chestnut, B. (1995). Deciphering media independence: The Gulf War debate in television and newspaper news. *Political Communication, 12,* 81–95.

Perez-Latre, F. J., & Sanchez-Tabernero, A. (2003). Leadership, an essential requirement for effecting change in media companies: An analysis of the Spanish market. *International Journal of Media Management, 5*(3), 198–208.

Picard, R. (2000). Changing business models on online content services: Their implications for multimedia and other content producers. *International Journal of Media Management, 2*(2), 60–68.

Picard, R. (2002). *The economics and financing of media companies.* New York, NY: Fordham University Press.

Picard, R. (2004). Environmental and market changes driving strategic planning in media firms. In R. G. Picard (Ed.), *Strategic responses to media market changes* (pp. 35–46). JIBS Research Reports No. 2004–2, Jönköping International Business School.

Picard, R. G., & van Weezel, A. (2008). Capital and control: Consequences of different forms of newspaper ownership. *International Journal on Media Management, 10*(1), 22–31.

Pollard, G. (1995). Job satisfaction among news workers: The influence of professionalism, perceptions of organizational structure, and social attributes. *Journalism and Mass Communication Quarterly, 72,* 682–697.

Ramstad, G. O. (1997). A model of structural analysis of the media market. *Journal of Media Economics, 10*(3), 45–50.

Rao, B. (2001). Broadband innovation and the customer experience imperative. *International Journal of Media Management, 3*(11), 56–65.

Redmond, J., & Trager, R. (2004). *Balancing on the wire: The art of managing media organizations* (2nd ed.). Cincinnati, OH: Atomic Dog.

Roberts, K. H., & Grabowski, M. (1996). Organizations, technology and structuring. In S. R. Clegg, C. Hardy, & W. R. Nord (Eds.), *Handbook of organization studies* (pp. 409–423). London, England: Sage.

Rogers, E. (1995). *Diffusion of innovations,* New York, NY: Free Press.

Rosen, S. (1981). The economics of superstars. *The American Economic Review, 71*(5), 845–858.

Rudner, R. S. (1966). *Philosophy of social science.* Englewood Cliffs, NJ: Prentice Hall.

Saksena, S., & Hollifield, C. A. (2002). U.S. newspapers and the development of online editions. *International Journal of Media Management, 4*(2), 75–84.

Savage, S., Madden, G., & Simpson, M. (1997). *Journal of Media Economics, 10*(1), 3–15.

Schein, E. H. (1992). *Organizational culture and leadership* (2nd ed.). San Francisco, CA: Jossey-Bass.

Sedman, D. (1998). Market parameters, marketing type, and technical standards: The introduction of the DVD. *Journal of Media Economics, 11*(1), 49–58.

Sylvie, G. (2003). A lesson from the *New York Times*: Timing and the management of cultural change. *International Journal of Media Management, 5*(4), 294–304.

Toren, N. (1969). Semi-professionalism and social work: A theoretical perspective. In A. Etzioni (Ed.), *The semi-professions and their organization* (pp. 141–195). New York, NY: Free Press.

Turner, J. H. (1993). *Classical sociological theory: A positivist's perspective.* Chicago, IL: Nelson Hall.

Turow, J. (1992). *Media systems in society: Understanding industries, strategies, and power.* New York, NY: Longman.

Wasko, J. (1998). Challenges to Hollywood's labor force in the 1990s. In G. Sussman & J. A. Lent (Eds.), *Global productions: Labor in the making of the "information society"* (pp. 173–190). Cresskill, NJ: Hampton.

Weaver, D. H., & Wilhoit, G. C. (1991). *The American journalist: A portrait of U.S. news people and their work.* Bloomington: Indiana University Press.

Weinstein, A. K. (1977). Foreign investments by service firms: The case of the multinational advertising agency. *Journal of International Business Studies, 8*(1), 83–91.

West, D. C. (1996). The determinants and consequences of multinational advertising agencies. *International Journal of Advertising, 15*(2), 128–139.

Wicks, J. L., Sylvie, G., Hollifield, C. A., Lacy, S., & Sohn, A. B. (2004). *Media management: A casebook approach* (3rd ed.). Mahwah, NJ: Erlbaum.

Wirth, M. O., & Bloch, H. (1995). Industrial organization theory and media industry analysis. *Journal of Media Economics, 8*(2), 15–26.

Yi, K., & Sung, Y. (2007). What to read in the morning? A niche analysis of free daily papers and paid papers in Korea. *International Journal on Media Management, 9*(4), 164–174.

Young, D. (2000). Modeling media markets: How important is market structure? *Journal of Media Economics, 13*(1), 27–44.

Notes

1. The review nature of this chapter calls for referencing many sources. Due to space restrictions, references indicating examples of research strains have been limited to the necessary minimum.

2. For a comprehensive overview of strategic management applied to media refer to Küng (2008).

3

The Management of the Creative Industries

FROM CONTENT TO CONTEXT

Chris Bilton

This volume is representative of a growing interest in management in the creative and media industries, based in part on a recognition that management and creation of content in these industries have become increasingly interdependent. In this chapter I will review the context for this merging of "managerial" and "creative" functions and then comment on some of the implications for management practice.

The immediate context for this merging of creativity and management is the devaluing of content, particularly online. In the late 1990s, online businesses followed the mantra "content is king." The success or failure of the early dot-com companies was seen to depend on a compelling idea. Today, with the massive oversupply of content, content is not king. Attention has shifted from the *what* of content to the *how* of delivery, branding, and customer relationships—in other words, toward management. Accustomed to receiving content for free, consumers can still be persuaded to pay for a premium service; iTunes offers a premium download service for music stripped of DRM (digital rights management) restrictions and with a supposedly CD quality. Spotify, which made its name by streaming free music paid for through advertising, recently launched a paid-for ad-free service. The band Radiohead made the headlines in 2008 by offering its *In Rainbows* album as a "pay-what-you-can" download—what was less commented upon at the time was the accompanying offer of a box set with artwork, vinyl and CD format album, and bonus CD as a premium product priced at £40 (see Eric Harvey, in this volume).

The Radiohead example points to a broader shift from raw content (music) to the packaging and benefits around the content. The massive oversupply of music on the Web (a 2008 industry survey found that of 13 million tracks available, 10 million did not sell a single copy) has increased competition to provide added value, for example in the form of "content about content" through services like Pandora and Last.fm.

Emerging business models for online music are the latest acceleration of a longer historical trend that undermines the integrity and authority of artistic content. To understand the emergent relationship between management and creativity we need to consider first the shift away from a model of unique artworks authored by individual artists toward a more complex model that embeds individual creativity in a broader system of cultural production.

The destruction of the aura and integrity of the individual artwork was associated with the forms of industrialized cultural production that emerged in the 1930s and 1940s. Where Adorno and Horkheimer (1947/1997) saw in the emergence of commercial mass culture a subjugation of art to the imperatives of industrial capitalism, the cultural industries policies of the 1980s used a similar argument to challenge the authority of traditional arts institutions and art forms, based on a democratization of cultural production and an expansive definition of culture that legitimized popular commercial culture. New technologies have added a new impetus to the democratization argument, with commentators like Chris Anderson (2006) describing a democratization of production and distribution, and corporations from Apple to Sony selling commercial products that promise to make everybody a cultural producer. Open-source software, user-generated content, and social networking sites allow creative roles to be distributed among consumers (see also Deuze and Fortunati, in this volume).

Whether this shift away from the autonomy of art and the canonical authority of cultural content amounts to empowerment or a further cycle of commodification, turning subcultural consumer creativity into a repackaged marketable product, is of course open to question. Critics on both sides have continued to debate the implications of consumer creativity—does this represent a new form of networked collective creativity or a fashionably postmodern take on consumerism? Where they converge is in recognizing that in the creative or cultural industries the creators of original content have had to concede their authority over cultural production to consumers and corporations.

A second historical strand to this decentering of content creation has been the rediscovery of craft in cultural production. William Morris described a separation of art from craft during the Industrial Revolution. According to Morris's idealized view of preindustrial culture, traditional artists had taken a pleasure and pride in the craft of their work. In an industrialized society, art was no longer integrated with everyday use and had become a commodity for commercial exchange (Morris, 1894). However, the sheer complexity of industrialized cultural production in the late 20th and early 21st centuries has introduced a new set of craft skills and new specializations in cultural work—a cursory glance at the credits on a film or CD will confirm the plethora of skilled craftspeople working in today's creative industries. There is no doubt a hierarchical division of labor between artists and craftspeople, and a huge differential in earnings. The artist Damien Hirst and the musician Prince are better known and better paid than the army of technicians and specialists who turn their ideas into crafted realities. But consumers are increasingly aware of the technical, crafted qualities of cultural products, exposed through reality television and the availability of quasiprofessional tools and software that allow them to craft their own cultural content. And as noted above, craft values—the production values in a piece of music, the technical quality of a photograph, the brushstrokes in an oil painting—may represent a critical difference between a ubiquitous DIY culture and the perception of premium quality, for which consumers are prepared to pay. Again, attention begins to shift from the *what* of content to the *how* of delivery and application. We can all have original ideas—but how well can we execute them?

A third and related historical trend has been a change in the way we approach cultural products, from considering them as unique, autonomous art objects toward having an awareness of cultural relativism and the role of consumers in shaping the meaning and value of cultural products. At a theoretical level there have been numerous developments in this direction from Roland Barthes's seminal essay on "the death of the author" (1977) and subsequent developments of structuralist theory in literary studies to audience theory in the work of John Fiske and Stuart Hall in media studies. In academic cultural studies beginning in the 1980s, attention shifted from cultural production to cultural consumption as the site where meaning and value are created (Fiske, 1989). More recently these theoretical strands have converged in postmodern theory, which confirms a pervasive relativism in the value of cultural products (Carey, 2005). The theoretical discussion of active audiences and consumer creativity has fed off practical developments in the creative industries, with a growing emphasis on interactivity, customer relationships, and engaging consumers in the active creation and re-creation of meaning, from YouTube to fan fiction and music samples and remixes. New technologies facilitate these second-generation cultural products, and the results of consumer creativity are very often repackaged and sold back to us or reincorporated into product advertising.

Finally, marketing and branding have emerged as cultural industries in their own right. The ubiquity of cultural content is merely an extension of a wider surplus of products in developed, industrialized markets. Branding and marketing have moved from being the process for differentiating generic products to being a product in their own right; in a saturated market, trademarks, logos, and brands require higher levels of investment and deliver higher levels of profit than traditional manufacturing. The international division of labor means that manufacture is very often undertaken using cheap labor in developing countries, with marketing (and profit) concentrated among a handful of global corporations. Customer-oriented marketing has become similarly important in the cultural sector, partly as a result of the market saturation alluded to above but also as a reflection of the growing managerialism and commercialization of the subsidized arts sector.

Marketing in the cultural industries focuses on the customer experience or "product surround" beyond cultural content. Building branded experiences around cultural content provides a measure of predictability and continuity in what is still a highly unpredictable and subjective process. And whereas a previous generation of gatekeepers in the cultural sector was able to control and exploit smaller cultural producers by restricting access to finance and markets, a more complex and competitive marketplace has brought in a newer and more diverse range of cultural intermediaries, competing to add value to cultural content through new forms of delivery and distribution. Whereas the old film studios or the major record labels were mainly concerned with providing access to content, the new gatekeepers like Amazon, Google, or Nokia use new technologies and business models to bundle content with other value-added services and sell content about content.

It is sometimes difficult to separate out new academic perspectives on the creative industries from observable economic and social trends in cultural markets. No doubt some of the trends summarized above have been exaggerated or polemicized by critics and commentators who regard them as desirable or dangerous depending on their political orientation. However, what is surely undeniable is that over the past 20 years economic, technological, social, and cultural changes have conspired to devalue cultural content and place a stronger emphasis on the services and systems that convert raw symbolic goods into meaningful and valuable experiences for consumers. Consequently creativity is closely linked to the management of cultural production and cultural distribution.

In the remainder of this chapter, we will consider the implications of these changes for management in the creative industries. First, to what extent are creative and managerial processes analogous and overlapping? Second, how are cultural entrepreneurs responding to the challenges outlined here? Finally, what might be the implications for cultural policies directed toward creativity?

Creative Management, Managed Creativity

Making an analogy between management and creativity is controversial. Managers have borrowed the language and lifestyles of artists; meanwhile creative organizations have had to become increasingly businesslike as a result of public sector accountability and private sector competition. The results have not been encouraging. "Creative management" can appear as a rather hollow rhetoric (Prichard, 2002), a way of legitimizing management by dressing up capitalism in a bohemian costume (Frank, 2001), or a parade of faddish consultancy and training projects signifying nothing (Schlesinger, 2007). It can be outright destructive, based on an infatuation with novelty and change for their own sakes, leading to a neglect of traditional skills and industries (Heartfield, 2001). "Managed creativity" on the other hand is associated with top-down interventions from regulators, funders, and investors; the imposition of deadlines and targets on necessarily unpredictable processes; a pursuit of short-term profit at the expense of a sustainable creative vision; and the subjugation of creative freedom to bureaucratic or managerialist imperatives. The love affair between creativity and management seems on this evidence to be a superficial one, a short-term flirtation with different sartorial and rhetorical styles. Beneath the shared casual dress code, fundamental divisions between artistic and managerial cultures remain.

One of the problems here is that the version of management imported into the arts has very often been highly uncreative; my own early experience of management training with a theater company in the 1980s involved an ex-military man instructing a room full of would-be creative entrepreneurs on the importance of petty cash vouchers. Conversely managers have tended to buy into the myth of unfettered, irresponsible artistic genius—a mythology that fits nicely with the cult of heroic leadership represented by "maverick" figures like Steve Jobs or Richard Branson. I have argued elsewhere that creative professionals and managers ignore their similarities in their enthusiastic embrace of mutual stereotypes and separations that are deeply ingrained in our education systems and in organizational cultures. I believe that management can be creative at a more fundamental level and that creative artists are effective self-managers (Bilton, 2007).

Artistic creativity involves an ability to make connections between different ways of thinking and seeing. Most cognitive definitions of creativity include this element of duality and paradox, between divergent and convergent thinking, between ideation and application, and between left-brain and right-brain thinking (Boden, 1994). Creative personalities must be tolerant of contradictions and able to make unexpected bisociative connections between previously incongruous frames of reference (Koestler, 1976). Consequently a lot of the competences we might associate with management—organizing, classifying, filtering, prioritizing, directing—are integral to certain aspects of the creative process. At a more empirical level, we can all identify examples of artists managing their own time and resources, directing their work process, and stepping in and out of creative and critical roles (they still might not know about petty cash vouchers). Separating out managerial and artistic functions can thus be seen as a highly uncreative way of thinking.

Managers too have to make connections between different processes and people, to create space within boundaries, and to release as well as control. Artistic creativity is a complex, multifaceted process—and more often than not a social process rather than an individual one—taking place within certain boundaries and constraints imposed both by the field or art world and by the artist's own decision making. If we accept this definition of creativity as a "managed" process, we can perhaps recognize that management too is (or should be) a creative process. Of course there are managers who will concentrate too hard on one part of the management process and overmanage or undermanage, just as there are artists who will fail to manage the connections between ideas and action or between their own vision and the art world around them. But more fundamentally, creative and managerial processes seem to be analogous, even if they may be seeking very different outcomes.

In today's creative industries, I have suggested that the boundaries between creativity—the making of original content—and the packaging and delivery of content have become blurred. Lawrence Lessig (2008) has described this as a remix culture, where the distinction between original content and various forms of exchange, collaboration, and imitation has become increasingly artificial. Lessig (2004) argues that this development has implications for the protection of intellectual property and a public domain or creative commons. I am more concerned here with the implications for the status and value of content and content creators. The rise of the superstar club DJ and the star producer or remixer during the 1980s and 1990s illustrated a shift in status from the visible performer toward the previously anonymous figures who made the performance possible. The club DJ is the music consumer turned producer. The success of J. K. Rowling's Harry Potter books is another example of a remix culture, skillfully drawing together genres and motifs from previous generations of children's fiction. Debates about Rowling's "originality" fail to recognize that her skill as a storyteller is to weave these derivative elements into a satisfying whole. Rowling is in this sense a manager of other people's creativity as much as an originator—her continued involvement in the films and merchandising has provided further evidence of her business acumen, and her roles as author and businesswoman seem in no way contradictory.

While new technologies have opened up the connections among production, distribution, and consumption in the creative industries, multitasking between managerial and creative tasks is not a new phenomenon. Indeed the idea of creativity as a separate, specialized function is itself a relatively new invention, dating back to the 19th century and Romantic theories of art and genius on the one hand and the specialization of labor and education as a result of industrialization on the other (Negus & Pickering, 2004). Further back we can recognize a longer tradition of creative management from the medieval craft guilds to the theater troupes of Shakespeare's time, including his own company, through to Paul DiMaggio's (1986) cultural entrepreneurs and showmen of the 19th century and the Victorian actor-managers like Henry Irving. New technologies have triggered a new generation of cultural entrepreneurs, but they are rediscovering traditions and unities that are historically embedded in cultural work. Academic distinctions between autonomous art and controlling managerialism overlook the synergies and connections between artists and managers in the art world and in the daily practice of artists. Certainly tensions and contradictions between freedom and control exist in both creative practice and management, but for artists and managers, negotiating these dilemmas is part of the job.

Rethinking the Value Chain

So far I have argued for a convergence between creativity and management. This reflects both the historical embeddedness of artistic work in broader systems of exchange and the more recent technologies of production and distribution, which have undermined the integrity and authority of content and content creators. The shift from content to context in contemporary media presents a new challenge for managers, in relation to the value chain.

Michael Porter's (1985) value chain is perhaps the best known framework for analyzing business. The model is based on a single firm, breaking up the different stages in production processes, and is used in various ways—to analyze the connection and consistency in a firm's processes and competences, to highlight areas in which the firm is vulnerable to competitors, and to identify "value chain competences" or a value chain position based on the firm's particular competitive strengths.

More recently it has been suggested that the value chain needs to be modified to suit more diversified and fragmented industrial systems (Norman & Ramirez, 1993; Prahalad & Krishnan, 2008)—nowhere more so than in the creative and media industries. Here creative and media enterprises have moved from value chains to value networks, based on clusters of firms and individuals working together. Disintermediation and reintermediation further disrupt the value chain, with new technologies and new markets reconfiguring or destroying the old value chain relationships. Disintermediation refers to shortcuts that allow certain parts of the chain to be bypassed or made redundant. With artists increasingly able to deal directly with consumers online, retailers are especially vulnerable—the traditional record store, caught between online retailers and digital download services (legal and illegal), is a good example. Reintermediation refers to the introduction of new intermediaries, often from outside the existing value chain. Today mobile phone companies, Internet service providers, and software companies have emerged as new gatekeepers to challenge broadcasters, publishers, and record labels in their respective spheres of influence.

Many of these changes in the value chain reflect industrial restructuring, usually summarized under the heading of *post-Fordism*. The term describes a shift from vertically integrated firms to networks of smaller, specialized firms collaborating together, a shift from mass production to customization, and a shift in the balance of power from producers to consumers, driven by changing technologies, changing markets, legal and political challenges to monopolies, and the emergence of a more sophisticated and discriminating consumer. Again, this restructuring is especially obvious in the creative industries (Storper, 1994).

Partly in response to these external changes but also following their own internal logic, value chains and business models in the creative and media industries have undergone similar changes. I have already alluded to the tradition of artist-managers and cultural entrepreneurs. This tradition of self-management in the cultural sector is partly a necessity, especially for smaller organizations. Independent theater companies have to book their own venues and sell their own tickets. Unsigned bands must do their own marketing and put out their own music. New technologies have simplified this process of self-management and multitasking, self-employed entrepreneurship. Artists and creative businesses are used to moving up and down the value chain taking on different functions that might have been allocated to separate departments in a larger, more conventional firm. Post-Fordist restructuring amplifies and accelerates these tendencies rather than creating them.

Even some larger cultural organizations tend toward a devolved management style. Cultural organizations, especially in the public sector, are characterized by flat hierarchies and a relatively collaborative approach to decision making—viewed from the outside it is often difficult to identify who is leading whom. Leadership in these organizations is distributed through the system rather than concentrated in senior management. And where there is a more overtly hierarchical structure—as in the handful of major global corporations that dominate creative and media markets—there is still a residual preference for senior managers with a track record as practitioners, even if their previous "practical" experience appears increasingly disconnected from their competence as managers.

But it is at the other end of the scale, in the small independent businesses and self-employed individuals who make up the cultural production sector, that the nature of self-managed creative work is most evident. The complexity, specialization, and individualization of skills and labor in cultural production are reflected in high levels of self-employment and "microbusinesses." Microenterprises and individuals converge around temporary projects—the project-based, flexible, and unpredictable nature of creative projects makes this more efficient than working in large, permanent organizations. Advertising, film, and television have long been characterized by this mode of working, with networks of specialists collaborating for one project, breaking up, and regrouping around the next one.

All of these trends take us away from Porter's (1985) value chain toward a more flexible, overlapping set of skills and competences, shared across and between enterprises and individuals. In this fragmented system, even the most specialized of workers need to know a little bit about the other businesses and individuals in the project or network. Even if they themselves are not multitasking, they are doing so collectively (see also Chris Hackley and Amy Tiwsakul, in this volume). In order to work effectively within a network, as opposed to an integrated firm, creative and media workers must know about more than their own corner of the specific business or project; as self-employed entrepreneurs and sole traders mature into networks of project-based enterprise, "know-who" becomes as important as "know-how."

In terms of the distinction between creativity and management, in this reconfigured, networked value constellation, the lines that separate creatives from managers cannot easily be drawn. The stereotypical polarization of "creatives" and "suits" is increasingly outdated in contemporary creative and media businesses (which is not to say it does not still exist). Media organizations tend to break open "talent silos" and encourage their creative teams to be more informed about management priorities and vice versa. In broadcasting and advertising, the *creative* label is as likely to be applied to a senior manager or strategist as to a copywriter or producer (Bilton, 2009). A senior manager at one of Britain's best known advertising agencies recently talked me through the agency's decision to pitch to clients wearing jeans instead of suits—the roles of creative and manager can be taken on and off to produce the desired impression on the client.

Love Thy Enemy

A collapsing of the distinction between content and context, a historical tradition of multitasking cultural entrepreneurship, and a restructuring of the value chain have made the dividing lines between creating and managing in the creative industries increasingly difficult to draw. Yet much of our policy and practice—and our academic discourse—continues to treat management and creativity as separate functions.

Some of the hostility between creative and managerial disciplines stems from our compartmentalized higher education system. This dates back to reforms of higher education in the late 19th century in Europe and the United States. Does interdisciplinarity lead to a loss of focus and purpose, a fudging of intellectual traditions? Certainly in schools in the United Kingdom, there is some evidence that the teaching of creative arts subjects is being diluted and instrumentalized, as if creativity, innovation, and entrepreneurship were interchangeable. On the other hand once young people move to the university they are encouraged to specialize in their disciplines and schools, and students in the arts and humanities and students of business and management retreat into their respective departments. It would surely make more sense to reverse this. Allow children to experience the intrinsic value of the arts and to develop their critical and intellectual faculties at a formative stage rather than training them to be junior entrepreneurs; then, once they move to university, let the arts and business specialists mix and learn from each other. Certainly in my own experience of teaching, these cross-disciplinary learning environments can be highly productive. The restructuring of the creative industries described in this chapter (and elsewhere in this book) suggests that the creative industries require creatives who can manage and managers who can be creative. Students' career destinations and their experiences of working reflect this.

There are also implications here for policy. Government policies on the creative industries still tend to treat the creative industries as a strange hybrid of magical creativity and bolted-on management processes and competences. Even the U.K. government's popular definition of the creative industries separates out the generation and exploitation of intellectual property and is implicitly advocating a traditional value chain in which artists generate content and managers exploit it. There is a danger here that we equate creativity with novelty—actually creativity requires "novelty with a purpose" or "novelty with value"—and the direction and management of creative ideas and talent are no less integral to the creative process than their discovery and release. This chapter argues that the generation and exploitation of intellectual property bleed into each other—in a remix culture it is possible to both break a copyright and create a new one at the same time. Recycling and repackaging old ideas can—if it is done so imaginatively—be no less creative than generating new ones. In fact given the oversupply of ideas and content alluded to above, we could say that policymakers need to invest in systems of cultural distribution and exchange rather than in centers of cultural production.

One important implication for cultural policy, already alluded to, is the need to reestablish a public domain within which ideas can be freely exchanged and developed without the constraints of copyright. This is in part a return to the old ideals of the public sphere and deliberative democracy, but it is also a practical attempt to facilitate the generation and regeneration of creative content. The aim of intellectual property law is to foster innovation by providing incentives to creators in the form of exclusive rights to profit from their inventions for a limited period, and to foster an exchange of ideas and information among the people both to stimulate future innovation and for the public good. Our current copyright laws have exponentially extended the "limited" time and scope of protection and reduced the access to copyrighted material—even to material that nobody seems to own or want. Further extensions to the term of copyright and moves toward the bundling of rights in all media will (in theory) allow corporations to invest in the next generation of content creators. But at the same time this will restrict the public domain and the accessibility of ideas. We need to find a better balance between providing economic incentives for rights holders and providing cultural resources for rights creators.

Finally, creative organizations need to find ways of breaking down the barriers between creative and management functions. I have argued that this is already happening, notably in advertising (Bilton, 2009). The BBC recently instituted a program of "cultural change" under the leadership of Greg Dyke, designed to introduce a more creative approach to management and mobilize the entire organization around a set of core creative values (Schlesinger, 2010). The jury is out as to whether the attempt has been successful. More recently the Royal Shakespeare Company has launched its own model of creative organizational culture, based on the principles of ensemble acting (Bilton & Cummings, 2010). By treating the organization as a project among all members of staff, much like an ensemble of actors in the rehearsal room, the senior managers hope to bridge the gap between creative and administrative staff. There are traces here of the new management discourse cited by Boltanski and Chiapello (2005) with its emphasis on shared vision, flexibility, and creativity. The project appears to be bringing the organization closer together and building a genuine sense of rapport that extends outward to a new sense of connection with audiences and local communities.

Readers of this chapter may continue to be skeptical about the "creativity" of management. They will point to the many examples of misdirected top-down interventions into creative organizations or the crass misappropriation of artistic metaphors to give a "cool" gloss to business as usual (Frank, 1997; McGuigan, 2009). More damningly, they can also highlight the exploitative "soft control" exerted over creative workers in small independent enterprises through a culture of self-reliant individualism and entrepreneurial machismo. Divisions and hierarchies still exist in the creative sector, and the fact that these inequalities are dressed up in the language of creative freedom and independence makes them all the more insidious. The purpose of this chapter is not to dispute these continuing oppositions and barriers but to find a way through them. A first step will be to recognize that both creativity and management are complex, multifaceted processes that rely on collaboration and connection. Connecting creativity and management in organizations, in education, and in cultural policies is a necessary corrective to a divisive and individualistic corporate culture. Just as content creators depend on the systems of production and distribution, which add value to their work, managers need to connect creative thinking to their strategies and organizations. Distinguishing genuine collaboration from window dressing will not be easy. But learning from those we have considered our enemies and opposites may be more valuable than fighting against them.

References

Adorno, T., and Horkheimer, M. (1997). The culture industry as mass deception (J. Cumming, Trans.). In *Dialectic of enlightenment* (pp. 120–167). London, England: Verso. (Original work published 1947)

Anderson, C. (2006). *The long tail.* New York, NY: Hyperion.

Barthes, R. (1977). The death of the author. In *Image-music-text* (pp. 142–148). London, England: Fontana.

Bilton, C. (2007). *Management and creativity: From creative industries to creative management.* Oxford, England: Blackwell.

Bilton, C. (2009). Relocating creativity in advertising: From aesthetic specialisation to strategic integration? In A. C. Pratt & P. Jeffcutt (Eds.), *Creativity, innovation and the cultural economy* (pp. 23–40). Abingdon, England: Routledge.

Bilton, C., & Cummings, S. (2010). *Creative strategy: Reconnecting business and innovation.* Chichester, England: Wiley.

Boden, M. A. (1994). What is creativity? In Margaret Boden (Ed.), *Dimensions of creativity* (pp. 75–117). Cambridge, MA: MIT Press.

Boltanski, L., & Chiapello, E. (2005). *The new spirit of capitalism.* London, England: Verso.

Carey, J. (2005). *What good are the arts?* London, England: Faber.

DiMaggio, P. J. (1986). Cultural entrepreneurship in nineteenth century Boston. In P. J. Dimaggio (Ed.), *Non-profit enterprise in the arts: Studies in mission and constraint* (pp. 41–61). New York, NY: Oxford University Press.

Fiske, J. (1989). Active audiences. In *Television culture* (pp. 62–83). London, England: Routledge.

Frank, T. (1997). *The conquest of cool: Business culture, counterculture and the rise of hip consumerism.* Chicago, IL: University of Chicago Press.

Frank, T. (2001). *One market under God: Extreme capitalism, market populism, and the end of economic democracy.* London, England: Secker & Warburg.

Heartfield, J. (2001). *Great expectations: The creative industries in the new economy.* London, England: Design Agenda.

Koestler, A. (1976). *The act of creation.* London, England: Hutchinson. (Original work published 1964)

Lessig, L. (2004). *Free culture: How big media uses technology and the law to lock down culture and control creativity.* New York, NY: Penguin.

Lessig, L. (2008). *Remix: Making art and commerce thrive in the hybrid economy.* New York, NY: Penguin.

McGuigan, J. (2009). *Cool capitalism.* London, England: Pluto Press.

Morris, W. (1894). Useful work versus useless toil. In A. L. Morton (Ed.), *Political writings of William Morris* (pp. 102–103). London, England: Lawrence & Wishart.

Negus, K., & Pickering, M. (2004). *Creativity, communication and cultural value.* London, England: Sage.

Norman, R., & Ramirez, R. (1993). From value chain to value constellation. *Harvard Business Review,* July/August, 65–77.

Porter, M. E. (1985). *Competitive advantage: Creating and sustaining superior performance.* New York, NY: Free Press.

Prahalad, C. K., & Krishnan, M. S. (2008). *The new age of innovation: Driving cocreated value through global networks.* Chicago, IL: McGraw-Hill Professional.

Prichard, C. (2002). Creative selves? Critically reading "creativity" in management discourse. *Creativity and Innovation Management, 11*(4), 265–276.

Schlesinger, P. (2007). Creativity: From discourse to doctrine? *Screen, 48*(3), 377–387.

Schlesinger, P. (2010). "The most creative organisation in the world": The BBC, "creativity" and management style. *International Journal of Cultural Policy, 16*(3).

Storper, M. (1994). The transition to flexible specialization in the US film industry: External economies, the division of labour and the crossing of industrial divides. In Ash Amin (Ed.), *Post-Fordism: A reader* (pp. 195–226). Oxford, England: Blackwell.

4 Managing Strategy and Maximizing Innovation in Media Organizations

Lucy Küng

T his chapter looks at the issues of strategy, creativity, and innovation in media firms. At first glance readers may question the connection between these elements—how does creativity connect with strategy, for example? The goal of the following pages is to demonstrate how closely linked these elements are, how crucial they are for the success of media organizations, and the priority they represent for managers working in them.

The Strategic Environment

A leitmotiv throughout this book is the fast-changing context of the media industry. All strategic actions are context dependent—that is, driven by the strategic environment that surrounds an organization. Indeed, Porter (1980, 1985) sees the task of aligning an organization with its strategic environment as the essence of competitive strategy. There are other ways to view the task of strategy management, as we shall see, but to kick off this chapter and inform the subsequent discussion of creativity and innovation, it is worth first reviewing key changes—and challenges—in the strategic environment facing media firms at the current time.

Technological Change

The first major dimension of change in the media industry's strategic context concerns technology. The media industry tends to define itself in terms of content but in fact is just as intimately involved with technology—it is a technology industry as much as it is a cultural one. The media's relationship with technology is symbiotic: It owes its very existence to technological inventions dating back to printing and moving forward through a steady stream of advances in creative, recording, reproduction, storing, and distribution technologies.

Viewed longitudinally, technology is probably the most powerful influence on strategy in the media sector, and the quality of an organization's response to changes in this domain is probably one of the most important determinants of strategic outcomes. Also viewed longitudinally, the pattern of technology development for the sector is consistent: Technology gives and technology takes away, but it seldom takes everything away. Technological innovations supplement, rather than replace, previous technologies. The previous medium is not destroyed but progressively undermined.

Technological advances create new products and services that in turn create new sectors of the media industry and fuel increases in usage and spending on media products. At the same time existing markets and segments are eroded, and business models are pushed to adapt.

The introduction of moveable type in 1448 disrupted the printing industry then based on carved wooden blocks. The invention of the microphone and sound recording led to radio broadcasting and recorded music but had a negative effect on live performances. Television created a new segment of the mass media but led to the demise of the comic book as a major entertainment product for children in the United States and ultimately caused newspapers' share of total advertising revenue to fall from 90% in the 1940s to 20% by the 1960s.

The constantly shifting "technological carpet" leads to one of the core strategic challenges for the industry—adaptation. The media industry's success in adjusting to the emergence of new technologies and the erosion of established products is mixed. While it is easy to criticize media companies for failing to respond adequately to new technologies, they do no better or worse than peers in other industries. Retrospective analysis of the largest U.S. firms indicates a repeat pattern by which some of the largest, best-resourced, and best-managed firms decline and even disappear, to be superseded by smaller players or newcomers, as a result of technological discontinuities (Utterback, 1994).

This results from inertial pressures within the incumbent, and a specific dynamic is involved (Tushman & Nelson, 1990; Tushman & O'Reilly, 1997; Tushman & Smith, 2002). In stable environments a market-leading organization focuses its resources on strengthening its lead by extending its core competencies and engaging in continuous incremental innovation. Inevitably structures, processes, and resource deployments also become focused around these activities. The more successful a firm is, the more confirmation it receives that its current priorities, systems, and strategies are correct. The more complacent it becomes, the more likely inertia will set in since there is little apparent need to change.

Inertia is not problematic until a technology transition takes place and technologies and markets shift. Organizations need to change, but the processes, systems, strategies, and assumptions that have brought success for so long have become institutionalized and are hard to alter. The incumbent cannot reinvent itself and cedes its leadership position to new players.

This pattern is not inevitable; clearly it is affected by the degree of inertia within an organization and also by the nature of the technological change. Not all technology transitions are identical. Some bring only incremental alterations to the status quo—evolution rather than revolution—that do not require substantial changes of direction. The move from typewriters to word processors to personal computers is an example.

Others, for example digitalization and the Internet, are revolutionary and have brought tremendous upheaval. Sectors such as the music industry, newspapers, and network television, which displayed all the inertial pressures described above, have been damaged deeply by their inability to find strategic solutions and/or implement the scope of organizational change necessary to master such challenges.

Evolution of Media Content Models

A second challenge in the current strategic environment concerns the dramatic evolution in media content models. This is an iterative process somewhat similar to the process of technology development described above. A new content model emerges, displacing but not destroying the previous one.

From the 1950s onward the media industry was characterized by mass media content models. These were based on products designed to reach large cross-sectional audiences and technologies that allow massive duplication at low cost for huge audiences. They provided portmanteau content that appealed to broad swathes of the population.

Mass media models are based on scarcity. When broadcasting frequencies are rationed, or when newspaper presses represent tremendous capital investments, media products must appeal to the broadest markets possible. In the 1980s, technological advances ranging from satellite and cable distribution to the Internet and digital cameras reduced the barriers to entry in content creation, production, duplication, and distribution. This allowed the emergence of content creation for specific market segments. MTV, CNN, and the Weather Channel are classic examples of such niche content.

Not surprisingly, audiences have demonstrated a clear preference for media content that matches their interests more closely than the portmanteau fare that was the norm during previous decades. In the United Kingdom between 1993 and 2003 the viewing share of nonterrestrial channels (effectively those offering niche content) increased from 6% to 33% (at the expense of the mass market networks).

In addition to the mass and niche content models comes a third content category, that involving social-network and participatory content. This broad category spans a broad spectrum including blogs, tweets, wikis, forums, photos, videos, and podcasts. Some of the strongest products—Facebook and YouTube—offer a combination of professional and user-generated content and have become central to the lives of younger media consumers.

As media products these are hybrids and hard to categorize. Communication and community functions are as important as content. They are designed to look amateur but are extremely professional. Their popularity poses a challenge for the established media industry that depends on the aggregation of mass audiences, especially as major consumer brands are beginning to advertise on the most popular sites.

Media Overload, Multitasking, Time Shifting, and Space Shifting

The third big area of change concerns consumers' relationship with media content. As the number of niche products continues to grow, as mass market content competes more aggressively for public attention, as peer content increases, and as more and more devices are capable of displaying media content, the media options available to consumers are becoming unmanageable. Consumption is increasing, but time and financial budgets are not limitless and certainly not increasing in line with the number of products and channels available.

Consumption is also increasingly nonlinear, which has particular ramifications for the mass media business model. The more consumers record and store broadcast content and continue to consume according to their personal schedule, the more difficult the traditional advertising model becomes, especially when there is an option to avoid advertising entirely.

The Strategic Challenge— An Emergent Environment

What do these environmental challenges mean for managers in the media? How do they shape the task of managing media work? The first general point to make is that these developments have created a very different strategic environment, an emergent one that is very different from the stable environment mass media models are predicated on. Emergent environments are characterized by uncertainty: Industry boundaries are unclear (as is, for example, the case with the ongoing convergence among the media, telecoms, and personal computing industries), business models are evolving (as in free newspapers or television formats that generate additional revenue from telephone calls from viewers), consumer preferences are not well known, and competition can come from hitherto unknown players (think of Internet search engines or telecom companies as purveyors of news).

Emergent environments present a complex management challenge, particularly for incumbents encumbered by their legacy systems and processes. Existing players need to embrace new strategic directions to master new content competencies. They will need to be able to strategize more rapidly and make their organizations more flexible.

Media organizations are operating in mature sectors with rising costs, declining revenue, increasing competition for audience attention, and evolving technological platforms and media content models. The strategic challenge is one not simply of adaptation but also of adaptation with ever-scarcer resources. For established media organizations (the majority of the industry) it also leads to a constant stretching of all kinds of strategic resources. They find themselves needing to bridge a widening range of content categories across a broader range of platforms. This gives rise to tremendous strategic and organizational complexity, brings the risks of lack of strategic focus and overstretched resources, and places these organizations at a significant strategic disadvantage compared with new players who have the luxury of focusing their efforts on one area.

Ongoing Need for Creativity

Creativity is needed by all types of institutions but plays a particularly vital role in the media, where creativity is a strategic necessity. This stems from the intrinsic nature of cultural goods. Because each product is unique and customer demand is fickle, there is an incessant need for novelty. Viewed strategically, the higher the levels of product creativity, the greater the likelihood of market success and the stronger the competitive advantage.

The need for creativity, of course, extends much further than the content sphere (see also Chris Bilton, in this volume). All organizations need to become more creative when environments become more turbulent, especially when that turbulence involves emerging technologies (Yoffie, 1997). This is clearly the case with the media sector.

Socioconstructivist theories of organizational creativity (see Amabile, 1983, 1988, 1993, 1996) provide guidance to managers seeking to boost levels of creativity in their organization. Creativity from this perspective is understood as a social process rather than an individual psychological phenomenon. To occur and prosper, three elements need to be present in an organizational setting:

1. Creativity-relevant skills: cognitive skills such as the ability to understand complexities, to break "cognitive set" during problem solving, to suspend judgment, and to find relationships between apparently unrelated items.

2. Expertise: knowledge of the field coupled with the experience of problem solving.

3. Intrinsic motivation: a drive to engage in an activity for its own sake, expressed as involvement, curiosity, or satisfaction. Intrinsic motivation is important because when levels are high individuals are more likely to take risks, explore new solutions, and experiment.

Amabile's research has identified aspects of the environment that have a direct effect on levels of intrinsic motivation and therefore creativity. These include a clear statement that creativity is required and a creative challenge that is consistent, credible, and feasible; an appropriate level of resources needs to be available to the creative team (particularly there needs to be enough money to allow the team to concentrate on the task at hand, and deadlines need to be realistic), the project team should be composed in such a way that it represents a diversity of perspectives and backgrounds, and finally the team needs to be given autonomy to solve its problems or reach its goals.

Media managers therefore not only need to ensure their organizations are permanently adapting to developments in technology and new content models; they also must ensure that the microclimate for those engaged in responding to these challenges is constituted in a particular way—for example they need to create clarity and consistency in terms of the creative challenge, even when the environment that establishes that challenge is itself permanently evolving. They need to ensure adequate resources are available, even if across the organization resources are becoming increasingly strained. They need to ensure the organization possesses internally or can access externally the creative skills and expertise required to create successful products for emerging technologies and consumer tastes.

Designing Strategic Responses

The field of management theory is enormous. The study of management and the development of business schools gained critical mass in the 1960s, spurred by the increasing complexity of organizations, industrial production, and international business. At this time strategic theory tended to be a subset of a discipline known as business policy and constituted a relatively manageable group of internally consistent concepts. Since then the field has exploded—there are reputedly over a thousand academic journals dealing with management alone. This diversity and complexity provides a stimulating research field for scholars but a challenge for managers seeking to apply this theory to their organizations.

Figure 4.1 offers one way to reduce this complexity. It views strategic theory as falling into three broad categories that are placed on a continuum moving from rationalist approaches on the left-hand side, through adaptive approaches in the middle, and to interpretative approaches on the right. The concepts in these schools should not be viewed as mutually exclusive alternatives. Rather managers need to work across the spectrum—using rationalist tools to diagnose problems but using adaptive and interpretative ones to ensure appropriate solutions are developed and successfully implemented.

Rationalist approaches to strategy involve sequential analysis of the strategic environment and the evaluation of the extent to which organizational resources can be used to respond to opportunities and threats. They help managers grasp how environmental developments are changing the dynamics and structure of

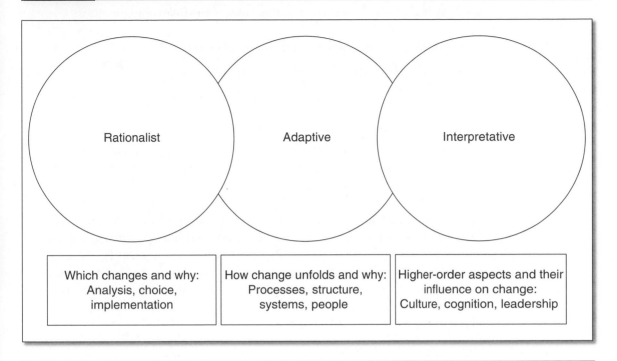

Figure 4.1   "Organizing" Strategic Theory

Rationalist

Adaptive

Interpretative

Which changes and why:
Analysis, choice,
implementation

How change unfolds and why:
Processes, structure,
systems, people

Higher-order aspects and their
influence on change:
Culture, cognition, leadership

Source: Adapted from Johnson (1987); Chaffee (1985)

their industry and how organizations should configure their strategies in response. Concepts in this school include Porter's (1980, 1985) five-forces framework and value chain.

Much of the research into strategy in the media works with rationalist tools. This has yielded fine-grained insights into shifts in the media landscape and into the drivers of firm behavior—for example, whether the number of joint ventures and alliances by media firms has increased, and if the search for specific strategy-relevant resources can explain this. The processes of management within media organizations and the organizational phenomena at play have, however, received less attention.

The adaptive school of strategy addresses a core distinction in strategy literature between strategy content and strategy process. Rationalist approaches focus on the content of strategy, on the strategic plan, and they seek to find a strategic position that will lead to optimal performance under specific environmental conditions through maximizing returns from resources and establishing competitive advantage. Adaptive approaches, however, see strategy as an ongoing process: Because environments are shifting constantly, strategic activity is a permanent process of reconciling and integrating an organization's external and internal worlds, by altering structure, people, and processes.

The interpretative school of strategy is well known to scholars but less familiar to managers, although they will be more than a little acquainted with the phenomena it deals with. For anyone who has been involved in a strategic change, the easiest way to grasp the relevance of this field is to take a moment to think back to such an event and then answer the following questions:

- Did the strategic change work out as planned?

- Which factors caused the most headaches?

- What, if anything, would you have done differently?

I have posed these questions many times to executives from the media and creative industries. Whatever the sector, whatever the nationality of those asked, the answers are invariably the same. Strategic projects seldom work out as planned. The factors that cause the most difficulties, the primary reason for the divergence between intended and actual results, tend to involve culture and mind-set. In retrospect the vast majority of those asked would have spent less time analyzing, planning, and writing documents and far more time working with those in the organization communicating, explaining the need to change, getting buy-in into the solutions, and even in some enlightened cases sharing the responsibility for diagnosing strategic problems and finding solutions with those in the organization who experience these problems or their effects daily.

The Importance of Managing the Social Architecture

The interpretative school focuses on exactly these elements, the implicit and unconscious aspects of organizational life such as beliefs, values, and emotions that can have a tremendous influence on strategic behavior. These are often underplayed or even ignored in strategic planning, partly because they are highly subjective and somewhat ethereal and partly because they concern phenomena that are difficult to access and interpret: how those working within organizations construe meaning out of events and phenomena, and the effects these processes of interpretation and sense making have on organizational outcomes. Time and time again we find that the most gifted managers in the media, from Greg Dyke at the BBC to John Lasseter at Pixar and Disney and even to Rupert Murdoch at News Corporation, have the ability to work with their organization's "social architecture" and use this to ensure strategic initiatives' success. Two elements are particularly important: cognition and culture.

Cognition

The issue of cognition often surfaces in press discussions of media industry strategic challenges. A "legacy mind-set" (i.e., old-fashioned thinking) has been seen as responsible for the industry's tendency to see new technology as a threat rather than as an opportunity, despite the fact that new media technologies ultimately do tend to create new markets and increased revenue for incumbents: The introduction of video, cable and satellite, video on demand, DVD, and home cinema technology has, for example, brought continued growth for the film industry over past decades.

Cognitive approaches to strategy explore how organizations' reactions to strategic events are driven by their members' "governing beliefs," which influence how organization members perceive and interpret the information from the environment. Simon's (1955) concept of bounded rationality is central to cognition theories: Human beings can never comprehend the world in its entirety or grasp every aspect of complex situations. We therefore reduce uncertainty and complexity by developing inferential heuristics—or rules of thumb based on previous experience. These simplify decision making by providing shortcuts but also bring the risk that our decisions are flawed, since we have only processed a limited amount of data and not reviewed every option open to us.

Thus, in any strategic situation we are inevitably working with incomplete and often conflicting information. The rules of thumb we develop will oversimplify the situation and probably introduce inaccuracies and errors. They will, for example, encourage us to focus on particular aspects of an issue, favor data that confirm our existing beliefs, and limit the range of solutions considered—all phenomena that seem relevant to the media industry's response to new technologies.

From Cognition to Culture

Cognition and culture are similar concepts. However, while both draw upon the same basic premise—that problem-solving and adaptive behavior is driven by a set of governing beliefs—there are important differences. In cognitive theory, beliefs and assumptions are accessible at surface level and therefore far easier for managers to change. Cultural assumptions are deeper and far harder to access and alter. Culture is the usual suspect cited when organizations experience difficulties implementing strategies, but while most recognize that culture is an impediment to strategic change, the concept itself remains vague. There is no shortage of examples of culture's impact on strategic initiatives in the media. The difficulties experienced by both the Sony BMG partnership and the AOL Time Warner merger have been ascribed in part to cultural differences. Meyer (2004) sees the complacent culture of the newspaper industry as partly responsible for its slow response to the threat of new technology and to seize the potential of user-generated content.

The essence of an organization's culture is contained in a set of interrelated unconscious assumptions that are shared by members of an organization. Schein (1992) defines culture as a pattern, shared by a group of organization members, of basic assumptions that develop as the group solves problems of external adaptation and internal integration. Culture is therefore the shared accumulated learning that is acquired as the group deals with its external environment and internal growth. This process gives rise to a set of tacit assumptions about how things do and should function that determine perceptions, thoughts, and feelings and function as shortcuts to decision making.

For Schein (1992) culture has three distinct but interconnected layers. The top layer comprises "artifacts"—behavior, dress style, rituals, publications, stories, and so on. These are easy to access but hard to interpret without prior understanding of the deeper levels. The second level comprises "espoused values"—officially expressed strategies, goals, and philosophies. This level of culture may appear to reveal a group's underlying beliefs but in reality represents how that group feels it should present itself publicly. This level of culture can be used to check hypotheses about underlying assumptions but will not represent them accurately. "Basic assumptions" are the third and deepest level of culture, and its essence. These are the unconscious, taken-for-granted beliefs, perceptions, and feelings about the organization and its environment that act as the ultimate source of values and drivers of actions and that contain the key to a culture and the tools by which the other levels—espoused values and artifacts—can be interpreted.

Managers seeking to implement strategic change need to access this level of an organization to explore what hindrance, or leverage, it may offer. They must also avoid falling into the trap of assuming that cultural (and cognitive) assumptions are inherently negative. Such assumptions can be a powerful lever for corporate renewal; they must, however, be understood first.

Cognitive and cultural assumptions affect how the environment and strategic plans are perceived. All other things being equal, provided the cultural assumptions are broadly correct and the strategies are appropriate, the organization will experience success. That success will reinforce the "rightness" of cultural assumptions. But as discussed above in connection to incumbent reactions to technology transitions, a strong culture forged through success can also become a liability in that it gives rise to a rigidity that impedes the ability to adapt. Cultural assumptions about correct responses to the problems of internal integration and external adaptation are formed and validated by success and passed on to new members as the "correct" way to feel and act. In this way an organization's culture is perpetuated. Yet should the competitive environment change markedly, members of the organization must change their core assumptions substantially, but such changes are hard to make (Schein, 1992).

From Theory to Practice: What Should Media Managers Do?

So what should managers in the media focus on to ensure they survive and succeed in the current environment? How can they respond to the developments described above and apply the strategic tools that have been discussed to manage their organizations better?

Forget the "Mass"

"Default" mass markets are evaporating inexorably, be they for national newspapers, national television channels, or other mass-market media. While particular vampire movies or finals of television talent shows might still achieve enormous audience figures, mass markets are fragmenting into smaller groups of consumers with specific tastes. Immediate strategic responses such as rebranding campaigns, redesigns, and promotions may provide short-term relief but also eat up financial resources and divert attention from the need to reconfigure the basic business.

Pressure on mass media models does not spell the end of critical mass: Mass media markets may simply be constituted differently—less around traditional portmanteau media offerings that provide something for everyone and more around niches that are magnified through the potential of global digital electronic networks. They may gather around franchises (Harry Potter, *Pop* or *American Idol*), talent (Madonna or the Rolling Stones), or slim national niches that become amplified globally.

Become Expert at Technological Change

Technological advances will continue to undermine established structures in the media industry. Adapting to changing technology will become a permanent facet of organizational life. Media firms need the capacity to judge how a new technology will affect them and the extent to which they can build on what they have or must access new competencies and resources. They must also make their organizations flexible and capable of adaptation. This may involve some combination of small project teams, response units that produce initial assessments of and/or responses to changes, and mechanisms that transfer learning to the parent.

By extension more attention will need to be given to organizational skills. Media members (professionals as well as scholars of media production) have long been obsessed with content competencies, but to flourish in the emerging environment all kinds of more prosaic organizational competencies will be required—project management, branding, management development, and most particularly leadership.

Learning is also central to adaptation. Companies must mine recent experiences to establish how much of the existing rule book has been rewritten and translate that learning into action (perhaps even learn what unofficial rules they have). Learning needs to be routinized to ensure it happens on a continual basis, and in an environment of increasing numbers of joint ventures, learning from new initiatives, internal or with partners, needs to be captured. A news organization, for example, needs to review how citizen journalism, social networking, and user-generated content can and should be integrated into its current content offerings and what implications this will have for it internally.

This requires technical and business skills but also the ability to shift cognitive frame. Organizations that best seize the potential of technological advance tend to be new players who may lack the advantages of brand, content assets, and financial reserves but who are also unencumbered by the legacy hindrances of mind-set. Some of the most creative new media organizations of the past decades—MTV, CNN, Endemol, and YouTube—emerged from underfunded beginnings to create new categories of media businesses. Arguably their newness and outsider situation allowed them to frame change in terms of a business opportunity rather than in terms of potential damage to existing ways of doing things. It is also noteworthy that the organization that found a commercially successful answer to digital downloading in the music business was Apple, far from a startup but an organization that was still an outsider to the music industry and therefore approached the problem with a different mind-set.

Understand Autonomy

A media organization needs to master the paradoxical demands of being able to reap the benefits of economies of scale and scope and cross-platform synergies and also provide small-scale autonomy to those tasked with creative projects.

The reason is that for the media industry autonomy appears to be first among equals of all the organizational elements that further creativity. The ability to synthesize autonomous small group creativity with the marketing and distribution capability of a large sophisticated organization is a consistent trait that distinguishes strong performers in the field. This means cutting bureaucratic sinews—creative people need the space to be creative. But as the theory discussed earlier demonstrates, autonomy needs to be carefully calibrated, and small groups operating autonomously still need to be well linked to the rest of the organization to ensure knowledge and learning can be transferred and creative potential can be fully exploited.

Tap Unexploited Reserves of Creativity

All media organizations need to be creative. And all media organizations—like any other institution—have reservoirs of unused creativity. Most creative individuals who have chosen to work in the media want to exercise their talents and will do so in the face of organizational obstacles. But an important element of managing creative organizations is not to strew unnecessary obstacles in the path of creativity. Theories of organizational creativity show how just about any employee can be more creative given the right circumstances. Levels of ongoing creativity can be raised through the appropriate management of a range of subtle interdependencies spanning team tasks, job descriptions, feedback, performance metrics, control mechanisms, and even business models.

Bearing that in mind, established media organizations who fear they will be outrun by new players in the digital economy should perhaps remember that hotshot new media companies do not have a higher creativity quotient than older ones. They simply place fewer blocks in the way of their people acting on their creative drive and insight. The "old" media have all the necessary resources to innovate and succeed—they just need to liberate them.

Further Reading

For a more detailed discussion of the issues covered in this chapter, see Küng, L. (2008). *Strategic management in the media: Theory to practice.* Los Angeles, CA: Sage.

References

Amabile, T. M. (1983). *The social psychology of creativity.* New York, NY: Springer.

Amabile, T. M. (1988). A model of creativity and innovation in organizations: Research in organizational behaviour. In B. M. Shaw & L. L. Cummings (Eds.), *Research in organizational behaviour* (10th ed., pp. 123–167). Greenwich, CT: JAI Press.

Amabile, T. M. (1993). Motivational synergy: Toward new conceptualizations of intrinsic and extrinsic motivation in the workplace. *Human Resource Management* Review, *3*(3), 185–201.

Amabile, T. M. (1996). *Creativity in context.* Boulder, CO: Westview Press.

Meyer, P. (2004). *The vanishing newspaper: Saving journalism in the information age.* Columbia: University of Missouri Press.

Porter, M. E. (1980). *Competitive strategy: Techniques for analyzing industries and competitors.* New York, NY: Free Press.

Porter, M. E. (1985). *Competitive advantage: Creating and sustaining superior performance.* New York, NY: Free Press.

Schein, E. H. (1992). *Organizational culture and leadership* (2nd ed.). San Francisco, CA: Jossey-Bass.

Simon, H. A. (1955). A behavioural model of rational choice. *Quarterly Journal of Economics, 69,* 99–118.

Tushman, M. L., & Anderson, P. (1986). Technological discontinuities and organizational environments. *Administrative Science Quarterly, 31,* 439.

Tushman, M. L., & Nelson, R. R. (1990). Introduction: Technology, organizations, and innovations. *Administrative Science Quarterly, 35,* 1–8.

Tushman, M. L., & O'Reilly, C. A., III. (1997). *Winning through innovation: A practical guide to leading organization change and renewal.* Boston, MA: Harvard Business School Press.

Tushman, M. L., & Smith, W. (2002). Organizational technology. In J. C. Baum (Ed.), *The Blackwell Companion to Organizations* (pp. 386–414). Oxford, England: Blackwell.

Utterback, J. M. (1994). *Mastering the dynamics of innovation.* Boston, MA: Harvard Business School Press.

Yoffie, D. B. (Ed.). (1997). *Competing in the age of digital convergence.* Boston, MA: Harvard Business School Press.

SECTION II

Media Work, Policy, and Economics

5 New Media Policies

Terry Flew

_____ **Introduction: Keynes, Schumpeter, and Marx**

While it may seem unusual to begin a discussion of new media and cultural policies with a discussion of old economists, a case can be made as to why the contributions of John Maynard Keynes, Joseph Schumpeter, and Karl Marx continue to be vitally relevant in shaping the intellectual parameters of the field. Keynes was the great 20th-century British economist whose theory of macroeconomic demand management provided the middle way between the free market capitalism that was in crisis with the 1930s global economic depression and state socialism and a centrally planned economy; his ideas have returned to global prominence since the financial crisis of 2008–2009. Less well known is Keynes's central place in what is today referred to as *cultural economics* or the economics of arts policy. During World War II, Keynes chaired the Council for the Encouragement of Music and the Arts (CEMA), which would become the Arts Council of Great Britain. Keynes was a great believer in the inherent qualities of the arts and always believed that the purpose of arts policy was to promote creative excellence, with the central role for government being provision of the financial and infrastructural scaffolding to ensure that this would always occur. At the same time, he believed that while the purpose of public patronage was to enable non-profit-making activities to take place, he saw good arts management as being central to ensuring the widest public access to and appreciation of music, drama, and the visual and performing arts (Skidelsky, 2000). In many ways, Keynes's attitude toward the arts echoed his wider social philosophy. For Keynes, the market economy was a reasonably effective vehicle for meeting most human needs, but for those higher-order goals and principles—such as artistic excellence or public welfare—what was needed was the wise and judicious use of public funds by experts who held the public good at heart and who were trained in the elite academies, and separated from the worlds of commerce and politics.

The Austrian economist Joseph Schumpeter was Keynes's contemporary, but his understanding of capitalism was profoundly different. Whereas Keynes identified long-term tendencies toward stagnation in capitalist economies in the absence of government expenditure to stimulate private investment (Bleaney, 1985), Schumpeter emphasized the role played by innovation and entrepreneurship in generating cycles of renewal in capitalist economies, as part of the process of what he termed *creative destruction*. At the same time, while innovation, private profit, entrepreneurship, and access to credit were the elements that Schumpeter saw as establishing the superiority of capitalism over socialism as an economic system—a debate that was very much alive around Schumpeter for all of his life—he was also aware that while "creative destruction fosters economic growth . . . it undercuts cherished human values . . . [and while] poverty brings misery . . . prosperity cannot assure peace of mind" (McCraw, 2007, p. 6). In his assessment of the strengths and weaknesses of capitalism in *Capitalism, Socialism and Democracy*, Schumpeter (1942/1970) observed that by promoting individualism and undercutting social relations of trust and reciprocity, capitalism increased the risks associated with personal error and failure. He was also aware of the ways in which material progress is a poor proxy for human happiness and how people may feel dissatisfied and worse off—and thus more inclined toward socialism—even if their personal economic circumstances are improving as an outcome of capitalist economic growth (McCraw, 2007).

Behind the debates between followers of Keynes and Schumpeter—which continue to this day—is the specter of Karl Marx. Without going into the complex questions of the relationship of Marxism to culture or Marxist cultural theory (see Artz, Macek, & Cloud, 2006; Nelson & Grossberg, 1988), there are three aspects of Marxism that are relevant here. First, there is Marx as the radical *critic of capitalist modernity*, whose vision of capitalism was as a relentlessly dynamic system that subordinated all other spheres to the expansionary principles of capital accumulation; this was an influence on the work of Schumpeter's theory of business cycles and "creative destruction." Both Marx and Schumpeter believed that capitalism was a dynamic system rather than one prone to stagnation, and neither would be surprised by Manuel Castells's (1996) observation that culture is today deeply embedded within the productive forces of contemporary capitalism. Second, there is the Marxist *critique of political economy*, which points to continuing inequalities of access and forms of exploitation in the cultural sphere, particularly as it is increasingly associated with capitalist commodity production (e.g., Golding & Murdock, 2004; Sparks & Calabrese, 2004). Finally, there is the Marxist *critique of alienation* under capitalism and the treatment of human labor as a commodity, where "the devaluation of the human world increases in direct relation to the increase of value of the world of things" (Marx, 1844/1982, p. 13).

Conventional wisdom would say these three economists allocated particular roles in relation to cultural policy. Although Keynes died before British arts policy was fully established, he had already flagged many of the themes that would be central to cultural economics, including the relationship between private patronage and state subsidy, tensions between promoting excellence and broadening access, the role of cities in the nurturing of creative talent, and the significance of regional diversity in arts funding policies (Skidelsky, 2000). More generally, Keynes was one of a generation of intellectuals who saw the arts as a higher-order social good, and he believed that as economists and social reformers could address the scourges of poverty, unemployment, and boom-bust cycles under capitalism, there would be more scope for a wider cross section of society to enjoy the arts as part of a better life for all. By contrast, Schumpeter's name is rarely mentioned in relation to arts and culture, but he is seen as a pioneer of what is today referred to as *innovation economics*. As Thomas McCraw (2007) observes in his biography of Schumpeter, his "signature legacy is his insight that innovation in the form of creative destruction is *the* driving force not only of capitalism but of material progress in general" (p. 495). Yet he was not a naïve defender of capitalism. He saw that material advancement was a poor proxy for human well-being and that the success of capitalism as an economic system could generate its own social critique by appearing to reduce everything to the status of commodities and cost-benefit calculus.

In some ways, Marxism has the most complex relationship to new media policies. While Marxist political parties and movements have been in decline in the West for many decades, the notion that capitalism has a double-edged nature, promoting growth and innovation while it also generates commodification and social *anomie*, has become a staple of a range of aesthetic-moral critiques of consumer society (e.g., Hamilton, 2005; Sennett, 2006). At the same time, the Marxist critique of alienation has itself become part of a *new spirit of capitalism*. Boltanski and Chiapello (2005) argue that one unexpected development of post-1960s critiques of capitalism, as the generator of "fake" commodified culture and a system that inhibits human freedom and creativity, has been the rise of discourses within both capitalist management and public policy that seek to harness participation, creativity, and individual autonomy for economic ends (Bilton, 2007). This has been accentuated by the rise of the Internet and digital media, particularly Web 2.0 technologies and user-created content where, as the Organisation for Economic Co-operation and Development (OECD, 2007) has described,

> the Internet as a new creative outlet has altered the economics of information production and led to the *democratization of media production* [emphasis added] and changes in the nature of communication and social relationships (sometimes referred to as the "rise—or return—of

the amateurs"). Changes in the way users produce, distribute, access and re-use information, knowledge and entertainment potentially gives rise to increased *user autonomy, increased participation and increased diversity* [emphasis added]. (p. 5)

Media managers and media policymakers are grappling with a new media environment marked by the shift from a 20th-century mass communications paradigm toward a model that has been referred to as a convergent media or Web 2.0 environment. Some features of this shift are indicated in Table 5.1.

Table 5.1	From Mass Communications Media to Convergent Media/Web 2.0	
	Mass Communications Media (20th Century)	**Convergent Media/ Web 2.0 (21st Century)**
Media distribution	Large-scale distribution; high barriers to entry for new entrants	Internet dramatically reduces barriers to entry based on distribution
Media production	Complex division of labor; critical role of media content gatekeepers and professionals	Easy-to-use Web 2.0 technologies give scope for individuals/small teams to be producers, editors, and distributors of media content
Media power	Asymmetrical power relationship—one-way communication flow	Greater empowerment of users/audiences enabled through interactivity and greater choice of media outlets
Media content	Tendency toward standardized mass appeal; content designed to maximize audience share—limited scope for market segmentation based on product differentiation	"Long tail" economics make much wider range of media content potentially profitable; demassification and segmentation of media content markets
Producer/consumer relationship	Mostly impersonal, anonymous, and commoditized (audiences as target mass markets)	Potential to be more personalized and driven by user communities and user-created content (UCC)

Source: Flew (2009, p. 88).

A Schumpeterian interpretation of such shifts may identify the emergence of a new techno-economic paradigm, as continuous waves of technological, product, and market innovation transform the mass media model into a new social media model (e.g., Perez, 2004). By contrast, a Keynesian interpretation may point to continuities as well as to changes, such as the continuing importance of the public service remit in the new media environment. This in turn would connect with the propensities of new media theorists to understand media change in terms of epochal shifts or in terms of graduated changes that are consistent with existing understandings of media and society, as well as whether they make optimistic or pessimistic appraisals of such changes. I have observed elsewhere (Flew, 2009) that new media discourse is often captured by an industry-generated *hype cycle,* where new technologies are routinely associated with radical and discontinuous change, which in turn generates a backlash and claims that this is simply *cyberbole* (Woolgar, 2002) and little or nothing has really changed.

New Media Policies: Shifting Balances Between Regulation and Promotion

Media policy has historically been associated with public interest regulation, where "the creation of regulatory agencies is viewed as the concrete expression of the spirit of democratic reform . . . established in response to the conflict between private corporations and the general public" (Horwitz, 1989, p. 23). Rationales for media regulation have included

- concerns about the impact of media content, particularly on children and "vulnerable" individuals;

- the capacity to use media for citizen formation and the development of a national cultural identity (Schudson, 1994);

- implied rights of public participation associated with the broadcasting spectrum being a common resource with competing public and private uses (Streeter, 1996);

- "public good" aspects of the media commodity, including nonrivalrous and nonexcludable elements of access and consumption (Hesmondhalgh, 2007);

- tendencies toward monopoly or oligopoly in media markets, with resulting entry barriers for new competitors and lack of content diversity (Picard, 1989); and

- the potential relationship between economic power and political power arising from concentration of ownership of the means of public communication.

A useful distinction can be made between *input-based* forms of policy intervention, which typically involve public support for the production of media content, and *output-based* forms, which typically involve regulating the conduct of private media organizations (Flew & Cunningham, 2002; see also Philip Napoli, in this volume). Media policy has historically differed from policies toward the creative and performing arts, not just in rationales for government support but also in the primary focus on regulating what are seen as media industries, rather than subsidizing creative individuals and organizations as artists.

At a comparative level, van Cuilenburg and McQuail (2003) have drawn attention to the great divergence after World War II between European and American approaches to media policy. The European model placed public service broadcasting at the center of the broadcast media system and generally saw media policy as being connected to the service of national social, political, and cultural objectives. By contrast, the U.S. model is almost exclusively centered on commercial media (the Public Broadcasting Service only emerged in the 1960s and has been at the margins of the American system), and the regulatory process takes a largely legal and statutory form with broadcasters having an arm's length relationship to the government of the day. The European model tended to align media policy with arts and cultural policy, particularly around questions of diversity, citizenship, and national identity and their relationship to media content, whereas U.S. media policy has tended to align with telecommunications policy around the legal dimensions of ownership, access, and the development of new services.

From the 1980s onward, there have been pressures toward deregulation of media policies, pressures toward opening up to new services enabled by digital technologies, and challenges to public service broadcasting. The media policy environment that has emerged has been one where "policy has generally to follow the logic of the marketplace and the technology and the wishes of consumers (and citizens) rather than impose its goals" (van Cuilenburg & McQuail, 2003, p. 200). The mass popularization of the Internet and digital media technologies since the 1990s has furthered such tendencies toward media policy driven by competition policy rather than cultural policy objectives, raising the question of whether media can continue to be seen as sufficiently distinct from other areas of business to warrant specialist regulation (Flew, 2006; Livingstone, Lunt, & Miller, 2007). But it is a mistake to focus one-sidedly on a loss of state capacity in the area of media policy, since what has been emerging are new debates about how best to stimulate domestic media content production in the context of globalization and media convergence. If media policy in the second half of the 20th century was shaped to a significant degree by priorities to develop national culture on the part of the protective or regulatory state (Mattelart, 1994; Neveu, 2004; Schlesinger, 1991, 1997), there have been from the 1990s onward new questions being asked about how the state can better enable innovation in digital media content production and distribution.

The 1990s saw a proliferation of information policy documents. The convergence of computing, telecommunication and media, and the mass popularization of the Internet acted as a stimulus for a plethora of national policy strategies to develop the information and communications technology (ICT) sectors and to enable social, economic, and cultural adaptation to the emergent global information society (Henten & Skouby, 2005). These policy documents tended to have a three-part structure: The first priority was to develop the high-speed broadband Internet infrastructure, the second was to promote "national champions" in the ICT sectors, and the third was to focus on how to adapt society and culture to the new technological imperatives. A major gap in 1990s information policy discourses, which the dot-com crash of 2001 brutally exposed, was around media content. While much attention had been given to the importance of developing the "fat pipes" of broadband Internet, very little discussion had occurred about how online content would be used and what transformations might occur in the production, consumption, and use of media accessed through the Internet. There was a strong tendency to view online as a new distribution channel for existing media content that would be produced by established media businesses. What became apparent in the early 2000s was that globalization was squeezing margins in the ICT sectors no less than in manufacturing, and national information policies that hitched economic fortunes to the ICT bandwagon lacked the scope to be socially inclusive and to stimulate innovation and creativity.

The rise of *creative industries* policy discourse can be understood in this context. Drawing upon cultural policy work undertaken in the 1990s on *cultural industries* value chains, creative industries strategies sought to build links among the arts, the media, and the ICT sectors and to identify new opportunities for cultural sectors in national innovation policy strategies. Creative industries strategies first developed in the United Kingdom in the late 1990s under Tony Blair's "New Labour" government but were adopted with varying degrees of commitment in the European Union, Australia, New Zealand, Singapore, Taiwan, Korea, and China. There was also significant uptake by international agencies such as the United Nations Conference on Trade and Development (UNCTAD) and the United Nations Educational, Scientific and Cultural Organization (UNESCO) (Cunningham, 2009; Flew, 2007), as well as a range of initiatives by city and regional governments, which is where interest has been strongest in the United States (Wyszomirski, 2008). Creative industries policy strategies have been based on the premise that, in an age of globally mobile capital, commodities, information, and talented and skilled individuals, it is the cultural or "software" side of the ICT sectors that can generate distinctive forms of intellectual property and sustainable competitive advantage.

One economic underpinning of the rise of creative industries is a growing awareness that *disruptive innovation* in the digital economy (transformational shifts as distinct from incremental improvements, and the creation of completely new products, services, and markets rather than improvements of existing ones) increasingly occurs at the margins, through startups and small-to-medium enterprises, rather than through the large corporations and publicly funded flagships that have been the traditional focus of both arts and media policy and national innovation strategies (Cunningham, 2005; Dodgson, Gann, & Salter, 2005). There has also been the shift in cultural policy dynamics toward the *subnational levels of cities and regions* (Schuster, 2002), with the *creative cities* agenda in particular drawing attention to the relationship of arts, media, and cultural policy to the emergence of creative milieux, or cities and regions that become catalysts for innovation and the development of agglomerations of expertise in media and cultural production (Scott, 2008). Both of these trends have been linked to the new ways in which, as cultural economist David Throsby (2008) notes, "governments have searched for ways to surf the wave of the new information economy, looking to the creative industries broadly defined as sources of innovation to feed economic growth and employment creation at both national and local levels," which has in turn enabled "the arts [to] be seen as part of a wider and more dynamic sphere of economic activity, with links through to the information and knowledge economies, fostering creativity, embracing new technologies and feeding innovation" (p. 229).

An example of how this has developed in practice can be seen with the creation of the Creative Industries Innovation Centre (CIIC) in Australia. The CIIC was established at the University of Technology, Sydney, in 2009 as a joint initiative between Innovation Minister Kim Carr and Arts Minister Peter Garrett, with a specific remit to "assist firms in the creative industries sector to make a larger contribution to the Australian economy." It aims to "enable small and medium sized businesses to improve their productivity and competitiveness by providing professional business advisory and development services" and to "build collaboration between researchers and businesses, and assist creative businesses to access the latest technologies and market specific information" (Enterprise Connect, 2009). The question of how to reconcile creative industries innovation agendas with the traditional remit of arts, media, and cultural policy has been an ongoing research concern of the Australian Research Council (ARC) Centre of Excellence for Creative Industries and Innovation (CCI), headquartered at the Queensland University of Technology. The CCI was first established with ARC funding in 2003 when the conservative government headed by John Howard was in power, but it has had its funding renewed under the Labor government of Kevin Rudd, suggesting that a degree of political bipartisanship has emerged in Australia around the economic contribution of the creative industries.

Policy Settings in the 2010s: Questioning Neoliberalism

The study of media policy draws attention to three recurring questions. First, there is the question of where to set boundaries between media policy and other policy domains. A distinction is often drawn between print and broadcast media, on the basis that the former has traditionally had significant freedom from government controls (at least in the English-speaking world), whereas licensing requirements as well as social concerns have seen more extensive regulation of radio and television. Media policy has frequently been pulled into the domains of cultural policy, particularly around questions of how to promote local audiovisual media content, but has also been aligned with telecommunications policy, particularly with the rise of the Internet and the convergence of media with computing and communications networks. In the context of convergence, media policy has gravitated into the domain of national information policy strategies, with digital content being identified as a new growth industry (OECD, 1998). The second issue is the relationship among media policy, media regulation, and media governance. Freedman (2008) defines *media policy* as "the development of goals and norms leading to the creation of instruments that are designed to shape the structure and behavior of media systems" (p. 14). This definition is broader than that for *media regulation*, which refers to the application of media policy principles by specialist agencies such as the Federal Communications Commission in the United States or Ofcom in Great Britain, but narrower than *media governance*, which incorporates informal as well as formal means of shaping media systems and refers to the role of supranational as well as national policy agencies (e.g., the role of agencies of global media policy such as the World Trade Organization and the World Intellectual Property Organization; Raboy, 2002). Finally, there are the *politics of media policy*, or the extent to which the forms that media institutions and policy settings take arise not so much as the result of neutral policy expertise as the exercise of power in and through the policy process. In his historical account of the shaping of U.S. broadcasting, Streeter (1996) argued that policy discourses that appear neutral between competing interests have already been shaped by and are "dependent on extensive and ongoing collective activities . . . that typically involve favoring some people and values at the expense of others" (p. xii).

Observing the interaction between political power and the policy process raises the question of the extent to which the conduct of media policy should be seen as reflective of established political and ideological positions and interests. Recent work on media policy has in many cases been strongly influenced by neo-Marxist political economy. David Harvey's (2005) account of the rise of *neoliberalism* as a global ideological project has been particularly influential. Harvey argues that neoliberalism was designed to shift power and resources to corporations and wealthy elites through the privatization of public assets, removal of "public interest" regulations over large corporations, and tax cuts targeted toward the highest-income earners. He defines neoliberalism as

> a theory of political economic practices that proposes that human well being can best be advanced by liberating individual entrepreneurial freedoms and skills within an institutional framework characterized by strong private property rights, free market, and free trade. The role of the state is to create and preserve an institutional framework appropriate to such practices. (Harvey, 2005, p. 2)

Hesmondhalgh (2007) and Freedman (2008) have argued that media policy in the 1990s and 2000s largely involved the implementation of neoliberalism. For Hesmondhalgh (2007), the rise of media and cultural industries to greater prominence coincided with the "Great Downturn" of the world economy in the 1970s and 1980s, generating a policy response focused on *marketization*, or "the process by which market exchange increasingly came to permeate the cultural industries and related sectors" (p. 110). Through a series of waves of such principles being advanced through the global system, Hesmondhalgh argued that "neo-liberalism and the neo-classical conception of the market have made huge advances in the cultural sphere," so "strong traditions of public ownership and regulation . . . were abandoned or severely limited during the neo-liberal turn" (p. 135). Freedman's (2008) account of the politics of media policy in the United States and Britain proposed that the period from the 1980s onward marked a decisive shift from pluralism to neoliberalism in media policy, associated primarily with "a much narrower and more consumer-oriented role for the media," and "conceptualizing media policy . . . towards a focus on the largely economic benefits that may accrue from the exploitation of the media industries" (p. 219). From this perspective, the turn toward creative industries policy discourse as a factor shaping media policy is simply an extension of neoliberal ideologies. Miller (2009) argues that "neo-liberalism is at the core of the creative industries" and that "neoliberalism [has] understood people exclusively through the precepts of selfishness [and] it exercised power on people by governing them through market imperatives" (pp. 270, 271; see also Toby Miller, in this volume).

I would argue that this interpretation of media policy in the 1990s and 2000s as largely involving the enactment of neoliberal principles in the media space, to the benefit of large media conglomerates and at the expense of the public interest, is one-sided and misleading. The term *neoliberal* itself raises issues, as it implies a relationship to liberalism as a political and philosophical tradition that has many dimensions and cannot be reduced to a Marxist caricature of bourgeois ideology. If we take the work of Keynes as an example, he was clearly a liberal who drew on longstanding classical traditions, but his work was central to the development of economic strategies for the reformist left in the post–World War II period. In so far as the economic downturn of the 1970s and 1980s exposed limits to Keynesian demand management policies, the monetarist and laissez-faire responses associated with authors such as Friedrich von Hayek and Milton Friedman were only one response. Others argued for an extension of Keynesian economics to the supply side through activist industrial and labor market policies, drawing on concepts developed through post-Keynesian economics (e.g., Arestis, Dunn, & Sawyer, 1999; Keen, 2001; Lazonick, 1991) and applied in the welfare capitalist states of Europe and Scandinavia (Esping-Anderson, 1990). Jessop and Sum (2006) observed that neoliberalism represents only one possible response to the decline of the post–World War II Keynesian welfare state model, with European neocorporatism and East Asian neostatism being equally important responses (cf. Perraton & Clift, 2004). It has also been observed that—*contra* Harvey (2005)—neoliberalism has little value in explaining the balance of political-economic forces in China (Kipnis, 2007; Nonini, 2008). In relation to creative industries policies, Cunningham (2009) has noted that it is misleading to focus solely on the experience of the Blair and Brown New Labour governments in Britain, as a variety of forms of interventionist media industry policies developed under the signs of creative industries and the creative economy have been emerging throughout Europe, Asia, and the developing world.

The other feature of new media policies in the 2000s and going into the 2010s is the extent to which the media as policy object is radically changing. In the 20th-century era of mass communications media, there were a relatively small number of powerful media producers and distributors and a large number of relatively powerless media consumers. The public interest in media policy entailed a commitment on the part of government to protecting the latter in the face of unequal power relations with the former, whether through regulatory interventions to safeguard against some forms of content, commitments to stimulate certain types of media content production (e.g., local content, children's programming), or, in the case of public service broadcasting, taking up a custodial role in the management of the airwaves and how they are to be used. In the 1980s and 1990s, this protective state role was challenged by positions that can be termed *neoliberal*—although they can also be *left-libertarian*—that wondered why the state should seek to guide consumer behavior, particularly in a context of multiple media channels and content proliferation. In the 2000s, there was further blurring of lines not only between media forms but also between media producers and consumers and between media professionals and so-called pro-ams utilizing social media and distributing user-crested content (Bruns, 2008; Jenkins, 2006). Media industry leader Jordan Levin (Holt & Perren, 2009) describes this process in the following terms:

> What we are presently experiencing is the shift away from a top-down business model being imposed on consumers by the producers and distributors of media to a bottom-up business model emerging out of the consumption behavior of media users. The era in which a privileged few accessed tools to facilitate the publishing of content for distribution over exclusive distribution networks reaching the masses is being eroded by both efficient production tools and peer-to-peer communications that can provide anyone with the ability to communicate their ideas to anyone else, any where, any time. (p. 258)

In such an innovative milieu, we may be tempted to ditch the statism and dirigisme of cultural policy with its Keynesian overtones of the protective state and look instead to the "gales of creative destruction" identified by Joseph Schumpeter as the raison d'etre of capitalist culture. But just as it is one-sided to see new media policies as abandoning a role for government as an enabler of digital media content, it is also a mistake to simply adopt a laissez-faire approach to established media institutions and professions. Moreover, the Marxist critique of capitalism, which continues to be developed through the political economy of communication, reminds us of the extent to which the market itself will not redress questions of inequality of access on a national or a global scale, even if digital media technologies promise new opportunities for popular engagement and consumer cocreation of media content. The most valuable insights into new media policies will come from a capacity to synthesize an understanding of the political economy of new media, the wellsprings of creativity and innovation, and the enabling role of the nation-state.

References

Arestis, P., Dunn, S., & Sawyer, M. (1999). Post-Keynesian economics and its critics. *Journal of Post-Keynesian Economics, 21*(4), 527–549.

Artz, L., Macek, S., and Cloud, D. (Eds.). (2006). *Marxism and communication studies.* New York, NY: Peter Lang.

Australian Research Council Centre of Excellence for Creative Industries and Innovation. (2009). *About CCI.* Retrieved from http://www.cci.edu.au/about/

Bilton, C. (2007). *Management and creativity: From creative industries to creative management.* Oxford, England: Blackwell.

Bleaney, M. (1985). *The rise and fall of Keynesian economics.* Basingstoke, England: Macmillan.

Boltanski, L., & Chiapello, E. (2005). *The new spirit of capitalism* (G. Elliott, Trans.). London, England: Verso.

Bruns, A. (2008). *Blogs, Wikipedia, Second Life and beyond: From production to produsage.* New York, NY: Peter Lang.

Castells, M. (1996). *The rise of the network society* (Vol. 1 of *The information age: Economy, society and culture*). Malden, MA: Blackwell.

Cunningham, S. (2005). Creative enterprises. In J. Hartley (Ed.), *Creative industries* (pp. 282–298). Malden, MA: Blackwell.

Cunningham, S. (2009). Trojan horse or Rorschach blot? Creative industries discourse around the world. *International Journal of Cultural Policy, 15*(4), 375–386.

Dodgson, M., Gann, D., & Salter, A. (2005). *Think, play, do: Technology, innovation, and organization.* Oxford, England: Oxford University Press.

Enterprise Connect. (2009). *Creative Industries Innovation Centre.* Retrieved from http://www.enterpriseconnect.gov.au/Innovation/Pages/CreativeIndustries InnovationCentre.aspx

Esping-Anderson, G. (1990). *The three worlds of welfare capitalism.* Cambridge, England: Polity Press.

Flew, T. (2006). The social contract and beyond in broadcast media policy. *Television and New Media, 7*(3), 282–305.

Flew, T. (2007). *Understanding global media.* Basingstoke, England: Palgrave Macmillan.

Flew, T. (2009). Democracy, participation and convergent media: Case studies in contemporary online news journalism in Australia. *Communications, Politics and Culture, 42*(2), 87–115.

Flew, T., & Cunningham, S. (2002). Policy. In T. Miller (Ed.), *Television studies* (pp. 50–53). London, England: BFI.

Freedman, D. (2008). *The politics of media policy.* Cambridge, England: Polity Press.

Golding, P., & Murdock, G. (2004). Dismantling the digital divide: Rethinking the dynamics of participation and exclusion. In C. Sparks & A. Calabrese (Eds.), *Towards a political economy of culture: Capitalism and communication in the 21st century* (pp. 244–260). Lanham, MD: Rowman & Littlefield.

Hamilton, C. (2005). *Affluenza.* Sydney, Australia: Allen & Unwin.

Harvey, D. (2005). *A brief history of neoliberalism.* Oxford, England: Oxford University Press.

Henten, A., & Skouby, K. E. (2005). New media and trade policy. In L. Lievrouw & S. Livingstone (Eds.), *Handbook of new media* (2nd ed., pp. 386–404). Thousand Oaks, CA: Sage.

Hesmondhalgh, D. (2007). *The cultural industries.* London, England: Sage.

Holt, J. & Perren, A. (Eds.). (2009). *Media industries: History, theory, and method.* Malden: Wiley-Blackwell.

Horwitz, R. (1989). *The irony of regulatory reform: The deregulation of American telecommunications.* New York, NY: Oxford University Press.

Jenkins, H. (2006). *Convergence culture: Where old and new media collide.* New York: New York University Press.

Jessop, B., and Sum, N.-L. (2006). *Beyond the regulation approach: Putting capitalist economies in their place.* Cheltenham, England: Edward Elgar.

Keen, S. (2001). *Debunking economics: The naked emperor of the social sciences.* London, England: Zed Books.

Kipnis, A. (2007). Neo-liberalism reified: *Suzhi* discourse and tropes of neo-liberalism in the People's Republic of China. *Journal of the Royal Anthropological Institute, 13,* 383–400.

Lazonick, W. (1991). *Business organization and the myth of the market economy.* New York, NY: Cambridge University Press.

Livingstone, S., Lunt, P., & Miller, L. (2007). Citizens and consumers: Discursive debates during and after the Communications Act 2003. *Media, Culture and Society, 29*(4), 613–638.

Marx, K. (1982). Labour and alienation. In A. Giddens & D. Held (Eds.), *Classes, power and conflict: Classical and contemporary debates* (pp. 12–19). Basingstoke, England: Macmillan. (Original work published 1844)

Mattelart, A. (1994). *Mapping world communication: War, progress, culture.* Minneapolis: University of Minnesota Press.

McCraw, T. (2007). *Prophet of innovation: Joseph Schumpeter and creative destruction.* Cambridge, MA: Harvard University Press.

Miller, T. (2009). Afterword: Albert and Michael's recombinant DNA. *Continuum: Journal of Media and Cultural Studies, 23*(2), 269–275.

Nelson, C., & Grossberg, L. (Eds.). (1988). *Marxism and the interpretation of culture.* Urbana: University of Illinois Press.

Neveu, E. (2004). Government, the state and media. In J. H. Downing, D. McQuail, P. Schlesinger, & E. Wartella (Eds.), *The SAGE Handbook of Media Studies* (pp. 331–350). Thousand Oaks, CA: Sage.

Nonini, D. (2008). Is China becoming neo-liberal? *Critique of Anthropology, 28*(2), 145–176.

Organisation for Economic Co-operation and Development. (1998). *Content as a new growth industry.* Paris, France: Author.

Organisation for Economic Co-operation and Development. (2007). *Participative Web: User-created content*. Working Group on the Information Economy. Paris, France: Author.

Perez, C. (2004). Technological revolutions, paradigm shifts and socio-institutional change. In E. Reinert (Ed.), *Globalization, economic development and inequality, an alternative perspective* (pp. 217–242). Cheltenham, England: Edward Elgar.

Perraton, J., & Clift, B. (2004). So where are national capitalisms now? In J. Perraton & B. Clift (Eds.), *Where are national capitalisms now?* (pp. 195–260). Basingstoke, England: Palgrave Macmillan.

Picard, R. (1989). *Media economics: Concepts and issues*. Newbury Park, CA: Sage.

Raboy, M. (2002). Media policy in the new communication environment. In M. Raboy (Ed.), *Global media policy in the new millennium* (pp. 3–16). Luton, England: University of Luton Press.

Schlesinger, P. (1991). *Media, state and nation: Political violence and collective identity*. London, England: Sage.

Schlesinger, P. (1997). From cultural defence to political culture: Media, politics, and collective identity in the European Union. *Media, Culture and Society, 19*(3), 369–391.

Schudson, M. (1994). Culture and the integration of modern societies. *International Social Science Journal, 46*(1), 63–80.

Schumpeter, J. (1970). *Capitalism, socialism and democracy*. London, England: Allen & Unwin. (Original work published 1942)

Schuster, J. M. (2002). Sub-national cultural policy—where the action is? Mapping state cultural policy in the United States. *International Journal of Cultural Policy, 8*(2), 181–196.

Scott, A. (2008). Cultural economy: Retrospect and prospect. In H. Anheier & Y. Raj Isar (Eds.), *The cultural economy* (Cultures and Globalization Series, pp. 307–323). Los Angeles, CA: Sage.

Sennett, R. (2006). *The culture of the new capitalism*. New Haven, CT: Yale University Press.

Skidelsky, R. (2000). *John Maynard Keynes: Fighting for Britain 1937–1946* (Vol. 3 of *John Maynard Keynes*). London, England: Macmillan.

Sparks, C., & Calabrese, A. (Eds.). (2004). *Towards a political economy of culture: Capitalism and communication in the 21st century*. Lanham, MD: Rowman & Littlefield.

Streeter, T. (1996). *Selling the air: A critique of the policy of commercial broadcasting in the United States*. Chicago, IL: University of Chicago Press.

Throsby, D. (2008). Modeling the cultural industries. *International Journal of Cultural Policy, 14*(3), 217–232.

United Nations Commission on Trade, Aid and Development. (2008). *The creative economy report*. Geneva, Switzerland: Author.

van Cuilenburg, J., & McQuail, D. (2003). Media policy paradigm shifts: Towards a new communications policy paradigm. *European Journal of Communication, 18*(2), 181–207.

Woolgar, S. (2002). Five rules of virtuality. In S. Woolgar (Ed.), *Virtual society? Technology, cyberbole, reality* (pp. 1–22). Oxford, England: Oxford University Press.

Wyszomirski, M. J. (2008). The local creative economy in the United States of America. In H. Anheier & Y. Raj Isar (Eds.), *The cultural economy* (Cultures and Globalization Series, pp. 199–212). Los Angeles, CA: Sage.

6

Global Deregulation and Media Corporations

Philip M. Napoli

The regulatory environment has a wide range of effects on the structure and behavior of media corporations, which in turn have a variety of effects on the nature of media work and the management of media organizations. The overall trend internationally over the past 30 or so years has been one of gradual deregulation of the media sector. Technological changes that have, in the estimation of many policymakers, contributed to a more competitive, more diverse, and more pluralistic media environment have been the key drivers of this deregulatory trend. The rise of technologies such as cable and satellite television, low-power FM radio, and, more recently, the Internet has reduced barriers to entry into the media sector, loosened bottlenecks in the paths to reaching media audiences, and blurred traditional technological distinctions underlying different platform-specific regulatory models. These developments have provided the impetus for regulators to loosen various media regulations, in an effort to maintain a regulatory environment that is reflective of contemporary economic and technological conditions. There are, of course, differing opinions as to if, or to what extent, deregulation is a necessary or appropriate response to the changes affecting the contemporary media environment, and these points of contention (detailed below) continue to be argued by advocates and opponents of further media deregulation.

This chapter considers the relationship between deregulation and media corporations in terms of the two broad categories of regulatory intervention—structural regulation and behavioral regulation (see also Terry Flew, in this volume). Drawing upon examples from both the United States and Europe, this chapter pays particular attention to the forces that have compelled this deregulatory trend over the past 30 years, the effects of this deregulatory trend on media markets and media corporations, and the dynamics of the contemporary media environment and how they are affecting the regulatory treatment of media corporations. As this chapter will illustrate, the dramatic changes affecting today's media environment are throwing well-established rationales for the regulation of media industries into a state of turmoil, the outcomes of which, at this point, remain unclear.

The Parameters and Principles of Media Regulation

Before exploring the dynamics of media deregulation, how they have affected media corporations, and how they are being affected by contemporary economic and technological developments, it is important to outline the basic parameters of media regulation. Generally, we can identify two broad categories of media regulation. The first of these is structural regulation. Structural regulation refers to those regulations directed at the structure of media organizations and media markets. The most common form of structural regulation is regulation directed at media ownership. There is a long history of regulatory bodies imposing a wide range of media ownership regulations, ranging from regulations that limit or restrict foreign ownership of media outlets, to regulations that limit horizontal or vertical integration within media industry sectors, to regulations that seek to promote or protect the ownership of media outlets by women or minority groups (see, e.g., Commission of the European Communities, 2007; Federal Communications Commission [FCC], 2008). Key rationales for such structural regulations have included economic objectives such as preserving and promoting competition in the media marketplace, as well as noneconomic objectives such as preserving and promoting diversity, pluralism, and localism in media markets (see, e.g., Commission of the European Communities, 2007; FCC, 2008; Napoli, 2001, 2007).

The second broad category of media regulation is behavioral regulation. Behavioral regulations are those regulations that, naturally, are directed at the behavior of media outlets. Most often, these behavioral regulations have taken the form of regulations directed at media content. Thus, for instance, regulators have placed restrictions on the levels of sexuality, violence, and adult language contained within media content and on the cross-border flows of foreign media content. Regulators also have required certain types of content, such as minimum levels of news, public affairs, domestically produced, or educational children's programming. Thus, as should be clear, content regulations can either restrict or promote certain forms of content. Rationales for such regulations have included the protection of children from adult content and the protection of national cultures, along with the broader notion that certain types of media outlets have public service obligations to provide information that contributes to a diverse, pluralistic marketplace of ideas and the effective functioning of the democratic process (see, e.g., Commission of the European Communities, 2007; Napoli, 2001, 2007).

Behavioral regulations that have addressed media organization practices beyond the realm of content creation and distribution have included areas such as community outreach and the gathering and usage of audience data. The latter area has become a focal point of concern in recent years, as the Web and other inherently interactive media technologies (such as DVRs) are providing content providers and advertisers with a wide range of new tools and opportunities to gather information about media audiences and to use this information to deliver more targeted advertisements—in some cases without the audiences' knowledge or consent that such information is being gathered and analyzed (see Andrejevic, 2007; Napoli, in press). Here, obviously, the central policy concern is consumer privacy (Cohen, 1996).

As should be clear, structural and behavioral regulations often overlap in terms of the goals they seek to achieve. Both often are directed at preserving and promoting policy principles such as diversity and pluralism. They simply go about pursuing these goals differently. We see this, for example, in the way that the European Union distinguishes between *internal media pluralism* and *external media pluralism*. Internal media pluralism in this case refers to "an obligation with respect to programme requirements or structural obligations, such as the composition of management bodies or bodies responsible for programme/content selection" (Commission of the European Communities, 2007, p. 8)—essentially, pluralism achievable via behavioral regulations. External media pluralism, in contrast, refers to "having many competing and diverse channels or titles controlled by many different players" (Commission of the European Communities, 2007, p. 8)—pluralism achievable via structural regulations.

Some argue that structural regulations are simply a more indirect way of achieving the goals of behavioral regulation. That is, structural regulations often are seen as a mechanism for affecting media content—in ways, it could be argued, that effectively circumvent restrictions against direct regulation of media content (see Napoli, 2001). Others, however, argue that structural regulations serve policy principles such as diversity, pluralism, competition, and localism independently of whether they have any explicitly measurable effects on content (e.g., Baker, 2006). From this standpoint, simply diffusing the capacity to communicate as widely as possible is fundamental to a democratic public sphere and thus to the normative goals of media regulators.

And finally, it is important to recognize the perspective of many media regulators and policy scholars that it is, in fact, the *absence* of such structural and behavioral regulations that is most conducive to achieving desired levels of pluralism, competition, diversity, and localism. From this perspective, a media marketplace free of such government interventions can best be counted on to most effectively serve the diverse information needs of the citizenry and to provide the most diverse array of content options (see, e.g., Owen, 1975; Pool, 1984).

_____ Media Deregulation and Media Corporations

The combination of a profound confidence in market mechanisms to produce the range of content that best serves the informational and cultural needs and interests of the citizenry (see above) and a technological environment that rapidly breeds new delivery platforms—ranging from cable and satellite television to VCRs and DVD players to low-power FM radio to the Web—and, consequently, new, additional mechanisms for the potential enhancement of competition, diversity, pluralism, and localism has meant that the past 30 years have been characterized by a steady trend toward the deregulation of media markets and media corporations, in the realms of both structural and behavioral regulation.

Structural Deregulation and Media Corporations

In terms of structural regulation, the gradual relaxation of media ownership restrictions and the gradual migration from state to private, commercial ownership of media outlets that has taken place in many countries around the world have had a profound effect on the structure and behavior of media corporations. Specifically, we have seen the loosening or eliminating of both horizontal and vertical ownership restrictions in the broadcast television, broadcast radio, and cable television sectors. In the United States, for instance, national radio station ownership caps have been eliminated, as have vertical ownership limits related to cable television networks and cable television systems, as well as line-of-business restrictions preventing local co-ownership of telecommunications and video programming service providers. National and local broadcast television station ownership caps have been relaxed, as have limitations on broadcast station–newspaper cross-ownership (see FCC, 2008).

In Europe, the past 30 years have seen a widespread privatization and commercialization of media ownership (see, e.g., Harcourt, 1998; Hitchens, 2006), given the extent to which government-operated public service media long have been a much more prominent component of the media sector in Europe than in the United States. In 1989, the European Commission's *Television Without Frontiers Directive* (Council of the European Commission, 1989) spurred a substantial amount of horizontal integration within media sectors (Harcourt, 1998). Increased vertical integration and cross-media concentration followed in the late 1990s as a result of the relaxation of a variety of cross-media ownership restrictions (Harcourt, 1998).

Together, these trends have contributed to the rise of the modern, cross-platform, global media conglomerate (see Gershon, 1996). Such entities have been a focal point of concern, advocacy, and analysis for media industry and policy scholars, public interest organizations, and some policymakers over the past three decades (see, e.g., Bagdikian, 2004; Herman & Chomsky, 1988; Klinenberg, 2007). A variety of potential harms have been associated with the increased horizontal and vertical integration associated with structural deregulation, ranging from diminished diversity of available ideas and viewpoints as a result of fewer owners to diminished innovation, risk taking, and quality in content as a result of the increased prominence in content creation of large, publicly held, and bureaucratized media organizations.

_____ Behavioral Deregulation and Media Corporations

This deregulatory trend also took hold (if not quite as powerfully as in the realm of structural regulation) in the realm of behavioral regulation. In the United States, for instance, the past 30 years have seen the elimination of a wide range of content regulations that once were imposed on broadcast licensees. Perhaps the most famous example is the elimination of the well-known Fairness Doctrine in the late 1980s. The Fairness Doctrine required that broadcasters provide coverage of controversial issues of public importance, but in a balanced manner, in order that opposing perspectives on the issues were given the opportunity to be heard. Other content requirements, such as the provision of minimum levels of local news and public affairs programming, and rules requiring broadcasters to provide public figures with airtime to respond to political editorials or personal attacks, also have been eliminated. Today, requirements for minimum levels of educational children's programming are virtually the only substantive affirmative content requirement remaining for U.S. broadcast licensees. It is important to note, however, that this deregulatory trend has been less pronounced in the realm of content _restrictions,_ where regulations on broadcast indecency remain in effect, though they are perhaps applied less rigorously than in years past.

In Europe, behavioral deregulation focused primarily on eliminating national-level restrictions affecting the flow of programming across European nations. These efforts began with the _Television Without Frontiers Directive_ (implemented in 1989), which sought to create a single European television market by eliminating restrictions that individual countries had placed on the importation of foreign television networks, channels, and programming (see Council of the European Commission, 1989). As a result of this deregulatory initiative, individual content distributors possessed much greater freedom—and choice—in terms of the range of content options available to them to provide to their audiences.

As has been the case in terms of structural deregulation, the effects on media corporations of behavioral deregulation have been profound. For example, in the United States, research has compellingly demonstrated that the rise of the very popular, and lucrative, talk radio format can be attributed largely to the elimination of the Fairness Doctrine (Hazlett & Sosa, 1997). Once radio stations were freed of Fairness Doctrine obligations, they were able to pursue much more politically oriented (and overtly ideological) programming without concerns over having to respond to multiple burdensome Fairness Doctrine complaints. In this regard, political talk radio programs such as Rush Limbaugh's essentially owe their existence to the elimination of the Fairness Doctrine.

Media Deregulation and the New Media Environment

Today, the dramatically destabilizing effects of the Internet as a platform for the production and distribution of content are contributing to a reconsideration of the rationales for both structural and behavioral media regulation, as the dynamics of media markets and the relationship between media corporations and audiences are in the midst of profound change.

Looking first at structural (i.e., ownership) regulation, we now find ourselves amidst both a reconsideration of the viability of large media conglomerates by media industry strategists and a reconsideration as to whether concentration of media ownership merits continued attention from regulators. From a strategic standpoint, the appeal of the large-scale media conglomerate has been undermined by the fact that many of the economies of scale and scope that were anticipated to arise from ever greater horizontal and vertical integration failed to materialize in some industry sectors to the extent that was anticipated. Also failing to materialize—to a much greater extent—were the much ballyhooed benefits of "synergy," which were expected to arise from the ability of media conglomerates to effectively develop and promote media properties across the variety of media platforms and outlets across which they had an ownership stake (Friedman, 2009; Roberts, 2009). Media strategists today seem less convinced that bigger is necessarily better. Today, those units of large, multiplatform media corporations that are being hardest hit by the destabilizing effects of the Internet and the ongoing economic crisis are being cast off in an effort to shed those organizational components imposing the greatest drag on profitability (see, e.g., Friedman, 2009). Of course, whether this scenario is a function of the true failure of horizontal and vertical integration and conglomeration as organizational strategies and the inherent value in content creation residing in smaller, more decentralized organizational contexts, or whether it is purely a function of today's challenging economic climate, is difficult to determine.

From a regulatory standpoint, the apparently declining economic imperatives toward greater concentration of ownership and the emerging technological environment in which individual media content producers and distributors now stand on closer-to-equal footing with traditional media corporations, and in which long-standing line-of-business restrictions separating traditional media sectors are blurring as a result of digital convergence, have left policymakers speculating as to whether structural regulations that are focused on the ownership of media outlets within or across narrowly defined media sectors serve a meaningful purpose any longer (see, e.g., Commission of the European Communities, 2007; FCC, 2008).

There are those, however, who would argue that, while the traditional *dangers* associated with concentration of media ownership are, thanks to the Web, no longer a legitimate concern, the potential *benefits* of concentration to traditional media corporations are essential at this particular point in time in order to preserve their viability. From this perspective, deregulation allowing further media concentration is essential to preserving traditional media in the face of the dramatically reconfigured competitive environment imposed by the Web, in which media corporations must now essentially compete with every individual with Internet access for audience attention. As audience attention and advertising dollars migrate to the Web, traditional media sectors such as newspapers and broadcast television are increasingly suffering. And although these sectors have diversified into the online space, the bottom line is that the nature of the Web as a content production and distribution platform has meant that neither content nor audiences have yet to be able to be monetized to the extent they have been able to be monetized on traditional media platforms (for a detailed discussion of these issues, see Napoli, in press).

As a result, today we see scenarios in which regulators are reconsidering long-held stances against further concentration of ownership within traditional media sectors. In the United States, for instance, even FCC Commissioner Michael Copps, who led the charge against further relaxation of media ownership restrictions for much of this past decade, has begun to express a willingness to, for example, consider relaxing restrictions on broadcast station–newspaper cross-ownership. His reconsideration is based on the premise that these struggling media platforms need to be able to pursue all available strategic options (such as maximizing economies of scope across newspaper and broadcast operations) in order to maintain their viability in this dramatically reconfigured media environment (Eggerton, 2009).

And, while one could question whether the preservation of established, though possibly outmoded, business models is an appropriate policy priority for communications regulators (see, e.g., Cooper, 2009), the fact that the bulk of the economic resources devoted to the production of the kind of news and information that regulators long have held as central to a well-functioning marketplace of ideas remain contained within such traditional media complicates the analytical calculus to some extent. Some policy scholars have gone so far as to argue that the preservation and promotion of industry and organizational structures that facilitate the production of such content should be seen as the central objective of media ownership regulations (Candeub, 2008). The point here is that the Web has not yet, according to many observers, served as a platform that adequately supports the production of rigorous, professional news reporting; investigative journalism; and thorough, well-researched analysis (see, e.g., Starr, 2009).

Certainly, some would disagree with this proposition, arguing that the wealth of user-generated content being supported by the Web is, in the aggregate, effectively serving the information needs of democracy, and is doing so while often utilizing innovative production models that frequently eschew the potentially corrupting effects of the commercial business models that have come to dominate the traditional media (see, e.g., Benkler, 2006). However, as long as the perception persists that the new media environment is not as hospitable to, or as conducive to, the production of various forms of rigorous journalism, then this logic toward allowing greater ownership concentration in order to preserve traditional media is likely to gain momentum. In sum, an increasingly prevalent perspective in contemporary media regulation is that new technologies such as the Web have alleviated the dangers traditionally associated with media concentration while (somewhat ironically) at the same time creating a powerful imperative for allowing greater media concentration to take place.

Of course, one could also argue that the recent turn away from ownership concentration in some sectors as a strategic imperative, and the financial damage that has been wrought upon those media corporations that pursued this strategic imperative, represents exactly the kind of evidence on behalf of restricting concentration of media ownership that advocates of ownership regulations long have been seeking. In this case, the fact that media corporations today exhibit weaker tendencies toward pursuing greater concentration of ownership does not mean that regulations preventing such activities are unnecessary or irrelevant.

Just as the rationales for structural regulation are, in some ways, under assault by contemporary economic and technological changes, so too is the underlying logic that has supported various strands of content-focused behavioral regulation. Content regulations have historically been applied to traditional electronic media such as broadcast radio and television and, to a much lesser degree, cable and satellite television. And, in new media contexts such as the Web, we also have seen the emergence of both successful and unsuccessful efforts to impose content regulations on online content providers. In some national contexts (such as the United States), efforts to impose content regulations online have been directed at issues such as adult content. In addition, in recent years the issue of "network neutrality" has been a focal point of online content regulation debates. Network neutrality refers to the notion that online service providers should not be allowed to discriminate in terms of the Web sites to which subscribers have access or in terms of the speed at which sites can be accessed. Whether such regulations are a necessary and appropriate way of pursuing policy objectives and whether such regulations represent permissible intrusions upon the speech rights of Internet service providers are issues that remain very much up for debate (see, e.g., Ammori, 2008–2009).

It is important to recognize that the underlying justifications for many content regulations were based in large part on the technological characteristics of particular media. Thus, for instance, broadcast regulation has been justified largely on the basis of the scarcity of the broadcast spectrum (see, e.g., Hettich, 2008). Today, however, challenges to such technologically based justifications arise from the ongoing convergence of media platforms—particularly in terms of the extent to which content produced across various media (broadcast television, cable and satellite television, radio, print) is now available online (Hettich, 2008). As a recent study prepared for the European

Commission noted, "Technological and economic changes . . . are affecting established media and communications sectors. . . . Traditional policy approaches . . . that were developed in an earlier era are being strained by these changes and there is a growing need to develop policy approaches appropriate for the contemporary and future environment" (K. U. Leuven, Jönköping International Business School, Central European University, & Ernst & Young Consultancy, 2009, p. 9).

In such an environment, sector-specific behavioral regulations lose some of their logical consistency, and the somewhat fragile house of cards of technology-specific regulatory justifications begins to crumble (see, e.g., Thierer, 2007). Consider, for instance, the various programming requirements and restrictions that many nations have placed on their broadcast sector. The fact that broadcast programming can—and increasingly is—viewed via platforms that are free of such regulations (e.g., cable television, the Web) raises the question of whether broadcast programming can and should be regulated in a manner that is supposedly reflective of the unique technical characteristics of the broadcast platform, when in fact a shrinking proportion of the audience is actually relying on the broadcast platform to access this programming. Policymakers have, consequently, recognized the need for greater consistency across platforms in terms of the regulatory models that are developed and employed (see, e.g., Commission of the European Communities, 2005). At this point, however, there seems to be as much interest among regulators in migrating broadcast-era systems of content regulation to new media platforms (particularly in Europe) as there is interest in abandoning broadcast-era systems of content regulation in the face of these new content delivery platforms (see, e.g., Hettich, 2008).

This issue of logical consistency is compounded by more pragmatic concerns related to jurisdictional boundaries and implementation approaches. As content migrates to global-reach media technologies such as the Web, the logic of national-level content regulations becomes more difficult to justify and enforce. How, for instance, can U.S. regulators regulate content available via the Web in the United States but produced and distributed from Asia? And can traditional top-down forms of content regulation, such as government-mandated programming restrictions, continue to be effectively justified in an interactive media environment in which audiences are increasingly empowered to control the inflow of content, via tools such as V-chips and Web filtering software? It would seem that less intrusive mechanisms than direct government intervention for effectively protecting children from potentially harmful content are now available.

One can increasingly question the necessity of affirmative requirements for any category of content provider when today's media environment seems to offer easy access to such a wide array of content types and sources. Thus, for instance, does it make sense to force broadcasters to provide certain forms of socially beneficial content (such as news and public affairs programming) when there may be so many other media sources providing content that can potentially serve as substitutes for such programming? To some extent, the special regulatory attention devoted to broadcast content has always been premised on its unique *pervasiveness* (read: popularity and influence). In today's highly fragmented media environment, broadcasting's privileged position in this regard is now very much in decline. Along similar lines, it has been interesting to see in the United States how both the policymaking and the policy advocacy communities have essentially begun to abandon community access television (local, community-based cable television programming mandated by local franchising authorities) in the face of the wide array of forms of local community expression and information exchange that can be cultivated online. Examples such as this illustrate the way that the increasingly fragmented media environment undermines regulatory approaches that impose specific affirmative content regulations on individual media platforms.

Finally, it should be noted that, as much as the new media environment is challenging traditional rationales for content-focused behavioral regulation, it is also inspiring increased interest in other areas of behavioral regulation— such as the realm of privacy of audiences' media consumption. As was noted above, today's highly interactive media environment provides unprecedented opportunities for content providers and advertisers to gather information about audiences (Napoli, in press). This has spawned a debate over whether more intensive government regulation and/or industry self-regulation are necessary to restrict the gathering and usage of information related to audiences' media usage. In the United States, in keeping with the general trend that has been discussed here, the Federal Trade Commission (2009) has proposed a set of self-regulatory principles related to audience privacy and information gathering that the agency hopes will be adopted by the media and advertising industries. This, however, has not stopped the U.S. Congress from devoting a substantial amount of scrutiny in recent years to online information gathering practices such as behavioral targeting and deep packet inspection (see, e.g., U.S. House of Representatives, 2008). In Europe, the European Commission has become similarly increasingly attentive to protecting online privacy, threatening to impose regulations unless industry self-regulation becomes more stringent (Williams, 2009).

Conclusion

In sum, many of the traditional logics of both structural and behavioral regulation of media corporations have, in recent years, been increasingly challenged by the evolutionary path of our media environment. This situation has introduced some further incentives for deregulation beyond those that already characterized the pre-Internet regulatory environment. As the Web becomes an increasingly important mechanism by which content is distributed and accessed, and as the traditional strict sender-receiver dynamic that long has characterized the relationship between media corporations and their audiences continues to unravel, regulatory approaches to media corporations and the networks over which they operate will require continued reconsideration.

We are only just beginning to understand the complex interactions between traditional media corporations and individual "users" in new media spaces. And we are certainly only just beginning to thoroughly examine the regulatory implications of these altered dynamics (see, e.g., Benkler, 2006; Napoli, in press; Wunsch-Vincent & Vickery, 2007).

Research that focuses on the nature of media work can make valuable contributions to these policy discussions, particularly in terms of contributing to a greater understanding of the interactions between "professional" media production and user-generated content, in terms of the inroads that user-generated content is making into the strategies and tactics employed by media organizations, and in terms of enhancing our understanding of how the resources devoted to the production and distribution of various content forms (particularly those considered highly valuable by policymakers) are being redistributed across old and new media platforms. Ultimately, as media work extends beyond traditional media organizations, the thinking of media policymakers needs to do the same.

References

Ammori, M. (2008–2009). Beyond content neutrality: Understanding content-based promotion of democratic speech. *Federal Communications Law Journal, 61,* 273–324.

Andrejevic, M. (2007). *iSpy: Surveillance and power in the interactive era.* Lawrence: University Press of Kansas.

Bagdikian, B. H. (2004). *The new media monopoly.* Boston, MA: Beacon Press.

Baker, C. E. (2006). *Media concentration and democracy: Why ownership matters.* New York, NY: Cambridge University Press.

Benkler, Y. (2006). *The wealth of networks: How social production transforms markets and freedom.* New Haven, CT: Yale University Press.

Candeub, A. (2008). Media ownership regulation, the First Amendment, and democracy's future. *UC Davis Law Review, 41,* 1547–1611.

Cohen, J. E. (1996). A right to read anonymously: A closer look at "copyright management" in cyberspace. *Connecticut Law Review, 28,* 981–1039.

Commission of the European Communities. (2005, June). *i2010—A European information society for growth and employment.* Retrieved from http://ec.europa.eu/information_society/eeurope/i2010/index_en.htm

Commission of the European Communities. (2007, January). *Media pluralism in the Member States of the European Union.* Retrieved from http://ec.europa.eu/information_society/media_taskforce/doc/pluralism/media_pluralism_swp_en.pdf

Commission of the European Communities. (2008, April). *Preparing Europe's digital future.* Retrieved from http://ec.europa.eu/information_society/eeurope/i2010/docs/annual_report/2008/i2010_mid-term_review_en.pdf

Cooper, M. (2009). The future of journalism is not in the past: Reframing the debate over how to "save" journalism. Donald McGannon Communication Research

Center Working Paper. Retrieved from http://www.fordham.edu/images/
undergraduate/communications/the%20future%20of%20journalism-huff.pdf

Council of the European Commission. (1989). *Television without frontiers directive.*
Retrieved from http://eur-lex.europa.eu/LexUriServ/site/en/consleg/1989/L/
01989L0552-19970730-en.pdf

Eggerton, J. (2009, March 26). Copps: FCC may need to revisit newspaper/broadcast
cross-ownership. *Broadcasting & Cable.* Retrieved from http://www.broadcasting
cable.com/article/190754-Copps_FCC_May_Need_To_Revisit_Newspaper_
Broadcast_Cross_Ownership.php

Federal Communications Commission. (2008). *2006 Quadrennial regulatory review—
Review of the commission's broadcast ownership rules and other rules pursuant to
Section 202 of the Telecommunications Act of 1996,* 71 Fed. Reg. 45,511.

Federal Trade Commission. (2009, February). *Self-regulatory principles for online
behavioral advertising.* FTC Staff Report. Retrieved from http://www.ftc.gov/
opa/2009/02/behavad.shtm

Friedman, W. (2009, May 29). Time Warner divorces AOL, corporate "synergy" now
passé. *TV Watch.* Retrieved from http://www.mediapost.com/publications/?fa=
Articles.showArticle&art_aid=106985&passFuseAction=PublicationsSearch.show
SearchReslts&art_searched=synergy&page_number=0&searchTab=all

Gershon, R. A. (1996). *The transnational media corporation: Global messages and
free market competition.* Mahwah, NJ: Erlbaum.

Harcourt, A. (1998). The European Commission and the regulation of the media
industry. *Cardozo Arts & Entertainment Law Journal, 16,* 425–449.

Hazlett, T. W., & Sosa, D. W. (1997). Was the Fairness Doctrine a "chilling effect"?
Evidence from the post-deregulation radio market. *Journal of Legal Studies, 26,*
279–301.

Herman, E. S., & Chomsky, N. (1988). *Manufacturing consent: The political economy of the mass media.* New York, NY: Pantheon.

Hettich, P. (2008). YouTube to be regulated? The FCC sites tight, while European
broadcast regulators make the grab for the Internet. *St. John's Law Review, 82,*
1447–1508.

Hitchens, L. (2006). *Broadcasting pluralism and diversity: A comparative study of
policy and regulation.* Oxford, England: Hart.

Klinenberg, E. (2007). *Fighting for air: The battle to control America's media.*
New York, NY: Metropolitan Books.

K. U. Leuven, Jönköping International Business School, Central European University,
& Ernst & Young Consultancy. (2009, April). *Independent study on indicators
for media pluralism in the member states—towards a risk-based approach.*
Report prepared for the European Commission, Directorate-General Information
Society and Media.

Napoli, P. M. (2001). *Foundations of communications policy: Principles and process
in the regulation of electronic media.* Cresskill, NJ: Hampton Press.

Napoli, P. M. (Ed.). (2007). *Media diversity and localism: Meaning and metrics.*
Mahwah, NJ: Erlbaum.

Napoli, P. M. (in press). *Audience evolution: New technologies and the transformation of media audiences.* New York, NY: Columbia University Press.

Owen, B. M. (1975). *Economics and freedom of expression.* Cambridge, MA:
Ballinger.

Pool, I. (1984). *Technologies of freedom: On free speech in an electronic age.* Cambridge, MA: Belknap Press.

Roberts, J. L. (2009, May 5). Big media, R.I.P.: Media conglomerates were supposed to take over the world. So why are they dying? *Newsweek.* Retrieved from http://www.newsweek.com/id/195961

Starr, P. (2009, March 4). Goodbye to the age of newspapers (hello to a new era of corruption). *The New Republic.* Retrieved from http://www.tnr.com/article/goodbye-the-age-newspapers-hello-new-era-corruption

Thierer, A. (2007). Why regulate broadcasting? Toward a consistent First Amendment standard for the information age. *CommLaw Conspectus, 15,* 431–482.

U.S. House of Representatives. (2008, July 17). *Committee on Energy and Commerce: Hearing on what your broadband provider knows about your Web use: Deep packet inspection and communications laws and policies.* Retrieved from http://archives.energycommerce.house.gov/cmte_mtgs/110-ti-hrg.071708 .DeepPacket.shtml

Williams, C. (2009, March 31). EU issues ultimatum in internet privacy. *The Register.* Retrieved from http://www.theregister.co.uk/2009/03/31/kuneva_behavioural/

Wunsch-Vincent, S., & Vickery, G. (2007). *Participative Web: User-created content.* Report prepared for the OECD Committee for Information, Computer and Communications Policy. Paris, France: Organisation for Economic Co-operation and Development.

7 The New International Division of Cultural Labor[1, 2]

Toby Miller

Management studies have taken an innovative—one might say *progressive*—turn in recent times.[3] Many managers and students of management are no longer either instrumentalist accumulators or human-relations softheads. They are even questioning the power dynamics of controlling employees! Change is also afoot for labor studies. More and more workers are transcending craft-union modes of organization in the context of calls for flexibility and lifelong learning. Taylorism and Fordism are not dead: Scientific management rears its ugly head every day and in every way, at the same time as secure employment remains the hope of many. But massive changes are taking place in the division of labor. Many of them are evident in the cultural sphere, especially the media.

In this chapter, I explain the division of labor; theorize its global cultural aspects; offer a case study of U.S. film, television, and electronic games; and outline worker resistance to casual media labor.

In the 18th century, the first great theorist of the division of labor, Adam Smith, took pin making as his key example:

> One man draws out the wire, another straightens it, a third cuts it, a fourth points it, a fifth grinds it at the top for receiving the head; to make the head requires three distinct operations; to put it on is a peculiar business, to whiten the pins is another; it is even a trade by itself to put them into the paper . . .
>
> The division of labor . . . occasions, in every art, a proportionable increase of the productive powers of labor. (Smith, 1970, p. 110)

Today, the expression *division of labor* is used to describe sectoral differences in an economy, the occupations and skills of a labor force, and the organization of tasks within a firm. Neoclassical economists suggest that wages increase with age, at a diminishing rate; unemployment and earnings are related to skills; already highly trained people benefit from ongoing training; the market determines the division of labor; and human-capital investments are less predictably valuable than more material ones (Becker, 1983, p. 16). Most labor-economics theory is based on these assumptions as applied to the United States, with little regard for empirical evidence from elsewhere (Hamermesh, 2002) or for theories based on labor as a *source* of value, rather than a brake on it.

Marxism offers a different story from this supply-and-demand magic. Its methods involve talking to people, visiting places, uncovering the past, and adding and subtracting actually existing numbers. This is what it finds. Objects and services obtain their surplus value as commodities through exploitation of the value derived from the labor that makes them. Once these commodities enter circulation with a price, they attain exchange value. The power gained by capitalism, through ever-widening exchange, includes both surplus value, realized as profit, and authority over the conditions and possibilities of labor, embodied as workplace power. The division of labor is the mechanism for linking productivity, exploitation, and social control. As its subdivisions multiply and spread geographically, capital acquires a talent for hiding the cooperation of labor that constitutes it, and expands its reach to counter redistributive gains made by workers through political activity (Marx, 1906, pp. 49, 83). Smith himself saw that the market must be extended internationally in order to sustain the division of labor, and the International Monetary Fund (2000) positions the division of labor at the center of globalization, in keeping with Smith's desire for a worldwide factory and mercantile republic (Mattelart, 2002).

The development of surplus production and the division of labor correspond to four distinct phases of trading history. In the 14th and 15th centuries, a mercantile system arose from calculations, appropriations, and exchanges of climate, geography, flora, fauna, and people. Exchanges of goods turned into exchanges of labor. As food commodities made their way around the globe, so did workers, often as slaves. When machinery was developed, work split into an industrial mode. Between the 16th and 18th centuries, cities grew into manufacturing sites, populations urbanized, and wages displaced farming as the basis of subsistence (Lang & Hines, 1993). This is the moment of Smith's famous pin-making example.

At the same time, new forms of labor were institutionalized in empire. During the 18th and 19th centuries, manufacturing went on at the center, with food, raw materials, and slaves imported from the periphery or shuffled around it. In the 20th century, assembly-line control, with its quid pro quo of sufficient wages to buy the products being assembled, became a Fordist paradigm. The labor force was divided between blue-collar workers, who undertook tasks on the line, and white-collar workers, who observed and timed them (Scott, 1998). Differences of opinion emerged about the significance of the balance of trade to a country's well-being. Mercantilists thought it should be controlled, but free traders wanted market forces to rule, in accordance with factor endowments and an international division of labor. Keynesian responses to the 1930s Depression made protectionism a more legitimate position in economic theory, until stagflation emerged from the transnational phase that commenced after the war (Cohen, 1991; Keynes, 1957; Strange, 1995; Wallerstein, 1989). By the mid-1980s, offshore production by multinationals exceeded trade between states for the first time. Since then, the global capitalist economy has depended on the integration of production processes; even when geographically dispersed, they remain governed by states and parastatal institutions in the service of capital accumulation. Life cycle models of international products suggest that they are first made and consumed in the center, in a major industrial economy; then exported to the periphery; and finally produced and consumed "out there," once technology is standardized and savings can be made on the labor front.

Hence the idea of a New International Division of Labor (NIDL), which discloses that developing markets for labor and sales, and the shift from the spatial *sen*sitivities of electrics to the spatial *in*sensitivities of electronics, have pushed businesses beyond treating Third World countries as suppliers of raw materials to looking on them as shadow-setters of the price of work, competing among themselves and with the First World for employment. As production split across continents, the prior division of the globe into a small number of empires and satellites and a majority of underdeveloped countries has been compromised. Fröbel, Heinrichs, and Kreye (1980) christened this trend the NIDL. Whereas the old IDL had kept labor costs down through the formal and informal slavery of colonialism (the trade in people and indentureship) and importation of cheap raw materials with value added in the metropole, successful action by the working class at the center redistributed income. The response from capital was to export production to the Third World, focusing increasingly on young women workers.

So how does the division of labor affect culture and the media? Artists, musicians, poets, and scholars traveled across royal courts, salons, and universities for many centuries prior to capitalism. But that revolution in social relations in Europe and the United States was accompanied by both new methods and new meanings associated with the exchange of bodies, ideologies, images, and money. Culture, which had previously referred to tending land, came to *personify* instrumentalism at the same time as *negating* it: On the one hand, there was the industrialization of agriculture; on the other, the tutoring of individual taste. For example, German, French, and Spanish dictionaries of the 18th century testify to a movement of the word *culture* in the direction of spiritual cultivation and away from animal husbandry. With the spread of literacy and publishing, and the advent of customs and laws that were shared, administered, and understood through the printed word, cultural texts supplemented and supplanted physical force as sources of authority. As the Industrial Revolution moved populations to cities, food was imported and new textual forms were exchanged, for both practical and entertainment purposes. Along came a society of consumers and an art world. There was an obvious corollary in labor terms: the emergence of *poligrafi* in 15th-century Venice and hacks in 18th-century London, who wrote popular books about conduct—instructions on daily life. Thus began a division of cultural labor in the modern sense (Benhabib, 2002; Briggs & Burke, 2002; de Pedro, 1991, 1999; Williams, 1983).

Industrialization and public education created new forms of media work in the 20th century. By midcentury, Fritz Machlup, neoclassical prophet of the knowledge society, was developing typologies of postindustrial work that would help make the United States a research leader by focusing its efforts within an opportunity-cost paradigm of intense pragmatism. His *Production and Distribution of Knowledge in the United States* (1962) became a bedside essential for the emerging ideologists of human capital. It showed how the research-and-development emphasis of U.S. industry, state, and education was crucial to its further development as an economy and a society.

Machlup's ideas caught on with both left and right in the United States. Most important (if improbable) for the study of the media and culture, they appealed to Barry Goldwater, Ronald Reagan, and others in the mid-1960s who were railing against the "Great Society" ideas of liberalism. Their defeat at the 1964 presidential election, seemingly a death rattle for the right, was soon followed by Reagan's 1966 campaign for the governorship of California, which he launched with the following words: "I propose . . . 'A Creative Society' . . . to discover, enlist and mobilize the incredibly rich human resources of California [through] innumerable people of creative talent." The idea of a "Creative Society" became central to Reagan's campaign. His rhetoric publicly birthed today's idea of using technology to unlock the creativity lurking in individuals, thereby permitting them to become happy and productive. And with the First World losing manufacturing jobs because of the NIDL from the 1970s, culture became a core employment site in the Global North. Many new occupations within the First World now come from the culture and media sector. Their connection is knowledge, information, emotion, and communication (Hardt & Negri, 2000; also see Folbre, 2003).

Daniel Bell discerns four changes in the Global North's economy from production to services:

- The preeminence of professionalism and technique.

- The importance of theory to innovate and generate public policies.

- The formation of a discourse of the future.

- New intellectual technologies that help make decisions (Mattelart, 2003).

The new turn since that time has further ramified Machlup's and Bell's prescriptions, with the First World recognizing that its economic future lies in finance capital and ideology rather than agriculture and manufacturing— seeking revenue from innovation and intellectual property, not minerals or masses. Hence former U.S. Secretary of State and master of the dark art of international relations Henry Kissinger's consulting firm advised that the United States must "win the battle of the world's information flows, dominating the airwaves as Great Britain once ruled the seas" (Rothkopf, 1997, pp. 38, 47). India's venerable last gasp of Nehruvianism, its Planning Commission, has a committee for creative industries. The United Nations

Educational, Scientific and Cultural Organization's (UNESCO, 2002) Global Alliance for Cultural Diversity heralds creative industries. China, which foresees an end to relying on cheap manufacturing labor to obtain economic growth, has announced new policies that follow the prescription (Keane, 2006). This is a technocratic vision dominated by experts, a world of modernity, rationality, and the ability to apply reason to problems and seek salvation in the secular. Such theorists as Joel Kotkin (2001) merrily predict a U.S. economy dictated by "an aristocracy of talent" (p. 22).

Manuel Castells suggests we inhabit an epoch of networks of knowledge workers, effectively a ruling class operating through technique and technology (see also Geert Lovink and Ned Rossiter, in this volume). This is not the daily society of humanity but a society, after Gilles Deleuze and Félix Guattari, of control (Mattelart, 2003). Castells discerns two economic models at work here. In the first system, the Anglo-Saxon one, services substitute for manufactures, with finance displacing physical labor. The second model, from Japan and Germany, combines the two, rather than substituting one for the other (Hardt & Negri, 2000). For their part, Michael Hardt and Antonio Negri (2000) developed the idea of immaterial labor to describe the tendency to exchange information, knowledge, and emotion, filtered through the computer and its methods of invigilation and abstracted from physical work. The problem with this approach is that it misrecognizes the number of cultural occupations that are monumentally material—consider the health and safety risks endured by camera operators, stunt people, models, singers, transport captains, set carpenters, cell phone testers, caterers, and computer *habitués*.

The culture industries comprise: music; sports; museums; education; the manufacture and recycling of computers, televisions, electronic games, and telephones; and the production and distribution of texts from film, TV, radio, music, the press, and electronic games. Within these sectors lie the following groups of workers, albeit with much overlap:

- Creators, such as musicians, directors, writers, journalists, Web designers, and technical workers, who make new art and ideas.

- Artisans, including sound engineers, editors, cinematographers, carpenters, and electricians, who communicate the art and ideas of others and provide infrastructural services.

- Impresarios, who connect proprietors and executives to creators.

- Proprietors and executives, who control employment and investment and negotiate with states.

- Critics, who create new interpretations.

- Audiences, whose labor as workers pays for content, whose labor as interpreters gives it meaning, and whose labor as imaginary people is its alibi.

These groups operate within specific institutional contexts:

- Private bureaucracies, controlling investment and distribution.
- Public bureaucracies, offering what capitalism cannot.
- Small businesses, run by charismatic individuals.
- Networks, fluid associations formed to undertake specific projects.

Private bureaucracies continue to control most of the cultural and copyright industries, frequently in collaboration with less formal networks, while public bureaucracies experience pressure to comport themselves in an increasingly commercial manner (Hesmondhalgh, 2002).

A group of analysts has applied these ideas and the model of manufacturing migrating from Western Europe to Asia to suggest that we are now in a New International Division of Cultural Labor (NICL).[4] I outline below how this has had an impact on the media.[5]

Film and Television

Since the demise of Hollywood's production-line studio system of making movies, which dominated between about 1920 and 1970 but was eroding by the late 1950s, the industry has been a pioneer in the loose model of employment beloved of contemporary management: Jobs are constantly ending, starting, and moving (Jones, 2002). This is a shift from lifelong employment to casual labor. Hollywood exemplifies "flexible specialization" in its economic commitment to "permanent innovation" and inflexible control in its political commitment to dominate its industry (Piore & Sabel, 1984, p. 17). The key difference is that Hollywood has sustained a form of partially craft-based, horizontal unionization to protect workers from the caprice and exploitation of capital, rather than an enterprise-based system, even though there is no consistent vertical employment in a long-standing firm. Within this context, workers and bosses strike complex, transitory arrangements on a project basis via temporary associations, with small numbers of divers hands involved at each stage other than production and sizeable crews functioning both together and semi-autonomously. Places and networks matter in terms of textual cues, policy incentives, educational support, financing, and skills (DeFillippi & Arthur, 1998). Work may be subject to local, national, regional, and international fetishization of each component, matching the way that the labor undertaken is largely fetishized away from the final text. Conventional organizational charts are inadequate to the task, especially if one seeks to elude the conventions of hierarchy through capital whilst recognizing the eternal presence of managerial surveillance. Business leeches want flexibility in the numbers they employ, the technology they use, the place where they produce, and the amount that they pay—and inflexibility of ownership and control (Eisenmann & Bower, 2000).

In 2002, there were 3,500 film and television companies in Southern California (Jones, 2002). Perhaps 0.1% of these firms hired over a thousand people, while about 75% had no more than four employees. This makes the industry look dispersed and open. But Hollywood is in a period of decentralized accumulation that is still accumulative (Wayne, 2003). The power and logic of domination by a small number of vast entities are achieved via a huge globalizing network of subcontracted firms and individuals, mediated through unions, employer associations, education, and the state. The specifics vary with the genre under discussion—for example, television soap operas and sports may be covered by teams that are kept together for entire seasons in order to minimize the transaction costs incurred in starting ventures anew, whereas movie companies may exist for just a few weeks. In addition, Hollywood has shifted its signification, such that it is effectively one part of a diversified system for recycling texts in different salesrooms and one (flagship) component of conglomerate activity.

To offer a personal instance of media labor, when I migrated to the United States in 1993, interviewers for broadcast TV stations' news shows would come to my apartment to ask me questions as a team: a full complement of sound recordist, camera operator, lighting technician, and journalist. Now they are rolled into one person. More content must be produced from fewer resources, and more and more multiskilling and multitasking are required. In my example, the journalist has taken over the other jobs. Editing is also being scooped up into the new concept of the "preditor," who is both producer and editor. And if journalists work for companies like NBC, they often write copy for several Web sites *and* provide different edited versions of the original story for MSNBC, CNBC, CNBC Africa, CNBC Europe, and CNBC Asia, in addition to the parent network and individual channels in various countries.

On the reality-television side, format sales exploit the NICL. Modeled on the 1950s U.S. game show, textual formats are traded in both regulated and pirated ways, with multinational firms moving easily between high moralism and sharp practice. The Format Recognition and Protection Association represents over a hundred TV companies worldwide that charge for reuse of their intellectual property. Agile format firms, aware that local-content regulations are designed to stymie imports, point out to small nation–based companies that protect local industries and culture through quotas that buying a format and customizing it may satisfy such policies (Moran, 2006).

Not all format exchanges go easily. A famous case concerns the 1999 Mexican program *TeleChobis,* an unauthorized TV Azteca version of the BBC children's program *Teletubbies* (1997–2001). *Teletubbies* was screening on Azteca's rival, Televisa. Azteca responded by introducing many national signifiers and live children to its copycat *TeleChobis*—but was ultimately defeated by intellectual-property regimes (Kraidy, 2005). Such edgy conduct is not the unique province of the Third World, of course. A leaked 2008 memo from inside ABC showed how high up within the delightful "family values" domain of Disney lurk executives who are content to pick and choose their adherence to the law and lore of formats that they import to exploit the NICL (Holmwood, 2008).

Digital Games[6]

Electronic games incarnate the centralized labor of production and the decentralized labor of interpretation that constitute the NICL, as evidenced in Hong Kong participants hybridizing games into local forms of popular culture via references to local films and comic books in the arcade argot of play, and by redisposal inside cultural production, with comic book artists drawing on the games.

Big publishers develop exploitative labor practices as their power increases via the destruction and purchase of small businesses and insertion into the NICL. Rockstar, for instance, is a New York company with studios in Britain, Canada, Japan, and Austria, where talent has been purchased from innovative small businesses. It made *Grand Theft Auto* and *Max Payne*. Rockstar's game process may start when someone builds a demonstration model and shows it to the firm, which previews it to the press and plans to ready the game for Christmas sales. By March, it only has 6 months left. Workers are required to be present 60 hours a week, with the promise of a bonus when the game is shipped. Then management insists on changes. By June, people are working 80 hours a week. Then the company finds the product won't be available by Christmas. It shifts shipment to March but keeps everyone working at the same rate. The bonus migrates months into the future.

At the vast multinational Electronic Arts (EA), which makes *The Sims, Harry Potter, Battlefield, Rock Band,* and many sports games, workers are under monumental pressure in terms of the need both to create more and more product for the global market and to compete with other workers at home and offshore. In 2004, ea_spouse anonymously posted a vibrant account of grotesque exploitation experienced by her fiancé and others at EA, via *LiveJournal*. She eloquently ripped back the veneer of joyous cybertarianism from games development, noting that EA's claim to blend aesthetics and technology, as per its name and corporate trademark ("Challenge Everything"), belied both its treatment of workers and its products. Regarding labor: "To any EA executive that happens to read this, I have a good challenge for you: how about safe and sane labor practices for the people on whose backs you walk for your millions?" Regarding texts: "Churning out one licensed football game after another doesn't sound like challenging much of anything to me; it sounds like a money farm." Then she detailed the exploitation: A putatively limited "precrunch" is announced, such that 48-hour weeks are required, with the alibi that months of this obviate the need for a real "crunch" at the conclusion of development; the precrunch goes on beyond its deadline; then 72-hour work weeks are mandated; that crunch passes its promised end; illness and irritability strike; then a new crunch is announced, whereby everyone must work 85- to 91-hour weeks, 9 a.m.–10 p.m. Monday–Sunday inclusive, with the occasional Saturday evening off after 6:30. There is no overtime or leave in return for this massive expenditure of talent and time. The workers discern no measurable impact from the crunch other than on themselves—so many errors are made from fatigue that time is needed to correct them. Turnover among engineering workers can run at 50%.

Yet *Fortune* magazine ranks EA among the "100 Best Companies to Work For," and it is 91st among corporations that "try hard to do right by their staff" as measured by the Great Place to Work® Institute in San Francisco. EA described itself to *Fortune* as "a one-class society," and its vice president of human resources advised that "most creativity comes at one of two times: when your back is up against the wall or in a time of calm." In case readers found this firing squad analogy alarming, *Fortune* reassured them that workers could "refresh their energy with free espresso or by playing volleyball and basket-ball." In 2007, the firm ranked 62nd in the magazine's "List of Industry Stars."

Meanwhile, ea_spouse's brave intervention (as we say on the left) or out-burst (as they say elsewhere) generated febrile and substantial responses to *LiveJournal*, such as calls for unionization, appeals to federal and state labor machinery, confirmation that EA was horrendous but by no means aberrant, frustration that the bourgeois press was disinclined to report the situation, denunciations of asinine managerialism and private-sector bureaucracy ("The average game company manager is quite possibly the worst qualified leader of people in the world"), and a recognition of how intellectual-property rights make labor disposable ("I'm beginning to think that EA is really nothing more than a licensing warehouse. [T]hey'll always be able to recruit naïve talent to slave away . . . alienating talent is not a big problem for them"). But labor sol-idarity remains compromised by job threats from around the world and nondisclosure agreements, which chill conversations across employment silos.

Of course, the concept of a division of labor applied to games does not end with production. The Political Economy Research Institute's 2004 *Misfortune 100: Top Corporate Air Polluters in the United States* placed media owners at numbers 1, 3, 16, 22, and 39. The relevant multinational corporations have denied responsibility for the postconsumption histories of their danger-ous products. Many recycling programs that corporations sponsor in the United States rely on customers paying them to take away these poisonous goods. The Environmental Protection Agency has been largely silent on the topic, and the United States has used the World Trade Organization to counter efforts at diminishing pollution from this equipment. So at the other end of the NICL, games end up as recycling fodder, along with the materials they are played on, and present significant labor questions. Sixteen-year-old girls leave villages in northern China to work in effectively indentured com-pounds run by Japanese, Taiwanese, and U.S. businesses in the south to build computers used for games. A year or so later, preteen girls pick away without protection at discarded First World computers full of leaded glass in order to find precious metals and then dump the remains in landfills. The metals are sold to recyclers, who do not use landfills or labor in the Global North (apart from U.S. prisons) because of environmental and industrial legislation contra the destruction to soil, water, and workers that is caused by the dozens of poisonous chemicals and gases in these dangerous machines. More than 130,000 personal computers a day are thrown out around the world, leading to millions of pounds of toxic waste (Maxwell & Miller, 2008, 2009).

Conclusion

When a multinational firm invests in a particular national formation, it always already sows the seeds of insecurity, because such companies are ever-ready to move on when tax incentives or other factors of production beckon—or they threaten to do so, thereby generating anxiety and obedience in the proletariat. In Western Europe and Japan, contingent media labor is responding by taking shape as a deconstructive, resistive entity. The precariat/précaires/precari@s/precari goes under the sign of San Precario, who guards the spirit of the "flashing lights of life." Since 2001, the EuroMayDay Network has organized precariat parades in 20 European cities, featuring "contortionists of flexibility . . . high-wire artists of mobility . . . [and] jugglers of credit," along with apparitions by San Precario to protect his children against evil bosses (Foti, 2005).

We inhabit a world where flexibility is the megasign of affluence and precariousness its flipside. One person's calculated risk is another's burden of labor, inequality is represented as the outcome of a moral test, and the young are supposed to regard insecurity as an opportunity rather than a constraint.

Negri (2007) refers to people mired in contingent media work as the cognitariat[7] because they have considerable educational attainment and great facility with cultural technologies and genres. The cognitariat plays key roles in the production and circulation of goods and services, through both creation and coordination. Today's "culturalization of production" may *en*able these intellectuals, by placing them at the center of world economies, but it also *dis*ables them, because it does so under conditions of flexible production and ideologies of "freedom." This new proletariat is not defined in terms of factories, manufacturing, or opposition to ruling-class power and ideology. Indeed, it is formed from those whose immediate forebears, with similar or less cultural capital, were the salariat, and confident of guaranteed health care and retirement income. It lacks both the organization of the traditional working class and the political entrée of the old middle class.

What used to be the fate of artists and musicians—where "making cool stuff" and working with relative autonomy were meant to outweigh ongoing employment—has become a norm across virtually every sector of the economy. The outcome is contingent labor as a way of life—the triumph of the

NICL. Progressive managers need to account for the postindustrial standing of cultural workers and reject a neoliberal embrace of casualized labor. There would be no culture, no media, without labor. It is not X-factor inefficiency. It is the beating heart of creativity and social justice.

References

Becker, G. S. (1983). *Human capital: A theoretical, and empirical analysis, with special reference to education* (2nd ed.). Chicago, IL: University of Chicago Press.

Benhabib, S. (2002). *The claims of culture: Equality and diversity in the global era.* Princeton, NJ: Princeton University Press.

Briggs, A., & Burke, P. (2002). *A social history of the media: From Gutenberg to the Internet.* Cambridge, England: Polity Press.

Cohen, R. (1991). *Contested domains: Debates in international labor studies.* London, England: Zed Books.

de Pedro, J. P. (1991). Concepto y otros aspectos del patrimonio cultural en la Constitución. En *Estudios sobre la Constitución Española: Homenaje al Profesor Eduardo Garcia de Enterria* (pp. 1551–1572). Madrid, Spain: Editorial Civitas, S. A.

de Pedro, J. P. (1999). Democracy and cultural difference in the Spanish Constitution of 1978. In C. J. Greenhouse with R. Kheshti (Eds.), *Democracy and ethnography: Constructing identities in multicultural liberal states* (pp. 61–80). Albany: State University of New York Press.

DeFillippi, R. J., & Arthur, M. B. (1998). Paradox in project-based enterprise: The case of film making. *California Management Review, 40,* 125–138.

Eisenmann, T. R., & Bower, J. L. (2000). The entrepreneurial M-form: Strategic integration in global media firms. *Organization Science, 11*(3), 348–355.

Folbre, N. (2003). *El trabajo afectivo* (MediaLabMadrid, Trans.). Retrieved from http://republicart.net/

Foti, A. (2005). *MAYDAY MAYDAY: Euro flex workers, time to get a move on!* Retrieved from http://republicart.net/

Fröbel, F., Heinrichs, J., & Kreye, O. (1980). *The New International Division of Labor: Structural unemployment in industrialised countries and industrialisation in developing countries* (P. Burgess, Trans.). Cambridge, England: Cambridge University Press.

Hamermesh, D. S. (2002). International labor economics. *Journal of Labor Economics, 20*(4), 709–732.

Hardt, M., & Negri, A. (2000). *Empire.* Cambridge, MA: Harvard University Press.

Hesmondhalgh, D. (2002). *The cultural industries.* London, England: Sage.

Holmwood, L. (2008, August 15). Don't steal TV formats, ABC is warned. *The Guardian.* Retrieved from http://www.guardian.co.uk/media/2008/aug/15/television.usa

International Monetary Fund. (2000). *Globalization: Threat or opportunity?* Retrieved from http://www.imf.org/external/np/exr/ib/2000/041200to.htm

Jones, C. (2002). Careers in project networks: The case of the film industry. In M. B. Arthur & D. M. Rousseau (Eds.), *The boundaryless career: A new employment principle for a new organizational era* (pp. 58–75). New York, NY: Oxford University Press.

Keane, M. (2006). From made in China to created in China. *International Journal of Cultural Studies, 9*(3), 285–296.

Keynes, J. M. (1957). *The general theory of employment interest and money.* London, England: Macmillan.

Kotkin, J. (2001). *The new geography: How the digital revolution is reshaping the American landscape.* New York, NY: Random House.

Kraidy, M. M. (2005). *Hybridity, or the cultural logic of globalization.* Philadelphia, PA: Temple University Press.

Lang, T., & Hines, C. (1993). *The new protectionism: Protecting the future against free trade.* New York, NY: New Press.

Machlup, F. (1962). *The production and distribution of knowledge in the United States.* Princeton, NJ: Princeton University Press.

Marx, K. (1906). *Capital: A critique of political economy* (S. Moore & E. Aveling, Trans., & F. Engels, Ed.). New York, NY: Modern Library.

Mattelart, A. (2002). An archaeology of the global era: Constructing a belief (S. Taponier with P. Schlesinger, Trans.). *Media Culture & Society, 24*(5), 591–612.

Mattelart, A. (2003). *The Information Society: An introduction* (S. G. Taponier & J. A. Cohen, Trans.). London, England: Sage.

Maxwell, R., & Miller, T. (2008). Creative industries or wasteful ones? *Urban China, 33,* 122.

Maxwell, R., & Miller, T. (2009). Talking rubbish: Green citizenship, media, and the environment. In T. Boyce & J. Lewis (Eds.), *Climate change and the media* (pp. 17–27). New York, NY: Peter Lang.

Miller, T. (1990a). Mission Impossible: How do you Turn Indooroopilly into Africa? In J. Dawson & B. Molloy (Eds.), *Queensland images in film and television* (pp. 122–131). St. Lucia: University of Queensland Press.

Miller, T. (1990b). Mission Impossible and the New International Division of Labor. *Metro, 82,* 21–28.

Miller, T. (2008). Anyone for games? Via the New International Division of Cultural Labor. In H. K. Anheier & Y. R. Israr (Eds.), A. Paul (Assoc. Ed.), & S. Cunningham (Guest Ed.), *The cultural economy* (pp. 227–240). London, England: Sage.

Miller, T., Govil, N., McMurria, J., & Maxwell, R. (2001). *Global Hollywood.* London, England: British Film Institute.

Miller, T., Govil, N., McMurria, J., Maxwell, R., & Wang, T. (2005). *Global Hollywood 2.* London, England: British Film Institute.

Miller, T., Lawrence, G., McKay, J., & Rowe, D. (2001). *Globalization and sport: Playing the world.* London, England: Sage.

Moran, A. (with Malbon, J.). (2006). *Understanding the global TV format.* Bristol, England: Intellect.

Negri, A. (2007). *Goodbye mister socialism.* Paris, France: Seuil.

Piore, M. J., & Sabel, C. F. (1984). *The second industrial divide: Possibilities for prosperity.* New York, NY: Basic Books.

Reagan, R. (1966, April 19). *The creative society.* Speech at the University of Southern California. Retrieved from http://www.freerepublic.com/focus/news/742041/posts

Rothkopf, D. (1997). In praise of cultural imperialism. *Foreign Policy, 107,* 38–53.

Scott, A. J. (1998). *Regions and the world economy: The coming shape of global production, competition, and political order.* Oxford, England: Oxford University Press.

Smith, A. (1970). *The wealth of nations, Books I–III* (A. Skinner, Ed.). Harmondsworth, England: Penguin.

Strange, S. (1995). The limits of politics. *Government and Opposition, 30*(3), 291–311.

Toffler, A. (1983). *Previews and premises.* New York, NY: William Morrow.

United Nations Educational, Scientific and Cultural Organization. (2002). *Culture and UNESCO.* Paris, France: Author.

Wallerstein, I. (1989). Culture as the ideological battleground of the modern world-system. *Hitotsubashi Journal of Social Studies, 21*(1), 5–22.

Wayne, M. (2003). *Marxism and media studies: Key concepts and contemporary trends.* London, England: Pluto Press.

Williams, R. (1983). *Keywords: A vocabulary of culture and society* (2nd ed.). New York, NY: Oxford University Press.

Notes

1. Thanks to the editor for his helpful and encouraging comments.

2. Editor's note: Parts of this chapter were previously published as Miller, T. (2009). "Step away from the croissant": Media studies 3.0. In D. Hesmondhalgh & J. Toynbee (Eds.), *The media and social theory* (pp. 213–230). London, England: Routledge.

3. See http://www.criticalmanagement.org/?q=en and http://group.aomonline .org/cms.

4. Miller, 1990a, 1990b; Miller, Govil, McMurria, & Maxwell, 2001; Miller, Govil, McMurria, Maxwell, & Wang, 2005; Miller, Lawrence, McKay, & Rowe, 2001.

5. This section draws on work cited in Miller et al., 2005.

6. This section draws on work cited in Miller, 2008.

7. Ironically, this term derives from a reactionary (Toffler, 1983).

SECTION III

Media Professions

8 Journalism in a Network

Jane B. Singer

The occupation of journalism has changed very dramatically very fast. Until the 1990s, journalists produced content for a single outlet, such as a newspaper or television program, and they produced it in a single format—printed words, say, or sound, or moving images. Most of them worked in stable media industries that, thanks largely to a lucrative advertising-based revenue model, had been highly profitable for decades if not centuries, and they had something close to a monopoly on providing news to the public. Outside the newsroom, almost all their work-related communication was with sources; only rarely did they interact directly with readers, viewers, or listeners—and when they did, they generally spoke for their media outlet rather than for themselves as individuals.

None of those things is true today.

This chapter surveys changes to journalism since the rise of the Internet as a popular medium, as well as the challenges of managing the transition. It touches on shifts in journalists' tasks, roles and self-perceptions, and occupational culture. The overarching message for those preparing to enter, manage, and study the media workforce is to be flexible. More change is the only thing you can count on.

Changing Tasks

Perhaps the most obvious change to journalism has involved the introduction and rapid incorporation of new tasks and the tools needed to accomplish them. Journalists always have been storytellers, and they still are. The best journalists are the most skillful at that core task. In the past, they developed, nurtured, and refined that skill within a single mode of expression; a writer honed the ability to choose and use just the right words, a photojournalist became adept at capturing the most compelling images, and so on.

Today, skillful storytelling requires knowing how to tell stories across different media—and, importantly, knowing which medium is most effective for which type of story or even for which component of a single story.

Christine Young, an investigative reporter at the Middletown *Times Herald-Record*, a 70,000-circulation newspaper in New York's Hudson Valley, had a powerful story to tell about a man locked behind bars for 20 years for a murder Young was sure he did not commit. Had she held her job at the time of the murder, she would have told it with words, supplemented by a few images from a staff photographer. But Young's investigation took place in the late 2000s. Her story, which won an Online News Association award for outstanding investigation by a small Web site (http://thr-investigations.com/lebrewjones/), was built using a greatly enhanced tool kit. Videos enable us to see and hear the victim's mother, the prisoner's brother, and others whose experiences and emotions enrich the story. Interactive maps and timelines let us sift through the clues. Links take us to digitized versions of the autopsy report and evidence list, among other documents and background information. Each piece contributes to an immensely compelling narrative—one that resulted in freedom for a man who never should have lost it.

This multimedia story, like many others that go beyond routine coverage, was a team enterprise, requiring collaboration and coordination to produce. Young worked with photographers, videographers, graphic artists, programmers, and editors, a total of 10 people in all—some wearing multiple hats. For example, photographer John Pertel also served as Web site designer, multimedia producer, videographer, and video editor. He is the sort of "multiskilled" journalist whom editors increasingly seek to hire: ones fluent in a much wider range of "languages" than in the past, including text, images, sound, and animation.

This story did not incorporate material from users, but working closely with both content and contributors from outside the newsroom is another, arguably even more significant, change in journalistic tasks. The creation of "j-blogs," individual or collective blogs by journalists, has provided a way to cross the sometimes restrictive parameters of conventional news storytelling, enabling journalists to develop and express a personal voice; equally important, it has created a forum for an exchange of ideas with users. J-blogs were virtually nonexistent a few years ago; today, it is hard to find a news Web site without them (Bivings Group, 2007). In addition, most sites provide opportunities for a wide and widening range of "participatory news" options (Deuze, 2006), from comments on stories to recommendation systems to user blogs. Many more options are certain to appear between the time I write this line and the time you read it.

The motives of newsroom managers for opening up the media space typically have been some combination of the democratic—a belief in the value of civic discussion about the issues of the day—and the economic; a user engaged in conversation with journalists or other users is more likely to return repeatedly to the Web site to continue talking, thus building traffic and, by extension, the potential for advertising revenue. In reality, however, much of the discussion has been somewhere south of civil (Hermida & Thurman, 2008; Singer & Ashman, 2009), and journalists have had to take on the additional task of online moderator. This new job involves everything from keeping the conversation on track to discouraging or outright deleting the most obnoxious of the detours.

The key word for all these tasks, in fact, is *additional*. New storytelling platforms, new tools and formats, new collaborations, and new responsibilities for user contributions all come on top of the newswork expected of earlier generations of journalists. And they are just the most tangible of the ongoing transformations.

Changing Roles and Self-Perceptions

Less tangible but at least as important are associated changes in journalists' roles and self-perceptions. The role of "moderator" is one manifestation of a broader change in the traditional journalistic role of gatekeeping. That information-management role involves "the process by which the vast array of potential news messages are winnowed, shaped, and prodded into those few that are actually transmitted by news media" (Shoemaker, Eichholz, Kim, & Wrigley, 2001, p. 233). More fundamentally, it describes a world in which the journalist controls the flow of information to the public. That world no longer exists.

In response, journalists have adjusted their self-perceptions in two related ways. One has involved an assertion of boundaries between themselves and other content providers in the open environment of the Internet; journalists have sought to define who they are and what makes them distinct. The other has entailed new thinking about the role they play in this world; here, journalists are evolving new definitions of what they do.

An answer to the question of who is a journalist is far less straightforward than it once was. Bloggers and others who have never set foot in a newsroom can and do legitimately claim some of the same occupational turf (Lowrey, 2006). Access to a printing press or broadcast transmitter isn't required; anyone can "publish," "broadcast," or otherwise disseminate information easily and cheaply online. Access to information sources can't be it, either, as vast storehouses of information are a click away, as are millions of other people. That storytelling ability discussed above is important, and not everyone is good at constructing a compelling narrative . . . but a great many fine writers clearly are not journalists.

Increasingly, journalists are instead defining themselves in terms of professional norms, standards, and practices that, they say, are only sporadically shared by those outside the newsroom. Many relate to the fundamental journalistic norm of truth telling. Others have more to do with relationships between journalists and their audiences or sources.

Some of the norms involve gathering information. Examples include obtaining verification or other collaborating evidence, seeking multiple perspectives to provide balance, and acting as an observer of, rather than an active participant in, whatever is being covered. Another set of norms relates to conveying information once it has been obtained. Journalists cannot hide behind the anonymity afforded by pseudonyms, as users who contribute to their Web sites often do. They have ethical obligations to acknowledge and correct their errors, to find ways to minimize the harm their words or images can cause, and to be accountable for their actions; users, they say, do not necessarily feel such obligations. In short, journalists have assigned themselves a responsibility to behave in a certain way, and they say that responsibility separates them from those who do not share it.

There is an obvious irony here: These are precisely the sorts of things that critics say journalists do *not* do, at least not consistently. Nonetheless, journalists generally see such attributes and practices as not only crucial but also self-defining—even though they know they sometimes fail to live up to their own standards.

If the question of who is a journalist is difficult to answer, the question of what is journalism may be even harder. The second, somewhat different, response of journalists to the loss of control over the flow of online information has been to redefine the core function of journalism in society, shifting it to one that is less about gatekeeping and more about sense making (Kovach & Rosenstiel, 2001; Singer, 1997). As the role of watchdog is taken up by other members of the online community, journalists are reclaiming the broader role of guide dog. In this view, journalism involves not just making information available but making it understandable, meaningful, and, ultimately, individually and collectively useful. Journalism is about providing context, analysis, and interpretation—a shift away from strict objectivity toward something that includes and invites reflection on, and engagement with, the information provided. In many ways, such journalism also is more personal, and there is a clear trend toward the development of individual journalists' public personas (Pew Project for Excellence in Journalism, 2009a). These emerging newsroom personalities, not incidentally, are increasingly being used as branding or marketing tools by their employers, as media outlets more explicitly position themselves as a collective of distinct individual voices rather than a monolithic journalistic entity.

Of course, journalism has always been about analysis and interpretation, as well as the presentation of "facts"; the current changes are arguably just ones of emphasis, with greater weight placed on guidance than in the past. More thoroughly novel—and harder for journalists to accommodate within existing self-perceptions—is the role of community participant. Both providing information and interpreting information are collaborative enterprises online and likely to become even more so as media Web sites integrate additional user contributions in an expanding range of formats.

The role of moderator mentioned above is only one aspect of participation. As journalism becomes a conversation rather than a lecture (Gillmor, 2006), journalists discover they have to engage in that conversation themselves—for instance, as bloggers or social networkers—and look for ways to engage others (see also Charles H. Davis, in this volume). They find themselves serving as the hosts of something resembling a gigantic virtual dinner party: keeping the discussion flowing; ensuring there is enough nourishment, in sufficient variety, to keep all the guests happy; steering together people who might enjoy one another's company; and, if necessary, heading off or breaking up any fights.

This is a novel role for journalists, and it takes some getting used to. It is an especially challenging transition for those who see the practice of journalism as necessitating a certain distance from people outside the newsroom, including sources and audience members. Such a change is not simply about taking on new roles; it is about adapting to an entirely new occupational culture.

Changing Culture

To recap, journalists see themselves as people who draw on particular skills to perform particular tasks in fulfilling particular social roles—and all those things are changing rapidly and dramatically, forcing practitioners to change their perceptions of who they are and what they do. Together, such changes contribute to a massive shift in the occupational culture of journalism.

The notion of fluidity—which applies to the entire journalistic enterprise, including products, processes, and structures of all sorts, from social to physical to economic—may be useful in considering this ongoing cultural change and the difficulty of managing its negotiation. Journalism once had clear boundaries. We have already discussed the erosion of definitional boundaries around who is and is not a journalist. There also were boundaries of time; journalists worked to a deadline, after which the presses had to roll or the program had to air. There were boundaries of space; journalism was produced within a newsroom and processed by editors who worked in it. There were boundaries around the product itself, too; journalism came neatly packaged within the pages of a newspaper or the minutes of a news show. Reaching the back page or the last minute meant there was no more news.

The Internet breached all those boundaries. Deadlines are continuous, and stories are updated whenever new information becomes available. Content of all sorts flows in from everywhere and everyone, and even the bits produced by journalists no longer necessarily are routed through a newsroom (or an editor) before appearing online. The unmanaged and perhaps unmanageable nature of the network itself, with its myriad intertwined links and updates every nanosecond, creates an essentially infinite, unbounded product.

To accommodate these changes, many news organizations also have dissolved long-standing physical boundaries within the newsroom. Newsrooms worldwide have been radically reconfigured to accommodate creation of a continuous, participatory, multiplatform product (see also Mark Deuze and Leopoldina Fortunati, in this volume). Physical and organizational structures designed to handle the old assembly-line process of making news—reporters in one part of the newsroom, copy editors in another, city editors in a third, visual journalists stuck in a far corner—are vanishing. They are being replaced by content-area clusters or other arrangements intended to facilitate the dissemination of content through digital platforms throughout the day and the channeling of selected portions of that material to legacy products, such as the newspaper, to meet their deadlines.

Collaborative decision making erases old divisions of labor in the newsroom and, increasingly, draws on external input, as well. The latter is an especially controversial challenge to the occupational culture of journalists, who are quite protective of their status as the ones who decide what constitutes news—and quite wary about online usage data or comment volume being allowed to drive those decisions, a practice derisively labeled "traffic whoring" (Singer & Ashman, 2009).

None of these cultural changes, which together take most journalists well outside their comfort zones, has been easy. They typically mean more work, and unfamiliar work at that; many journalists have balked or protested, as individuals or through trade unions such as the Newspaper Guild in America or the National Union of Journalists in Britain. Concerns about increased workload are inevitably tied to concerns about quality: More (and more varied) content must be created, on a never-ending deadline, using new and constantly changing tools.

And if all that weren't enough, the business model that has sustained journalism for centuries appears to be unworkable online, knocking the economic underpinnings of news organizations out from under them. Some long-standing news outlets have folded; others have drastically scaled back operations or have turned to online-only distribution. Many newspeople have found themselves without a full-time job, becoming journeyman journalists who work for short periods on particular projects—or leaving the profession altogether.

"Even before the recession, the fundamental question facing journalism was whether the news industry could win a race against the clock for survival: could it find new ways to underwrite the gathering of news online, while using the declining revenue of the old platforms to finance the transition?" observers at the Pew Project for Excellence in Journalism (2009b) wrote in 2009. The fundamental questions facing journalism are where the money is to come from, how it is to be spent, and whether it will be enough to cover the costs of gathering and disseminating quality information. As of this writing, those questions are unanswered.

Fluidity always brings uncertainty, or at least less certainty than a fixed and stable environment affords. The shape of familiar things has changed dramatically, as we have seen; the shape of things still to come is unclear. Which skills, tasks, roles, principles, or practices will remain vital; which will be transformed and in what ways; and which will become relics of a past that looks increasingly unlike the present, let alone the future? What will journalists expect of themselves, and what will others expect of them?

What sorts of collaborations will prove valuable, and how will they be nurtured, strengthened, and extended? What cultural and economic structures will emerge to sustain journalism—and what will happen to our democratic society if they do not?

Managing these enormous simultaneous changes, adapting an entire occupational culture to accommodate them, finding and implementing sustainable new business models, and coping with pervasive uncertainty at every step of the way are Herculean tasks. Media workers and researchers face the challenge of understanding this volatile occupation and helping it move forward, sometimes reluctantly, often slowly, yet also inevitably. Are you ready?

References

The Bivings Group. (2007, July 19). *American newspapers and the Internet: Threat or opportunity?* Retrieved from http://www.bivingsreport.com/wp-content/uploads/2007/08/newspaperstudy_22.pdf

Deuze, M. (2006). Participation, remediation, bricolage: Considering principal components of a digital culture. *The Information Society, 22*(2), 63–75.

Gillmor, D. (2006). *We the media: Grassroots journalism by the people, for the people.* Sebastopol, CA: O'Reilly Media.

Hermida, A., & Thurman, N. (2008). A clash of cultures: The integration of user-generated content within professional journalistic frameworks at British newspaper Websites. *Journalism Practice, 2*(3), 343–356.

Kovach, B., & Rosenstiel, T. (2001). *The elements of journalism: What newspeople should know and the public should expect.* New York, NY: Crown.

Lowrey, W. (2006). Mapping the journalism-blogging relationship. *Journalism, 7*(4), 477–500.

Pew Project for Excellence in Journalism. (2009a). *Overview: Major trends.* The State of the News Media 2009. Retrieved from http://www.stateofthemedia.org/2009/narrative_overview_majortrends.php?cat=1&media=1

Pew Project for Excellence in Journalism. (2009b). *Overview: Introduction.* The State of the News Media 2009. Retrieved from http://www.stateofthemedia.org/2009/narrative_overview_intro.php?media=1&cat=0

Shoemaker, P. J., Eichholz, M., Kim, E., & Wrigley, B. (2001). Individual and routine forces in gatekeeping. *Journalism & Mass Communication Quarterly, 78*(2), 233–246.

Singer, J. B. (1997). Still guarding the gate? The newspaper journalist's role in an online world. *Convergence: The International Journal of Research Into New Media Technologies, 3*(1), 72–89.

Singer, J. B., & Ashman, I. (2009). "Comment is free, but facts are sacred": User-generated content and ethical constructs at the *Guardian. Journal of Mass Media Ethics, 24*(1), 3–21.

9

Atypical Newswork, Atypical Media Management

Mark Deuze and Leopoldina Fortunati

Contingency defines the lived experience of many, if not most, media professionals today. Of all the professions in the media production industries (such as advertising, film and TV, and digital game development), the labor market for journalism has arguably been the most stable for the longest time, particularly regarding newspapers as employing (until the late 1990s) the majority of the editorial workforce. This is rapidly changing, however. In April 2006, the International Federation of Journalists (IFJ) released a report on the labor conditions of journalists around the world, concluding that "journalists and media workers are increasingly being employed in atypical and contingent employment relationships—casual employment, use of contract work and the rise of the use of triangular, ambiguous and disguised employment." At the time, atypical newswork made up around one third of the membership of IFJ affiliates, and it can be considered to be growing rapidly—as newspapers, magazines, and local broadcast stations around the world are either scaling down their content operations or closing their doors altogether. The percentage of atypical employment is significantly higher among newcomers in the industry and among those working in television and online. This not only suggests growing numbers of freelancers in the news industry—although that certainly has been the case. Even among contracted employees, many are doing freelance work—for other titles at the same corporate parent or by repurposing story ideas and materials across more media channels not necessarily owned by the original employer (Deuze, 2009). Some reporters are still permanently employed, but most others only parachute in for a period of time to work on a certain aspect of a project (a special issue or supplement, a specific program or reportage, a part of a news Web site); several people move in and out of projects and temporary labor arrangements all the time, and many if not most media workers swim in what Hesmondhalgh (2007) considers a pool of underutilized talent. Contemporary trends in new media technologies, changes in the ownership structures and production networks of cultural industries, an ongoing hyper-fragmentation of media audiences, and a gradual convergence of production and consumption in an increasingly participatory media culture contribute to this precariousness (Deuze, 2007; Jenkins, 2006).

Loss of Control

The increased contingency in work and employment does not mean media professionals are without power or without resources to counteract. But beyond the casualization of labor, a significant factor handicapping practitioners in making effective use of their power—to unionize or otherwise collectively take action—is the contemporary shift in resources away from journalists to their audiences (Fortunati & Deuze, 2010). These two factors deeply affecting the work and management of journalists' careers tend to get amplified by the ongoing computerization and convergence of newswork. The implementation of such computerized information processes in the news industry signals the shift of journalism from being a liberal profession—requiring a highly specialized and elite talent base—to becoming a simple labor—that is, a labor that requires a limited number of family and social resources to be produced and that from a technical point of view might be done by anyone. This shift implies a loss of authority and control on the part of journalists over their work—which is one of the foundational elements in their sense of professionalism (Beam, 2006). This sense of shared control and peer review used to be the benchmark of what it means to be a professional journalist. The results of journalists' work are primarily judged by their bosses and their clients, two audiences that often have different, if not contradictory, interests. Moreover, this judgment is expressed in a situation in which journalists are paying the price of the unfinished revolution introduced by the information process in newsrooms: the news-producing consumer (often constructed as a competitor-colleague: a "citizen journalist").

The advent of the Internet has in fact opened the door to a new role of audiences that the journalistic sector has not been able to handle in an appropriate way. As research across Europe in recent years by one of the authors shows (Fortunati et al., 2009), publishers and editors have not succeeded in taking advantage of the contribution of audiences, because they did not invest at the organizational level regarding new professional roles inside the newsrooms with the task to monitor, moderate, select, and convey the opinions and comments coming from the audience into the newsrooms. They preferred to confine audiences' voices, generally publishing them in separated and specific places mainly inside the forums of online newspapers, without interacting with them and without including them in their editorial strategy. Research in other aspects of news organizations making the transition to digital and online suggests similar outcomes: a lack of managerial commitment and organizational investment, the prevalence of turf wars over synergy or collaboration, and empowering innovations taking place largely at the hands of a select few enterprising individuals within the company—not supported by their colleagues, management, or even (most of) the audience (Deuze, 2004; Paterson & Domingo, 2008).

The combination of workforce casualization, a difficult economic context for advertising-supported media (such as newspapers and broadcast news programming), and the power shift from journalists to audiences and employers makes for a particularly challenging set of parameters for the management of firms and careers in journalism.

The Problems of Management

In many if not most countries, a drive toward convergence of formerly distinct news operations has been a staple of the business. Generally, such managerial initiatives have been initiated as a consequence of (or a push to) the ongoing integration, consolidation, and concentration of media ownership. It is important to note that the concentration of media ownership with the deliberate goal to integrate different departments and sections of the industry into cross-media enterprises is and always has been a top-down strategy, to the point that in a study carried out recently in 11 European countries on journalism and the Internet it came out that the majority of the journalists interviewed did not appear to be informed about other multimedia initiatives such as radio, TV, and SMS, WAP, MMS, or PDA news produced by their media organization.

Studying the institutional and cultural contours of innovation at two Dutch newspapers owned by publisher PCM, Ybema (2003) typified management strategies in this context as "postalgic," noting how the industry's executives tend to come up with all kinds of far-reaching plans and futuristic ideals that are primarily interpreted by the journalists involved as unfair criticisms on their work. The direct result is the cultivation of some kind of nostalgia about the "good old days" among reporters and editors, which in turn leads to resistance to the proposed changes in the newsroom. A survey among hundreds of managers and journalists at U.S. daily newspapers about change initiatives shows that the implementation thereof caused conflict and hurt morale (Gade, 2004). Gade found in this survey how journalists appreciate the difficult and complex situation management is in today but still question the factors motivating change. This overall lack of (shared) vision or clarity of goals pursued in managerial innovation was also noticed in a study conducted in 2000 among news organizations and managers in Denmark, Sweden, The Netherlands, Austria, and Switzerland (Bierhoff, Deuze, & De Vreese, 2000; see also Bozena I. Mierzejewska, in this volume), while in the more recent European study mentioned above some managerial problems in the implementation of the Internet emerged.

In a critical assessment of the competences and skills on the level of management responsible for the implementation of convergence, Killebrew (2004) found most managers were not equipped to deal with these changes in their newsrooms. Managers have been told to implement change, argues Killebrew, but most have not been given the tools to successfully integrate converged (or multimedia) journalism into the workplace. Quinn's (2005) work on management and convergence journalism is based on "best practices"–based case study research in newsrooms in the United States, Finland, the United Kingdom, and Hong Kong. Emphasizing the need for investment in communication, training, incentives, and rewards, Quinn makes a compelling case in favor of convergence—but only if it is done by organizations, managers, and journalists with access to significant resources, which is regrettably exactly what the business lacks at this point in time.

Although these and other studies suggest journalists are not necessarily opposed to change, they do tend to be cautious and skeptical toward changes in the institutional and organizational arrangements of their work, as lessons learned in the past suggest that such changes tend to go hand in hand with downsizing, layoffs, and having to do more with a smaller staff, a lower budget, and fewer resources. This in turn has consequences for the quality of the news that gets produced, as documented by numerous studies—for example by Avilés, Bienvenido, Sanders, and Harrison (2004) at television newsrooms in Spain and Britain and by Boczkowski (2004) in several U.S. print newsrooms (see also Pablo Boczkowski, in this volume).

McKercher (2002) argues that technological convergence and corporate concentration must be understood as part of the strategy of media owners to acquire new sources for profit, extending their control over the relations of production and distribution of news and aiming to undermine the collective bargaining position of journalists through their unions by shifting toward a model of individualized and contingent contracts. Gall (2000) further notes that the introduction of such personal contracts in the news industry, though allowing individual journalists some freedom to negotiate their own terms and conditions of employment, in fact has resulted in a deterioration of the working conditions of journalists: lower wages, less job security, and more contingent labor relationships (variable hours, job rotation, and flextime). Similarly, Marjoribanks (2003) notes that the contemporary organization of work in transnational and converged news enterprises has allowed for the creation of a more flexible, multiskilled, and highly moveable—at least in the eyes of management—workforce.

Convergence Journalism

A structure of convergent multimedia news organizations has been emerging since the mid-1990s, with companies all over the world opting for at least some form of cross-media cooperation or synergy among formerly separated staffers, newsrooms, and departments. Researchers involved in studying and observing convergence journalism ventures around the world note, however, how the biggest obstacles to seamless integration always boil down to cultural clashes. This goes especially for the print reporters, citing their deep distrust of broadcast journalists' work routines, their skepticism about the quality of newswork when it involves having to do stand-ups for television or write blurbs for the Web, and their critical view of the quality and level of experience of their television and online counterparts.

On the other side, television people reportedly feel their print colleagues are conservative, slow, and oblivious to the wants and needs of their audiences (for instance as expressed through market research, sales figures, and daily ratings). Fortunati (2003) found, however, that in Italy many print journalists were aspiring to work for television channels for the wider popularity that TV could offer along with a higher retribution. Killebrew (2004) even reports how news managers charged with implementing the convergence processes often seem unprepared, skeptical, and ill prepared for the job. In effect they are required to produce technological and organizational innovations while the cultures that should sustain, support, and shape these changes are not still existing. These kinds of mutual stereotypes are not just the products of a stressful and confusing convergence experience but are exponents of the historical separation of different professional identities and work cultures—which also suggests that interpersonal relationships and communication across the different media can be considered the essentials in any managerial tool kit (Quinn, 2005; see also Jane B. Singer, in this volume).

There is always a large part of unspoken "knowledge in practice" at work inside any media company, in the context of which it is difficult to enact or inspire new ways of doing things during the convergence process, and which thus can become a terrible inertia or resistance against any proposed changes. Furthermore, this ongoing reorganization of newswork requires a different type of journalist with multimedia skills and competences—including taking the coproducing consumers seriously. As with television news before, such cross-media approaches will transform news. Given the historical context of news transformations, this will most likely occur in the packaging of news first and in the content later (Nerone & Barnhurst, 2003).

Reporters and Editors

A survey by multimedia consulting firm Innovation—commissioned by the World Association of Newspapers—conducted in 2001 among media executives worldwide cited as the biggest obstacle to media convergence the individualistic nature of journalists (mentioned by 31% of all respondents). Using data from representative surveys among U.S. journalists, Beam (2006) found that "rank-and-file journalists are more dubious about the business goals and priorities of their organization than are their supervisors" (p. 180), showing that journalists in general tend to be more satisfied with their jobs if they perceive that their employer values "good journalism" over profit.

Research by Russo (1998) additionally suggests that journalists identify themselves more easily with the profession of journalism than, for example, with the medium or media company that employs them. Journalists (and news managers) entering the changing and pressured industry today have to work in and through historically and socially constructed shared routines, knowledge, and "values that experienced members of a group transmit to newcomers through socialization and [that are] used to shape a group's processes, material output, and ability to survive" (Mierzjewska & Hollifield, 2006, p. 46). In this context, who journalists are becomes a fundamental element in understanding careers and companies in journalism.

Comparing results from surveys among journalists in 21 countries, Weaver (1998) found support for claims that the characteristics of journalists, including their demographics, are largely similar worldwide. Comparing findings from recent surveys among journalists in five countries—The Netherlands, Germany, Great Britain, Australia, and the United States—several striking conclusions can be drawn, most notably regarding the general homogeneity among journalists in these different but equivalent countries:

- Journalists tend to share a distinct middle-class background.

- Journalists are generally college educated.

- Journalists have socioeconomic backgrounds firmly grounded in the dominant cultural and ethnic sectors of society, and thus newsrooms exhibit an overall low minority representation.

- There exists a distinct glass ceiling in terms of gender issues: Women are overrepresented in "feminine" news beats (lifestyle, education, fashion, health and beauty) and are underrepresented in managerial functions.

- Reporters and editors in modern Western democracies hold similar views on what is important in their work (in recent years, for example, privileging interpretation over breaking news as the most crucial aspect of their jobs).

Although it seems safe to argue that the professional group of journalists tends to be populated by generally the same kind of people as in the past, female journalists in Europe and to some extent North America today have begun to outnumber their male counterparts—particularly in the lowest positions in the professional hierarchy (Witt-Barthel, 2007).

Most journalists today still work for traditional print media, newspapers in particular, although reports over time show that the fields of broadcasting and new media are gaining ground in terms of new openings and jobs offered to newcomers. Magazine, broadcasting, and online newsrooms tend to be significantly smaller in staff size than newspaper newsrooms, and the work for these news media gets done almost exclusively on a contract-by-contract, freelance, or stringer basis. The recent European survey, already mentioned, shows that the journalists interviewed do not perceive the recent innovations in their working environment as a process that can enhance their political roles, understood as defense of democracy, control on politicians, influence on public opinion and the political agenda, and analysis and interpretation of complex issues (Fortunati et al., 2009).

Considering the primacy of the individual journalist and his or her traditional orientation toward peers rather than publics or employers, it is fascinating to note a conclusion from Journalism.org's 2009 *State of the News Media* report in the United States, suggesting that "power is shifting to the individual journalist and away, by degrees, from journalistic institutions. . . . Through search, e-mail, blogs, social media and more, consumers are gravitating to the work of individual writers and voices, and away somewhat from institutional brand. Journalists who have left legacy news organizations are attracting funding to create their own websites."

The individualization of newswork as implied by a new capitalist culture of workforce flexibility, the ongoing information processes of convergence and computerization, and the emergence of audiences increasingly focused on individual rather than institutional voices may prove to be a fertile ground for future professionals to explore. One of the key areas in this future development of the field is, for example, the intrinsic weakness of online information: its unreliability. Journalists are uniquely equipped with the skills and mind-set critically needed in the validation of information online. This, combined with their individual and perhaps idiosyncratic added value as well as professional self-perception, is at the very least an interesting, even if unresolved, trend.

Discussion

Journalists today enter a workforce that is built on the heyday of the 20th-century era of omnipresent mass media but that is expected to perform in a contemporary news ecology where individualization, globalization, and the pervasive role of corresponding networked technologies challenge all the assumptions traditional news making is based on. When considering the current developments in the lived reality of newswork, evidence can be found both of things staying the same and of trends producing profound change. Technology further amplifies these trends as it primarily gets introduced in news organizations to standardize existing ways of doing things and to act as a cost-cutting measure by enabling reporters to do more general work with less specialized staff or resources (other than portable, networked equipment). Within organizations, newsroom socialization has long been a staple of the production of culture. As part of this, the routinization of newswork becomes a crucial strategy in managing the accelerated news flow—a flow further supercharged by the addition of citizens as producers next to consumers of news through online platforms.

All the processes analyzed in this chapter suggest that we are witnessing a shift toward a new stage of industrialization in the news sector. The gradual transition toward a postindustrial and precarious organization of labor in journalism is the result of a business strategy that through the computerization of newsrooms and the development of convergence has consistently aimed to reduce costs and effect more managerial control over reporters and editors. Atypical newswork and atypical media management describe the increasing weakening of the journalistic profession with its craft tradition in the production of news, the presence and prestige of the byline, and the art to write, shoot, record, edit, and produce an authoritative narrative. Journalism today, as it is practiced in most mainstream news organizations, is being reduced to a simple form of labor, where journalists (from the perspective of management) are cast as flexible, multiskilled, and highly moveable newsworkers. The enforcement of this postindustrialization process is bringing to this sector, as well as to the other industrial sectors, standardization, homogenization, and uniformity of the labor force (as also reflected in the coherence and isomorphism of news stories around the world) with the purpose of obtaining its interchangeability (thus the need to have anonymous, nonspecialized journalists, for example). In this stage there is also a new role of audiences—perhaps emerging as an unexpected side effect of the ongoing convergence in the sector—one with which managers have not yet decided how to deal. These "new" audiences of producing consumers, or "prosumers," can prove to be a disruptive force for established business models in news, but they also may represent a wealth of people available to work without being paid.

These processes certainly have the effect of provoking an inevitable devaluation of the quality of news. This further development of the commodification and serialization of news is related not only to a strategy of cost reduction but also to the formalization of less freedom for journalists. Elsewhere we have argued (Fortunati & Deuze, 2010) how this may bring about a situation of a journalism without journalists. If this catastrophe comes true, perhaps this is the time to signal for individual journalists an alternative route to professionalism and the production of quality public information: outside of the institutions that thus far have defined the news as a business and a commodity.

References

Avilés, J., Bienvenido, L., Sanders, K., & Harrison, J. (2004). Journalists at digital television newsrooms in Britain and Spain: Workflow and multi-skilling in a competitive environment. *Journalism Studies, 5*(1), 87–100.

Beam, R. (2006). Organizational goals and priorities and the job satisfaction of U.S. journalists. *Journalism Quarterly, 83*(1), 169–185.

Bierhoff, J., Deuze, M., & De Vreese, C. (2000). *Media innovation, professional debate and media training: A European analysis.* European Journalism Center Report. Retrieved from https://scholarworks.iu.edu/dspace/handle/2022/6601

Boczkowski, P. (2004). *Digitizing the news: Innovation in online newspapers.* Boston, MA: MIT Press.

Deuze, M. (2004). What is multimedia journalism? *Journalism Studies, 5*(2), 139–152.

Deuze, M. (2007). *Media work*. Cambridge, England: Polity Press.

Deuze, M. (2009). Technology and the individual journalist: Agency beyond imitation and change. In B. Zelizer (Ed.), *The changing faces of journalism: Tabloidization, technology and truthiness* (pp. 82–98). London, England: Routledge.

Du Gay, P. (2000). *In praise of bureaucracy*. London, England: Sage.

Fortunati, L. (2003). The information society at the service of tradition. In C. MacKeogh & P. Preston (Eds.), *Strategies of inclusion: Gender in the information society: Vol. II. Experiences from private and voluntary sector initiatives* (pp. 283–302). Center for Technology and Society. Trondheim, Norway: Norwegian University of Science and Technology.

Fortunati, L., & Deuze, M. (2010). Journalism without journalists. In G. Meikle & G. Redden (Eds.), *News online: Transformation and continuity*. Basingstoke, England: Palgrave Macmillan.

Fortunati, L., Sarrica, M., Balcytiene, A., Harro-Loit, H., Macgregor, P., Roussou, N., et al. (2009). The influence of the Internet on European journalism. *Journal of Computer-Mediated Communication, 14*(4), 928–963.

Gade, P. (2004). Newspapers and organizational development: Management and journalist perceptions of newsroom cultural change. *Journalism Monographs, 6*.

Gall, G. (2000). New technology, the labour process and employment relations in the provincial newspaper industry. *New Technology, Work and Employment, 15*(2), 94–107.

Hesmondhalgh, D. (2007). *The cultural industries* (2nd ed.). London, England: Sage.

International Federation of Journalists. (2006). *The changing nature of work: A global survey and case study of atypical work in the media industry*. Research report. Retrieved from http://www.ifj.org/pdfs/ILOReport070606.pdf

Jenkins, H. (2006). *Convergence culture: Where old and new media collide*. New York: New York University Press.

Journalism.org. (2009). *The state of the news media*. Project for Excellence in Journalism. Retrieved from http://www.stateofthemedia.org/2009/narrative_overview_majortrends.php?cat=1&media=1/

Killebrew, K. (2004). *Managing media convergence: Pathways to journalistic cooperation*. Malden, MA: Blackwell.

Marjoribanks, T. (2003). Strategising technological innovation. In S. Cottle (Ed.), *Media organization and production* (pp. 59–75). London, England: Sage.

McKercher, C. (2002). *Newsworkers unite: Labor, convergence and North American newspapers*. Lanham, MD: Rowman & Littlefield.

Mierzjewska, B., & Hollifield, C. A. (2006). Theoretical approaches to media management research. In A. B. Albarran, S. M. Chan-Olmsted, & M. O. Wirth (Eds.), *Handbook of media management and economics* (pp. 37–66). Mahwah, NJ: Erlbaum.

Nerone, J., & Barnhurst, K. G. (2003). US newspaper types, the newsroom, and the division of labor. *Journalism Studies, 4*(4), 435–449.

Paterson, C., & Domingo, D. (Eds.). (2008). *Making online news*. New York, NY: Peter Lang.

Russo, T. C. (1998). Organizational and professional identification: A case of newspaper journalists. *Management Communication Quarterly, 12*(1), 72–111.

Quinn, S. (2005). *Convergence journalism*. New York, NY: Peter Lang.

Weaver, D. (Ed.). (1998). *The global journalist: News people around the world.* Cresskill, NJ: Hampton Press.

Witt-Barthel, A. (2007). *EFJ survey: Women journalists in the European integration process.* Brussels, Belgium: European Federation of Journalists.

Ybema, S. (2003). *De koers van de krant.* Amsterdam, The Netherlands: Vrije Universiteit.

10 On the Wisdom of Ignorance

KNOWLEDGE AND THE MANAGEMENT OF CONTEMPORARY NEWS ORGANIZATIONS

Pablo J. Boczkowski

In the fall of 2008 I received a kind invitation from Mark Deuze "to contribute an essay on how [I] see [my] work contributing to our understanding of the management of media work." More specifically, Mark suggested that this essay answer the following question: "What should media managers know about your work, and how could or should it influence their work?" I must confess that my initial reaction was not positive. This reaction was, in part, informed by the experience of teaching my research for a few years in executive education programs organized by the Media Management Center at Northwestern University. Managers often participate in these programs, or enter into conversations with consultants, expecting palatable diagnoses of the typical problems they might face in their workplaces and empowering strategies that are guaranteed to solve these problems when implemented. Whether these expectations are adequate and helpful and what the role of programs and consultants is in fostering them are beside the point. Since, as pragmatist scholars have long noted, "situations defined as real are real in their consequences" (Thomas & Thomas, 1917/1970), these expectations tend to frame discussions about media management. In contrast, I found it

Author's note: I thank Mark Deuze for inviting me to share my ideas in the context of this volume and for his infinite patience. This essay elaborates on arguments presented more extensively in my book, *News at Work: Imitation in an Age of Information Abundance* (Chicago, University of Chicago Press, 2010), and in related articles (Boczkowski, 2009a, 2009b, 2009c; Boczkowski & de Santos, 2007). The ideas regarding the managerial implications of these arguments benefited from a most stimulating conversation with Howard Rheingold. I also thank Keith Hampton for suggesting that I think about the Fitzgerald story in the context of my recent research. Needless to say, any shortcomings and misunderstandings contained in this essay are my sole responsibility.

very difficult to frame my research in these terms, which resulted in dissatis-faction between the audience and me.

But it is now undeniable that the news industry is affected by a momentous crisis of economic sustainability. The ideas imparted in executive education programs and consulting engagements have been unable to make a dent in this state of affairs, despite the promissory language in which they are usually couched and the hefty fees that are frequently charged to access them. Hence, as I further considered Mark's invitation, I realized that perhaps the current cli-mate might afford an opportunity to change the tone and—paraphrasing the title of Clay Shirky's (2009) much circulated blog post—think the unthinkable. Thus, I decided to write this essay by presenting an unpleasant diagnosis of some key trends in the knowledge space of contemporary journalism and offering an unrealistic suggestion to alleviate them. Expecting the unreason-able might be a stance worth exploring in these interesting times.

To get things started, I examine a peculiar field experiment undertaken recently by a young researcher across the Atlantic.

A Field Experiment on Contemporary Knowledge Practices in Newswork

Famed music composer Maurice Jarre died on March 28, 2009. Shane Fitzgerald, then a college student in Dublin, Ireland, decided to take advantage of this tragic event to run a field experiment. Taking into account his position and resources, Fitzgerald's objective was overly ambitious. It was also devas-tatingly simple. According to the readers' editor of British newspaper *The Guardian*, Fitzgerald described his objective as follows: "My aim was to show that an undergraduate university student in Ireland can influence what news-papers are doing around the world and also that the reliance of newspapers on the internet can lead to some faults" (Butterworth, 2009, para. 10). How did Fitzgerald go about pursuing this aim? According to a handful of press accounts, this is what happened (Butterworth, 2009; Carbery, 2009; Pogatchnik, 2009). Shortly after learning that Jarre had passed away, Fitzgerald fabricated an eminently quotable phrase and inserted it into Jarre's biography on Wikipedia. This phrase "had no referenced sources and was therefore taken down by moderators of Wikipedia within minutes. However, Fitzgerald put it back a few more times until it was finally left up on the site for more than 24 hours" (Carbery, 2009, para. 10). In the next couple of days the phrase—or parts of it—appeared in numerous blogs and also "in obituaries published in the *Guardian,* [in] the *London Independent,* on the *BBC Music Magazine* website and in Indian and Australian newspapers" (Carbery, 2009, para. 3). The fabricated quote stayed on these publications and sites for weeks. Then, Fitzgerald contacted the main newspapers to inform them of the hoax. In a widely reproduced Associated Press report, Fitzgerald stated, "I am 100 percent convinced that if I hadn't come forward, that quote would have gone down in history as something Maurice Jarre said, instead of something I made up" (Pogatchnik, 2009, para. 7).

The most common reactions to this revelation among news organizations affected by this hoax were to correct the mistake or do nothing. To the best of my knowledge, only *The Guardian* publicly reflected on its implications. According to Siobhain Butterworth (2009), the readers' editor, "*The Guardian* commissioned an obituary writer on the morning of 30 March, giving him only a few hours to produce a substantial piece on Jarre's life for the following day's paper" (para. 2). Wikipedia was one of the sources that the writer utilized for the article. This included reproducing the Fitzgerald phrase and placing it in a prominent location within the obituary. The writer proceeded in this way even though it violated *The Guardian*'s editorial code, which "advises that when quotes are taken from another publication, journalists should acknowledge the source. The guidance is less strictly adhered to in obituaries, features and blogs than it is in news stories, and it wasn't followed here" (Butterworth, 2009, para. 7).

How are we to interpret the findings from Fitzgerald's experiment? Contrasting what happened with a counterfactual scenario brings into sharp relief the dynamics that caused the observed patterns of action. Imagine for a moment that the news industry got stuck in, for instance, the 1960s. In this hypothetical situation, journalists at *The Guardian* and similar news organizations would have tackled the task of writing Jarre's obituary by relying on their own memory; their newspaper's own archive; conversations with some colleagues and, maybe, a couple of experts; and perusal of a handful of books. The outcome of these knowledge practices would have been the production of more diverse obituary pieces on Jarre across news organizations than was the case in the aftermath of Fitzgerald's experiment. The dynamics in question are simple. On the one hand, the reliance on more publicly available knowledge is tied to less diversity in content across the media field. The adjective *public* denotes not only that this knowledge is available to all the players in the field but also that each player knows that the others can access this knowledge as well. On the other hand, the reliance on less publicly available knowledge (whether residing in one's head, one's personal network of contacts, or the newspaper's "morgue") results in more diversity of content across the media field. More is less versus less is more.

How common are the kinds of processes made visible by Fitzgerald's experiment? Anecdotal evidence suggests a disheartening answer. Looking for information about this experiment, time and again I found that the above-mentioned report from the Associated Press was reprinted in a number of outlets, several of them leading online news sources in America, such as Yahoo! News, MSNBC.com, ABC News, SFGate.com (the online site of the *San Francisco Chronicle*), and *The Seattle Times*. In turn, this report served as the factual basis on which numerous bloggers shared their opinion about the causes and consequences of what had happened, thus vastly amplifying the presence of this account. Beyond this anecdote, as I demonstrate in the next section, systematic analyses of knowledge practices in contemporary journalism suggest that the dynamics illuminated by Fitzgerald's experiment are quite common.

More Information, Less News

Scholars have long analyzed the pervasiveness in journalism of monitoring the competition and imitating some of the content discovered through monitoring (Donsbach, 1999; Graber, 1971; Halloran, Elliot, & Murdock, 1970; Reinemann, 2004; Tuchman, 1978; Velthuis, 2006). Schudson (2003) maintains, "News institutions monitor one another all the time" (p. 109). According to Bourdieu (1998), this is because journalists often operate under the assumption that "to know what to say, you have to know what everyone else has said" (p. 18). Learning through monitoring often fuels imitation. In his landmark dissertation research on social control in the newsroom, Breed (1955) already noted "the tendency of many papers to feature the same stories atop their front pages, to the exclusion of others" (p. 277). Two decades later, Crouse (1972/2003) offered a detailed portrait of "the notorious phenomenon of 'pack journalism,'" in which "a group of reporters were assigned to follow a single candidate for weeks or months at a time, like a pack of hounds sicked on a fox" (p. 7).

Studies conclude that there has been a recent intensification of preexisting monitoring and imitation habits in contemporary journalistic work (Bourdieu, 1998; Gans, 2003; Klinenberg, 2002; Norris, 2000; Shoemaker & Reese, 1996). Commenting about the contemporary media landscape in the United States, Rosenstiel (2005) argues, "The explosion in [news] outlets has not meant more reporters doing original shoe-leather reporting. Instead, more people are involved in taking material that is secondhand and repackaging it" (p. 701). Thus, he concludes, "This emphasis on synthesis is the new pack journalism" (p. 706). In his ethnography of editorial work on German news sites, Quandt (2008) shows that "the journalists constantly monitor the output of their . . . competitors in order to check their news in relation to what the others offer" (p. 90).

In light of this intensification of monitoring and imitation, it is not surprising to find evidence of homogenization in the resulting news stories. To Schudson (2003), "The stories one reads in one publication are likely to bear a stronger resemblance to the stories in the next publication than they would have in the past" (p. 109). Surveying the recent evolution of the news industry in the United States, Journalism.org's 2006 *State of the News Media* report argues, "The new paradox of journalism is more outlets covering fewer stories," and its 2008 edition concludes that "2007 became a year notable for the narrowness of the news agenda." This narrowness of the news agenda is such that a year earlier, in the 2007 edition of the report, we read the following:

Visitors could spend the good part of a day just following the links for a single news story. If someone were to actually do that, though, the value might be disappointing. With no editing process, related stories automatically pop up from all different outlets. In some cases the reports are nearly identical wire stories carried in different outlets.

To further understand these processes of monitoring and imitation in journalistic work and their impact on the resulting news stories, I undertook a series of studies between 2005 and 2007. More precisely, I directed a research team that examined (a) the daily practices of editorial work in the two leading print newspapers of Argentina, *Clarín* and *La Nación*, and in their online counterparts, Clarin.com and Lanacion.com; (b) the selection and editorial construction of the top stories of the day in these outlets; (c) the patterns of popularity of online news stories as expressed in the most-clicked stories on their respective sites; and (d) the habits and experiences of the consumers of online news. (See Appendix A in Boczkowski, in press, for detailed methodological information on these studies.)

This research showed the intense and constant monitoring of online news sites among both online and print staffers. For instance, one editor at Clarin.com commented that he looked at competitors' sites "all the time. . . . I don't want to miss anything of what they have" (personal communication, December 15, 2005). Comparable monitoring practices were also an important component of the work routines of Lanacion.com journalists in charge of producing breaking news. A staffer who wrote about politics said, "I continuously look at Clarin.com, and [local news sites] Infobae.com, Ambito.com, Perfil.com, and Urgente24.com. . . . I have a lot of windows opened [on the computer screen] and I keep looking" (personal communication, December 18, 2006).

Journalists who worked in the print *Clarín* and *La Nación* newsrooms said that online media had increasingly occupied a larger and more important role in their monitoring routines. Julio Blanck, one of three editors-in-chief at *Clarín*, regularly monitored Clarin.com during the workday: "I do it a lot. . . . I look at Clarin.com all the time to see what [news] it has" (personal communication, December 14, 2006). Fernando Rodriguez, an editor on the metro desk of the print *La Nación*, looked at local online news sites "every ten minutes. . . . I have [their window tabs] at the bottom of the screen and keep clicking" (personal communication, March 20, 2007). Rodriguez recalled situations in which monitoring the competition had led to a discovery that affected his news budget. For instance, a short time before our conversation took place, there had been a verdict in a judicial case that "was a production of Clarin.com, which then triggered our own search [of information]. It did not show up in the wires . . . until 10:30 in the evening" (ibid.).

The comments by Rodriguez tie monitoring and imitation: When a journalist learned that a story had been published by the competition, it substantively increased the likelihood that she would publish it too. An editor at Clarin.com noted, "If a piece of news has been published by [the competition], then we also have to publish it. Perhaps it is not very important, so we lower it [referring to placement on the home page], but we publish it anyway. If they have it, we have it too" (personal communication, July 28, 2005). Imitation also affected issues of editorial construction. Recalling a developing story, a Clarin.com staffer said, "When we defined the headline and the lead we were going to use, the first thing we did was to look at the sites of Lanacion.com and Infobae.com to see theirs" (personal communication, July 28, 2005). He added, "This is something that happens almost naturally. 'This is how we frame the story, in principle; let's see how the others do it [before publishing]'" (ibid.).

This puts in place a replication logic in which a journalist selects or frames a story in part because others have already selected it or framed it in a particular way. This, in turn, contributes to an echo chamber effect on the media landscape. This effect leads to the belief, expressed in a phrase commonly heard during observations and interviews, that "everybody has the same." A Clarin.com staffer stated, "There is a reality and it is that all [online] newspapers . . . have the same [news]" (personal communication, October 5, 2005). A colleague in the print newsroom shared a related thought: "A phrase that you hear frequently in newsrooms is that today everybody has the same [news stories]" (personal communication, March 21, 2007).

These monitoring and imitation dynamics are consistent with the results of a content analysis of the main stories published by *Clarín* and *La Nación* on their front pages between 1995 and 2005 and the top stories published on the home pages of Clarin.com and Lanacion.com in 2005. The analysis revealed the existence of a sizeable and significant increase of similarity in the selection of news stories on print front pages during this period. It also indicated a high level of similarity in the selection of news stories on online home pages in 2005, a level that is comparable to that of the front pages of *Clarín* and *La Nación* for the same year. In addition, the analysis showed a rise in similarity in the editorial construction of the news for both print and online during this period. These results suggest that the effects of increased imitation affect both print and online outlets.

These effects did not go unnoticed among the more than 60 consumers of online news interviewed for this research. Pablo, a 27-year-old lawyer, stated, "If you go to an [online] newspaper [site, it] is like going to all [of the others]. . . . The [main] headlines of the day and the news in general are the same" (personal communication, February 21, 2007). Natalia, a 23-year-old college student, concurred with Pablo: "The most important news [is published in] all newspapers" (personal communication, December 18, 2006). Moreover, several consumers said that the similarity in the selection of stories extended to the broader media landscape. For instance, according to Manuel, a 27-year-old computer technician, "Everybody has the same news and that makes it boring, monotonous, with no variety. Buying a newspaper ends up like buying any other one" (personal communication, March 29, 2007). Norberto, a 62-year-old accountant who devoted significant amounts of time to the news since retiring from his job, characterized cross-media patterns of content similarity with a great degree of frustration: "The media . . . take a lot of advantage of the other's harvest. . . . During the day I listen to radio programs . . . and they . . . comment on the news that they read on the newspaper just like I do" (personal communication, January 19, 2007).

The vast majority of consumers reacted negatively to the loss of content diversity. Esteban, a 35-year-old Web designer, said that in the current environment "everything becomes homogenized . . . [whereas] the ideal thing is that each one retains its profile" (personal communication, January 16, 2007). Lorena, a 29-year-old teacher of Spanish as a second language, noted, "It's always better to have difference. The single, monolithic voice—no!" (personal communication, March 2, 2007). Gerardo, a 48-year-old engineer, concurred with Esteban and Lorena: "I don't like the homogeneity [of things]; it tends to make everything uniform, alike. It seems boring to me" (personal communication, April 10, 2007).

This dominant reaction of dislike was tied to an overwhelmingly negative affect. Some, like Vanina, a 40-year-old teacher, expressed their feelings in a rather visceral fashion. She said that a scenario marked by an increasingly similar supply of news stories by the leading media "gives me stomach pain because there is that sense of [something] monopolistic, that there are two [news organizations] telling you the same story. . . . It gives me a feeling of claustrophobia . . . of confinement" (personal communication, February 22, 2007). Others, like Alexis, a 37-year-old psychiatrist, talked about their emotions in a distant and intellectualized way: "It provokes a very moderate irritation in a context . . . in which we can't trust in anybody or anything anymore, in which everything has some sort of interest [behind it], and nothing is as genuine as what it seems. . . . Then, I say, 'Well, that's all there is'" (personal communication, December 26, 2007).

In addition to the stated dislike and negative affect associated with the perception of growing homogenization in the news provided by the leading media outlets, an analysis of the most-clicked stories on Clarin.com and Lanacion.com showed a much lower level of homogenization in the stories that consumers read most frequently than in the stories that journalists consider most newsworthy. These results also indicate the existence of different thematic distributions in the selection patterns of journalists and consumers. The choices of journalists are concentrated on national, business, economics, and international topics, and those of consumers center on sports, entertainment, and crime subjects. Thus, the rise of imitation in news production does not appear to match consumer preferences. Additional studies undertaken in the United States, Latin America, and Europe showed a similar kind of mismatch between the editorial offerings of the leading online news sites and the preferences of the consumers of these outlets (Boczkowski, Mitchelstein, & Walter, 2009; Boczkowski & Peer, 2008). These patterns of news production and consumption exist despite the distaste of journalists (who rarely enter the occupation to replicate someone else's stories), the dissatisfaction of consumers, and their detrimental implications for the watchdog function of the press and contribution to the diversity of ideas in the public sphere. Why?

The Connection Between
Knowledge and Imitation

The evolution of online news toward increased volume and frequency of publication has made the knowledge space of journalistic work substantively more transparent than previously. That is, using a computer connected to the Internet gives any journalist access to much deeper and wider knowledge of the stories that competitors are working on as well as of publicly available sources of information (from government sites to Wikipedia to whatever can be found through Google searches) than previously. Furthermore, in a media landscape signaled by a continuous production cycle, this knowledge is also more actionable than previously. In the world of print and broadcast news of half a century ago, journalists knew less about what their competitors were doing and about publicly available information repositories than they do today. This knowledge space was therefore quite opaque: Journalists resorted less to publicly available information, such as wire copy, and more to interpersonal networks, such as sources that rendered information that was private (in the sense that it was not widely available to others). In addition, given the discontinuous production cycle, even when they learned about the competition, many times they could not use this knowledge to alter their own products. Today's journalists know far more about what their competitors are working on, have greater access to a much wider array of publicly available information, and have an easier time utilizing this knowledge in their own production processes. As was evident in the past two sections, the widespread use of this knowledge has been tied to the rise in imitative activity and the homogenization of the resulting stories.

This transformation in the knowledge space of editorial work does not determine the actions of journalists. (My research shows that there are patterns of variation by type of content and medium.) But it creates structural conditions that become consequential in relation to a number of local factors that vary from organization to organization and from unit to unit within an organization. Due to space limitations, I focus on four such factors that my research has shown to be particularly salient: (a) the orientation toward colleagues, (b) the management of reputation, (c) the character of work processes, and (d) the representation of the consumers. Regarding the first factor, the classic ethnographies of news production established the extent to which journalists, using Robert Darnton's (1975) apt formulation, "really wr[i]te for one another" (p. 176). The more this orientation is prevalent for a journalist, the more she will be inclined to spend time monitoring the competition and producing content that will be considered valuable among her peers. Concerning the second factor, journalists often manage their reputations in part by conforming to the perceived consensus. As Sharon Dunwoody (1980) wrote almost 30 years ago,

> Each journalist knows that his editor is watching the competitive newspapers and wire services and is evaluating what he produces *in relation to* [emphasis in the original] what the competition publishes. If he produces

something different, he may be in trouble; at the very least he will have to defend his choice. But if all competitors produce the same story for the day, then each editor assumes his reporter has done a good job. (p. 17)

In light of these tendencies, the increased transparency of the knowledge space can often be linked to increased imitation of competitors and other players in the media field. Third, there has been an acceleration in the flow of news production, a rise in the expectation regarding the volume of stories to be finished on an average workday, and either a stasis or a decrease in the temporal and material resources available to produce these stories. These transformations in work processes also contribute to turn the transparency of the knowledge space into a fertile terrain for the rise of imitation. Finally, and this pertains only to the sphere of online news, journalists tend to conceive of their public as expecting broad coverage of current events and fast dissemination of the resulting stories, or they would migrate to competitors' sites. With the other factors, this combination of comprehensiveness and timeliness shapes taking advantage of a more transparent knowledge space in the direction of increased imitation.

Given that these transformations in knowledge and imitation are negative for journalists, consumers, and society at large, what managerial path could be pursued to effect change? A first step might be to recognize that taking advantage of greater knowledge opportunities is not always beneficial. Situations exist in which there is wisdom in the pursuit of ignorance, and this appears to be one of them. Once this first step has been taken, the likelihood of rendering the knowledge space more opaque than it has become might increase by trying to counter the four factors identified above. Among other actions, this would involve decreasing the orientation that journalists have toward their colleagues and substituting it with a greater commitment to uniqueness in the production of news. It might entail making the culture less risk averse and sending clear signals that reputations should be made—and unmade—largely on the kind of originality that can only emerge from nonconformity. It could also require the alteration of work processes. In the case of online news sites, this could be done by reducing the volume of stories carried by the site or by providing direct feeds from wires of the vast majority of the stories and concentrating the editorial resources on high-quality coverage of a handful of key stories. Finally, it would also imply a problematization of the dominant representation of the ideal-typical consumer who, based on her clicking behavior and stated experience, seems to expect far more original news coverage than she normally encounters. None of these suggestions are easily deployable or even highly realistic. But, as noted in the introduction, a myriad of deployable and realistic suggestions do not seem to have helped the industry very much in recent years.

Concluding Remarks

"What should media managers know about [my] work, and how could or should it influence their work?" In a nutshell, recent transformations in the condition of knowledge that mark the contemporary journalistic field have been tied to major changes in journalistic practice. The advent of cable television news and, especially, the rise of online news have triggered major increases in the volume of news stories available and in the frequency of their dissemination. These developments are part of a larger trend toward an explosion in the amount of mediated information—increasingly through digital media—available in organizations and households.[1] Ours has become an age of information abundance. This, in turn, has had the unintended consequence of making the knowledge space of competition far less opaque than previously. That is, today's journalists have far more knowledge of the stories deemed newsworthy by their competitors than a few decades ago. Confronted with this condition of increased knowledge, quite often journalists take advantage of the ease of information reproduction and the continuous dissemination cycle to imitate what their counterparts in other organizations do. This leads to a decrease in the content diversity of the resulting stories they author. The aggregate result amounts to an emerging crisis of news homogeneity that is distinct from, but contributes to, the crisis of economic sustainability in the industry. This state of affairs is not only unwelcome by journalists and detrimental for the polity but also bad for business since it fosters interpretive dislike and negative affect among news consumers.

How could these ideas influence the behavior of managers in news organizations? My suggestion is straightforward, albeit admittedly romantic: Since more has become less, less might eventually turn into more. Rather than directly and indirectly fostering the acquisition of public knowledge that is often tied to a generic editorial offering, managers should encourage the conscious ignorance of this knowledge and the gathering of unique information that is privately known and can thus contribute to a differentiated news product. After all, there might be some wisdom in the active pursuit of ignorance.

References

Boczkowski, P. (2009a). *Materiality and mimicry in the journalistic field*. In B. Zelizer (Ed.), *The changing faces of journalism* (pp. 56–67). New York, NY: Routledge.

Boczkowski, P. (2009b). Rethinking hard and soft news production: From common ground to divergent paths. *Journal of Communication, 59*, 98–116.

Boczkowski, P. (2009c). Technology, monitoring and imitation in contemporary news work. *Communication, Culture & Critique, 2*, 39–59.

Boczkowski, P. (in press). *News at work: Imitation in an age of information abundance*. Chicago, IL: University of Chicago Press.

Boczkowski, P., & de Santos, M. (2007). When more media equals less news: Patterns of content homogenization in Argentina's leading print and online newspapers. *Political Communication, 24,* 167–190.

Boczkowski, P., Mitchelstein, E., & Walter, M. (2009). *The news choices of journalists and consumers in an era of digital media and global information flows: Latin America and Europe in comparative perspective.* Paper presented at the XXVIII International Congress of the Latin American Studies Association, Rio de Janeiro, Brazil, June 11–14.

Boczkowski, P., & Peer, L. (2008). *The choice gap: The divergent online news preferences of journalists and consumers.* Paper presented at the annual meeting of the International Communication Association, Montreal, Canada, May.

Bourdieu, P. (1998). *On television.* New York, NY: The New Press.

Breed, W. (1955). Newspaper "opinion leaders" and the processes of standardization. *Journalism Quarterly, 32*(Summer), 277–284.

Butterworth, S. (2009, May 4). Open door: The readers' editor on . . . web hoaxes and the pitfalls of quick journalism. *The Guardian.* Retrieved from http://guardian.co.uk/commentisfree/2009/may/04/journalism-obituaries-shane-fitzgerald

Carbery, G. (2009, May6). Student's Wikipedia hoax quote used worldwide in newspaper obituaries. The Irish Times. Retrieved from http://www.irishtimes.com/newspaper/ireland/2009/0506/1224245992919_pf/html

Crouse, T. (2003). *The boys on the bus.* New York, NY: Random House. (Original work published 1972)

Darnton, R. (1975). Writing news and telling stories. *Daedalus, 104*(Spring), 175–194.

Donsbach, W. (1999). Journalism research. In H.-B. Brosius & C. Holtz-Bacha (Eds.), *German communication yearbook* (pp. 159–180). Cresskill, NJ: Hampton Press.

Dunwoody, S. (1980). The science writing inner club: A communication link between science and lay people. *Science, Technology & Human Values, 5,* 14–22.

Gans, H. (2003). *Democracy and the news.* New York, NY: Oxford University Press.

Graber, D. (1971). The press as public opinion resource during the 1968 presidential campaign. *Public Opinion Quarterly, 35,* 162–182.

Halloran, J., Elliot, P., & Murdock, G. (1970). *Demonstrations and communication: A case study.* Harmondsworth, England: Penguin Books.

Journalism.org. (2006). *The state of the news media.* Project for Excellence in Journalism. Retrieved from http://www.stateofthemedia.org/2006/

Journalism.org. (2007). *The state of the news media.* Project for Excellence in Journalism. Retrieved from http://www.stateofthemedia.org/2007/

Journalism.org. (2008). *The state of the news media.* Project for Excellence in Journalism. Retrieved from http://www.stateofthemedia.org/2008/

Klinenberg, E. (2002). *Heat wave.* Chicago, IL: University of Chicago Press.

Neuman, W. R. (2009). *The flow of mediated culture: Trends in supply and demand, 1960–2005.* Paper presented at the annual meeting of the American Sociological Association, San Francisco, California, August 7–11.

Norris, P. (2000). *A virtuous circle.* Cambridge, England: Cambridge University Press.

Pogatchnik, S. (2009). Irish student hoaxes world's media with fake quote. *SFGate.com.* Retrieved from http://www.sfgate.com/cgi-bin/article.cgi?f=/n/a/2009/05/11/international/i090708D96.DTL

Quandt, T. (2008). News tuning and content management: An observation study of old and new routines in German online newsrooms In C. A. Paterson & D. Domingo (Eds.), *Making online news: The ethnography of new media production* (pp. 77–97). New York, NY: Peter Lang.

Reinemann, C. (2004). Routine reliance revisited: Exploring media importance for German political journalists. *Journalism & Mass Communication Quarterly, 81,* 857–876.

Rosenstiel, T. (2005). Political polling and the new media culture: A case of more being less. *Public Opinion Quarterly, 69,* 698–715.

Schudson, M. (2003). *The sociology of news.* New York, NY: W. W. Norton.

Shirky, C. (2009). *Newspapers and thinking the unthinkable.* Retrieved from http://www.shirky.com/weblog/2009/03/newspapers-and-thinking-the-unthinkable/

Shoemaker, P., & Reese, S. (1996). *Mediating the message: Theories of influences on mass media content.* New York, NY: Longman.

Thomas, W., & Thomas, D. (1970). Situations defined as real are real in their consequences. In G. Stone & H. Farberman (Eds.), *Social psychology through symbolic interaction* (pp. 54–155). Waltham, MA: Xerox. (Original work published 1917)

Tuchman, G. (1978). *Making news.* New York, NY: Free Press.

Velthuis, O. (2006). Inside a world of spin: Four days at the World Trade Organization. *Ethnography, 7,* 125–150.

Note

1. See Neuman, 2009, for a heroic attempt to measure the "flow of mediated culture" in American households.

11 Understanding Multinational Media Management

Tim Marjoribanks

Management is a critical dimension of any organizational context. It involves relations of power and authority within organizations, as well as cooperative and contested relations between organizations, and also raises, at particular moments, forms of resistance and struggle within organizations. In seeking to understand what commercial media organizations do, and why, it is vital to engage with questions of management. And, in a context in which many major media organizations are increasingly operating beyond the boundaries of the nation-state, so too there is a need to analyze and understand multinational media management.

Over many years, much debate has arisen about multinational media organizations and the effects of their products, often discussed in the context of globalization. For example, important interventions have focused on the concentration of ownership and power (Bagdikian, 2004; Schiller, 1999). Debates have also emerged, often with a link to the work of German philosopher Jürgen Habermas, considering the connection between global media and a global public sphere (Couldry & Dreher, 2007; Fraser, 2007). There have also been significant arguments around cultural imperialism, with concerns emerging about the impact of globalization of content on local cultural practices and about the ongoing viability of local media industries (Boyd-Barrett, 2006; Jin, 2007; Rai & Cottle, 2007). Such literature is of critical importance, identifying key features of media organizations in the production and dissemination of information and knowledge in a global information society.

What is also required is analysis of what goes on inside multinational media organizations in terms of managerial practice. As research by Cottle (2003a), Deuze (2007), Flew (2007), and Küng (2008), among others, reveals, such analyses are critical if we are to get a full picture of the organizational complexity, negotiations, and contests that underlie the activities of multinational media corporations. In this chapter, I will engage with examples of research that has explored managerial practice within multinational media corporations. Overall, it will become evident that a full account of the organization, practices, and effects of multinational media must engage with the opportunities and constraints that managers work with in their everyday practice.

In this chapter, I consider five critical issues relating to management in multinational media corporations. First, I present key contextual features of the multinational media market. Second, I argue that a new institutional model provides an important theoretical framework for engaging with management in multinational media corporations. Third, I consider literature that has examined key dimensions of multinational media corporations from a macro perspective, focusing on the relations they form with other organizations. Fourth, I engage with literature that has analyzed managerial practices within media organizations. Fifth, and finally, I consider some of the implications of this research for multinational media management. Through this discussion, I argue that in the context of trends indicating that multinational media corporations are key players in the global media market, an understanding of their operation requires analysis of management practice inside the organization at the local level.

Setting the Scene: The Dynamics of Multinational Media Corporations

The contemporary commercial media landscape is dominated by a small number of multinational media organizations. While media organizations including News Corporation (Australia/United States), Bertelsmann (Germany), Time Warner (United States), and Walt Disney (United States) have their origins in specific national contexts, during the second half of the 20th century and into the 21st century they have become increasingly international in their activities. For example, in 2008, Time Warner, then the world's largest media conglomerate, had sales of U.S. $46,984 million, 87,000 employees, and a presence in the United States, Asia, Oceania, Canada, Latin America, and Europe. Walt Disney had sales of U.S. $37,843 million and 150,000 employees in 2008, while Bertelsmann, with 102,397 employees in 2007 and €18.758 billion in revenue, operates in more than 50 countries. Meanwhile, News Corporation, now based primarily in the United States but with its origins in Australia, in 2008 had sales of U.S. $32,996 million, 64,000 employees, and operations distributed across the United States, Europe, Asia, Oceania, Canada, and Latin America, making it then third largest global media conglomerate behind Time Warner and Walt Disney (data from hoovers.com; Balnaves, Donald, & Donald, 2001). As Balnaves, Donald, and Donald write, while the United States is at the center of the global media economy, these corporations and their competitors "have their sights set on global markets, public access, and exploitable archives of films, programming, music, and text" (p. 60).

In addition to the sheer size of these organizations, it is important to recognize the diversity of organizational forms they take and the wide range of operations they are involved in, as these in turn pose challenges for managerial practice. For example, as Winseck (2008) notes, from the 1980s through the

2000s, there has been a series of processes involving vertical integration between U.S. television networks and Hollywood studios, with the resulting corporations engaging in international activity across diverse platforms. Winseck also notes the transnational ownership structures of some media organizations. For example, although ultimately ill fated, in 2000, the French conglomerate Vivendi purchased Universal Studios in the United States for U.S. $35 billion (Winseck, 2008). As another example, News Corporation has interests in a range of countries around the world, including those it has developed itself and others that it has bought from local owners (Marjoribanks, 2000). Specific challenges that arise in contexts such as these include managing across diverse platforms and bringing together organizations that were not only previously independent but also operating in different national contexts, often with very different forms of organizational practice.

Multinational media corporations may also be involved in relationships with nonmedia organizations. As Arsenault and Castells (2008) identify, in addition to the emergence of "denser connections between transnational and local media organizations" (p. 722), multinational media organizations engage in varying partnerships, alliances, and cross-investments with other industries, including financial, technological, and political organizations (Arsenault & Castells, 2008). Management then confronts challenges in operating not only across a diversity of media but also across varied industries.

This overview of multinational media gives an indication of the size of these organizations, and of the various organizational relationships they create. The significance of such multinational organizations relates to features including the centrality of media organizations in contemporary societies, their actual and potential capacity to influence public debate, the direct importing of programming, and the international "diffus[ion] of a corporate-driven media model" (Arsenault & Castells, 2008, p. 722). Given these factors, it is vital to engage with the management practices that shape them. Additionally, it is extremely likely that anyone seeking a career in the mainstream commercial media at some point works either for or with a company (wholly or partly) owned by one of these multinational corporations.

Analyzing Management in Multinational Media Corporations

Given a context in which multinational media organizations are increasingly significant, critical issues arise over how best to analyze them. Here I focus on developing a new institutional approach, arguing that it provides a framework that facilitates our understanding of multinational media management.

To start, it is important to situate media organizations within their social, political, and economic context. Here, the work of Manuel Castells (2000) on the emergence of a global network society is instructive. As Castells argues, we are living through a period of fundamental societal transformation in which all aspects of life are being transformed. Vital to such transformation processes is the centrality of information to a globalizing society, and the significant role of networks as a means of social, political, and economic organization. In such a context, as media corporations operate as key sites for the production and distribution of information, they become critical as sites of economic, social, and political power. Related to this, in Castells's analysis, organizational practice across all forms of industry, including media, is undergoing profound transformation, in particular from hierarchical and rigid organization to networked, fluid, and flexible forms of organization.

Castells's (2000) network approach suggests that, to understand management practice in multinational media corporations, there is a need for an analytic approach that can capture relationships that exist both within and between media organizations and between media corporations and other organizations. In this regard, an approach drawing on the insights of new institutionalism, in particular emphasizing relationships, processes, and embeddedness, is particularly appropriate as an analytic framework. While not explicitly discussing multinational media organizations, Simon Cottle provides an important starting point for such an analysis when he proposes that, if we are to understand organizational practice in media organizations, there is a need to analyze the interaction of relations at the macro, meso, and micro levels of the organization. Specifically, Cottle (2003b) argues,

> Complexities and levels of media production include, at the *micro-level,* the cultural milieux and interactions of producers situated within norm-governed and hierarchical production settings and the relationships entered into with technologies, professional colleagues and outside sources; at the *meso-level,* impinging organizational cultures, corporate strategies and editorial policies informing production practices and the reproduction of conventionalized (and changing) cultural forms; and, at the *macro-level,* surrounding regulatory, technological and competitive environments conditioning the operations and output of media organizations globally and locally. (p. 24)

While Cottle separates out these different dimensions for analytic purposes, it is also important to be aware that they intersect with each other. For example, what is possible for journalists to achieve at the micro level of everyday organizational practice is influenced by regulatory, technological, and competitive environments at the macro level (for other approaches emphasizing similar issues see Bennett, 2004; Benson, 2006; Flew, 2007).

Building on these approaches, a central insight of new institutional approaches is to argue that organizations are embedded in institutional environments, "the socially constructed normative worlds in which organizations exist" (Orru, Woolsey Biggart, & Hamilton, 1991, p. 361; see also Campbell, 2004; Duina, 2006). Central to these institutional environments are a range of organizations, including other media and nonmedia organizations, and the state, including in particular the legal system (Bennett, 2004; Marjoribanks, 2000, 2003; Marjoribanks & Kenyon, 2003). The notion of embedment also indicates that it is critical to pay attention to relations and practices at the local level, even as media organizations become increasingly multinational (Flew, 2007). Finally, in the context of organizational practice, new institutional approaches emphasize "the significance of the interaction of the worldviews of workplace actors, their social and institutional contexts and historical contingency in explaining transformations in workplace relations" and in explaining management practice (Marjoribanks, 2003, p. 62). In this regard, new institutional approaches demand an analysis of boundaries, within and between organizations, as key sites of contest and struggle (Lamont & Molnar, 2002). Combined, these interventions suggest a number of key points that should contribute to studying and understanding multinational media management:

- There is a need to analyze the relationships among micro, meso, and macro internal and external practices relevant to the organization.

- There is a need to analyze the interactions of the perceptions, experiences, and worldviews of organizational actors, including managers and those whom they manage, and to analyze the boundary struggles that occur among these actors.

- There is a need to focus not only on internal organizational relations but also on the external environment, taking account of other media corporations; regulators, including the state; and other organizations.

- There is a need to analyze management as part of organizational practice that is embedded in specific institutional environments, meaning there is a need to examine management at the local level and on a case-by-case basis, even as tendencies toward common forms of multinational management become more prevalent.

Holding this analytic framework together is the argument that media organizations and the individuals who constitute them are not freely floating actors, able to act or to develop strategy and practices in any way they wish. Rather, multinational media corporations, and their managers, are embedded in a set of internal and external social, political, and economic relations that provide both opportunities for action and forms of constraint.

Having established an analytic model for engaging with multinational media management, we can now turn attention to the external institutional context within which these organizations are embedded, before turning our attention to the internal practices of management in more specific detail.

External Organizational Issues for Multinational Media Management

The work of scholars in disciplines including sociology, media, political science, management, and economics, among others, provides crucial insights into the forms of organizational practice being undertaken by multinational media organizations and the contexts that influence such behavior. Amelia Arsenault and Manuel Castells (2008), for example, identify four major trends evident in multinational media corporations. First, media ownership is increasingly concentrated; second, multinational media corporations use an increasingly diverse range of platforms to deliver content; third, customization and segmentation of audiences are encouraged to promote advertising revenue; and fourth, achieving economies of synergy that take advantage of the changing communications environment is crucial to success.

Having identified these general trends among multinational media, Arsenault and Castells point to the increasing significance of networks as a form of organizational structure for multinational media organizations. Crucial to the success of these processes is the capacity of multinational media organizations to "connect to the global network of mediated communications" (Arsenault & Castells, 2008, p. 722; see also Castells & Arsenault, 2008), through a range of relationships including partnerships, alliances, and cross-investments, as well as mergers and takeovers. Identifying a similar trend, Balnaves et al. (2001) write that although commercial media corporations are competitors, "they come together to further common interests at particular moments, and then break apart again and reconfigure when political and economic circumstances change" (p. 60).

In addition to analyzing relations between media corporations, the concept of networked relations can also be used as a means for analyzing relations within media organizations. For example, Eric Louw (2001) cites Rupert Murdoch's News Corporation as a specific example of a successful networked media organization:

[In News Corporation] we find multiple (and proliferating) styles of control and decision-making being tolerated in different parts of the network, so long as those at the centre of the web can gain some benefit from allowing a particular practice and/or organizational arrangement to exist in a part of their networked "empire." In addition, the various . . . empires are not discrete—they can simultaneously overlap, intersect, cooperate, or even be in conflict with each other in an ever-shifting feudal-like *mélange* of networked power relationships. (p. 64)

What these examples suggest is that managers in multinational media corporations have a critical role to play in creating and maintaining networks, both internally and in the relations of media organizations with other organizations.

Given the requirements of a new institutional approach, it is important to note that the capacity to form and connect to such networks is influenced by elements of the external institutional environment, including in particular the regulatory regime. As Flew (2007) notes,

> Media organizations are . . . subject to a series of technical, marketplace and conduct regulations over elements of ownership, content and performance, both as general forms of industry regulation (for example, laws to ensure competitive markets), and regulations that are specific to the media, by virtue of their unique role as an instrument of public communication. (p. 171)

Such regulations may either enable or constrain particular actions. One example of constraint arose in the late 1990s when News Corporation attempted to purchase the English Premier League football club, Manchester United. While many at the time thought the takeover was a foregone conclusion, state regulators prevented it on the basis that it constituted anti-competitive behavior (Hamil, Michie, Oughton, & Warby, 2000). While media corporations seek partnerships, alliances, and other forms of relationship, they are not completely free to act as they wish.

This literature on the external institutional contexts within which multinational media corporations are operating provides important lessons for management. In particular, it indicates that managers are operating in an increasingly fluid and dynamic organizational context, where they must seek opportunities to become part of networks for particular projects or goals, and that once those projects or goals are accomplished, networks may be dissolved and new ones created. While media corporations still exhibit formal hierarchies, managers need to be open to creating relationships with a range of organizations in a flexible and fluid fashion. At the same time, they are not completely free to act as they like. In addition to resource constraints, national-level regulations (among other external factors) can either enable or constrain forms of action. As we turn our attention now to managerial action within media corporations, it is critical that we keep in mind this external environment and the opportunities and constraints it provides for managers in their everyday practice.

Management Practice Within Multinational Media Corporations

In the following section, I explore technological innovation and journalism standards as two examples of the challenges that face multinational media corporations in their everyday managerial practices. In discussing these examples, it is important to keep in mind the external environment as discussed above, and to consider how the different dimensions intersect with each other.

Technological Innovation

A crucial set of challenges for multinational media corporations relates to processes of managing the introduction of new technology into the workplace.

As researchers including Pablo Boczkowski (2004), Mark Deuze (2007), Eric Klinenberg (2005), and Gillian Ursell (2001) have shown, when analyzing technological innovation in media organizations and across media platforms, it is critical to avoid technological determinism, which suggests that technology determines organizational outcomes. To the contrary, as these researchers have shown, while technology is highly influential in media organization practice, its operation is the outcome of the intersection of social, political, and organizational practice, including issues such as who decided to introduce technology, when and how, and the ongoing processes over time through which technological change is implemented.

As an example of how these processes unfold in multinational contexts, it is instructive to consider transformations that have occurred within News Corporation over a number of decades. Under the leadership of Rupert Murdoch (2008), News Corporation has been a media leader in terms of globally innovative practice in relation to technology. To take newspapers as one example, from the 1970s to the present, in countries including Australia, the United States, and the United Kingdom, News Corporation has sought to develop a "best practice" model of implementing technological innovation across its multinational holdings (Marjoribanks, 2000, 2003). At the same time, management has had to be aware of the specifics of local contexts in introducing such change. This has resulted in change processes involving important similarities and variations. At a general level, for example, key common outcomes across its newspaper interests have been the introduction of similar technologies across its newspaper holdings and a generalized intensification of managerial control over workplace production practices. At the same time, there have also been important variations. These have included differences in whether change has been accomplished smoothly or in the context of major upheaval and workplace struggle. In seeking to understand such variation, it is important to recognize that processes of technological innovation are influenced by the specific histories of local workplaces, including the perceptions of organizational actors, while the local and national political and policy context also has an important impact on how change proceeds. For example, a history of conflict-based workplace relations at *The Times* (London) contributed to a violent process of workplace change, whereas more paternalistic workplace relations at *The Advertiser* in Adelaide, Australia, contributed to a less conflict-based process of change there. Such contests also raise crucial issues around boundary struggles, as media workers either embrace or reject change linked in part to their perceptions of whether or not their boundaries of expertise and authority are being enhanced or constricted (Marjoribanks, 2000, 2003).

Another significant dimension of the change process in this context has concerned other organizations following in the footsteps of News Corporation. For example, management at the *Financial Times* in London was able to use transformations at News Corporation as an underlying threat to its workforce in pursuing technological innovation in its own organization. In particular, management at the *Financial Times* was able to go to its workforce with a change agenda and to argue that, if the workforce did not comply peacefully with managerial requirements, then change would be pushed through by force as had occurred at News Corporation. In a similar fashion, experiences in one part of News Corporation have influenced other parts of the News Corporation network. For example, after changes occurred in London, with a move from Fleet Street to Wapping, there was widespread discussion in the holdings of News in Australia of the possibility of a "Wapping South" emerging. This again was a threat that management in Australia could use to pursue its change agenda. In both instances, management and other members of the organization are involved in processes of inter- and cross-organizational learning (Marjoribanks, 2000, 2003).

Based on such research, a number of key lessons emerge that can inform managerial practice. First, technological innovation involves an interrelated set of internal and external organizational relations that need to be managed. Second, it is important to recognize that technological innovation is a process. While it may be possible to identify a moment when specific technology is introduced, a range of other elements are involved both prior to and after that moment. This includes, for example, issues such as who is involved in negotiations about innovation, what training is provided, how the consequences of new technology for the workforce are managed, and the state of the broader political and policy context. Such issues, in turn, are influenced by the specific history of the organization. This again raises challenges for management of change. While there may be a desire to introduce technology across a multinational organization in a uniform and best-practice mode, depending on factors such as local workplace context, whether change has been introduced elsewhere and with what effect, and broader political settlements, what is appropriate in one context may, or may not, be appropriate in another.

Regulating Standards

As a second example, we can consider the regulation of standards of journalistic practice through both defamation law and ombudsmen. The significance of standards regulation for management and for other media workers is that it raises questions about the competence of members of the workforce and has the potential to put producers, editors, journalists, legal advisors, and ombudsmen in conflict with each other (Nolan & Marjoribanks, 2007).

Defamation law regulates the publication by media of material harmful to reputation by balancing the promotion of free speech and the protection of reputation. While defamation law exists in many countries, there are significant variations in how it has developed over time. For example, at a general level, defamation law in the United States favors freedom of speech to a greater extent than in the United Kingdom and Australia. In both the United Kingdom and Australia in recent years, however, the courts have broadened the opportunities for speech by developing a form of privilege defense for journalists in the context of stories that cannot be proven to be true by legal standards but that were published based on "responsible journalism" about a matter of public interest (Kenyon & Marjoribanks, 2008, p. 376). As Kenyon and Marjoribanks have noted, this has potentially significant repercussions for multinational media management and journalistic practice:

> Debates around responsible news production sit uneasily between the local or national contexts in which many producers practice, and the transnational syndicated or online audiences that receive their content. . . . With greater international dispersal of content there is increased potential for different understandings of what constitutes good journalism to be applied to the same content. (p. 373)

For managers in multinational media corporations, a key challenge then becomes one of being aware that in particular contexts the same content may be held accountable to different legal standards, thereby requiring managers to work to put in place organizational strategies around creative practice and standards to manage this issue.

Just as defamation law is one means of regulating standards, so too are ombudsmen used by news organizations as an internal form of regulation aimed at promoting journalistic standards. While ombudsmen have been introduced at least in part as a means to promote standards, they are considered by many journalists and other media workers as problematic constraints on professional self-regulation of standards (Nolan & Marjoribanks, 2007; Van Dalen & Deuze, 2006). They therefore have the potential to become a site of struggle and resistance within organizations, based on conceptions of professional boundaries and status. One of the critical challenges that such forms of internal regulation raises concerns variation between sites across national boundaries in terms of professional practice and expectations. Such concerns become particularly heightened for multinational media organizations with a potentially mobile workforce moving from one site to another and needing to be aware of differences in local standards and practices.

In the case of both defamation law and ombudsmen, a key challenge for managers is that many journalists and other media workers consider these forms of regulation as improperly encroaching on their area of professional competence. Managers need to be aware of practices at the local level and, even as they attempt to introduce organization-wide practices, be responsive to those local practices.

Conclusion

The discussion in this chapter provides a basis for identifying three key insights into challenges that confront management in multinational media organizations:

- First, managers need to be aware of and responsive to local institutional and organizational contexts, even when operating in multinational contexts.

- Second, managers need to be aware that the perceptions and under-standings of media workers around professional boundaries have a significant impact on their engagement with change processes.

- Third, in managing organizational processes, managers need to be aware of the relationships among micro, meso, and macro dimensions of organizational behavior and practice.

What emerges centrally when considering these processes is that, while many media organizations are increasingly operating in multinational contexts, local practice and local context remain of vital significance. This in turn means that while media organizations may seek to develop global and international strategies, whether relating to technology, standards, or other issues, there needs to be flexibility to respond to local organizational practices and cultures. As such, any tendency toward development of a general best-practice strategy in multinational media corporations needs to recognize the continuing significance of local experience and practice.

References

Arsenault, A., & Castells, M. (2008). The structure and dynamics of global multi-media business networks. *International Journal of Communication, 2,* 707–748.

Bagdikian, B. H. (2004). *The new media monopoly.* Boston, MA: Beacon Press.

Balnaves, M., Donald, J., & Donald, S. H. (2001). *The global media atlas.* London, England: British Film Institute.

Bennett, W. L. (2004). Global media and politics: Transnational communication regimes and civic cultures. *Annual Review of Political Science, 7,* 125–148.

Benson, R. (2006). News media as a "journalistic field": What Bourdieu adds to new institutionalism, and vice versa. *Political Communication, 23*(2), 187–202.

Boczkowski, P. J. (2004). *Digitizing the news: Innovation in online newspapers.* Cambridge, MA: MIT Press.

Boyd-Barrett, O. (2006). Cyberspace, globalization and empire. *Global Media and Communication, 2*(1), 21–41.

Campbell, J. L. (2004). *Institutional change and globalization.* Princeton, NJ: Princeton University Press.

Castells, M. (2000). Materials for an exploratory theory of the network society. *British Journal of Sociology, 51*(1), 5–24.

Castells, M., & Arsenault, A. (2008). Switching power: Rupert Murdoch and the global business of media politics: A sociological analysis. *International Sociology, 23,* 488–513.

Cottle, S. (Ed.). (2003a). *Media organization and production.* London, England: Sage.

Cottle, S. (2003b). Media organization and production: Mapping the field. In S. Cottle (Ed.), *Media organization and production* (pp. 3–24). London, England: Sage.

Couldry, N., & Dreher, T. (2007). Globalization and the public sphere: Exploring the space of community media in Sydney. *Global Media and Communication, 3*(1), 79–100.

Deuze, M. (2007). *Media work.* Cambridge, England: Polity.

Duina, F. (2006). *The social construction of free trade: The European Union, NAFTA, and Mercosur.* Princeton, NJ: Princeton University Press.

Flew, T. (2007). *Understanding global media.* Houndmills, England: Palgrave Macmillan.

Fraser, N. (2007). Transnationalizing the public sphere. On the legitimacy and efficacy of public opinion in a post-Westphalian world. *Theory, Culture and Society, 24*(4), 7–30.

Hamil, S., Michie, J., Oughton, C., & Warby, S. (Eds.). (2000). *Football in the digital age: Whose game is it anyway?* Edinburgh, Scotland: Mainstream.

Hoovers.com (2010). Hoover's Inc. <hoovers.com>

Jin, D. Y. (2007). Reinterpretation of cultural imperialism: Emerging domestic market vs continuing US dominance. *Media, Culture and Society, 29*(5), 753–771.

Kenyon, A. T., & Marjoribanks, T. (2008). The future of "responsible journalism." Defamation law, public debate and news production. *Journalism Practice, 2*(3), 372–385.

Klinenberg, E. (2005). Convergence: News production in a digital age. *The Annals of the American Academy of Political and Social Science, 597,* 48–64.

Küng, L. (2008). *Strategic management in the media industry: Theory to practice.* London, England: Sage.

Lamont, M., & Molnar, V. (2002). The study of boundaries in the social sciences. *Annual Review of Sociology, 28,* 167–195.

Louw, E. P. (2001). *The media and cultural production.* London, England: Sage.

Marjoribanks, T. (2000). *News Corporation, technology and the workplace: Global strategies, local change.* Cambridge, England: Cambridge University Press.

Marjoribanks, T. (2003). Strategizing technological innovation: The case of News Corporation. In S. Cottle (Ed.), *Media organization and production* (pp. 59–75). London, England: Sage.

Marjoribanks, T., & Kenyon, A. T. (2003). Negotiating news: Journalistic practice and defamation law in Australia and the US. *Australian Journalism Review, 25*(2), 71–90.

Murdoch, R. (2008). *The golden age of freedom: The 2008 Boyer lectures.* Sydney, Australia: ABC Books.

Nolan, D., & Marjoribanks, T. (2007). Regulating standards: Ombudsmen in newspaper journalism. *Joint Conference Proceeding of the TASA/SAANZ Conference: Public Sociologies: Lessons and Trans-Tasman Connections,* University of Auckland. Available from http://www.tasa.org.au/conference

Orru, M., Woolsey Biggart, N., & Hamilton, G. (1991). Organizational isomorphism in East Asia. In W. Powell & P. DiMaggio (Eds.), *The new institutionalism in organizational analysis* (pp. 361–389). Chicago, IL: University of Chicago Press.

Rai, M., & Cottle, S. (2007). Global mediations: On the changing ecology of satellite television news. *Global Media and Communication, 3*(1), 51–78.

Schiller, D. (1999). *Digital capitalism: Networking the global market system.* Cambridge, MA: MIT Press.

Ursell, G. (2001). Dumbing down or shaping up? New technologies, new media, new journalism. *Journalism, 2*(2), 175–196.

Van Dalen, A., & Deuze, M. (2006). Advocates or ambassadors? Newspaper ombudsmen in The Netherlands. *European Journal of Communication, 21*(4), 457–475.

Winseck, D. (2008). The state of media ownership and media markets: Competition or concentration and why should we care? *Sociology Compass, 2*(1), 34–47.

12 The Organization of Film and Television Production

Keith Randle

Film and television are different industries with some important similarities and overlaps in their production and labor processes. This chapter explores the way in which the creation of films and TV programs is achieved by bringing together people with a very diverse range of skills, knowledge, and occupations into a project-based production process. It examines the implications of this for those working and managing in these industries.

A key difference between film and television lies in their distribution and exhibition of content. TV programs and advertisements are *broadcast:* sent simultaneously to multiple recipients with some TV products—for example, sports or news—being broadcast live. Films, on the other hand, once produced, have historically been distributed by road to cinemas where they are exhibited to audiences who are able to watch one of a limited number of copies in existence, thus constraining the size of the audience at any given time.

This historical difference is fundamentally related to the technologies employed by the two industries. However, convergence, through the application of digital technologies to both film and television, is having a revolutionary impact on them and has led to digitization being described as a "disruptive technology," at least when applied to the global film industry (Culkin, Morawetz, & Randle, 2007). However, all sectors of the film and television industries are in a process of change that is deeper than at any time in the past. Technological change will continue to have a major impact on the organization of these industries, the nature of both work and management within them, and the search for new business models for the foreseeable future (Culkin & Randle, 2004).

To be accurate, what we are comparing above are the *cinema* and television industries. If we see the *film industry* as concerned simply with the production of content for cinema and we simultaneously focus on the production phase of television excluding the broadcasting of programs, then the two industries intersect with employers drawing on a common pool of labor and production services made up of a large number of freelance workers and small and micro businesses. It is this production phase in particular that the chapter will focus on.

The Production Process: From Conception to Exhibition

The film and television industries are linked by a production process that is broadly similar across all sectors and that, technology notwithstanding, has changed very little over the past century. This process has a number of common stages: preproduction, production, and postproduction.

In preproduction projects are conceived; ideas are generated, written, and developed; finance is assembled; and cast and key creative roles are appointed. Production is perhaps the best-known and -represented stage where a crew (or crews) is brought to a studio and/or to one or more other locations, in order to capture a performance by actors on film or video or, increasingly with the development of digitization, hard disk. In postproduction content is edited and sometimes computerized, special effects are added, music tracks are synchronized, and titles and credits are added.

The finished product is then duplicated before being distributed through a widening range of platforms, which can include broadcast television, cable or satellite, video or DVD, and onboard aircraft, and is increasingly sent to mobile devices such as telephones or streamed via the Internet onto computer screens. The term *exhibition* tends to be reserved for the showing of films on cinema screens.

Despite these differences there is a degree of crossover in production and postproduction between film and television, which means that individuals (at least in those countries where there is a national film industry) working in production or postproduction may find themselves working on products for exhibition in the cinema or for broadcasting on television. This is perhaps most obvious in the case of TV drama productions where the companies that make the programs may be competing to employ the same crew members (e.g., camera, lighting, sound, hair and makeup, set design, or production assistants) as feature film production companies. It is least obvious in, for example, television news where crews may be permanently employed in-house, although many broadcasters do outsource news coverage to independent companies.

The similarity of this production process crosses not only the boundaries between film and TV but also those between nations, while recognizing that differing local institutional contexts nevertheless do lead to variety in labor market practices (Blair, Culkin, & Randle, 2003).

Hollywood's Dominance Under Threat?

The international film industry is dominated by Hollywood, with U.S. companies owning between 40% and 90% of the movies shown in most parts of the world (Miller, Govil, McMurria, Maxwell, & Wang, 2005). In contrast, film in much of the rest of the world is described as comprising national "cottage industries." Even in the United Kingdom, with an enviable reputation for high-quality film production over the course of the 20th century, the government's own Culture, Media and Sport Committee has referred to its industry in these terms.[1]

However, the U.S. industry does not only dominate through the export of its films. Employment relations across disparate territories also emulate the Hollywood model, with the United Kingdom as one of the earliest adopters. First in the United Kingdom's film industry and then in its oldest public broadcaster the BBC, stable hierarchies and internal labor markets have been replaced by "boundaryless external labour markets, where a growing group of skilled professionals and experts flexibly supplies an industry of a few big companies and many small producers" (Deuze, 2007, p. 189). In the United Kingdom the percentage of the broadcasting workforce that was freelance rose from 39% to 54% between 1989 and 1994 (Platman, 2004).

Hollywood has recently had its other dominant position, as a key location for the production of the world's movies and TV content, threatened by what has been termed *runaway production*[2] (Miller et al., 2005; Randle & Culkin, 2009). Tax credits or lower labor costs provide the motivation to producers to move their filmmaking to other parts of the world. A survey of 1,075 U.S. film and television projects in 1998 showed more than a quarter involved runaway production, with the majority accounted for by production for television (Scott, 2005). Ten years later, the percentage of runaway productions from the United States is estimated at over 50%.

There is some question as to whether this tendency benefits the nations to which production moves. Will it allow them to develop their own production capacity and consequently their own national industries, or is this transitory, lost as soon as another territory becomes economically attractive (Miller et al., 2005)? The latter seems more likely when financial capital is able to enter and leave national film industries with ease. In both the United Kingdom and Canada inward investment has been withdrawn almost overnight where economic incentives are not sufficiently attractive, leaving a production service industry struggling to survive (Morawetz, Hardy, Haslam, & Randle, 2007). The consensus seems to be that while there is some dissipation of Los Angeles as a center for global moviemaking, impacting to a greater or lesser extent on U.S. film workers, the unarguable dominance of the United States in the export of film and television products remains unchallenged.

Precarious Labor? Making a Living and Building a Career in Film and Television Production

The Impact of Structural Change on the Workforce

One fundamental development in the organization of these industries is the fragmentation that has given rise to their "hourglass" shape, with a relatively large number of people employed (often full-time and permanently) by a small number of broadcasters, cable and satellite TV companies, and film majors—while others are employed by small or micro businesses in production or postproduction, often as freelancers or temporary staff. In the United States by 2004 over four fifths of jobs in film and television were in establishments with 20 or more workers, even though most companies in the industry had fewer than 5 employees (Deuze, 2007).

The film and television industries are sometimes seen as emblematic of the future for employment in a global information society where knowledge-based, highly skilled work allies with increasing employment opportunities (Blair, Grey, & Randle, 2001; Lash & Urry, 1994). This more positive scenario, however, contrasts with the characterization of the 1990s as the decade in which the growth of a variety of "atypical"—that is, contingent and flexible—contractual working arrangements took off. Film and TV work is generally precarious, involving increasingly freelance project-based, or casualized, work (Deuze, 2007; Randle & Culkin, 2009; see also Toby Miller, in this volume). The dominant employment model for the U.S. film industry is, and has for some time been, "casual employment on a project-by-project basis rather than attachment to a single employer" (Grey & Seeber, 1996, p. 7). Other national film and television industries have adopted this model of casualization.

The labor markets for creative labor as a whole have changed dramatically as cultural organizations have turned to a marketized and outsourced approach to managing their operations (McKinlay & Smith, 2009). However, there are exceptions (Haunschild, 2003), and we must be careful not to assume that the models described here of short-term, outsourced, freelance, and network-based approaches to employment are universal or inevitable across the creative and cultural industries or that institutions operate free of state or cultural contexts. Recent reviews of this development in work organizations more generally point to permanent positions as enduring alongside models of flexible production (Doogan, 2001).

The entertainment industries are attractive to young people and are characterized by an oversupply of willing entrants. Barriers to entry are low—particularly as the cost of sophisticated equipment falls—but barriers to success are high. The nature of the employment system, which has resulted in new entrants often agreeing to work for free for up to perhaps a year, means that the social composition of the workforce is likely to be shaped by the ability of entrants to draw on financial support from family members, or their own resources, or to negotiate a tricky portfolio of part-time, temporary, and casual employment frequently in the service sectors (Randle & Culkin, 2009). Watson (2008) provides considerable evidence that in the United Kingdom the extent of free working suggests significant illegal employment practices where minimum-wage regulations are being flouted.

There is evidence that those working in these industries comprise, if not a continuum from "entrepreneur to underclass" (Randle, 2009), at the very least an "A list" and a "B list" of talent and crew, where members of the latter group have to rely on work outside of their preferred occupation to make a living (Christopherson, 2009; see also Susan Christopherson, in this volume). This in turn has implications for those entering the workforce and trying to gain the necessary experience required to build a career. The core, whose income derives from continuous work in the entertainment industries, is in decline while there is a growing periphery in the context of an expanding workforce between 1991 and 2002. Furthermore, for those existing on the margins between the creative and mainstream economies, the struggle to retain a foothold in the industry remains paramount and requires the maintenance of an occupational identity in the face of its continual erosion (Randle & Culkin, 2009).

Employee Strategies for Reducing Uncertainty

In both the United Kingdom and the United States (and often elsewhere in primary film and TV production regions such as Eastern Europe, New Zealand, and Australia) the most noticeable recent shift from permanent employment in medium or large firms to independent contractors or self-employment is in the broadcast television sector (Christopherson, 2009; Grugulis & Stoyanova, 2009). In the United Kingdom changes to competitive and regulative conditions in TV have made for an increasingly uncertain environment for television production workers, which is experienced as a problem for the majority (Dex, Willis, Paterson, & Shepherd, 2000). Individuals cope with precarity in media work by diversifying income sources, collecting information, considering leaving the sector, and building informal networks. As permanent staff size has declined in television and casualization increases, despite the lowered barriers to entry referred to earlier, it has become more difficult to gain a foothold in the industry. At the same time earnings have fallen, working terms and conditions have continued to deteriorate (Ursell, 2000), and trade union organization has been undermined (McKinlay & Quinn, 1999).

However, if precariousness has been built on a combination of technological change and convergence, uncertain financing, and fragmentation of employment, to new entrants in the industry it tends to be experienced as a form of "precarious stability" (Blair, 2001) or "structured uncertainty" (Randle & Culkin, 2009). On the one hand, individual film or television workers are powerless to ameliorate the structural conditions or major events that can have a disproportionate impact on the ability to find work. On the other, as Randle and Culkin (2009) noted while tracking the impact of the events of 9/11, the 2001 Screen Actors Guild commercial strike, and the increasing incidence of runaway production on a panel of Hollywood film workers, they are able to employ a range of strategies in an attempt to ensure some continuity in employment and a steady income stream.

On this theme Blair (2003) describes how film workers form what she calls "Semi Permanent Work Groups" (SPWGs), moving as a department or team from one project to the next with the onus being on the generally most experienced and, we may assume, best-networked member to find a stream of projects to keep other members of the crew employed. Blair (2009) proposes the term *active networking* as "a means of capturing the dynamic and conscious, yet structured process of networking and the interpersonal webs which are reproduced by that process" (p. 132). What this term implies is a strategic engagement in the networking process with wider social and economic structures both enabling and constraining actors.

Networking remains an extremely important skill, process, or behavior in these sectors, where recruitment is often on the basis of who you know and your reputation (Blair, 2001). Trust is frequently mentioned as a vital intervening variable. When projects are "green lit," have to be staffed quickly, and may not last more than a few weeks, those responsible for production need to have a degree of certainty that a crew member will be technically competent and will also "fit in" with others on the crew. Consequently, those in positions to make recommendations do not do so lightly as a recommendation that turns out to be ill-judged will rebound on them by diminishing their own reputation.

The outcome is that while the networks mediating employment are a source of stability and decreasing uncertainty for some, they can be a source of exclusion for others. Hunt (2007) refers to Hollywood as "an insular industry that white males have traditionally dominated, where employment opportunities rest squarely on personal networks steeped in gender, race and age" (p. 14). Specific groups such as women, ethnic minorities, people with disabilities, and the economically marginalized are routinely excluded from employment in the U.K. film and TV industries. An increasingly fragmented and deregulated industry creates a paradox where, in a post–mass broadcasting age, studios and TV companies must orientate on niche audiences with specialized products. This requires a diverse creative input, for example Asian writers and researchers to work on programs for these audiences, yet the informal mechanisms and networks that pervade the industry can form impenetrable barriers to these very same people. Similar conclusions can be drawn in, for example, the U.S. context.[3]

Once again we need to remain cautious about sweeping generalizations as temporal and institutional contexts are vital to our understanding of creative work. All creative industries, always high risk, are not high risk in the same way, with the media industries becoming more risky since the mid-1990s and with opportunities to earn a livelihood or build a career deteriorating (Christopherson, 2009; see also Susan Christopherson, in this volume).

Acquiring Skills and Developing a Career

Without the benefits of an internal labor market within the firm, a key issue after "getting in" is "getting on," moving up the occupational ladder or making a career in the industry (Randle & Culkin, 2009). An example might be making the move from camera operator to director of photography (the head of the camera department). This can often mean returning to a previous, more precarious stage of employment and working for free or for "copy and credit" to gain experience, make new contacts, and establish a new professional identity.

The increasing predominance of freelance working throws up a range of managerial issues, with that of training and skills development being key (Grugulis & Stoyanova, 2009). Historically in the United States, the United Kingdom, and elsewhere the dissipated system of permanent employment in major studios or public service broadcasters formed a robust system of apprenticeships and on-the-job training. This has largely gone, and the onus is now on the individual to ensure that he or she has the skills employers require in what can be seen as part of a wider societal move toward individualization, which in turn has led the push toward a managerial emphasis on individual creative entrepreneurship (Storey, Salaman, & Platman, 2005) and what Castells (2000) calls "self-programmable labor" (p. 12) as one of the key elements of the contemporary network society.

Ensuring that employers in key industries have access to a pool of appropriately skilled labor has frequently required the state to intervene in the labor market in order to compensate for this move from employer to individual employee responsibility for skills acquisition. In most countries media training is now predominantly carried out by colleges, universities, and a range of private sector training companies and equipment manufacturers, with the individual taking on the responsibility for seeking out appropriate training and arranging finance for initial training and often for professional development too.

_____ Conclusion: Runaway Production, Runaway Jobs

While new technologies and financial arrangements have added to the footloose nature of film and television production, allowing it to move more easily between international boundaries, jobs—especially permanent full-time positions—have become more elusive. If film and television are emblematic of the creative media industries in all their guises, it has also been argued that they are indicative of the future of labor and management much more broadly. If so, they should serve to act as a guide to both prospective entrants and those charged with managing in these sectors (and perhaps others) as to what the future may hold. What should be evident from this chapter is that ongoing changes in the organization of film and television production are creating industries characterized by both precariousness and its close companion in this case—individualization. As has been pointed out elsewhere (Randle & Culkin, 2009), where larger corporations in the creative industries choose to delegate business risk to small firms, freelancers, and the self-employed, they are effectively transferring that risk to the household. This will inevitably have a major impact on the experience of work and management, on careers, and on lives more generally.

Where uncertainty and insecurity pervade film and television work, informal recruitment mechanisms prevail, and new entrants are expected to work for free, achieving diversity in employment will be an uphill struggle and nepotism will remain a key characteristic of employment. Family life patterns are distorted by a long-hours culture, and maintaining work-life boundaries provides a challenge within project work perennially struggling against deadlines. As training and skill acquisition increasingly become the responsibility of the individual creative media worker, periodic skills shortages and skills gaps are likely to confront management. In many ways as the internal labor markets and tight union control of the media industries dissipate and managers regain the "right to manage" in a more individualistic environment, their role can be seen as increasingly important, but as yet there is relatively little research reporting, for example, the experiences and views of this group in managing freelance workers (Platman, 2004). These industries will survive the global recession at the end of the first decade of the 21st century, though no doubt changes to technology, regulation, and industry structure will continue to have an impact on the experience of work—a challenge to both management and those trying to manage their own careers within them.

References

Blair, H. (2001). "You're only as good as your last job": The labor process and labor market in the British film industry. *Work, Employment and Society, 15*(1), 149–169.

Blair, H. (2003). Winning and losing in flexible labour markets: The formation and operation of networks of interdependence in the UK film industry. *Sociology, 37*(4), 677–694.

Blair, H. (2009). Active networking: Action, social structure and the process of networking. In A. McKinlay & C. Smith (Eds.), *Creative labour: Working in the creative industries* (pp. 116–134). Basingstoke, England: Palgrave Macmillan.

Blair, H., Culkin, C., & Randle, K. (2003). Comparison of local labour market processes in the US and UK film industries. *International Journal of Human Resource Management, 14*(4), 6l9–633.

Blair, H., Grey, S., & Randle, K. (2001). Working in film: Employment in a project-based industry. *Personnel Review, 30*(1&2), 170–185.

Castells, M. (2000). Materials for an exploratory theory of the network society. *British Journal of Sociology, 51*(1), 5–24.

Christopherson, S. (2009). Working in the creative economy: Risk, adaptation, and the persistence of exclusionary networks. In A. McKinlay & C. Smith (Eds.), *Creative labour: Working in the creative industries* (pp. 72–90). Basingstoke, England: Palgrave Macmillan.

Culkin, N., Morawetz, N., & Randle, K. (2007). Digital cinema as disruptive technology: Exploring new business models in the age of digital distribution. In S. van der Graaf & W. Washida (Eds.), *Information communication technologies and emerging business strategies* (pp. 160–178). New York, NY: Idea Group.

Culkin, N., & Randle, K. (2004). Digital cinema: Opportunities and challenges. *Convergence, 9*(4), 79–98.

Deuze, M. (2007). *Media work.* Cambridge, England: Polity Press.

Dex, S., Willis, J., Paterson, R., & Shepherd, E. (2000). Freelance workers and contract uncertainty: The effects of contractual changes in the television industry. *Work, Employment & Society, 14*(2), 283–305.

Doogan, K. (2001). Insecurity and long-term employment. *Work, Employment and Society, 15*(3), 419–441.

Grey, L., & Seeber, R. (1996). The industry and the unions: An overview. In L. Gray & R. Seeber (Eds.), *Under the stars* (pp. 15–49). New York, NY: ILR Press.

Grugulis, I., & Stoyanova, D. (2009). "I don't know where you learn them": Skills in film and TV. In A. McKinlay & C. Smith (Eds.), *Creative labour* (pp. 135–155). Basingstoke, England: Palgrave Macmillan.

Haunschild, A. (2003). Managing employment relationships in flexible labour markets: The case of German repertory theatres. *Human Relations, 56*(8), 899–929.

Hunt, D. (2007). *Whose stories are we telling?* The 2007 Hollywood Writers Report. Los Angeles, CA: Writers Guild of America West.

Lash, S., & Urry, J. (1994). *Economies of signs and space.* London, England: Sage.

McKinlay, A., & Quinn, B. (1999). Management, technology and work in commercial broadcasting, c. 1979–98. *New Technology, Work and Employment, 14*(1), 2–17.

McKinlay, A., & Smith, C. (Eds.). (2009). *Creative labour.* Basingstoke, England: Palgrave Macmillan.

Miller, T., Govil, N., McMurria, J., Maxwell, R., & Wang, T. (2005). *Global Hollywood 2.* London, England: BFI.

Morawetz, N., Hardy, J., Haslam, C., & Randle, K. (2007). Finance, policy and industrial dynamics—The rise of co-productions in the film industry. *Industry and Innovation, 14*(4), 421–443.

Platman, K. (2004). Portfolio careers and the search for flexibility in later life. *Work, Employment and Society, 18*(3), 573–599.

Randle, K. (2009). "Freelancers in the creative media industries: Between entrepreneur and underclass?" *International Labour Process Conference,* Edinburgh, April 6–8, 2009.

Randle, K., & Culkin, C. (2009). Getting in and getting on in Hollywood: Freelance careers in an uncertain industry. In A. McKinlay & C. Smith (Eds.), *Creative labour* (pp. 93–115). Basingstoke, England: Palgrave Macmillan.

Scott, A. (2005). *On Hollywood.* Princeton, NJ: Princeton University Press.

Storey, J., Salaman, G., & Platman, K. (2005). Living with enterprise in an enterprise economy: Freelance and contract workers in the media. *Human Relations, 58*(8), 1033–1054.

Ursell, G. (2000). Television production: Issues of exploitation, commodification and subjectivity in UK television labour markets. *Media, Culture and Society, 22*(6), 805–825.

Watson, M. (2008). *Young unpaid workers in popular industries.* Submission to the Low Pay Commission: Consultation for the Annual Report on the National Minimum Wage 2008. Retrieved from http://www.lowpay.gov.uk

Notes

1. See http://www.publications.parliament.uk/pa/cm200203/cmselect/cmcumeds/667/66706.htm.

2. Runaway production is the tendency for Hollywood-financed films to be made in, for example, Canada, Australia, Italy, the People's Republic of China, the Czech Republic, South Africa, India, Britain, Mexico, and Southeast Asia.

3. See, for example, http://www.moviesbywomen.com.

13 Producing Filmed Entertainment

Alisa Perren

In recent years, the costs of producing and distributing media have dropped so steeply that anyone with access to an iPhone and the Internet can produce and distribute a short film or webisode for a few dollars. Concurrently, there has emerged a cacophony of voices that loudly trumpet the possibilities for fame and fortune in this brave new digital world. Yet in spite of such marketing promises and technological possibilities, the opportunities available to those hoping to make a living from producing feature films and television series remain elusive at best. By no means has the ease of online distribution translated into workable business models. Nor, in most instances, has the ability to gain an online audience enabled individuals to build careers in the traditional film and television industries. Indeed, the lowered barriers to entry and simultaneous proliferation of content have only made it more challenging for both media companies and individuals to profit from their creations.

Factors such as growing piracy enabled by the diffusion of broadband, ever-mounting production and marketing costs, the stagnation of the DVD market, the continuing fragmentation of the media marketplace, and the broader global economic crisis have placed long-standing business models for fictional film and television in jeopardy.[1] The fragility of these business models, in turn, has contributed to heightened instability and uncertainty for media producers. Consequently, those in charge of managing commercial media productions have employed several measures in their efforts to ensure the viability of their projects in the marketplace. This essay surveys four prominent strategies that those producing commercially oriented narrative feature films and prime-time television programs have used as a means of cutting costs while differentiating their content from "amateur" productions: (a) renegotiating relations with unionized labor or employing more nonunion staff; (b) adopting the most sophisticated, high-end production and postproduction technologies; (c) taking advantage of tax incentives and rebates offered in locations around the world; and (d) assessing the ability to effectively market projects across multiple platforms and media outlets before initiating production.

The focus here is on strategies employed by North American entities. However, given the transnational nature of production and distribution, the examples offered below easily apply to many other national and regional contexts. This essay illustrates how decisions made with regard to labor, technology, locations, and marketing are having a substantial impact not only on the opportunities and constraints facing those working in production but also on the types of commercial film and television content shown on various screens.

Labor

Most feature films and prime-time television series are developed by what trade publication *Variety* calls "indie prods" or independent production companies. While conglomerates or deep-pocketed investors typically provide the money and therefore retain the copyright to these projects, companies such as Jerry Bruckheimer Films (*Cold Case; Pirates of the Caribbean*) and Imagine Entertainment (*24; Angels & Demons*) oversee the actual development, production, and postproduction processes. Executives at media conglomerates such as Disney, Sony, Fox, Paramount, Time Warner, and Universal certainly provide ample creative input (or the much dreaded "notes"), but the scheduling, budgeting, hiring, and location scouting are typically undertaken by these so-called independent production companies. Oftentimes production companies are actively involved in securing financing and advising on marketing as well. Such is the decentralized nature of production in the contemporary post-Fordist environment (Caldwell, 2008; Curtin, 1996).

This decentralized structure means that, with the exception of a production company's core office staff, most film and television employees are hired on a project-by-project basis. In other words, most production workers labor for long stretches while a project is either shooting or in postproduction but then find themselves unemployed for varying lengths of time. Although relationships and reputation count in terms of getting the next job, that does not mean that those who work in production and postproduction will move smoothly from one position to the next. From 2007 to 2009, as the economic climate worsened and the threat of or actual strikes occurred, many production workers found themselves either without employment for longer stretches than usual or forced to take lesser-paying jobs to make ends meet. For example, in Los Angeles from January to March 2009, between 70% and 80% of technicians and film crew workers were unemployed (Gumbel, 2009).

The project-based nature of production has been standard for the film and television business since the breakdown of the studio system in the 1950s (Bordwell, Staiger, & Thompson, 1985). However, since the 1990s, this long-standing instability has been magnified due to the rise of digital technologies and the development of new program forms such as reality television and computer-generated animation. Whereas many of those fortunate enough to gain positions working in the production of fictional prime-time television series and studio-financed films are able to reap the benefits of guild and union protections (DGA, WGA, IATSE[2], etc.), many working in newer fields such as reality television series and animated films, as well as "indie" feature projects, are not similarly protected.[3]

Even the protections offered by union or guild memberships are far less than they used to be. This is in large part because the organization that acts on behalf of the media conglomerates, AMPTP,[4] has successfully employed a "divide and conquer" strategy in its negotiations with labor organizations. Each union or guild meets with AMPTP on a separate timeline, thereby weakening their ability to bargain collectively. For example, in the latest round of contract negotiations, the WGA wrangled first with AMPTP, followed by the DGA, then AFTRA, and then, more than a year later, SAG.[5]

One example of how contentiousness between labor unions has worked to the financial benefit of the conglomerates and to the disadvantage of media workers can be seen in the way the two major organizations representing actors, SAG and AFTRA, negotiated with AMPTP in 2008–2009. For decades, SAG has been the more powerful organization. Any projects that are shot on film and distributed by AMPTP companies have to be SAG signatories. Any projects undertaken by AFTRA have to be shot electronically (in other words, they cannot be shot on film). For as long as digital technologies were viewed as inferior by the industry, SAG retained the advantage on prime-time television series. However, by 2008, the distinctions between film and digital video were far less apparent, and thus SAG's past advantage, especially in the particularly lucrative arena of prime-time television, was no more (Littleton, 2009b).

Significantly, AFTRA's greater willingness to sign a contract before SAG would settle had an impact not only on the broader labor market but also on industry-wide production practices, technological choices, and television aesthetics. AFTRA's eagerness to settle quickly and for less favorable terms than those pursued by SAG meant that those producers shooting pilots in 2009 opted to use AFTRA contracts. In doing so, producers committed themselves to shooting these series digitally for the length of the series' run.[6] In effect, AMPTP members bypassed SAG and proceeded apace with their television season. AMPTP was able to weaken SAG's power at the same time that it lowered its own production costs.[7] Costs were lowered not only because AFTRA's terms were seen as more favorable by AMPTP but also because shooting digitally is both less expensive and more efficient than shooting on film.[8]

At the same time that production companies have kept their costs down by employing these types of complicated labor negotiations, they have also limited their expenses on other projects by increasingly turning to nonunion labor. The protections offered to those in newer areas such as reality television, special effects, and animation are significantly less than those available to older professions such as cinematography and editing. Yet digital effects and reality TV are among the fastest-growing areas of work in commercial media production. As a result, along with entry-level assistant positions, these areas are where many of those fresh out of film school begin their careers. Initially, the opportunity to work on a major commercial production may sound seductive to many young and eager filmmakers-to-be. And, in fact, on occasion these positions do pay reasonably well. However, the 80-plus-hour workweeks of repetitive, often mind-numbing labor prove incredibly draining.[9] Further, jobs in many of these newer areas, especially reality television, are viewed with disdain by some working in other sectors of the industry (e.g., fictional series television). This makes it even more challenging for those breaking in through many of the newer areas to transition into other, more prestigious—and unionized—forms of work.

While the promise of ascending to higher levels of management entices some to forge ahead, others burn out well before they reach their 30s. The lack of union support for these newer fields makes them even more precarious. Even more troubling is the always-lingering possibility that this type of work will be "outsourced" to other countries. Animation and special effects work are particularly likely to shift to other parts of the United States or beyond U.S. borders depending on the rebate and incentive programs on offer at a given time.

With more and more fields of work lacking strong union protection, a caste system in production has become even more prominent of late. There are significant economic and cultural schisms not only between different types of labor but also between older and younger workers in the same field. Some media analysts believe that this structure, in which an extremely small number of individuals earn stunning sums of money while the rest struggle, might become still more magnified in the ensuing years as more content shifts to online distribution (McNary, 2008; Simmons, 2009). This is the case for a variety of reasons, including a decrease in the number of union productions, smaller residuals on offer through new media outlets than via traditional syndication, and lower pay scales for online video relative to traditional media. Cumulatively, the emerging situation threatens to further diminish the "middle class" of media makers.

Technology

In addition to these mounting stresses placed on labor, production workers face the additional pressure to become or remain conversant in the latest technologies. While it may be easier than ever for one person to develop, shoot, and edit a production on his or her own with low-end equipment, large-scale productions require keeping up with the newest technologies (e.g., new HD, or high-definition, cameras or the latest editing programs). One must be able to commit both time and money to attend training workshops, trade shows, markets, and festivals to keep abreast of the latest resources and to cultivate contacts for future work.[10]

Recently, media companies have placed a growing emphasis on newer technologies such as HD and 3-D as a means of product differentiation, thereby making greater demands on workers and companies alike. Producers and conglomerates have increasingly recognized that motion pictures targeted for theatrical release need to "show" their production values through 3-D as well as more elaborate special effects. Some companies, such as DreamWorks Animation (*Monsters vs Aliens,* 2009), have committed to producing all future theatrical films in 3-D (Debruge, 2009a).[11] A widely held belief is that by heightening the spectacle in films, moviegoers will be willing to pay to see movies in theaters.[12] This emphasis impacts employment opportunities because it both necessitates that media workers be conversant in the most up-to-date technologies and leads to the production of certain types of films at the expense of others.

Movies that don't prove viable for effects and 3-D, such as the "indies" that have been a central focus of specialty divisions like Miramax and Fox Searchlight, have become less important to media conglomerates in the 2000s (McClintock, 2009). During 2008–2009, several conglomerates shut down or significantly reduced the number of releases coming from their specialty divisions. Paramount Vantage, Warner Independent (Time Warner), Picturehouse (Time Warner), and Fox Atomic (News Corp.) were closed while Focus (Universal), Miramax (Disney), and New Line (Time Warner) all reduced their output. Meanwhile, many of the big-budget divisions of the conglomerates reduced the number of films they financed as well. For example, in 1995, Disney released 37 films; in 2008, the number had declined to 19. Similarly, in 1995, Sony released 31 films; in 2008, the number was down to 18.[13]

A reduction in output, of course, translates to a reduction in jobs. Certainly the opportunities for earning a living by working on motion picture production have long been far more limited than those available in television. However, these developments promise to make finding employment—especially well-paying employment—in the theatrically oriented film business even more challenging. Though production in the low-budget film scene is as vibrant as it has ever been, specialized distributors such as the Independent Film Channel, Sony Pictures Classics, and Magnolia typically have substantial leverage over sellers. A high supply of films, combined with a shrinking number of buyers, means that those making films often celebrate receiving a paycheck as small as $10,000 (Horn, 2009). Such a sum is scarcely enough to compensate those who worked on these projects, many of whom either deferred compensation or were paid scale in the hopes that a lucrative deal could be struck down the road. Such deals remain few and far between these days, however (Swart & Holdsworth, 2009).

Locations

Even as media companies attempt to lower costs by cutting production and acquisitions, they also try to reduce budgets by taking advantage of incentive programs offered by different cities and countries around the world. Though film productions have been shot on location for decades, television production was, until the 1990s, largely centered in the Los Angeles area (and, to a lesser extent, New York). However, this began to change as a wide range of places started to offer more aggressive tax rebates and production credits in an effort to entice companies already panicked by rising budgets.

Among the states that have approved these incentives are Massachusetts, Hawaii, Texas, Rhode Island, and Louisiana. Such programs appear to have worked in drawing productions away from Southern California. In the 2009 pilot season alone, 42 of the 103 television pilots were shot outside of Los Angeles. Overall, the production of pilots has declined by nearly 42% since 2005 (Littleton, 2009a). Similarly, the number of big-budget feature films shot in Los Angeles went from 71 in 1996 to 21 in 2008 (Gumbel, 2009).[14]

Many projects have left the United States altogether. British Columbia, in particular, has benefited from runaway production activities. In 2009, it trailed only Los Angeles and New York in production days. Further, 75% of its projects came from the United States (McDonald, 2009). Movies such as *Watchmen* and *The Incredible Hulk* and television series such as *Smallville* and *Battlestar Galactica* were lured to Canada by the lower costs associated with shooting there.

At times, incentive programs can be seen as diversifying the types of stories told and images shown on screen; programs like *Friday Night Lights* (Texas), *Burn Notice* (Miami), and *In Plain Sight* (New Mexico) readily exploit their distinctive settings in their narratives. This is less true with many Canadian productions, which often strive to make their locations look like Anywhere, USA. In addition to introducing more varied landscapes and settings, location shooting often brings money into new communities and strengthens the base of below-the-line workers in new regions.[15] However, runaway production also proves problematic because it further heightens job insecurity for below-the-line workers. Those based in traditional production locales such as New York or Los Angeles have witnessed many of their jobs move out-of-state or out-of-country. Meanwhile, those within any other locality benefit only for as long as the incentive program remains in place. Should a given state or region adjust its incentive program, producers will often swiftly move on to the next cost-effective locale—taking along most of the job opportunities they brought with them.

In general, the shifts in financing and production practices associated with the growth of incentive programs further heighten the instability being felt by those involved in film and television production. Whether one resides in a major production center such as Los Angeles or the latest hot spot such as Michigan (where producers have been seduced by a substantial 42% tax rebate), workers are forced to figure out ways to sustain themselves during unpredictable down periods (Egan, 2009).[16]

Creating and Marketing a Multimedia, Multiplatform Identity _____

There are two notable ways that some have responded to the industrial shifts discussed here. First, many people increasingly balance better-paying commercially oriented projects (often of the high-concept variety) with lower-paying "projects of passion." Often individuals will work at a lower level (e.g., second assistant director) on a well-financed project. Then, during their off time or on weekends, they will take on a more prominent role (e.g., primary editor) on a small-scale but artistically ambitious project. As this description indicates, art and commerce are often compartmentalized by contemporary media workers. The dream always remains, of course, that the "side project" will turn into that next "little indie that could," thereby enabling greater autonomy and originality in future projects.

Even if such projects fail to gain any traction beyond the festival circuit or local competitions, they frequently become a way for industry workers to build up or diversify their reels and résumés. At present, guild or union rules and long-standing institutional traditions frequently prohibit working in multiple roles on a given project (e.g., both grip and first assistant director). This might seem counterintuitive considering that it is now more possible than ever before for amateur media makers to write, produce, and edit their own projects with minimal expense and little assistance from others. Nonetheless, for the most part, rigid hierarchies remain in place in most of the established areas of professional film and television production. "Old media" institutions and organizations continue to perpetuate the cultivation of single skill sets for varied reasons. These include older generations fighting to protect their own ever-more fragile turf and managers who, already pressed for time and resources, have little ability or desire to implement substantive structural changes. Thus the onus is placed on individuals to simultaneously be able to serve the highly specialized demands of older (often better-paying) companies while developing a diverse set of skills for promising, but frequently less financially sound, new media operations.

Second, many people are increasingly trying to "brand" themselves and the kinds of work they do (see also Chris Hackley and Amy Tiwsakul, in this volume). Given the ever-expanding supply of labor and the shrinking number of jobs available, it has become imperative for those aspiring to move up in the business to cultivate a clear identity for themselves. This identity can begin to be crafted from early experiences in internships, which are the primary means by which individuals begin their careers within the film and television industries. The particular brand identity one develops can relate to specific tasks (e.g., trained on high-end effects software) as well as to specific types of work (e.g., skilled at polishing dialogue for romantic comedies). It is important to add that one cannot simply possess these skills but must be able to *show others* that he or she possesses such abilities through self-promotion via social networks (e.g., LinkedIn) and in-person networking events (e.g., local film and television association meetings; see also Charles H. Davis, in this volume).

Significantly, the growth of transmedia storytelling has, of late, been accompanied by the expansion of transmedia marketing practices (Jenkins, 2005). Thus, another rapidly expanding area for those seeking work in production and postproduction has been in generating promotional content—trailers, promos, Web sites, and so on—designed to support or tie in to large corporate media brands across a variety of platforms. For those looking for some degree of stability in media production, one of the safer areas to look for employment is in the creation of promotional materials (see also Chris Bilton, in this volume).

To a certain extent, an emphasis on "personal branding" fits in with the ever-growing emphasis on branding that has developed throughout the media industries in the last few decades. Companies (Syfy, Bravo) and projects (*American Idol, Batman*) cultivate brands as a means of breaking out from the clutter. In this commodified landscape, why wouldn't media workers be expected to behave in the same way?

It might seem odd to conclude with an emphasis on the importance of marketing to those working in production. Yet regardless of whether one is speaking of a company, a project, or a person, selling has become ever-more central from day one. Media producers have little chance of procuring production financing unless they anticipate and plan effective marketing strategies from the earliest days of a project's development. Similarly, the prospects for media workers' success in making films and television series are to a large degree dependent on their ability to establish a clear identity for themselves and their abilities both in person and online. Those individuals seeking to navigate the highly insecure terrain of contemporary film and television can benefit by recognizing the ways that marketability factors into both production—and hiring—decisions.

References

Bordwell, D., Staiger, J., & Thompson, K. (1985). *The classical Hollywood cinema: Film style & mode of production to 1960*. New York, NY: Columbia University Press.

Caldwell, J. (2008). *Production culture: Industrial reflexivity and critical practice in film & television*. Durham, NC: Duke University Press.

Click on Detroit. (2009, July 3). *Film tax incentive program at risk*. Retrieved from http://www.clickondetroit.com/news/19937450/detail.html

Curtin, M. (1996). On edge: Culture industries in the neo-network era. In R. Ohmann (Ed.), *Making & selling culture* (pp. 181–202). Hanover, NH: Wesleyan University Press.

Debruge, P. (2009a, May 27). DreamWorks animates its output. *Variety*. Retrieved from http://www.variety.com/article/VR1118004228.html?categoryid=13& cs=1&nid=2562

Debruge, P. (2009b, July 6). HR pros get creative in down economy. *Variety*. Retrieved from http://www.variety.com/article/VR1118005690.html?categoryid=3668& cs=1&nid=2562

Egan, J. (2009, June 12). Hawaii incentives supplement nature. *Variety*. Retrieved from http://www.variety.com/article/VR1118004901.html?categoryid=3659& cs=1&nid=2562

Garrett, D. (2009, July 6). Job hunters go back to school. *Variety*. Retrieved from http://www.variety.com/article/VR1118005691.html?categoryid=3668&cs=1& nid=2562

Gumbel, A. (2009, April 27). Hollywood feels the pinch: Film production at standstill. *The Guardian*. Retrieved from http://www.guardian.co.uk/film/2009/apr/27/hollywood-film-industry

Holt, J., & Perren, A. (Eds.). (2009). *Media industries: History, theory, and method*. Malden, MA: Wiley-Blackwell.

Horn, J. (2009, May 12). The living-room TV, not Cannes, may be independent film's best friend. *Los Angeles Times*. Retrieved from http://articles.latimes.com/2009/may/12/entertainment/et-cannesvod12?pg=1

Jenkins, H. (2005). *Convergence culture: Where old and new media collide*. New York: New York University Press.

Littleton, C. (2009a, June 10). Pilots flying from LA. *Variety*. Retrieved from http://www.variety.com/article/VR1118004782.html?categoryid=14&cs=1&nid=2562

Littleton, C. (2009b, June 26). TV: A matter of life and def. *Variety*. Retrieved from http://www.variety.com/article/VR1118005455.html?categoryid=14&cs=1&nid=2562

McClintock, P. (2009, May 1). Specialty biz: What just happened?. *Variety*. Retrieved from http://www.variety.com/article/VR1118003089.html?categoryid=13&cs=1&nid=2562

McDonald, K. A. (2009, May 11). British Columbia lures big productions. *Variety*. Retrieved from http://www.variety.com/article/VR1118003490.html?categoryid=3621&cs=1&nid=2562

McNary, D. (2008, December 12). SAG leaders ponder life sans strike. *Daily Variety*. Retrieved from LexisNexis database.

McNary, D. (2009, July 10). AFTRA, SAG merger still far off. *Variety*. Retrieved from http://www.variety.com/article/VR1118005879.html?categoryid=18&cs=1&nid=2562

Schuker, L. A. E. (2009, March 20). Can 3-D save Hollywood? *The Wall Street Journal*. Retrieved from http://online.wsj.com/article/SB123751033980990723.html?mod=dist_smartbrief

Simmons, L. (2009, November 24). Actors will vote on strike. *Adweek*. Retrieved from LexisNexis database.

Smith, S., & Forsom, A. (2009, July 6). Careers in entertainment get competitive. *Variety*. Retrieved from http://www.variety.com/article/VR1118005689.html?categoryid=3668&ref=ra&cs=1

Swart, S., & Holdsworth, N. (2009, May 22). Cannes signals new industry model. *Variety*. Retrieved from http://www.variety.com/article/VR1118004096.html?categoryid=3620&cs=1&nid=2562

Variety. (2009, June 10). Timeline: SAG's contract dispute. Retrieved from http://www.variety.com/article/VR1118004766.html?categoryid=18&cs=1&nid=2562

Notes

1. In Holt and Perren (2009) 21 prominent scholars with backgrounds in communication, media studies, and cultural studies survey the key reasons why and how the media industries are facing heightened instability and uncertainty.

2. DGA stands for Directors Guild of America, WGA for Writers Guild of America, and IATSE for International Alliance of Theatrical Stage Employees, Moving Picture Technicians, Artists and Allied Crafts of the United States, Its Territories, and Canada.

3. The minimum rates available for members of each union are available on their respective Web sites. For example, see http://www.sag.org/content/theatrical-film-contracts.

4. AMPTP stands for the Alliance of Motion Picture and Television Producers. This name is a bit misleading, as the organization actually represents the interests of the major media conglomerates, not producers per se. Among the interests that AMPTP represents are Fox, Paramount, Disney, Sony, Warner Bros., CBS, and Universal.

5. AFTRA stands for American Federation of Television and Radio Artists; SAG for Screen Actors Guild. AFTRA members approved their deal in July 2008; SAG members in June 2009. For key moments in the negotiations, see *Variety* (2009).

6. The only way a production company could sign later with SAG is if it switched to shooting on film (Littleton, 2009b).

7. Approximately $20,000 per episode can be saved by shooting digitally. Further, more footage can be shot and there is no delay between production and post-production because no time is needed for film processing (Littleton, 2009b).

8. As of July 2009, SAG had 120,000 members while AFTRA had 70,000. There are 44,000 dual SAG-AFTRA members. Though both SAG and AFTRA cover certain areas of television and new media, the most notable differences are that AFTRA doesn't cover theatrical motion pictures and SAG doesn't cover radio. SAG historically has covered predominantly prime-time television series, while AFTRA has covered much of daytime television. For a discussion of the contentiousness between the two organizations, see McNary (2009).

9. In *Production Cultures,* Caldwell (2008) calls these work environments "digital sweatshops."

10. For a discussion of some of the job hunting strategies being used by film and television workers, see Debruge (2009b), Garrett (2009), and Smith and Forsom (2009).

11. According to *The Wall Street Journal,* Hollywood plans to release an estimated 45 3-D films between 2009 and 2011 (Schuker, 2009).

12. An emphasis on spectacle is also perceived as one means of combating piracy.

13. Data regarding releases come from http://www.the-numbers.com/market/Distributors/. Releases from specialty divisions are not included here.

14. For the first quarter of 2009, only two big-budget studio films, *Iron Man 2* and *Alice in Wonderland,* were shot in Los Angeles.

15. Often above-the-line crew members only remain in a city for the duration of the shoot.

16. Though Michigan's incentive program has helped attract a number of productions, including HBO's *Hung* (2009–) and Paramount's *Up in the Air* (2009), as of this writing, the program's long-term viability remains in question. Michigan's economy has been particularly hard hit by the financial crisis, which has led some to call for a reduction or elimination of the incentive program. See Click on Detroit (2009).

14 New Firms in the Screen-Based Media Industry

STARTUPS, SELF-EMPLOYMENT, AND STANDING RESERVE

Charles H. Davis

Self-employment may be seen either as a survival strategy for those who cannot find any other means of earning an income or as evidence of entrepreneurial spirit and a desire to be one's own boss.

—Organisation for Economic Co-operation
and Development, 2009, para. 1.

Media industries display very high rates of new firm formation. In the English-speaking world, large populations of self-employed individuals and microenterprises have emerged in the screen-based media industry, notably in the creative content, software, and technical craft and services segments of film and video production, postproduction, and Internet publishing.[1] A look at processes and outcomes of new firm formation in the screen industry sheds light on some of the deeper issues and challenges of innovation, growth, public policy, and work and employment in the cultural economy (see also Susan Christopherson, in this volume).

As in many other countries, the emergence of indigenous firms in creative industries is encouraged in Canada for the sake of art and commerce—as a way to support cultural sovereignty, as well as to pursue the rewards of an economically viable cultural sector. Although most students who enter the screen-based media industry are not motivated by conventional entrepreneurial aspirations, increasingly media students are encouraged to develop career strategies embracing self-employment or active entrepreneurship that seeks to create a successful firm. Many circumstances are encouraging this turn toward business and enterprise among emerging media workers. Industry associations publish reports emphasizing media firms' outstanding needs in business, management, and marketing (i.e., Women in Film and Television, 2004). Government agencies publish career-management manuals for cultural workers that point out requirements for competencies in project management, business planning, marketing, financial and legal matters, and strategy (Cultural Human Resources Council, 2009). Popular television shows such as the BBC's *Dragons' Den* bring favorable attention to entrepreneurship (Boyle & Magor, 2008). Students may take courses in entrepreneurship and media management that often are offered in media or business schools. Involvement with digital media often puts film, television, and journalism students into contact with students in faculties of business, engineering, and computer science who are aware of the culture and practices of venturing in the information-technology industry. And the modest prospects of finding full-time salaried employment in the film or television industry in Canada are well known to students by the time they graduate.

What are we to make of the proliferation of self-employment and microenterprises in the screen media industry? The research literature offers three diverging views on media self-employment and entrepreneurship, each leading to a rather different perspective on management of media work and business practices in small media firms. First, unusually high levels of new firm formation in various media industry branches suggest that the industry renews itself on a regular basis, implying presence of entrepreneurial opportunity in the industry. Thus, despite high levels of ownership concentration, an abundant supply of startups ensures innovation, employment, and economic growth. Second, the "Hollywood model" of vertical disintegration is often presented as the paradigmatic way to organize production in cultural industries, accommodating diverse creative, self-reliant, nonstandard, gratifying lifestyles through flexible project-based self-employment (although at the cost of workers' income insecurity). Third, expanding populations of precarious media freelancers and self-employed workers serve as a cultural proletariat or reserve army of labor: workers who are always on call, readily exploitable by larger or more powerful incumbents, with little prospect of attaining economic security.

In this chapter I discuss the range of entrepreneurial dynamics in the screen media industry. As in other industries, growth-oriented new ventures are a small minority among small or new firms in the media sector. Most new or small media firms are lifestyle or survival vehicles. Although some will grow and develop into larger firms, the majority lack the resources and capabilities for growth. Nevertheless, self-employment requires an enterprising outlook and self-management behavior on the part of the worker.

Untangling Self-Employment, Small-Business Ownership, and Entrepreneurship

Entrepreneurs create, define, discover, and exploit opportunities (Zahra, Sapienza, & Davidsson, 2006), and scholarly research on entrepreneurship seeks to explain how, by whom, and with what effects this happens (Shane & Venkataraman, 2000). Entrepreneurship researchers distinguish between greater and lesser degrees of entrepreneurial behavior. Thus distinctions are made between major entrepreneurship—risky introduction of new economic activities that lead to a change in the marketplace—and minor forms of entrepreneurship that entail lower risk, less innovation, or simpler forms of business such as freelancing, franchising, or business as usual (Dale, 1991; Davidsson, 2005; Eckhardt & Shane, 2003).

In contrast, most of the literature on "enterprising selves" in the media industry focuses on formerly salaried workers who have been forced into self-employment (Baines & Robson, 2001; Neff, Wissinger, & Zukin, 2005; Paterson, 2001; Saundry, 1998). Accounts of these workers emphasize how they adopt business paraphernalia such as self-branding but do not embrace "the underpinning psychology of business" and generally do not prosper as businesses (Storey, Salaman, & Platman, 2005; see also Alisa Perren, in this volume). These individuals can be considered survival entrepreneurs.

Some self-employed persons are basically short-term employees without benefits, as when downsized employees are rehired on a limited-term contract basis as "consultants" (Dale, 1991). But most self-employed persons are owner-operators of small firms, especially microenterprises. Self-employment is widespread across many industries. About 78% of all firms in Canada are microenterprises—the "smallest of the small businesses" (Clinton, Totterdell, & Wood, 2006). In 2008, about 2.6 million Canadians were self-employed—that is, they owned businesses with or without employees.

Growth is not the primary objective of most microentrepreneurs, as evidenced by the many "push" and "pull" factors that motivate self-employment (Wiklund, Davidsson, & Delmar, 2003). Loss of employment, unemployability, parenting or elder care responsibilities, need for a second income, semiretirement, and professional and personal aspirations and lifestyle preferences are very important considerations in choice of career and employment mode (Beaucage, Laplante, & Légaré, 2004; Delage, 2002). The latter considerations are particularly germane in creative industries, which many individuals enter because they find the work intrinsically rewarding—or at least more rewarding than available paid employment.

In Canada, workers with more than $30,000 in nonsalaried earned income must register as firms, which by definition have the capacity to make a profit and incur business expense and risk. Tax authorities make a clear distinction between self-employed persons and employed individuals. This is necessary because self-employed persons must pay value-added tax on business transactions and until 2010 were ineligible for public employment insurance. Attributes considered by the Canada Revenue Agency to indicate self-employment include ownership and maintenance of necessary tools and equipment, absence of security or benefits, discretion to hire helpers and subcontractors, maintenance of one's own work space, maintenance of a business presence, financial liability for completion of contracted work, and possibility to realize a profit or incur a loss. Since a firm with employees must contribute to their employment insurance and other benefits, adding to the firm's overhead costs, it is cheaper and less constraining to deal with independent contractors.

Self-employment reflects considerable variation in degree of entrepreneurial ambition, and self-employed persons bring a wide range of capabilities and resources to bear on new ventures, leading to widely varying performance outcomes. Microenterprises in general exhibit very low growth potential: Only 1% of microenterprises grow to the next size category of firm in 10 years (Industry Canada, 2001). Among the smallest firms in Canada, the factors that explain firm growth include entrepreneurial intent, higher levels of education, informal networking with customers and suppliers, business partnering behavior, product innovation, adoption of e-business technologies, managerial delegation, focus on the local market, and age (Papadaki & Chami, 2002). Growth-oriented ventures are generally initiated and led by persons who have experience and training in an industry and who prepare the venture and launch it with resources and a competent team (Friar & Meyer, 2003). These entrepreneurs identify or create an opportunity that supports an expectation of growth in spite of the risk involved. Since entrepreneurs who create firms and employ workers have to organize, motivate, and manage people around functional firm-level tasks, successful entrepreneurs need to be jacks-of-all-trades and bring a broad skill set to the endeavor, rather than deep but narrow subject matter expertise (Lazear, 2005). And because most self-employment is neither primarily growth-oriented nor supported by pronounced entrepreneurial capabilities or resources, self-employed persons generally earn lower incomes than their salaried counterparts, although they report higher levels of work satisfaction (Hamilton, 2000).

How do new entrants with enterprising capabilities identify and exploit openings? What kinds of niches are found or created in the mature segments of the media industry? How do "nonenterprising" self-employed persons fare in the media sector? One sees major differences in strategy, management capability, and performance among three kinds of the smallest media enterprises: firms that are created and resourced with growth objectives in mind, although they may not seek to maximize growth; ventures that, while not primarily driven by growth aspirations, are intended to create viable and valuable firms—we can call them self-reliant, lifestyle, or "transgressive" firms (after Fenwick, 2002), because these firms discount conventional corporate enterprise values; and sole-proprietor microenterprises that are formed for survival purposes. We may also expect differences between ventures designed to exploit new content and ventures designed to exploit new technologies or new organizational forms.

Self-Employment and Entrepreneurship in Screen-Based Media

Most management-oriented studies of media firms focus on large firms. With the exception of a scattered literature on Internet startups, media venturing has not received a great deal of attention. Fewer than 80 articles on media entrepreneurship were published between 1970 and 2005 (Hang & van Weezel, 2007).

Clearly, the industrial and geographic context of new firm formation is important. It is impossible to ignore the centrality of economically and politically powerful media conglomerates and their established suppliers. Most branches of the screen media industry are pyramids in which a few very large firms (globally integrated central studios, national broadcasters, or publishers) coexist with a relatively small population of medium-sized incumbents and very large numbers of microenterprises and freelancers.

The locus of entrepreneurial opportunity shifts among layers and segments of the media industry over time. Longitudinal analysis of media industries shows a great deal of volatility (entry and exit) through vertical disintegration due to technological discontinuities, regulatory intervention, and organizational innovation (Deuze, 2007). In North America this volatility has opened up opportunities for new entrants every decade. With the exception of publishing, media industries in the United States have exhibited very high rates of volatility since the 1950s, culminating in higher-than-average rates of volatility in the 1990s (Hoag, 2008). Funk's (2008) analysis of entrepreneurial opportunity in the U.S. broadcasting sector from the 1920s through the 1990s illustrates how openings have regularly appeared in vertically disintegrated layers of the industry.

Industry dynamics differ substantially in the transport, software, and content layers of the screen-based media industry, suggesting varying opportunities for entrepreneurial entry afforded by vertical disintegration and the emergence of new distribution channels. At present, new and young media firms have a significant impact on the media sector, perhaps more now than ever before, with the decline of protectionism, arrival of broadband distribution channels, and changing patterns of media consumption (McKelvie & Picard, 2008). Viable ventures emerge even in traditional media such as newspaper publishing (Achtenhagen, 2008). In digital media, research suggests a coevolutionary relationship between innovation in the software and creative content layers through the effects of market pull and technology push (McKelvie & Wiklund, 2008). When new industry segments open up, value networks of firms emerge that may number in the thousands of small specialist providers, as is currently the case among software application developers for mobile platforms (Funk, 2009).

The transport layer is scale intensive and so supports correspondingly larger firms, especially in the absence of regulation. The transport layer of the industry is dominated by large firms that control distribution infrastructure: broadcasting, cable, telecommunications carriage, and exhibition. In Canada, medium and large firms with more than 100 employees represent over 60% of the firms in most of these segments, according to the Business Register. To successfully enter a promising niche in the transport layer of the screen industry requires assembling a considerable package of financial, technological, and human resources. For example, for Toronto-based Globalive to enter the national wireless telephone business in 2009 required an outlay of several hundred million dollars, obtained from foreign backers, to win a spectrum license. The lowest barriers to entry in the transport layer are in the pay and specialty television and satellite broadcasting segments, where 70% of the firms in Canada are microenterprises according to the Business Register. The software or middleware layer of the screen industry is also in the middle in terms of the mix of firm sizes: In software publishing about 70% of the firms are microenterprises.

At the extreme end of the size spectrum are the creative content and technical craft segments of the industry: writers, performers, film and video producers, music publishers, audio recording studios, postproduction houses, and Internet publishers, where more than 85% of the firms are microenterprises. Many of these latter segments are not susceptible to economies of scale and so do not have a dominant market leader. The modest resources needed to enter the creative content and technical craft and service segments of the screen industry include skills that are generally acquired in a postsecondary institution, access to production equipment in some cases, and enough actionable social capital to obtain work.

The flexible or even precarious working conditions in the screen-based media industry are well known. Media labor precariousness has increased as graduates from postsecondary media and communication programs flood the labor market, and as senior individuals who have been made redundant in waves of industry consolidation and privatization set up shop. They enter a media labor market that is internally stratified by gender, age, and ethnicity (Bielby & Bielby, 1996, 2001; Christopherson, 2008). Collective bargaining arrangements support well-defined job roles and compensation scales in film and television, but not in other media industries such as advertising. In interactive digital media, collective bargaining has not emerged in North America. Instead, free agency and employment flexibility prevail, and fluid job roles, piecework, and on-the-job learning are widespread (Christopherson & van Jaarsveld, 2005).

These conditions lead to large numbers of freelancers and tiny firms. Although the predominance of big business in the media sector does not necessarily prevent entrepreneurs from entering, the high degree of labor flexibility is favorable to established firms. Concentration of financial and organizational resources among larger firms permits them to shift risks onto their suppliers, who procure crews and specialized inputs from geographically dispersed suppliers (Bilton, 1999; Canadian Film and Television Production Association, 2006). The availability of abundant lower-cost production talent in urban centers outside of Hollywood is an important driver of production outsourcing (Christopherson, 2005). Outsourced film and television production employs mainly domestic below-the-line labor and so does not directly support development of indigenous creative business capabilities, although Canadian independent film and television production firms benefit from having access to highly flexible and experienced production labor (Davis & Kaye, in press). Among small independent production firms, executive producers regard management of project-based production as a relatively unproblematic organizational capability compared to the business development, product development, relationship management, and marketing capabilities their firms need (Davis, Vladica, & Berkowitz, 2008). Firms with a dozen or fewer employees can easily expand project-based production by several orders of magnitude when production contracts are available without adding salaried employees. Smallness confers the advantage of flexibility. For example, in the Canadian independent film and television production sector, self-employed executive producers often partner on a project-by-project basis with larger established firms that supply overhead services, infrastructure, contacts, credibility with broadcasters, and creative involvement.

Flexibility, network-based production, and free agency are important functional characteristics of cultural or creative industries. Pioneered by the film industry, the Hollywood model of work organization is often presented as the vanguard of a new form of work organization required for high levels of creativity and innovation: Highly networked individuals configure and reconfigure on a project-by-project basis to produce unique, highly skill-intensive creative products (Grantham, 2000; Leadbeater, 2000). Flexible specialization induces "portfolio careers" characterized by periods of salaried employment interspersed with contract employment, self-employment, and unemployment (see Toby Miller, in this volume).

The literature on cultural and creative workers emphasizes time and again their desire for self-expression and creative control, as opposed to market or customer orientation, which is regarded as the hallmark of enterprise culture (Caves, 2000; Hirsch, 2000; Menger, 1999). The careers and work experiences of Toronto-area screenwriters illustrate the ways that portfolio careers incorporate elements of freelancing, self-employment, enterprise, and entrepreneurship. Most of the time screenwriters work on a project-by-project basis, and many combine screenwriting with other income-generating activities, especially producing, directing, show running, editing, acting, journalism, teaching, camera work, writing novels or nonfiction books or theatrical plays, corporate media, ownership of a production company, or entirely unrelated employment such as truck driving. The work of screenwriting thus combines a sequence of projects with a variety of customers or employers, providing great work variety. These microentrepreneurs of cultural production must manage many risks: income unpredictability, lack of benefits, intrusion of work into home life, demoralization and depression when work is short, constant revisions and criticism, isolation, and the fear of being out of step. For many screenwriters, however, the psychological rewards of cultural microentrepreneurship are as important as the financial rewards: freedom to set one's agenda and work odd hours, freedom from office politics, and the gratification of creative work.

Contingent creative careers are thus concurrently risky and seductive. They must be actively and effectively managed, requiring a great deal of self-awareness, self-discipline, and self-management (and some good fortune) on the part of the entrepreneur (Gold & Fraser, 2002). The individual bears principal responsibility for career path creation, for the maintenance of career momentum, for reinvention of his or her professional self over time, and for absorbing the risks of failure. The psychological rewards of success are attractive enough to motivate high levels of self-discipline as well as self-exploitation (Banks, 2006).

Most of the firms in the screen-based industry supply so-called humdrum inputs. A shortcoming of the research literature on media entrepreneurship and media self-employment is that it focuses primarily on the creative content and interactive digital segments, saying little about self-employment, new firm formation, and firm-level management in the wide range of craft, professional, technical, and service firms that support the screen-based media industry. For example, nearly 1,600 Greater Toronto Area firms are listed in the 2010 Ontario Media Development Corporation's Production Guide (http://www.omdc.on.ca/Page3597.aspx). These include production companies, investment and insurance firms, legal services, talent and recruitment agencies, unions and guilds, publicists, training institutions, production services (equipment rentals, props suppliers, transportation), and firms in the postproduction (animation, audio, closed captioning, editing, negative cutting, storage), distribution (bookers, theaters, marketing print delivery), and exhibition businesses (concessions, ticketing systems, broadcasters, digital channels, etc.). Collectively the capabilities and resources of these firms shape the evolution of screen-based industry in metropolitan Toronto through path dependence. Although legally independent, however, most of the firms in the industry are economically dependent, directly or indirectly, on the business success of a relatively small number of key industry players—in the case of Toronto, these are primarily domestic broadcasters, Hollywood studios, and established production firms, as well as a growing population of new media firms with customers in a variety of sectors.

When the industrial environment is volatile and the urban environment is economically diverse, entrepreneurs can enter a sector from a variety of directions. Bathelt (2004) identifies six origins of media firms in Leipzig, Germany: local startups, spin-offs from the university, unintentionally self-employed individuals, spinouts from public firms, and transplants and branches of establishments from elsewhere in Germany. Indergaard (2004) relates how individuals entered the New York interactive media industry from a broad range of industries: arts, corporate mass media, information technology, finance, and advertising. Britton (2007) discusses the importance of skills developed in the entertainment and business services sectors for the emergence of interactive digital media firms in Toronto.

But some entry points and institutional antecedents provide better initial advantage than others, supporting "dominance by birthright"—stronger performance than competitors (Klepper & Simons, 2000). For example, before starting their firm, most of the members of senior owner-management teams of the group of successful independent firms that produce children's programming in Canada had prior management experience at the senior level in domestic or foreign private or public media firms (Davis et al., 2008). Their startups were deliberate ventures that drew on irreplaceable prior experience and high-level contacts in the industry. Most video production firms started up by university graduates do not enjoy the same credibility, leverage, or social capital in industry. They are often required by broadcasters to partner with established firms.[2] On the other hand, film and video production firms established by recent graduates are more likely than older production firms to have access to digital media technical and cultural skills—attractive attributes in some growing markets. In this sense, a shift of demand toward interactive digital media presently provides an advantage to younger self-employed individuals and entrepreneurs who have pertinent cultural and social capital and recent links to postsecondary institutions.

Conclusion

In this chapter I have explored the implications of growing self-employment in the screen media sector, the shifting loci of opportunity for new entrants, and the range of entrepreneurial ambitions and capabilities at play. Vertical disintegration, outsourcing, downsizing, and low barriers to entry via postsecondary education have created large pools of flexible, free-agent, contingent media labor. Multiple factors encourage self-employed individuals in the media industry to develop minor or major degrees of self-identity as survival-seeking freelancers, self-employed creative persons, or entrepreneurs. While self-employed workers seek to make a living through content production, delivery of professional and technical services, and other firm-based media practices, they are not necessarily "enterprising" firms. Some media microenterprises grow into larger firms, depending on the skill or good fortune of the entrepreneur in locating or creating technological or market opportunities, but these more ambitious ventures require much greater access to resources than are available to the typical media microentrepreneur. Prospects for small-firm growth in the lower ranks of the creative content and technical craft segments of the film and television industry are constrained.

Relationships among art, commerce, and employment have substantially shifted in creative industries (Ellmeier, 2003). These industries present an ongoing economic conundrum. Should they be regarded as a welfare sector requiring permanent subsidy or as a set of stovepipe industries that might be made economically viable in some cases? Do they represent a sector with potential growth spillovers into other sectors, or are they the equivalent of a decentralized cultural research-and-development lab that nurtures innovation across wide swaths of the economy (Potts & Cunningham, 2008)? At issue is the path-creation capability of the population of very small firms in the media sector and the personal risks of perpetual membership in the standing reserve.

Since salaried employment in screen-based media is growing much less quickly than self-employment, I suggest that media education, which typically emphasizes inculcation of production skills and aesthetic conventions, needs to better prepare students for independent practice, including development of stronger capabilities for creation and management of viable new firms. More generally, encouragement of small business and entrepreneurship in media industries is a good idea. As microentrepreneurs, self-employed media workers need access to programs, support services, and infrastructure that provide incubation, training, investment, and business and market development. We must also keep in mind that promoting a microenterprise sector and improving self-management capabilities among self-employed media workers will not provide a general solution to the precariousness of labor in this industry. Media workers, like other contingent workers in the cultural industries, need income security, health insurance, and child care and retirement benefits (Gollmitzer & Murray, 2008). These public policy issues are only beginning to be raised in discussions about work in the creative economy in North America.

References

Achtenhagen, L. (2008). Understanding entrepreneurship in traditional media. *Journal of Media Business Studies, 5*(1), 123–142.

Baines, S., & Robson, L. (2001). Being self-employed or being enterprising? The case of creative work for the media industries. *Journal of Small Business and Enterprise Development, 8*(4), 349–362.

Banks, M. (2006). Moral economy and cultural work. *Sociology, 40*(3), 455–472.

Bathelt, H. (2004). Toward a multidimensional conception of clusters: The case of the Leipzig media industry, Germany. In D. Power & A. Scott (Eds.), *Cultural industries and the production of culture* (pp. 147–168). London, England: Routledge.

Beaucage, A., Laplante, N., & Légaré, R. (2004). Le passage au travail autonome: Choix impose ou choix qui s'impose? *Relations Industrielles, 59*(2), 345–378.

Bielby, D. D., & Bielby, W. T. (1996). Women and men in film: Gender inequality among writers in a culture industry. *Gender and Society, 10*(3), 248–270.

Bielby, D. D., & Bielby, W. T. (2001). Audience segmentation and age stratification among television writers. *Journal of Broadcasting and Electronic Media, 45*(3), 391–412.

Bilton, C. (1999). Risky business: The independent production sector in Britain's creative industries. *Cultural Policy, 6*(1), 17–39.

Boyle, R., & Magor, M. (2008). A nation of entrepreneurs? Television, social change, and the rise of the entrepreneur. *International Journal of Media and Cultural Politics, 4*(2), 125–144.

Britton, J. N. H. (2007). Path dependence and cluster adaptation: A case study of Toronto's new media industry. *International Journal of Entrepreneurship and Innovation Management, 7*(2–5), 272–297.

Canadian Film and Television Production Association. (2006). *Profile 2006. An economic report on the Canadian film and television production industry.* Ottawa, ON, Canada: Author.

Caves, R. (2000). *Creative industries: Contracts between art and commerce.* Cambridge, MA: Harvard University Press.

Christopherson, S. (2005). Divide and conquer: Regional competition in a concentrated media industry. In G. Elmer & M. Gasher (Eds.), *Contracting out Hollywood: Runaway productions and foreign location shooting.* Oxford, England: Rowman and Littlefield.

Christopherson, S. (2008). Beyond the self-expressive creative worker. *Theory, Culture, and Society, 25*(7–8), 73–95.

Christopherson, S., & van Jaarsveld, D. (2005). New media after the dot.com bust: The persistent influence of political institutions on work in cultural industries. *International Journal of Cultural Policy, 11*(1), 77–93.

Clinton, M., Totterdell, P., & Wood, S. (2006). A grounded theory of portfolio working: Experiencing the smallest of small businesses. *International Small Business Journal, 24*(2), 179–203.

Cultural Human Resources Council. (2009). *The art of managing your career. A Guide for the Canadian artist and the self-employed cultural worker.* Ottawa, ON, Canada: Author.

Dale, A. (1991). Self-employment and entrepreneurship: Notes on two problematic concepts. In R. Burrows (Ed.), *Deciphering self-employment* (pp. 35–51). London, England: Routledge.

Davidsson, P. (2005). *Researching entrepreneurship.* New York, NY: Springer.

Davis, C. H., & Kaye, J. (in press). International production outsourcing and the development of indigenous film and television capabilities—The case of Canada. In G. Elmer, C. H. Davis, J. Marchessault, & J. McCullough (Eds.), *Locating migrating media.* Lanham, MD: Lexington Books.

Davis, C. H., Vladica, F., & Berkowitz, I. (2008). Business capabilities of small entrepreneurial media firms: Independent production of children's television in Canada. *Journal of Media Business Studies, 5*(1), 9–39.

Delage, B. (2002). *Results from the Survey of Self-Employment in Canada.* Hull, QC: Human Resources Development Canada.

Deuze, M. (2007). *Media work.* Cambridge, England: Polity Press.

Eckhardt, J. T., & Shane, S. A. (2003). Opportunities and entrepreneurship. *Journal of Management, 29*(3), 333–349.

Ellmeier, A. (2003). Cultural entrepreneurialism: On the changing relationship between the arts, culture and employment. *The International Journal of Cultural Policy, 9*(1), 3–16.

Fenwick, T. J. (2002). Transgressive desires: New enterprising selves in the new capitalism. *Work, Employment and Society, 16*(4), 703–723.

Friar, J. H., & Meyer, M. H. (2003). Entrepreneurship and start-ups in the Boston region: Factors differentiating high-growth ventures from micro-ventures. *Small Business Economics, 21*, 145–152.

Funk, J. (2008). *Vertical disintegration and entrepreneurial opportunities: The case of the U.S. broadcasting sector.* Paper presented at the 25th Celebration Conference, Danish Research Unit on Industrial Dynamics, Copenhagen Business School.

Funk, J. (2009). The emerging value network in the mobile phone industry: The case of Japan and its implications for the rest of the world. *Telecommunications Policy, 33*, 4–18.

Gold, M., & Fraser, J. (2002). Managing self-management: Successful transitions to portfolio careers. *Work, Employment and Society, 16*(4), 579–597.

Gollmitzer, M., & Murray, C. (2008). *From economy to ecology: A policy framework for creative labour.* Vancouver, BC, Canada: Center of Expertise on Culture and Communities, Simon Fraser University.

Grantham, C. (2000). *The future of work: The promise of the new digital work society.* New York, NY: McGraw-Hill.

Hamilton, B. H. (2000). Does entrepreneurship pay? An empirical analysis of the returns to self-employment. *Journal of Political Economy, 108*(3), 604–631.

Hang, M., & van Weezel, A. (2007). Media and entrepreneurship: What do we know and where should we go? *Journal of Media Business Studies, 4*(1), 51–70.

Hirsch, P. M. (2000). Cultural industries revisited. *Organization Science, 11*(3), 356–361.

Hoag, A. (2008). Measuring media entrepreneurship. *International Journal on Media Management, 10,* 74–80.

Indergaard, M. (2004). *Silicon alley: The rise and fall of a new media district.* New York, NY: Routledge.

Industry Canada. (2001). *Microenterprises Survey 2000: A progress report.* Ottawa, ON: Author, Small Business Policy Branch.

Klepper, S., & Simons, K. L. (2000). Dominance by birthright: Entry of prior radio producers and competitive ramifications in the U.S. television receiver industry. *Strategic Management Journal, 21*(10–11), 997–1016.

Lazear, E. P. (2005). Entrepreneurship. *Journal of Labor Economics, 23*(4), 649–680.

Leadbeater, C. (2000). *Living on thin air.* London, England: Penguin.

McKelvie, A., & Picard, R. G. (2008). The growth and development of new and young media firms. *Journal of Media Business Studies, 5*(1), 1–8.

McKelvie, A., & Wiklund, J. (2008). Understanding innovation in new and young media firms. In C. Del Zotto & H. van Kranenburg (Eds.), *Management and innovation in the media industry* (pp. 15–35). Cheltenham, England: Edward Elgar.

Menger, P.-M. (1999). Artistic labor markets and careers. *Annual Review of Sociology, 25,* 541–574.

Neff, G., Wissinger, E., & Zukin, S. (2005). Entrepreneurial labor among cultural producers: "Cool" jobs in "hot" industries. *Social Semiotics, 15*(3), 307–333.

Organisation for Economic Co-operation and Development. (2009). *OECD Factbook 2009: Economic, environmental, and social statistics.* Retrieved from http://masetto.sourceoecd.org/vl=4816921/cl=12/nw=1/rpsv/factbook2009/06/01/04/index.htm

Papadaki, E., & Chami, B. (2002). *Growth determinants of micro businesses in Canada.* Ottawa, ON: Industry Canada, Small Business Policy Branch.

Paterson, R. (2001). Work histories in television. *Media, Culture and Society, 23,* 495–520.

Potts, J., & Cunningham, S. (2008). Four models of the creative industries. *International Journal of Cultural Policy, 14*(3), 233–247.

Saundry, R. (1998). The limits of flexibility: The case of UK television. *British Journal of Management, 9,* 151–162.

Shane, S., & Venkataraman, S. (2000). The promise of entrepreneurship as a field of research. *Academy of Management Review, 25*(1), 217–226.

Storey, J., Salaman, G., & Platman, K. (2005). Living with enterprise in an enterprise economy: Freelance and contract workers in the media. *Human Relations, 58,* 1033–1054.

Wiklund, J., Davidsson, P., & Delmar, F. (2003). What do they think and feel about growth? An expectancy-value approach to small business managers' attitudes toward growth. *Entrepreneurship Theory & Practice, 27*, 247–269.

Women in Film and Television. (2004). *Frame work: Employment in Canadian screen-based media—A national profile*. Toronto, ON, Canada: Author.

Zahra, S. A., Sapienza, H. J., & Davidsson, P. (2006). Entrepreneurship and dynamic capabilities: A review, model, and research agenda. *Journal of Management Studies, 43*(4), 917–955.

Notes

1. In this chapter, screen-based media encompass film, television, and interactive digital media. A microenterprise is defined in Canada as a firm with fewer than 5 employees, including "indeterminate" or zero-employee firms (i.e., self-employed individuals without employees). In other jurisdictions, microenterprises are defined as firms with fewer than 10 employees.

2. The Canadian film and television production industry was much more open to university graduates three decades earlier when several film students from Queen's University established a production firm that grew to become Alliance Atlantis, a major publicly traded Canadian media firm with broadcasting, distribution, and production interests until its takeover by Canwest and Goldman Sachs in 2007.

15 Connecting the Dots

STRUCTURE, STRATEGY, AND SUBJECTIVITY IN ENTERTAINMENT MEDIA

Susan Christopherson

About 50 years ago, in the mid-1950s, the U.S. media entertainment industries faced a crisis. The film workforce was aging, and there were no institutions in place to foster, train, and sustain a new generation of gaffers, best boys, actors, writers, and directors. Following the Paramount decision in 1948, which forced the major film studios to divest themselves of their exhibition houses (which had assured them of a market for their films), the studios also gradually divested themselves of a permanent workforce. They relied on self-employed freelancers to carry out production and focused on film finance and distribution. While this profit strategy was rational for the studios, the workforce was left adrift. Those workers with already established reputations reaped the benefits of being in a smaller pool, and incomes bifurcated between "known quantities" and new entrants trying to build careers (Christopherson & Storper, 1989).

At the same time, young people moved to work in network television, where a more immediate and frequently less scripted form of entertainment was developing, centered in New York rather than Los Angeles. With close ties to commercial production, television was more flexible and less hierarchical than filmmaking although it had a corporate base in the networks. Like filmmaking, however, TV lacked institutions that could sustain talented freelancers through spells of unemployment, help them build careers in a project-based industry, and provide them with pensions and health insurance.

The response to these challenges, one partially supported by employers of the freelance workforce, came from unions and professional guilds in film and television, which provided the governance institutions that enabled the freelance workforce to develop occupational skills and build careers in media entertainment. Not coincidentally, these institutions also protected the workforce from the risks attendant to a career as a self-employed worker.

In the early 2000s, the entertainment media industries face a challenge similar to that of the 1950s. The established unionized workforce is aging, and with fewer opportunities for work its ability to hang on to middle-class incomes is deteriorating. The unions that have bargained for the self-employed reasonably effectively over the past 50 years are not only less powerful but also fractured. They are pitted against one another as much as or more than against the now, once again, highly concentrated media entertainment employers.

And again, young people are moving outside the orbit of the established production processes and ways of working. Now, the move is to the world of new media and "unscripted" television, the arenas where work opportunities are increasing. While they complain about exploitation, lack of mentors, and the risks they face, these young workers have little recourse against the exploitation by their employers (Silver, 2005).

In this chapter I examine the labor demand and labor supply conditions that underpin the contemporary crisis facing the self-employed freelance workforce in film and television in the United States, looking particularly at the role of the producer, who stands between conglomerate demands for cost reduction and the production company whose members must produce a viable product. I also explore some implications of the changes occurring in the media entertainment industries, for the workforce and for industry governance. While some anticipate (and hope) that demand will rebound and once again emphasize high-value production in scripted television and feature film, all signs point to a longer-term transformation in product demand and declining bargaining power by collective bargaining organizations. This, in turn, implies further de-professionalization of the workforce and income bifurcation. Whether these changes stimulate union strategies that respond creatively to the contemporary market and its consequences for the workforce is yet to be seen. The import of this transformation for what is produced and how it is produced goes beyond worker bargaining power, however.

The media industries have relied on the unions and the associated industry institutions not only to "organize" a freelance workforce but also to organize and sustain the industry. So, this transition and crisis also has implications for the future quality and character of media production.

On the Demand Side: Changes in Structure and Strategy _____

The contemporary organizational structure of the entertainment media industry in the United States is difficult to depict in a simple, straightforward way. The industry is highly concentrated—at the point of product distribution and in particular product markets, including film and television. Just six firms control the gateways to consumer markets (Schatz, 2008). The major U.S.-based media conglomerates include (as of 2009) Disney, General Electric, National Amusements, News Corporation, Sony, and Time Warner. (Within General Electric and Sony, the media entertainment divisions are only small contributors to corporate profits.)

The deregulation of media industries that has occurred in the United States since the mid-1980s has enabled the conglomeration of formerly separate film and television industries and the subsequent acquisition of media entertainment corporations by nonmedia transnational firms such as General Electric, which owns NBC Television, Telemundo networks, numerous other cable networks, and Universal Studios. All the conglomerates set up internal markets in which they use the products they produce across their multiple media distribution outlets (Meehan, 2008; Schatz, 2008). This concentration, and decreasing competition among media distributors, has had significant effects on the bargaining power of independent producer-directors and of the workforce.

Together, conglomeration and control of multiple distribution markets in the United States, along with continued ability to collude in global markets (as well as emerging Internet markets), have limited competition. Those who produce media products must sell those products to one of a few firms that control distribution if they want their products to make money and reach an audience.

Concentrated conglomerate ownership has also affected decisions about the content of TV and film products. For example, in theatrical film, the conglomerates have moved from direct investment in a diverse portfolio of films for national and global markets to a more exclusive focus on global "blockbusters" aimed at a young male market. While extraordinarily expensive to make, these films appeal to that global audience which is most likely to go to a theater to see an action film and offer the potential for product spinoffs, particularly high-profit computer games, aimed at the same audience.

To fill out their distribution portfolios, media distributors rely on independently produced films, aimed at more limited (U.S.) markets: adults, women, families with young children, and so forth (Wasko, 2008). The studios have enough investment in these films (largely capital for marketing) to enable them to reap the benefits if one turns into a hit. These investments also enable the conglomerate distributors to use the film products within in their multiple distribution venues (network television, cable, pay-per-view, DVD sales, etc.) so as to recoup their investment. The film market has become strongly bifurcated. At the bottom, in terms of risk and revenue, are half of the approximately 500 films released in the United States every year. These films are made "on the cheap," with budgets between $5 million and $10 million, and have little if any money invested in marketing. The difference in profit potential among these product types is dramatic. "In 2005, the top five major studio releases alone earned more domestically than all of the 345 independent releases combined" (Schatz, 2008, p. 31).

Conglomerate ownership of television broadcast and cable networks has also had effects on production organization and market strategies within these industry segments. Historically, television has been the more stable of the film and television media entertainment industries, with large corporate organizations and long-running episodic programming. With mergers and acquisitions, the large corporate operations have been reduced, and production has been outsourced to production companies under contract to the distributor. In the contemporary television production environment, production risks fall substantially on the independent producer while the conglomerate distributor retains control through investment and by acting as a gatekeeper to the consumer market.[1]

In the short term, the media conglomerates face serious difficulties because of the fragmentation of advertising revenue and advertisers' flight from mass markets to the more targeted marketing opportunities offered by Internet search engines such as Google and social networking sites. They are also in a precarious financial position because of investments in mergers and acquisitions in the 1990s. Adding to their uncertainties, new types of media entertainment products have developed, such as videos shown on YouTube and other consumer-created content. While these products are innovative, they lie outside the mainstream profit-oriented media production and distribution system. These new "products," however, create flux and uncertainty in media entertainment, as well as suggest that new entrepreneurial opportunities are emerging.

There are some indications that the concentrated media may once again develop a more competitive structure if conglomerates have to sell off key assets because of financial distress. However, at this juncture, the media conglomerates continue to control those venues in which profits from production of content are possible. And, although they have made costly and unsuccessful moves to incorporate Internet distribution within their conglomerate structures, the major media distributors' ultimate aim is the convergence of the distribution formats under their ownership. The emergence of a television and film distribution "network" on the Internet, Hulu, a joint venture of two of the conglomerates, General Electric (NBC Universal) and News Corporation, suggests how this scenario may develop.

In the immediate future, however, conglomerates are under serious financial pressure and need to reduce the cost of filling their multiple television broadcast and cable networks to a minimum. Two prominent ways in which the conglomerates are responding to the revenue crisis are production budget control and production outsourcing to low-cost locations. By driving and sometimes determining the options available to producers and directors who need capital to finance their film and television projects and access to "eyeballs," the conglomerates directly and indirectly influence labor demand and the organization of work. In the new television production environment, cost reduction in the large corporate broadcast organizations and lower production budgets have been accompanied by dramatic expansion of low-end production, particularly in "nonfiction" programming, especially, but not exclusively, for cable television. Given the overall profile of film and television production, it is at the low end of television production that labor demand has increased since the late 1990s.

By contrast with the concentration in distribution, production of entertainment media is carried out in a vertically disintegrated system, organized around projects. This vertically disintegrated production organization is an inheritance of the industry production organization that emerged from the 1950s through the early 1980s, following the breakup of the "studio system." Until recently, production organization was governed fairly effectively via a balance of power between the (now) media conglomerates, represented by the Alliance of Motion Picture and Television Producers (AMPTP), and the guilds and unions representing the largely self-employed talent and craft workers who create film and television products.

The balance of power enabled the studios and TV networks to be assured of a professional, trained, and credentialed workforce that could renew itself over time. This governance system had serious drawbacks. For example, some unions attempted to limit labor supply (and drive up wages) by keeping workforce entrants in apprenticeship positions for many years. Nevertheless, the governance system enabled the workforce to build careers in a freelance industry environment, providing markers of experience and expertise such as the credit system. Hourly wages were high enough to compensate for long spells of unemployment and the continuous employment uncertainty that distinguishes a project-based industry. All of these governance mechanisms are at risk in the contemporary environment.

To better understand how governance institutions in media entertainment are being affected by conglomerate strategies to concentrate on the low end of content production and to control budgets, both directly and by outsourcing, we need to examine how these strategies are visited on the producer, the central executive in the production process. In the next section, I examine the changing role of the "middle man," the producer, focusing particularly on television production where cost cutting is being pursued most strenuously even as demand for programming remains strong.

The Changing Role of the Producer— More Responsibility, Less Creative Control

The producer is arguably the central figure in television production, with direct responsibility for a program's quality and viability. In conventional wisdom in fact, television is considered a producer's medium, in contrast to film, where the director is usually regarded as the key initiating talent. The film producer's role, though, is similar to that of the television producer as the primary "entrepreneur" behind the project, initiating and coordinating all phases of the production and with responsibility for project financing and personnel.

The role of producer may be combined with other production roles, such as writer or director, but it is the intermediary role of producer, between investors and distributors (the media conglomerates) and the production project company that makes it critical to interpreting how incentives and structural changes move from conglomerate distributor to the workforce.

Because of their entrepreneurial role, producers are keenly aware of the changes in the industry and the challenges they face. First, they are aware of the deterioration in the "infrastructure" that once supported the production process.

Recent interviews with producer-directors made clear that they see changes in the organizational infrastructure in which media products take shape: "The [broadcasting] networks are more unstable. The economics are just not there. They are empty. They are shells. They used to be full of people on contract. [Now] they want to work with people who are reliable and produce at the lowest price" (personal communication, September 9, 2007).

And from another producer-director who has worked in supplying programming in both commercial and public television: "I don't see the [economic] model. Budgets are lower and production values are lower. Schedules are crazy and you are expected to just churn out the stuff" (personal communication, September 5, 2007).

Interviews also indicated that producers who want to make quality television programs or feature films within low budgets engage in a variety of strategies. These strategies exemplify the changing bargaining power in the industry among conglomerates, independent producer-directors, and the workforce as it has emerged since the 1980s. They include tapping unconventional sources of financing—particularly place-based incentives, using simplified production methods made possible by new technologies, reducing the time allocated to direct production, increasing the reputation value of the product with financier-investors and potential distributors by going with the "tried-and-true" among the industry workforce, and tapping an expanded pool of multiskilled, nonunionized labor.

The Motion Picture Association of America, a trade association that represents the media conglomerates, has encouraged state governments to compete with one another to provide direct financing (through transferable tax credits) to productions, including low-end reality television (Christopherson & Rightor, 2010). According to one producer: "The power has shifted from the 'Creatives' to the 'Suits.' In other words, if you don't have a large incentive, you are not considered. Many projects are now budgeted with specific incentives in mind before a director is hired" (personal communication, September 9, 2007).

The Casting Data Report from the Screen Actors Guild (SAG) reports on roles (jobs) and days worked by production type. Between 2004 and 2006, the total number of roles (jobs) was up 10%, but the average number of days worked per role was down 7%. In nonepisodic television, average days worked declined by 19%. In addition, the largest increase in roles (jobs) was in the low-budget theatrical category (20.2%; Screen Actors Guild, 2007). The evidence from SAG is substantiated by anecdotal reports from production crews who describe intensified production schedules that shave days off by extending the workday to 13, 15, or even 18 hours and cutting the time allocated for crew "recovery" between shooting days.

The tried-and-true strategy regarding workforce talent also enables producers to carry out a production with some confidence in the skills of the production crew. It has had the side effect of reinforcing income bifurcation in the workforce and disadvantaging some workforce segments (women, minorities, young entrants) that are not integrated into established networks.

The demand for low-cost (meaning low-labor-cost) productions to fill time on conglomerate-owned cable networks has fostered the use of nonunionized labor, in an industry in which union density has been very high, especially by U.S. standards. In addition, production formats (most notably reality television) have emerged in which skilled labor inputs are minimized. The use of terminology such as *program planner* to replace *writer* or *participant* to replace *actor* obscures roles in the production process and avoids union jurisdiction. These changes in what production roles are named enable avoidance of employment contracts and shift accountability from the program distributor and producer to the individual who willingly participates in a program "event."

The availability of this flexible low-cost labor force is critical to the transformation of industry production methods and the popularity of "unscripted" reality television. This labor force is important not only because it provides cheap labor but also because it represents a sea change in attitudes toward how media work is done, what skills are required, and how a media worker acquires an income over time.

On the Supply Side: The Emergence of an Entrepreneurial Media Workforce—More "Wannabes" and a Generational Shift in Expectations

Despite the increasingly difficult production environment, the number of people who identify themselves as employed in media entertainment industries in the United States has increased steadily over the early 2000s. National employment in motion picture and video industry (television) firms (including production and postproduction) increased by 0.31% between 2002 and 2006.

From another perspective, statistics show dramatic increases in the numbers of people who identify themselves in key entertainment industry occupations. Between 2002 and 2006, there was a 14% increase in the number of individuals identified as producers and directors, a 7% increase in individuals identified as actors, and a 9% increase in camera operators for television and motion pictures.

The expansion of the entertainment media labor supply has been stimulated, in part, by the success of higher education media training programs. In these programs, which have proliferated in Los Angeles and New York as well as in other cities, students learn a wide variety of production skills and are introduced to new technologies that cross conventional union professional and craft jurisdictions. They learn how to produce on "shoestring" budgets and to work very rapidly and under severe time constraints. They learn to work in efficient multifunctional production teams. When they graduate, they are "hybrids": writer-directors, director–camera operator–editors, and, most important, all-purpose program producers who make up a flexible, independent contractor workforce perfectly suited to the high-growth segment of the media industry—production for cable television. In some respects, this workforce has more in common with its young colleagues in new media than it does with its elders who work in broadcast television and medium- to high-budget film (Batt, Christopherson, Rightor, & van Jaarsveld, 2001).

Although there has been a fractional increase in employment in companies employing more than one individual, much of the expansion in the workforce has taken place among freelancers. Individuals reporting themselves as self-employed in the motion picture and video industries (as reported by U.S. federal income tax filings) grew by 36% between 1997 and 2007 (according to U.S. Census figures). Although the entertainment media industries have always had a high proportion of freelance, self-employed workers, this proportion has expanded with the disintegration of corporate broadcast and cable network operations.

That this expanding self-employed workforce is not keeping up financially is indicated by output or profits per firm (which in this case refers to the self-employed worker). Over the period between 1997 and 2007, there was a 7% decrease in output per firm (ibid.). Given the bifurcation in incomes in the industry workforce and the impact of inflation on buying power over this period, this decrease reinforces anecdotal information that the larger, self-employed workforce in entertainment media has experienced income deterioration.

The expansion of the nonunionized freelance workforce combined with a shortage of higher-paying scripted television and feature film jobs and more demand for cheap unscripted programming for cable has created fissures within the workforce. These fissures are between talent and craft workers and between older established workers and younger workers and "wannabes" with only a tenuous hold on industry employment.

For example, changes in entertainment media production have been interpreted differently by the so-called talent, or "above-the-line" workforce, and the skilled craft workers who compose the "below-the-line" workforce. This difference in perception of the "problem" and what to do about it was manifested strongly in the 2008 writers' strike. At the top end of the creative entertainment media workforce, producers, writers, and directors complained about tighter production deadlines and budgets and the loss of creative control, as well as loss of residual payments that sustain them financially during the dry periods when they are not employed on a project. They attributed these changes directly to industry conglomeration and the decrease in competition.

According to one veteran filmmaker, "in cable, residuals [payments for each showing of the product] for writers, actors, and directors are a percent of the producer's gross. But if that producer is a network who self-deals the rights to their cable company . . . there is no compensation for that. Suddenly you discover that the eleven or twelve per cent gross residual among the three guilds that has been fought over for so many decades is virtually meaningless, as rights are simply self-dealt among related entities" (Hill, 2004, p. 20).

Anne-Marie Johnson of the Screen Actors Guild (2007) described the impact of these changes in her testimony at the Federal Communications Commission hearings:

> As actors, we find the continued consolidation of media companies has drastically limited our ability to individually bargain our personal services agreements. . . . The networks decide what the top-of-the show rates are, in a parallel practice. Some networks will even tell you they only pay 50 per cent of the going rate. Take it or leave it. This salary compression cripples the middle class actor's ability to make a living.

Craft workers, members of the International Alliance of Theatrical Stage Employees who do not receive residuals and have less investment in the creative content of a product, are concerned with keeping production rolling. They are big supporters of incentives to productions by states and cities because any work is better than no work. This position is understandable given that a makeup artist, script supervisor, gaffer, or best boy requires a certain number of days every year on unionized projects in order to maintain his health insurance and pension benefits. While this system of "vesting" worked to maintain a workforce over time, it now limits workers who would be better off combining work in different industries. The craft worker needs to work on unionized film or television projects in order to achieve workforce protections and always has to be available to do a unionized film or television job if one becomes available.

Thus, older workers find themselves in an industry with fewer opportunities for work, income, or creative expression. The collective bargaining they depended on to preserve their status in a project-oriented industry serves an ever-smaller slice of the workforce. Overall, there is evidence that the gap between the income of people employed in the entertainment media and the median income of all people employed in California (Entertainment Economy Institute & PMR Group, 2004) is decreasing. The incomes of the once highly paid talent are beginning to converge with those of the largely nonunionized workforce in the United States.

The Perspective of the Young Worker in the Low-Cost Production Industry

Young people entering the media entertainment industry come to their jobs with different experiences and expectations than their elders. They have very likely gained what technical skills they have from college courses or on-the-job experience as production assistants. They are typically drawn to the reality television format both because they are familiar with it and because that is where the jobs are. By contrast with scripted television or film, reality television has few professional roles and many hybrid jobs, the most important of which is "producer." The producer of a program stands in for a writer. The program producer takes hours of taped video footage and, often with the aid of an editor, turns that footage into a coherent narrative. Editing, writing, and producing roles have been hybridized into new occupational titles such as *producer* or *program developer*. For this work, the self-employed reality program developers are paid one third of the rate that unionized writers earn on a scripted program. Beginning producers on reality programs typically earn about $1,000 per week for a workweek that can run over 70 hours. Because they are independent contractors they have no access to the pension or health benefits that accrue to unionized workers in the industry (Wyatt, 2009). By contrast with the older professional workforce in scripted television and feature film, the goals of these young freelancers are defined in entrepreneurial rather than professional terms. Their goal is to develop a program "concept" and to sell it and reap rewards in the form of pay for intellectual property rather than salary, benefits, or residual payments (ibid.).

The customer for the product they develop is the media conglomerate firm. Even if they have investment capital, the conglomerate will decide whether the program fits with their corporate strategy.

So, the divide between the young program producers and their elders—actors, writers, and directors—is multidimensional, defined by occupational identification as well as experience, expectations, and attitudes toward collective bargaining. This divide is likely to grow if the trend toward low-end production continues.

Conclusions

The entertainment media industries have always had an entrepreneurial culture. From the beginning, adventurous people have set up small production companies, and technical crew members have established equipment supply companies. New ventures are a mainstay of industry practice. Alongside this entrepreneurial culture, however, was an occupational culture of profession and craft. This culture, underpinned by unions and guilds, provided for a skilled industry workforce with training and experience. It created institutions, such as the Motion Picture & Television Fund, to sustain workers during frequent periods of unemployment and aided them in building careers. It marketed the industry and its talent through the Academy of Motion Picture Arts and Sciences.

Since the early 2000s, the conception of what it means to work in the media entertainment industries has been shifting away from the occupational world of writers, directors, and actors and toward a model based on "the entrepreneurial self" (see Charles H. Davis, in this volume). Young media workers see their future in terms of developing and selling concepts for programs or games. They are producers and program developers rather than professionals. They are more invested in the product and less in the creative process.

The emergence of this media workforce, composed of entrepreneurs whose central capital is their time and energy, has accompanied shifts in what is being produced and how it is being produced. This chapter has attempted to make a case for looking to industry structure and firm strategy in formulating answers to these questions.

While this story raises broader theoretical issues, there is also the question of how the media entertainment industries will evolve at what looks like a critical turning point. What will emerge from the divide between an older, now threatened industry of feature film and scripted television and a new industry of nonfiction television and new media? The institutions that serve the workforce, unions and guilds, appear to have strategies that are organized around the interests of their older, more established members rather than the younger people entering an industry with decreasing opportunities for professional careers. They are primarily concerned to protect the fewer good jobs for their members and to seek out state and federal subsidies for producers, which ultimately profit the conglomerate distributors. They are, with rare exceptions, unwilling to confront the underlying problems, particularly industry conglomeration, that are changing what is produced and how it is produced and distributed. The entertainment media workforce of the 1950s faced a similar set of daunting challenges but managed to devise a set of innovative solutions that supported freelance career professionals in film and television for over 50 years. To devise those solutions it had to directly confront and understand how its industry was changing. The current situation will require a similar confrontation. At this juncture, the question of whether there is a bridge to institutions that can sustain the media entertainment workforce encompassed in both the old and new industries is compelling but still open.

References

Batt, R. S., Christopherson, S., Rightor, N., & van Jaarsveld, D. (2001). *Net working, work patterns and workforce policies for the new media industry.* Washington, DC: Economic Policy Institute.

Christopherson, S., & Rightor, N. (2010). The creative economy as "big business": Evaluating state strategies to lure filmmakers. *Journal of Planning Education and Research, 29*(3), 336–352.

Christopherson, S., & Storper, M. (1989). The effects of flexible specialization on industrial politics and the labour market. *Industrial and Labour Relations Review, 42*(3), 331.

Entertainment Economy Institute (EEI) & PMR Group. (2004). *California's entertainment workforce: Employment and earnings (1991–2002).* Los Angeles, CA: EEI.

Hill, L. (2004). Can media artists survive media consolidation? *The Journal of the Caucus of Television Producers, Writers and Directors, XXII,* 17–21.

Manly, L. (2005, June 20). Networks and the outside producer: Can they co-exist? *The New York Times,* pp. C1, C7.

Meehan, E. (2008). Ancillary markets—television: From challenge to safe haven. In P. MacDonald, & J. Wasko (Eds.), *The contemporary Hollywood film industry* (pp. 106–119). Oxford, England: Blackwell.

Reardon, M. (2006, October 3). Hollywood bashes media consolidation. *CNET News.* Retrieved from http://news.cnet.com/Hollywood-bashes-media-consolidation/2100-1026_3-6122447.html?tag=mncol

Schatz, T. (2008). The studio system and conglomerate Hollywood. In P. MacDonald & J. Wasko (Eds.), *The contemporary Hollywood film industry* (pp. 13–42). Oxford, England: Blackwell.

Screen Actors Guild. (2007). *Casting data report.* Retrieved from http://www.sag.org/content/studies-and-reports

Silver, J. (2005, April 11). Exploitation is more widespread than ever. *The Guardian.* Retrieved from http://www.guardian.co.uk/media/2005/apr/11/broadcasting.mondaymediasection

Ursell, G. (2000). Television production: Issues of exploitation, commodification and subjectivity in UK television labor markets. *Media, Culture and Society, 22*(6), 805–825.

Wasko, J. (2008). Financing and production: Creating the Hollywood film commodity. In P. MacDonald & J. Wasko (Eds.), *The contemporary Hollywood film industry* (pp. 43–62). Oxford, England: Blackwell.

Wyatt, E. (2009, July 23). Television fledgling keeps it real. *The New York Times.* Retrieved from http://www.nytimes.com/2009/07/26/arts/television/26wyat.html

Note

1. A Directors Guild of America representative, testifying before a U.S. Federal Communications Commission hearing in Los Angeles in October 2006, described the impact of concentration on television production. In his testimony he noted that in 1993, about 66% of network television programs came from independent producers while the networks produced 44%. In 2006, independent producers produced only 22% of network television while networks produced 76% (Reardon, 2006).

16

Advertising

STRUCTURE, AGENCY, OR AGENCEMENT?

Liz McFall

Scene A: Sterling Cooper creative team meeting

Ken	Why do moms give treats? There's no good reason.
Salvatore	My mom would come out to the truck with us. She'd break the Popsicle in half and give it to us like Jesus at the Last Supper.
Ken	Sounds cheap.
Peggy	No, my mother did it too; it was great.
Ken	In Vermont we made our own ice cream—it was a pain in the ass.
Peggy	Everyone breaks Popsicles in half.
Ken	So?
Peggy	You can do it all year-round; the ritual: It's like Communion.
Ken	It's kind of Catholic, isn't it?
Peggy	It's Christian, as in behavior, not religion. Let me tell you something. The Catholic Church knows how to sell things . . .

Scene B: Sterling Cooper pitch to Popsicle client

Peggy	When I was little my mother would take a twin Pop and break it in half and give one to me and one to my sister. We were completely equal in her eyes, beloved. Everyone does this with Popsicles, but they may not realize what it means. It has nothing to do with an ice cream truck on a hot summer day or the flavor or the color; it's a ritual—you *take it, break it, share it, love it* [unveils artwork showing a Jesus Christlike mom dispensing Popsicles].
Popsicle client	People do do that.
Peggy	This act of sharing is what a Popsicle is. It's the same treat from the freezer as it is from the truck. I don't care if it's snowing or if it's a hundred degrees—you can still *take it, break it, share it, love it*.
Popsicle client	[Looking at the artwork] I like the way she's handing out the Pops. The kids are excited, but the mom reminds me of something.
Peggy	No, this is original.
Popsicle client	Well, I can tell you this now, but we wanted something with the word *love* in it. When I ask, the first thing people say is "I love Popsicles."

Source: Weiner, Veith, & Taylor (2008).

They might be the stuff of television drama, but these scenes from cable network AMC's show *Mad Men* pack in a lot of clues for media managers and workers about creative advertising practice and about what a sociological perspective[1] can bring to an understanding of advertising processes. In this short chapter I will refer to these scenes in an attempt to offer a sociological account of how creative advertising works, both as a media practice and as a market device.

There is no shortage of social theories that could be brought to bear to account for what is going on in these two short scenes, and you wouldn't have to be too far advanced in a sociological education to see that there is more at play here than straightforward selling. In invoking religion, maternal care, and childhood memories Peggy locates the Popsicle pitch, subtly, but quite directly, in a social world. In doing so she creates a pitch with some punch, but she also, as far as centuries of critics, sociologists, and other commentators are concerned, does something else. What that something else is has been construed in a variety of different ways, and while there is not the space here to do justice to the nuances within the long history of advertising critique,[2] at core it seems to involve a transfer or exchange between one realm and another. This transfer is what Samuel Johnson was getting at when he remarked in the 18th century on the "improper disposition" of advertise-ments in combining the noble with the mundane, and it is what has exercised a range of 20th-century scholars who have derived inspiration from Marx's thesis on commodity fetishism to explain what advertising, especially creative or persuasive advertising, does.[3] At the crudest level, a value or quality that properly belongs in one place is imported into another in the service of com-mercial strategy. Advertising has been conceived as a mediator, a "bridge" that permits or encourages transfer between different "places," allowing, for example, cultural, aesthetic, social, or psychological qualities to "turn up" in the economy. From a critical, sociological perspective this exchange has been construed as one with largely negative consequences including the devalua-tion of art and culture, the decline of social institutions, the manipulation of individual fears and anxieties, the promotion of narcissistic individualism, and the encouragement of excessive consumption.[4]

This is a formidable burden of responsibility for advertising workers to shoulder. It clearly has some purchase judging by the accounts of former prac-titioners who have been drawn to critical writing and, sometimes through movements like "culture jamming," to critical action.[5] But while classic and contemporary critiques of advertising carry some weight, there is no consen-sus on advertising's influence—negative or positive—or the degree to which advertising, rather than commerce in general, should be held responsible. Sociological critiques of advertising are, in any event, really critiques of mar-ket society both in the systemic and totalizing overviews they offer and, more often than not, in their focus on the role and effects of advertising generally, rather than its practices and processes empirically.

The tendency to access advertising primarily through its texts or products began to give way in the 1990s as part of a broader resurgence of sociological interest in the practices, processes, and institutions that make up the economy.[6] Turning to the economy and to a more empirical, more ethnographic, more practice-based approach, however, unsettles some well-established ideas about advertising work. To characterize advertising as a bridging, mediating technology devised by cultural intermediaries (Bourdieu, 1984; McFall, 2002) relies on a conception of whatever it is that advertising workers are transfer-ring, blending, or "hybridizing" with the economic—cultural, symbolic, aes-thetic, or social values—as properly belonging to separate spheres. From a Frankfurt School perspective advertising is a "culture industry" that captures and transforms culture proper into a mass-produced and debased form, while for social theorists like Baudrillard (1988); Beck, Giddens, and Lash (1994); and Bourdieu (1984) advertising plays a lead role in blurring the boundaries between the cultural and economic spheres.

The problem with this, as I have argued elsewhere (McFall, 2004), is that while the distinction between the cultural and the economic is conceptually useful, it is actually very difficult to sustain in concrete practice. There may be good reasons for defending the distinction, but it is nevertheless an artificial one resulting from centuries of separating intellectual work that has sought to enforce and maintain an abstract, conceptual division between spheres of activity. When it comes to practice the distinction collapses as the cultural, symbolic bits are all mixed up with the commercial and economic. To return to the Popsicle example, Peggy may be importing childhood memories, religion, and ideals of mothering to add symbolic values to the product, but that doesn't change the fact that the Popsicle is already imbued with culture, meaning, and significance as a result of its history and its patterns of use. What makes Peggy's pitch successful is not that she's come up with an alluring but arbitrary cultural value, an "improper disposition"—rather it is that she has selectively condensed appealing aspects of the intersecting histories of product, client, and consumers in her pitch.

Advertising work is always already cultural in that it involves representing and repackaging select aspects of the social world.[7] Despite the manifest proximity to other forms of cultural production this is a characteristic not just of creative work but of media and account planning and management functions too. For this reason I have referred previously (McFall, 2004) to all forms of advertising work as constituent material practices that are necessarily made up of cultural and economic elements and entirely contingent upon material factors: technologies, techniques, rules, conventions, and budgets that substantially pattern the final advertising product. Thinking about advertising work as constituent draws upon anthropological perspectives that reject the idea that the cultural and economic ever function in practice as pure, separate, and autonomous realms. This goes some way toward addressing the critical fascination with advertising as singularly to blame for mixing things up that should be kept separate, but the idea of advertising as a constituent practice on its own does little else. The most promising route toward a better understanding of the character of advertising work both sociologically and from a media management perspective lies in the renewed emphasis on the material.

To try and explain what I mean by this it is worth considering another way of thinking sociologically about how advertising production might work. Perhaps the most central of all sociological concerns is the relationship between individuals and social worlds or, more conventionally, that between agency and structure. At the risk of caricaturing, sociological thought classically divides between those concerned with action and agency on the one hand and those concerned with structure and structural constraint on the other. Returning to the scenes from *Mad Men* once more, a sociological account focused on agency would light upon Peggy's individual drive and creative brilliance, her biography, and her reflexivity as the core factors shaping the campaign pitch; a more structural account, on the other hand, would primarily stress institutional factors such as the relationship between the agency and the client and the overriding need in a capitalist market society to create profit by whatever means necessary.

Admittedly, few sociologists would insist on either agency or structure as the sole determinant of the social world—or indeed the campaign pitch; most would see these factors as interacting to greater or lesser extents. Still, this leaves the agency-structure dualism intact and leaves sociology and social theory in the same blind alley that Norbert Elias remarked about as long ago as 1939. Individuals (agents), Elias (1939/2000) maintained, do not stand outside society (structure), and society cannot exist outside individuals. This seemingly obvious point is nevertheless frequently misunderstood. Elias is not just saying that the individual and society are related; his point is that they are part of the same whole, a network of interdependencies.

This may seem a long way from thinking about the management of advertising work, but maybe it is not. In recent years the upsurge in interest in refining a sociological understanding of the economy and economic practices has been reinforced by efforts to rethink the agency-structure dualism along more material and process-oriented lines. One of the more fruitful lines of inquiry arose initially from actor-network theory's (ANT's) attempt to rethink the sociological conception of the human agent as the prime source of social action. ANT proactively challenged the idea that agency, understood as the capacity to undertake voluntary willed action, could be contained in a human being.[8] Rather, agency was to be understood as materially endowed and distributed across networks of arrangements. Viewed this way, Peggy's idea may originate in Peggy, but its translation into a meaningful pitch or action involves materials, tools, equipment, organizational settings, the support of her agency colleagues, and so forth. It is these material processes of translation that produce social outcomes. From an ANT perspective, meaningful action is best traced through what Law (1999) called a "semiotics of materiality" (p. 4). Where traditional semiotics proceeded from the principle that social meaning is relational, the outcome of the differences between signs—we know what *black* is because we know what *white* is—a semiotics of materiality explores the network of relations among *all* materials.

The implications of this are worth unraveling. What it suggests is that managing advertising work is not about managing the transfer of value or meaning from one sphere to another or about managing the relations between individuals and advertising structures. Rather it is about understanding the material and distributed nature of the work and the processes and translations among different participants involved in production. Viewed up close, advertising work may be composed of constituent material practices where culture-like bits are blended with economy-like bits using specific materials, but this is not all there is to it. Equally significant are the shifting networks of organizational and institutional relations through which practitioners negotiate their work. Rather than thinking of these factors as the interaction of agency and structure, a process-oriented approach would define all these factors as party to the "agencement" of advertising.

Michel Callon (2005, 2007), among others,[9] has applied the term *agencement* to the study of markets and economic practices to emphasize the importance of the interconnections among "agencies" with the capacity for meaningful action. Agencies here are not simply human actors. In line with the distributed and material conception of agency in ANT, agencies are "made up of human bodies but also of prostheses, tools, equipment, technical devices, algorithms, etc." (Callon, 2005, p. 4). Agencements, then, are the human and nonhuman, material, social, technical, and textual assemblages that together form the source of all action. In an economic context, market agencements, like advertising, are hybrid, collective devices that *do* things; agencements make things happen.

Considering advertising as an agencement is more than just a clumsy way of saying that its production involves a complex assembly of different elements. It is a way of signaling the generative force of the connections among these elements. The connections themselves are what matters. Agencements include all the material, social, and technical elements of a given practice or device and the statements made about that practice such that all elements act in accordance with each other in the way that operating instructions are part of what makes a device work. The relationship among these different elements is performative. A performative act is one that creates a state of affairs by uttering it—as in the archetypal example "I pronounce you husband and wife." The statements, knowledge, and formulae that underpin a given market practice or device can be considered performative because they are part of what makes it succeed or fail. Statements, knowledge, and formulae, Callon (2007) concludes, discover worlds—be they advertising, credit markets, or whatever—that are themselves put into motion by the statements describing them. Economies and markets—and advertising and media environments—acquire their form through continual observation and experimentation. These ongoing adjustments between advertising knowledge and its material practices together make up the collective assembly, the agencement, of advertising.

By highlighting the performative character of the links among elements, agencement marks agency as intricately distributed and continually evolving. At the risk of laboring the example, considered as an agencement Peggy's pitch works because of the timely coincidence of the different elements. Thus her memories of being given Popsicles as a child, her knowledge of religion, her skills as a creative, and her capacity to link these to the client's brief all inform her ideas, but in order for her idea to become a successful pitch a range of other institutional factors are also required. Her endorsement by the agency as the lead creative, her ability to work with other members of the team to develop Salvatore's Last Supper image, the support from art and layout, account management, and finally the client's perspective on the product and so forth are all keen in translating the initial discussion into a successful pitch. The action here, notwithstanding the potency of the brilliant creative mind rhetoric, does not spring from a single source.

In the context of media management, what this means is dispensing with seductive fictions about brilliant individuals and recognizing instead the hybrid, material, and distributed character of advertising work. Advertising workers of course include the ever-diversifying range of media planning, research and account, and reputation and image management specialisms, as well as the creatives so heavily overrepresented in fictional and popular narratives. But the work of creatives is itself both glamorized and oversimplified when cast as an intermediary role reliant mainly on the capacity to transfer value and meaning from the "cultural" to the "economic." This neglects the significance to creative work of evolving and overlapping personal, social, and institutional networks and its dependence on the appropriate tools, technologies, and techniques from graphics packages and image libraries to office furniture (see also Chris Bilton, Bozena I. Mierzejewska, in this volume).

Negotiating through these networks and technologies involves understanding, for instance, product and competitor markets, institutional and professional associations, agency organization and staffing structures, industry standards, and conventions and how these impact advertising work in a rapidly changing environment. This technical and administrative knowledge may be less likely to be featured as the stuff of television drama, but it is as germane to the bulk of advertising production as the stereotypes about creative talent and elite consumers that have taken center stage in both dramatic and sociological portrayals of advertising business. A more pragmatic—if less romantic—approach to advertising and media management involves recognizing the material, collective, and distributed nature of the work. Describing and understanding how these constituent elements combine should form the basis of a sociologically informed approach to media management whether of an individual career portfolio or a transnational agency.

References

Baudrillard, J. (1988). Consumer society. In M. Poster (Ed.), *Selected writings* (pp. 32–59). Cambridge, England: Polity Press.

Beck, U., Giddens, A., & Lash, S. (1994). *Reflexive modernization, politics, tradition and aesthetics in modern social theory*. Cambridge, England: Polity Press.

Bourdieu, P. (1984). *Distinction: A critique of the judgement of taste*. London, England: Routledge.

Callon, M. (1998). *The laws of the market*. Oxford, England: Blackwell.

Callon, M. (2005). Why virtualism paves the way to political impotence: A reply to Daniel Miller's critique of *The Laws of the Markets*. *Economic Sociology: European Electronic Newsletter, 6*(2), 3–20.

Callon, M. (2007). What does it mean to say that economics is performative? In D. Mackenzie, F. Muniesa, & L. Sui (Eds.), *Do economists make markets?* (pp. 311–357). Princeton, NJ: Princeton University Press.

Callon, M., Millo, Y., & Muniesa, F. (2007). *Market devices*. Oxford, England: Blackwell.

du Gay, P., & Pryke, M. (Eds.). (2002). *Cultural economy*. London, England: Sage.

Elias, N. (2000). *The civilising process*. Oxford, England: Blackwell. (Original work published 1939)

Ewen, S. (1976). *Captains of consciousness: Advertising and the social roots of consumer culture*. New York, NY: McGraw-Hill.

Hardie, I., & Mackenzie, D. (2007). Assembling an economic actor: The *agencement* of a hedge fund. *Sociological Review, 55*(1), 57–80.

Haug, W. (1986). *Critique of commodity aesthetics*. Cambridge, England: Polity Press.

Law, J. (1999). After ANT: Complexity, naming and topology. In J. Law & J. Hassard (Eds.), *Actor network theory and after* (pp. 1–14). Oxford, England: Blackwell.

Leiss, W., Kline, S., Jhally, S., & Botterill, J. (2006). *Social communication in advertising* (3rd ed.). London, England: Routledge.

Mackenzie, D., Muniesa, F., & Sui, L. (Eds.). (2007). *Do economists make markets?* Princeton, NJ: Princeton University Press.

McFall, L. (2002). What about the old cultural intermediaries? An historical review of advertising producers. *Cultural Studies, 16*(4), 532–552.

McFall, L. (2004). *Advertising: A cultural economy.* London, England: Sage.

McFall, L. (2009). The agencement of industrial branch life assurance. *Journal of Cultural Economy, 2*(2–3), 49–65.

Miller, P. (2008). Calculating economic life. *Journal of Cultural Economy, 1*(1), 51–64.

Miller, P., & Rose, N. (1990). Governing economic life. *Economy and Society, 19*(1), 1–31.

Nixon, S. (1996). *Hard looks: Masculinities, spectatorship and contemporary consumption.* London, England: UCL Press.

Nixon, S. (2003). *Advertising cultures: Gender, commerce, creativity.* London, England: Sage.

Weiner, M., Veith, R. (Writers), & Taylor, A. (Director). (2008). The mountain king [Television series episode]. In M. Weiner (Executive producer), *Mad men.* North Vancouver, BC, Canada: Lionsgate Television.

Wernick, A. (1991). *Promotional culture: Advertising, ideology and symbolic expression.* London, England: Sage.

Notes

1. I use this term very broadly to include a range of critical academic perspectives including media, communication, and cultural studies analyses.

2. See Leiss, Kline, Jhally, and Botterill (2006) and McFall (2004) for overviews of critique.

3. For a more detailed overview of critique on the illogical juxtaposition of products and meanings or values in advertisements see McFall (2004), especially Chapters 1, 2, and 6.

4. For classic critiques of advertising see, for example, Ewen (1976), Haug (1986), and Wernick (1991).

5. For more on culture jamming see https://www.adbusters.org/.

6. Callon (1998), du Gay and Pryke (2002), and Miller and Rose (1990) offer perspectives on the new economic sociology; see McFall (2004) and Nixon (1996, 2003) for practice-based accounts of advertising (see also Sean Nixon, in this volume).

7. This representational labor may equally be characteristic of all forms of work including, for example, accounting and finance (see Miller, 2008).

8. See Law (1999) for an introduction to ANT; see Callon (1998) and Callon, Millo, and Muniesa (2007) for applications to markets.

9. For recent applications of the term to financial and consumer markets see Hardie and Mackenzie (2007); Mackenzie, Muniesa, and Sui (2007); and McFall (2009).

17

From Full-Service Agency to 3-D Marketing Consultants

"CREATIVITY" AND ORGANIZATIONAL CHANGE IN ADVERTISING

Sean Nixon

Even the most cursory look at the landscape of advertising reveals the transformed nature of the agency sector. The full-service agency of the 20th century no longer exists in a recognizable form, and the commission system that underpinned it has been replaced by new forms of financial remuneration, preeminently a fee-based system negotiated between agencies and clients for particular services. There has been the growth of new service providers and consultants in areas formerly integrated within service agencies. This includes, centrally, the functions of media buying, marketing and planning, and brand consultancy. Even the names of the new enterprises that have come to prominence in the sector reflect the decline of the old ideal of the service advertising agency. On the wane in the United Kingdom, for example, are agencies named after founding partners with their overtones of family capitalism. On the rise are the funky branded companies: Mother, Tomato, St. Luke's, Naked.

This transformation in the landscape of advertising as a business sector has been driven by a range of external factors. We can see these emerging in the 1990s, and it is in this period that the origin of the contemporary shape of advertising lies. Agencies found themselves facing competition from other groups of symbolic intermediaries in the areas of expertise that they had traditionally monopolized. One set of challenges came from management consultants who were increasingly offering their services to clients as the providers of rigorous strategic advice about brands. The consultancy firm McKinsey & Co., most notably, garnered a good deal of disapprobation from agencies for its aggressive moves into the communications field in the early 1990s ("Client Service Hangs on Dedication to Creativity," 1994; Marshall, 1994). Advertising agencies were also experiencing intensive competition from companies known as "media independents" in the researching, planning, and buying of media space as clients became more prepared to separate the media buying services, which they required, from the other core services, which they bought from agencies. This move by clients had profound consequences. As Mike Yershon noted, whereas in 1973 only the U.S. giant Unilever and a handful of other clients used media independents and did not, as a consequence, integrate their planning, buying, and creative work under one roof, by the early 1990s over half of all media buying was carried out at a different location from where the creative work was developed (Read, 1993). Many of the blue-chip clients were centrally involved in this process. In the year before May 1994, for example, £200 million worth of media business was centralized into media independents by Boots, British Gas, RHM, and Cadbury ("The Relationship Crisis," 1994).

Both forms of competition—but most clearly that coming from media independents—were related to a further significant set of external developments bearing on agency practice. These derived from changes in advertising media. Between 1988 and 1998 there was an acceleration of the process of media proliferation that had begun in the early 1980s. At the root of this was the policy-driven opening up of media markets—especially television markets—and the emergence of new media technologies and delivery systems. The scale of these developments was phenomenal. For example, to take the British example, in 1980 there was just one commercial television channel providing 88 minutes of advertising time a day. By 1993, this had risen to 15 channels offering in excess of 1,500 minutes each day. Similarly, in 1980, there were just 16 national newspapers and 1,400 consumer magazines. By 1992, this had become 23 newspapers, each typically heavily sectionalized, and 2,300 consumer magazines. Commercial radio stations had also risen from 26 in 1980 to 125 in 1992 (Read, 1993). Associated with this process of media proliferation was the rising cost of traditional advertising media, particularly television airtime. This rise in the cost of placing ads was the product of the concentration of media ownership, especially in the television industry. By 1997, for example, Carlton, Granada, and United controlled 70% of network TV sales in Britain, while on a global scale News Corporation, Time Warner, Seagram, Disney, and Viacom operated from their bases in the United States as an effective oligopoly with enormous power over media pricing (WPP, 1997). This concentration of ownership was itself a major spur to the growth of the large media buying groups that had increasingly taken over this function from full-service agencies. The size of these media buyers—which included companies like Zenith and Media Partnership—enabled them to generate lower media costs for clients in their negotiations with media owners.

The proliferation in the early 21st century of online media has continued to pose challenges to established agency structures and practices. Not only has it hastened the end of the commission system and the need for agencies to be "media agnostic" when it comes to the genesis of marketing solutions for their clients, but it has also clearly pushed the relative decline of the television commercial as the preeminent marketing form. Figures for expenditure on the "old" and "new" media give a sense of this shift. In the year 2005–2006, TV advertising expenditure in the United Kingdom, for example, fell by 4%, while revenue from online media increased by 45% in the same period (Bilton, 2009). TV, however, continues to remain an influential advertising medium. In 2006, expenditure on display adverting on TV in the United Kingdom stood at £3,929 million, far outstripping the £460 million spent on display advertising on the Internet (Fletcher, 2009). *Campaign,* the leading British advertising trade paper, made Cadbury's "Gorilla" television ad its campaign of the year in 2007. In a sign of the times, however, part of the success of the TV ad sprung from a clever viral campaign on YouTube that gave initial momentum to the ad. The absurd style of the commercial also echoed the quirky, home postings familiar on YouTube.

Reinventing the Agency

Addressing these heterogeneous challenges and, in particular, protecting the status of agencies as the preeminent suppliers of advertising and marketing services have been and continue to be a pressing concern for the major players in the advertising industry. In the mid- to late 1990s, it led, amongst other things, to a sustained reflection on the commercial role of advertising agencies. Some of the influential players in the London-based industry, for example, sought to reorder the kinds of commercial expertise that they offered clients and the way they conducted the business of advertising. Two influential agencies—Bartle Bogle Hegarty (BBH) and Howell Henry Chaldecott Lury (HHCL)—can serve as an illustration of this.

BBH had been formed in 1982 and was one of the most successful and strongly branded advertising agencies in Britain. It quickly gained a reputation as the producer of stylish advertising, particularly for its first and most significant client, Levi Strauss. By the mid-1990s the agency had matured into a significant player within the British advertising industry with a range of subsidiary companies and an office in Singapore. As the agency grew, it sought to address the challenges facing it and the agency sector more generally. Looming large in this was the foregrounding of its role as a trusted business partner to clients. In elaborating this vision, BBH claimed that the way agencies were often seen—and saw themselves—prevented them from fully developing this more expanded role. The agency argued that rather than positioning themselves as service providers, advertising agencies ought to become "specialist sources of creative excellence" (Bartle Bogle Hegarty [BBH], 1996, p. 3).

Part of the problem in effecting change for BBH stemmed from the way agencies charged for their services. Two forms of remuneration dominated within the industry. As I have already noted, these were commission-based and fee-based payments. Although media commission remained, in the mid-1990s, an important source of income for many agencies, income derived from fees and retainers paid by clients came close to matching it (see, inter alia, Hatfield, 1995; "Is Commission Really the Solution for Agencies?" 1995; Marshall, 1993). BBH, in line with a number of other agencies, sought to develop a form of financial compensation that better reflected the role agencies could play as all-around business partners to clients. To this end, it proposed the idea of the "agency salary":

> Our approach is simple. View the agency as a person. The clients who appoint BBH want the agency to become part of the team and to work in a spirit of real partnership. . . . Salary is not just a semantic re-expression of fees. It represents a different attitude to the issue. If an agency is to become part of the team and operate as a strategic partner, it cannot do so simply via the production and placement of the advertising. It must be able to contribute on a broader front, to take *initiatives outside the specific sphere of advertising development* [emphasis added]. . . . We are not seeking to pad out our income. We simply seek a method of remuneration that reflects the scale of our input, the quality of our output and allows us to deliver in breadth to the best of our ability. The fact that one agency may cost more or less than another does not, of itself, make a statement about which offers better value. (BBH, 1996, pp. 9–10)

BBH's advocacy of the idea of the agency salary was about more than the technical matter of how agencies were paid. As its powerful statement testifies, in focusing on the methods of agency remuneration it was seeking to dramatize its vision of agencies as trusted business partners able to operate across the full range of their clients' business and commercial needs. At the same time, the focus on financial compensation offered a way of institutionalizing this kind of relationship with clients through the financial contracts both parties entered into. The move formed part of BBH's ambition to become what it elsewhere called the "co-custodian" of its clients' brands and to be able to act as a trusted confidante over wider areas of a client's business, including product development. The agency had some success in pursuing this new kind of relationship and, in the case of its long-term client Levi Strauss, was represented on the board of the client company.

In pressing for this kind of influence, BBH made much of the distinctive expertise that it could bring to the client's commercial needs—expertise that set it apart from other agencies and, importantly, competitors such as management consultants. At the heart of this, as one of the earlier quotes indicated, was its provision of creativity and "creative excellence" (see also Chris Bilton, in this volume). What the agency understood by these terms, however, was something rather specific. On the one hand, BBH invoked it to connote the broad range of expertise and know-how that it could offer clients. Central to this was its ability to provide "creative original thinking" (Bogle, 1993, p. 1). This was thinking that could unlock the marketing and wider business problems of a client and pave the way for effective advertising or some other remedial strategy. Creativity and creative excellence, on the other hand, also encompassed the representational techniques that were evident in the press and television advertising that it produced for clients. In this latter sense, the agency saw itself as continuing the "creative revolution" in British advertising. The agency's reputation had been built on the stylish and highly aestheticized press, cinema, and television advertising that it produced in the mid-1980s. Defending this legacy and its particular ordering of the expertise that agencies could deliver was integral to how BBH understood creativity and creative excellence in the mid-1990s. In fact, it was this dual emphasis on creative *execution* and its capacity to generate creative *ideas* and *thinking* that characterized BBH's deployment of the rubric of creativity. The agency invoked these definitions at every opportunity, drawing attention, for example in a case study prepared for the Department of Trade and Industry (DTI), to its success at being voted international agency of the year for 3 consecutive years at the International Advertising Festival at Cannes for its creative work. Through moves of this kind, BBH positioned itself as close to the heart of the United Kingdom's reputation as a center of creative excellence.

BBH's concern to position itself as a supplier of creativity to clients and as an organization able to bring this expertise to bear across the full range of a client's business needs—not just press and television advertising—was closely shared by HHCL. HHCL had been formed in 1987 at the height of the boom in advertising expenditure of the mid- to late 1980s. By the mid-1990s the agency had achieved significant growth on the back of the steady accumulation of new business and was ranked 23rd in the listings of agencies in Britain based on billings. By the time it was named agency of the year for the second time in 1995 in the annual *Campaign* awards, it was the fastest growing of the top 50 agencies and had established itself as one of the most high-profile agencies in Britain. HHCL placed great emphasis on its iconoclastic approach to advertising and marketing and was self-consciously avant-garde. A central aspect of this concerned its ambition to operate, like BBH, not only in the area of advertising but across the broader field of marketing and communications. It christened this approach, with characteristic aplomb, "3-D marketing." The aim was to approach a client's marketing needs by developing a dialogue with target consumers across different media. As the agency put it,

> [3-D marketing] expands customer relationships into a series of interlocking experiences. The aim is no longer to align several "flat" media but to create an experience that actively links the customer, the media and the brand. In other words, the "brand experience" will exist beyond a set of mental constituents presented on flat media. (Howell Henry Chaldecott Lury [HHCL], 1994, p. 27)

The agency cited the example of Niketown, the U.S. company Nike's retailing emporium, as a good example of this kind of 3-D marketing where "shoes are just one expression of Nike-ness—one ride at the fair" (HHCL, 1994, p. 21). This conception of 3-D marketing went hand in hand with the agency's avant-gardism. On its Web site (hhcl.com, now defunct), HHCL described itself as being "particularly good at working with clients who need to *radically* [emphasis in the original] change the way they communicate with their various audiences." Elsewhere on the Web site it claimed to be "an innovative . . . marketing and communications agency, responsible for a number of high impact campaigns which have tested the boundaries of the acceptable in advertising." The agency's work was certainly distinctive. With widely praised campaigns for Britvic's Tango soft drink, the Automobile Association (AA), Mazda, and Golden Wonder, the agency developed a style of communication that was direct and highly cognizant of the conventions of marketing. This led, for example, in the case of its work for Tango to a campaign that cast the company's marketing director warning consumers to be on the lookout for "fake" Tango ads and a television commercial for Mazda that required the viewer to record the ad and then play it back frame by frame in order to see its message (*Campaign*, 1995).

HHCL's ambition to innovate in the work that it produced was also evident in the range of promotional techniques that it deployed. This linked up with its concern to operate across a broad front on behalf of the client. One dimension of this concerned its commitment to what it called "media creativity." This referred to the innovative and inventive use of advertising media. HHCL's emphasis on media creativity formed part of its vision of 3-D marketing and was allied to the agency's positioning of itself as a strategic partner to clients, one that was able to operate across different media and without a bias to the traditional media of press, television, and posters (Hatfield, 1994). This emphasis on the need to think beyond the limits of traditional advertising was integral to HHCL's accenting of the idea of creativity toward that of innovative and original thinking and strategy. Champions of the agency in the trade press often sought to draw a distinction between HHCL's strategy and that pursued by a more established agency like BBH. While differences certainly existed in the style of advertising and promotion produced by BBH and HHCL, commentators were guilty of overplaying them. Both agencies embraced a broader view of the marketing and service role that agencies should play as they sought to position themselves as trusted business partners to clients, and both were committed, as a consequence, to an approach to solving their clients' business needs that shifted press and television advertising out of its previously ensured centrality to the business of advertising.

Differences, however, did appear in the way the two agencies sought to institutionalize this consultancy model within their respective organizational processes. In the late 1990s, both HHCL and BBH embarked on major programs of organizational change in order to enable them to deliver the kind of service—and creativity—that their respective visions of the ad agency demanded. Central to these programs of organizational restructuring was the ambition to develop more dynamic and "creative" ways of working. Rather late in the day compared to many of the client companies they worked with, BBH and HHCL attempted to reorganize themselves along more entrepreneurial lines.

With characteristic bravura, HHCL announced the changes that it was making to its ways of working by rebranding itself as a marketing and communications company. The agency even produced a publication—titled *Marketing at a Point of Change*—to promote and give intellectual gloss to these changes (HHCL, 1994). Running through its slick language were pointers to the central organizational changes HHCL introduced in order to deliver this dynamic approach to working with clients. These were multifunctional or multidisciplinary project teams that were assigned to separate client accounts. This restructuring marked a significant change from the way agencies had conventionally been organized. The organizational model of the service agency had typically been a departmentalized and functionally driven structure. The core jobs central to the development of advertising and the servicing of clients were organized into discrete departments: an account handling department, an account planning department, a creative department, and a media buying and planning department. Overseen by the traffic department, the process of creating work for clients formally moved from department to department toward the final finished ad. In this sense, the project teams that the agency introduced aimed to restructure established ways of working in order to generate a more creative and innovative environment.

Bringing these new ways of working to life prompted HHCL to transform the built environment of the agency. After initially considering moving from its Kent House premises behind Oxford Street in London's West End, the agency instead hired a consultant to help it restructure the interior of the building. At the heart of the redesign was the principle of "romping" or "hot desking" in which staff were given a mobile phone and a locker and encouraged to occupy a range of spaces depending on what they were working on, rather than their own permanent desk. To this end, the interior of Kent House was remade as a "diversity of environments."

What was particularly striking about these moves is that they sent out a strong signal about how the agency saw all its key workers—not just art directors and copywriters—as the potential source of innovation and creativity. Project team working, in this sense, sought to liberate the creativity of all the core practitioners involved in the advertising process.

BBH took a similar approach to matters of organizational change and the pursuit of ways of working that could improve the conditions within the agency under which advertising work was generated. The agency hired the industrial psychologists Nicholson McBride in 1993 to help it bring about these changes. At the heart of the restructuring that followed this consultation was the introduction of cross-disciplinary project teams. BBH's decision to restructure itself along these lines, however, introduced a significant—and highly symbolic—modification to the project team structure, when the teams were established in May 1996. In setting them up, BBH explicitly excluded art directors and copywriters—the advertising creatives—from them. In doing so, the agency maintained the integrity of the creative department and the established system of pairing art directors and copywriters. This system of creative teams (a copywriter paired with an art director) had been pioneered by the New York agency Doyle Dane Bernbach (DDB) in the 1940s and quickly became the norm in Britain by the early 1960s. The pairing of art directors and copywriters was unique to creative jobs and was one of the features that gave these jobs their distinctive character. Explaining the logic behind maintaining the system of creative teams and the integrity of the creative department, Martin Smith, BBH's chairman, suggested "advertising ideas are usually the product of 2 creative people, a closed door and a great brief. Everything else we add to that very simple concept is done to help the creative team perform its task" (Richmond, 1993, p. 31). This defense of the separateness of creative teams within the organization was centrally tied in with BBH's vision of itself as a creative agency and the producer of creative advertising. Thus, while BBH attempted to "free up" the creativity of all its core workers, it retained a sense that creatives were a special case and the privileged source of creativity. This was different, as we have seen, from HHCL's approach. It attempted to give scope to other practitioners to become the source of creativity more broadly conceived and to erode the division of labor within the creative development process—though, it should be noted, HHCL still effectively paired creative teams within this more open structure. These different approaches carried discrete messages about the relative status and standing of creatives in each agency and were intimately bound up with the broader understanding of the kinds of commercial expertise each agency primarily saw itself as supplying.

Conclusion

The programs of organizational change established by BBH and HHCL in the late 1990s represented ambitious attempts to reinvent the advertising agency in an era when the institutional conditions that had underpinned its commercial viability and raison d'etre had effectively disappeared. In more recent years, as I noted earlier, newer agencies and communications consultants have deepened and extended this process of change. But they have done so in ways that owe a great deal to the innovations pioneered by agencies like BBH and HHCL in the late 1990s. These developments have effectively hollowed out the full-service agency, leaving advertising businesses to become less the sprawling octopuses of old and more spiders at the center of a network of experts, consultants, and suppliers of media, marketing, and creative services (see also Geert Lovink and Ned Rossiter, in this volume). There is an irony in all these developments, however—an irony in which we might see the ruse of history at work. Funky contemporary advertising businesses like Naked, Mother, and Tomato seek to be more than the mere suppliers of services for clients and to become strategic partners, integrated into the heart of their clients' businesses. While this might no longer involve being the close service providers of old, such a vision contains echoes of the ambition of the full-service agency of the mid- to late 20th century to be more than a supplier of ads and to be integrated into the "life-world" of its client.

References

Bartle Bogle Hegarty. (1996). *Business practice.* London, England: Author.

Bilton, C. (2009). Relocating creativity in advertising: From aesthetic specialisation to strategic innovation? In A. Pratt & P. Jeffcut (Eds.), *Creativity, innovation and the cultural economy* (pp. 23–40). London, England: Routledge.

Bogle, N. (1993, April). *IPA Newsfile,* p. 1.

Campaign. (1995, November 6). P. 17.

Client service hangs on dedication to creativity [Leader article]. (1994, July 15). *Campaign,* p. 29.

Fletcher, W. (2009). *Powers of persuasion.* Oxford, England: Oxford University Press.

Hatfield, S. (1994, November 4). Howell Henry puts good ideas before pretty execution. *Campaign,* p. 11.

Hatfield, S. (1995, January 20). Payment by commission is fair to clients and agencies. *Campaign,* p. 25.

Howell Henry Chaldecott Lury. (1994). *Marketing at a point of change.* London, England: Author, IPA Newsfile.

Is commission really the solution for agencies? [Leader article]. (1995, June 23). *Campaign,* p. 12.

Marshall, C. (1993, August 13). The latest state of play. *Campaign,* pp. 22–23.

Marshall, C. (1994, December 2). The clash of the gurus. *Campaign,* pp. 36–37.

Read, A. (1993, June 4). Ad clout or full-service? *Campaign,* pp. 32–33.

The relationship crisis [Leader article]. (1994, May 13). *Campaign,* pp. 30–31.

Richmond, S. (1993, June 25). Ad agencies business practices come up for trial. *Campaign,* p. 31.

WPP. (1997). *Annual report.* London, England: Author.

18 Advertising Management and Professional Identity in the Digital Age

*Chris Hackley and
Amy Rungpaka Tiwsakul*

Employment in advertising, like other creative and cultural industries, has typically been characterized by a reliance on informal networks, collegiate styles of management, and the use of project-based work teams (Deuze, 2007; Smith & McKinlay, 2009). An order of insecurity permeates careers in the field. This is particularly so for those charged with producing the creative content, the "creatives" (Hackley & Kover, 2007). Reputations depend on building credibility, often over a long period of time, through unpaid or low-paid work that helps the aspiring creative build up a book of work and gain entry into the inner circle of networked advertising professionals (McLeod, O'Donohoe, & Townley, 2009).

In spite of the difficulties of gaining entry to the advertising field, it remains attractive for many who feel that it is invested with social capital (Schwarzkopf, 2008). But the industry is facing a series of challenges that, some commentators argue, could spell the end for advertising as we know it, with unpredictable implications for professional identity and the labor process. It may be premature to call it the end of advertising—after all, the advertising business has always had to utilize changes in media technology as opportunities, rather than threats. The difference today is that it is facing challenges to its working practices on several fronts. Developments in digital and mobile communication technology for advertising have to be understood through a prism of increasing media concentration, fragmenting media audiences, and the rise of integrated marketing communications. The latter development, driven by holistic brand logic, in concert with the burgeoning possibilities for advertising of Web 2.0 and mobile, is blurring the distinction between promotion disciplines (Hackley, 2009a).

This is creating a convergence mentality in two senses. Media technology is moving toward convergence of devices so that all media engagement could happen through one, mobile, WAP-enabled device in the not-too-distant future (Sharma, Herzog, & Melfi, 2008). Concomitant with this, advertising professionals are under pressure to devise content solutions that fit the convergence landscape. This demands not only creative and strategic ability but also digital literacy across a range of media platforms. Therefore, professional networks have to range beyond their immediate discipline so individuals can, when required, supplement their own skills by calling on those of other specialists. In turn, this is pushing more agencies into project-based working since it is harder than ever for them to maintain the creative and technical skills in-house that are needed to deliver integrated, multiplatform campaigns.

In this short chapter we will outline some contradictions around the notion of professional identity in the context of changes in the advertising industry. We will suggest that the task of crafting a sense of professional identity in the field is being shaped by new technology and working practices. Aspiring advertising professionals have to respond to this complex working environment by making use of wider and deeper networks and creating a digital presence (see also Geert Lovink and Ned Rossiter, in this volume).

We acknowledge that there is a risk of conflating the career experiences and trajectories of creatives with those of account planners and account management. Nevertheless, for the purposes of this piece we feel this is justified in order to engage more generally with the management of the creative advertising development process. In addition, we feel that some of the trends apparent in the field are impacting all categories of worker, though perhaps not equally. None are immune to the effects of increased outsourcing and project-based working. What is more, the boundary lines between marketing communication disciplines are becoming increasingly blurred. Account executives or planners are sometimes directly or indirectly responsible for the creative content of campaigns (Hackley, 2003b; Peng & Hackley, 2007). With greater pressure for integrated media solutions there is more stress on all advertising professionals being able to think both strategically and creatively. One London agency, Mother,[1] has responded to this trend by flattening its structure and taking out the account management layer—it claims that all its account team members are creative (see also Sean Nixon, in this volume). This remains an exception but reflects a move toward more integrated, multiskilled, and flexible account teams.

Professional Identity in Advertising

A sense of identity generally is negotiated through an "internal-external dialectic" (Jenkins, 2004, p. 18). Who we say we are requires validation from external sources. These might consist of the standards, qualifications, values, and rewards that are constructed by professions to exclude outsiders and affirm hierarchies of membership. Such professional structures can obtain in creative occupations such as journalism, acting, and screenwriting, which have a tradition of strong unionization (McKinlay & Smith, 2009), as well as in traditional manufacturing or service production. In addition, there are the discourses that obtain in the wider world about that profession. Being a surgeon, for example, would probably elicit greater respect and social status than being an advertising professional.

In advertising, there are no enforced entry qualifications, and union power is low or zero. What is more, the legitimacy of each of the three main crafts of advertising—creative, planning, and account management—is often openly challenged on a day-to-day basis within agencies (Hackley, 2003a). The roles coexist in a state that could be described as creative tension, though some would describe it as permanent dysfunction. The three crafts bring very different sets of implicit assumptions to the work, and this sets them in opposition to each other in a battle for control over the creative advertising development process (Hackley, 2003c; Kover, 1995; Kover & Goldberg, 1995).

For the world at large, an advertising man (there are many highly successful and accomplished advertising women, but it is a male-dominated business) occupies a dubious status. Advertising is a form of communication that is regarded simultaneously with awe and contempt (Cook, 2001). Its practitioners are often regarded in a similar light. It is blamed for all manner of social evils, from anorexia to obesity, from alcohol-related illness and street disorder to general moral decay and the rise of a material lifestyle (Hackley, 2010). Yet we betray our fascination of it with television shows and Web sites devoted to the funniest, most shocking, or most beautiful advertisements. The most successful campaigns are credited with changing attitudes, creating cultural icons, and sometimes revolutionizing entire industries. The legendary Levi's 501 campaign by Bartle Bogle Hegarty in the 1980s, for example, was said to have increased sales in the denim jeans market as a whole by 600% (Hackley, 2005).

Stereotypical representations of the advertising industry in popular culture reflect its ambivalent cultural status. As Hackley and Kover (2007) point out, in movies such as *Mr. Blandings Builds His Dream House* and *What Women Want* the advertising professional is wealthy, privileged, and also maverick, cynical, and narcissistic. In *How to Get Ahead in Advertising* the central character is self-obsessed, insecure, mendacious, and half-crazy. In the current top-rated U.S. TV series *Two and a Half Men* the main character, played by Charlie Sheen, is shallow, hedonistic, materialistic, and selfish. He makes his living writing advertising jingles. As is typical for the advertising industry in the United States and the United Kingdom, Sheen's character is White, educated, and privileged. The planning and executive roles in advertising have, traditionally, often been taken by graduates of elite universities (Hackley, 2000), but this is not so true of the creative roles. McLeod et al. (2009) found that it is common for advertising creatives to describe their own origins as working or lower-middle class. Advertising offered a step up in class, based on talent.

The origins of advertising's social capital are difficult to pin down. No doubt the rapid growth in advertising revenue in the postwar period, as television ownership and viewing figures soared, helped. It gave the industry the scent of money and provided the resources for the much-celebrated creative revolution that shifted advertising from the realm of marketing to the fringes of modern art. Important advertising agencies such as Crawford's of London championed the idea that advertising creativity could contribute to the cultural economy (Schwarzkopf, 2008).

Because the resources available for constructing professional identity in advertising are so slim, workers have to construct their sense of professional identity anew every day. As one professional said, "We are only as good as the last thing we did . . ." (Deuze, 2007, p. 130). Advertising creatives lack a backstop of professional legitimacy so that even if they earn credit for their performance in one campaign, they have to reproduce that in the next. As one expressed, "I have to start from scratch every morning" (Hackley & Kover, 2007, p. 66). This lends a particular insecurity to the profession. Writers and artists can assert their identity as writers or artists even if they have never sold a piece of work. If they have had one success, it offers a lasting testament to their craft skills. When reputations are made in advertising they can confer legendary status on an individual, with wealth and job security to match. But these individuals are very few, and for the great majority, reputation has to be earned with each new job.

Nixon and Crewe (2004) refer to what they call "social splitting" (p. 143) to describe the way that creatives in advertising have to reconcile the contradiction of the cool, urbane image some outsiders hold of being an advertising creative and the intense rivalry and ruthless competition that obtains inside the industry. The situation is even more complex than this, since, as we have noted, advertising professionals can be regarded very negatively indeed. Attacks on advertising (see discussion in Hackley, 2007) reflected another perception of the industry as the science and art of manipulation, with a hidden oligarchy of highly educated and skilled technocrats pulling the strings of consumer behavior. This ambivalence, of course, might enhance its attractiveness to those who see a certain antiestablishment side to the advertising business.

Advertising Management and Working Practices

The working practices of advertising are clearly an important influence in labor processes in the industry. Advertising agencies, to differing degrees, have well-deserved reputations for being unorthodox, collegiate, and informal in the way work is organized and controlled, at least in comparison to labor processes in more formally bureaucratic industries. There can be considerable differences in emphasis between agencies, but the general approach in advertising agencies has changed remarkably little in 40 years (Feldwick, 2009) and is quite similar around the world (Hackley & Tiwsakul, 2008). The license to be creative is an important component shaping the character of advertising work, and the legitimacy of creativity in advertising is disputed not only within agencies but also in the wider industry. Today, advertising is a small, highly concentrated industry in which creative control over campaigns is contested between local agencies and the global headquarters of brand marketing corporations (Deuze, 2007).

Key ideas about the management of advertising have inscribed the creative component within the process model for advertising development. The first school of advertising copywriting was established at the Lord and Thomas agency in the early part of the 1900s under industry pioneer Albert D. Lasker. Lasker was inspired by the ideas of one of his employees, John E. Kennedy (1904), who argued that advertising was "salesmanship in print." As Hackley (2010; citing McDonald & Scott, 2007) discusses, ideas about advertising effectiveness, advertising research, and creativity were popularized by famous practitioners in the 1960s, such as Bill Bernbach's groundbreaking ideas on advertising creativity, David Ogilvy's notion of "brand personality," and Leo Burnett's use of dramatic realism. An influential idea about managing the advertising development process, called account planning (Hackley, 2003a), became well known in the 1960s and formalized the role of creativity as part of the value-creating process in advertising. Account planning may have preserved the existence of the creative agency in the face of pressures for more instrumental and accountable business communication (Feldwick, 2009, citing Fletcher, 2008). As a counterpoint to the creative side of the process and the craft skills of fine and graphic art, copywriting, music, and scriptwriting that go with that, a scientific vocabulary of marketing and consumer research and copy-testing techniques also emerged. These had to be mastered by agency professionals who became social researchers in the service of advertising (Hackley, 2002). The creative and scientific sides of advertising are perpetually in conflict, but they also act to mutually reinforce conventional working approaches.

_____ Concluding Comment: Digital Identities?

Individuals in creative industries have to utilize informal networks in order to learn about the job, build a reputation, and hear about work. Today, changes in the structure, technology, and working practices of the advertising industry mean that the networks have to be wider and deeper in order to gain access to a greater variety of skills. One implication of this is that individuals are utilizing Web 2.0 and mobile in a mirror image of the trend for agencies to market themselves at a personal level through interactive technology. It is already accepted in marketing that blogging is an effective strategy for gaining new business (Hackley, 2009b); in fact, there is a view in the advertising industry that blogging is the most important new business mechanism. Agencies offer advice, "think piece" articles, and case histories on their Web sites, sometimes with an entry point for hosted discussion. In this way, the traditional method of pitching for new business on the basis of a client brief is increasingly bypassed as potential clients can look at the agency's work and discuss projects over the Internet without any commitment.

Now, individuals as well as agencies are proving their digital credentials and creating an integrated shop window, networking forum, and new business pitch by setting up their own blog; http://joeadamfry.com/ is a recent example. This Web site showcases the skills of a talented young PhD student who is also a consultant in digital and creative advertising. The site acts as a business card, a shop window, and a permanent tool for dialogue with any interested party. It reflects a wider trend for the digitization of networking. Individual strategies for negotiating professional identity in advertising, then, are taking on some of the character of changes in the industry itself. While the digital revolution might be throwing advertising labor processes into a flux, it might also offer some solutions for entrepreneurial individuals.

References

Cook, G. (2001). *The discourse of advertising.* London, England: Routledge.

Deuze, M. (2007). *Media work.* Cambridge, England: Polity Press.

Feldwick, P. (2009). Account planning: Back to the future. *Market Leader, Quarter* 2(March), 55–57.

Fletcher, W. (2008). *Powers of persuasion.* New York, NY: Oxford University Press.

Hackley, C. (2000). Silent running: Tacit, discursive and psychological aspects of management in a top UK advertising agency. *British Journal of Management, 11*(3), 239–254.

Hackley, C. (2002). The panoptic role of advertising agencies in the production of consumer culture. *Consumption, Markets and Culture, 5*(3), 211–229.

Hackley, C. (2003a). Account planning: Current agency perspectives on an advertising enigma. *Journal of Advertising Research, 43*(2), 235–246.

Hackley, C. (2003b). From consumer insight to advertising strategy: The account planner's integrative role in creative advertising development. *Marketing Intelligence and Planning, 21*(7), 446–452.

Hackley, C. (2003c). How divergent beliefs cause account team conflict. *International Journal of Advertising, 22*(3), 313–332.

Hackley, C. (2005). *Advertising and promotion: Communicating brands.* London, England: Sage.

Hackley, C. (2007). Marketing psychology and the hidden persuaders. *Psychologist, 20*(8), 488–490.

Hackley, C. (2009a). *Advertising and promotion in integrated marketing communication* (2nd ed.). London, England: Sage.

Hackley, C. (2009b). *Marketing: A critical introduction.* London, England: Sage.

Hackley, C. (2010). Theorizing advertising: Managerial, scientific and cultural approaches. In P. MacLaran, M. Saren, & M. Tadajewski (Eds.), *Handbook of marketing theory* (pp. 89–108). London, England: Sage.

Hackley, C., & Kover, A. J. (2007). The trouble with creatives: Negotiating creative identity in advertising agencies. *International Journal of Advertising, 26*(1), 63–78.

Hackley, C., & Tiwsakul, A. R. (2008). Comparative management practices in international advertising agencies in the UK, Thailand and the USA. In C. Smith, B. McSweeney, & R. Fitzgerald (Eds.), *Remaking management: Between global and local* (pp. 586–626). Cambridge, England: Cambridge University Press.

Jenkins, R. (2004). *Social identity* (2nd ed.). London, England: Routledge.

Kennedy, J. E. (1904). *Reason why advertising plus intensive advertising.* TWI Press.

Kover, A. (1995). Copywriters' implicit theories of communication: An exploration. *Journal of Consumer Research, 21*(4), 596–611.

Kover, A. J., & Goldberg, S. M. (1995). The games copywriters play: Conflict, quasi-control, a new proposal. *Journal of Advertising Research, 35*(4), 52–68.

McDonald, C., & Scott, J. (2007). A brief history of advertising. In G. Tellis & T. Ambler (Eds.), *The Sage handbook of advertising* (pp. 17–34). London, England: Sage.

McKinlay, A., & Smith, C. (2009). *Creative labour: Working in the creative industries.* Basingstoke, England: Palgrave Macmillan.

McLeod, C., O'Donohoe, S., & Townley, B. (2009). The elephant in the room? Class and creative careers. *Human Relations, 62*(7), 1011–1039.

Nixon, S., & Crewe, B. (2004). Pleasure at work? Gender, consumption and work-based identities in the cultural industries. *Consumption, Markets and Culture, 7*(2), 129–147.

Peng, N., & Hackley, C. (2007). Political marketing communications planning in the UK and Taiwan: Comparative insights from leading practitioners. *Marketing Intelligence and Planning, 25*(5), 483–498.

Schwarzkopf, S. (2008). Creativity, capital and tacit knowledge: The Crawford agency and British advertising in the interwar years. *Journal of Cultural Economy, 1*(2), 181–197.

Sharma, C., Herzog, J., & Melfi, V. (2008). *Mobile advertising: Supercharge your brand in the exploding wireless market.* Hoboken, NJ: Wiley.

Smith, C., & McKinlay, A. (2009). Creative labour, content, contract and control. In A. McKinlay & C. Smith (Eds.), *Creative labour: Working in the creative industries* (pp. 29–50). Basingstoke, England: Palgrave Macmillan.

Note

1. http://www.motherlondon.com/

19 Managing Global Public Relations in the New Media Environment

Marina Vujnovic and Dean Kruckeberg

More than a decade ago, in his essay "A Manifesto for the Fast World" (1999), which Thomas L. Friedman had adapted from his subsequent book, *The Lexus and the Olive Tree: Understanding Globalization* (1999), this highly respected *New York Times* columnist described globalization as the new international system that succeeded the Cold War. But for at least a decade preceding Friedman's manifesto, globalization had become one of the most popular and challenging areas of inquiry for journalists, economists, political pundits, and scholars alike. Today, *globalization* has become a household word throughout much of the world, with elaborate discourses both from the political left and right and from those ranging from unbridled proponents, who enthusiastically extol the perceived benefits of globalization, to vehement antiglobalization activists, who direly warn society of the supposed cataclysmic consequences of this phenomenon.

Everyone, however, seems to agree that globalization is drastically changing our world, which is being ridden by the complexities of oftentimes contradictory processes of integration and disintegration—resulting in fundamental power shifts, both on the macro level of nation-states and on the micro level of local geographic communities.

This chapter focuses not on systemic global changes but rather on a major driving force of these globalization processes—that is, rapidly developing communication technologies that (a) allow and encourage the increasing compression of time and space, (b) make global communication unprohibitively inexpensive, (c) overwhelm people with information, and (d) intermingle traditional vetted sources of information with user-generated content (UGC) that may be suspect in source credibility and nontransparent regarding agenda. Particularly the Internet and its escalating use throughout the world has allowed for previously unimaginable opportunities for global networking. L'Etang (2008) argues that public relations itself partakes in initiating and stimulating globalization processes. These communicative opportunities for media professionals (including public relations practitioners in particular) are taken into consideration by media scholars (see in particular Lucy Küng, and Annet Aris, in this volume). The migration of people to online environments develops social interactions that have caught the attention of media practitioners who see value in reaching out to stakeholders with the intent to build communities. The importance of interactions online is increasingly recognized; as Deuze (2007) observes, "What people are doing online is a good indicator of how everyday life for a working professional (or those seeking to become one) in today's new capitalist economy has changed" (p. vii).

The advent of global public relations networks is a case in point. Since the late 1990s, globalization has been a major area of study among public relations scholars and has gotten increasing attention from practitioners. Although globalization is theorized primarily in terms of the consequences for public relations practice internationally, such theory building is oftentimes focused on globalization's impact on multinational corporations, and on public relations agencies that are serving growing numbers of international clients. Both scholars and public relations practitioners initiated discussions about the appropriate management of public relations in the global arena (Moreley, 2009; Sriramesh & Vercic, 2009). No consensus has been found on what would constitute appropriate management strategies in a globalized world context, and we want to add to that debate by exploring global networking communicative possibilities through new social media. We submit that this is an exciting time that affords unique opportunities for building networks and alliances in (the management of) public relations in international organizations.

But first, it is necessary to reexamine the concept of public(s). This concept has been both a means to advance public relations theory and practice and a point of recalcitrance, especially in today's new media environment. New media, and social networking in particular, have a unique potential to narrow the participatory gap that historically has existed within the concept of the "stakeholder" that has dominated public relations theory and practice for decades.

The Public(s) in the Internet and Social Networking Era

The term *stakeholder* is popular in the literature of several disciplines and professional areas as a way to define groups that have a stake in an organization and are critical for that organization's existence. Among the first to define stakeholders as individuals or groups that can affect or be affected by the organization was Freeman (1984). Grunig and Hunt (1984) also dealt with definitions of stakeholders and publics, including those whom they considered "nonpublics." In public relations, it is believed that stakeholders are created as a result of organizational activities and that groups can be mainly narrowed down to local communities and local organizations, including media (Werther & Chandler, 2006).

Although the term *stakeholder* has been useful in building public relations theory, it has serious weaknesses (Ihlen, 2008). These weaknesses have been accentuated with the rise of a networked "global community" in which it has become increasingly impossible to predict how and where public(s) will form and organize. At the same time, organizations themselves are networking with diverse publics and creating "virtual communities," which we term *private publics* that could exist as compasses for organizational activities in the global environment.

The conceptualization of public(s) as a stakeholder in public relations has had a long trajectory, as it was co-opted from other disciplines and originally from John Dewey. An early public relations textbook (Cutlip & Center, 1971) acknowledges this debt, noting both the concept's use as a plural (i.e., multiple publics) in public relations at that time and the term's genesis as both a singular and a plural noun. The authors defined *public* as a group of individuals tied together by some common bond of interest who share a sense of togetherness. John Dewey, in his 1927 work *The Public and Its Problems*, defined *public* as "a group of individuals who together are affected by a particular action or idea. Thus, each issue or problem creates its own public" (p. 128).

Public relations may have taken liberties with Dewey's concept. Although Cutlip and Center (1971) acknowledged the presence of a "general public," most contemporary public relations literature—in an effort to make public relations strategic—says this public does not even exist; that is, Newsom, Turk, and Kruckeberg (2010) note that there is no "general public." Grunig and his colleagues (e.g., Dozier, 1995) further segmented *public* into a non-public that is not affected by an organization's behavior, a latent public that is affected but not aware of this, an aware public, and an active public whose members organize to do something about their common problem.

Grunig and colleagues' original explication of "publics" has not been without criticism, albeit primarily because of their preoccupation with "strategic" publics. Within such a strategic frame, two macro worldviews have influenced the perception of the relative importance of publics—that is, *the world is good,* and thus the organization should seek harmony with its publics, and *the world is evil,* and therefore the organization must be protected from these inherently threatening and potentially harmful publics. Overwhelmingly, the mainstream contemporary public relations literature is based on the second worldview. This implicitly suggests a lack of concern for social responsibility, as "non-publics" tend to be dismissed as being of no concern to the organization because they apparently do not threaten or intend to harm the organization.

We argue that an organization's responsibility extends beyond these *strategic publics,* noting that an organization should view society as a larger social system in which the organization can coexist and seek harmony. An "organic theory" of public relations is needed that recognizes the complexity of contemporary global society and the threats to society at this macro level. Such an "organic model" of public relations would have benefits for every organization and for every individual (including "nonpublics") as well as for society at large (i.e., the "general public").

As a way to critique an all-too-easy framing of such a general public, public(s) should be investigated with more detail and nuance. Kruckeberg, Starck, and Vujnovic (2006), for example, examined "consumer communities," and Kruckeberg and Tsetsura (2008) identified myriad global communities that are or can easily become dysfunctional. Kruckeberg and Tsetsura (2008) say dramatic changes are raising questions about earlier social-scientific perspectives, "especially when considering the escalating development of three inter-related phenomena that have created the most profound, yet largely unappreciated and insufficiently measured, societal changes: 1) communication/transportation technology, which is an intervening variable that has encouraged: 2) its outcome, globalism and 3) globalism's obverse, multiculturalism, because of which a global society remains divisive and fragmented" (p. 14).

What a century ago had become national is now global; what a century ago was a resegmentation of citizens into specialized national communities has now become a global resegmentation representing those having seemingly infinite perspectives on multiple issues—demanding far greater knowledge and broader cultural understanding by practitioners; what had become inverted between public and private has become a confusing and potentially dangerous concoction of what is private, which can become globally public at a misplaced keystroke. "Active publics" who seek information and organize on the Internet may be easier than in the past to identify, to monitor, and to communicate with; however, these publics are equally accessing overwhelming amounts of conflicting information that is being inexpensively sent from myriad other potentially hostile sources.

We question the continuing utility of the concept of publics (plural) in an era of globalism, easy and immediate resegmentation into multiple worldwide publics, and the dangers of what was meant to be private becoming globally public in the viral environment of the Internet. With incendiary immediacy, volatile "publics" worldwide can form immediately and unpredictably, and they can act seemingly chaotically and with unforeseen power. It has become meaningless to identify "publics" (plural) and to attempt to distinguish among a nonpublic, a latent public, an aware public, and an active public.

In today's global media environment, we question the contemporary accuracy of Grunig and Repper's (1992) historical contention that public relations programs seldom will be effective if they are directed to a mass audience. Rather, in today's global milieu, the only truly "strategic" public is the "general public." New communication technology and its applications, such as the blogosphere, have given the general public the power to cause direct (negative and positive) consequences for organizations, in a way and with scope beyond the control of public relations practitioners. The time has come when public relations scholars and practitioners must reassess the importance of the general public.

Managing Global Public Relations: Impact of the New Social Media

The fragmentation of audiences in an era of converging media (Jenkins, 2006; Skinner, Compton, & Gasher, 2005) has occupied the minds of contemporary media scholars. Similarly, the future of public relations has been theorized in terms of the impact of the Internet on public relations management and practice (Culbertson & Chen, 1996; Epley, 1992; Wolcott, 1990). The management of global public relations has also been the focus of scholarly research, and Vercic, Grunig, and Grunig (1996) have suggested that the effectiveness of global public relations depends on sharing generic principles while accepting differences. However, the practice and management of public relations globally through the use of social media networks thus far has not been addressed in this context.

The historic conceptualization of stakeholders and diverse publics in the public relations literature is unsustainable. With globalization and the compression of time and space and abundant and inexpensive information, it is impossible to predict how publics will form, organize, and respond to organizational activities. Rather, organizations should enter existing global networking organizations and corporations (e.g., PR Newswire or Communispace) and embrace social media such as blogging, YouTube, Twitter, Facebook, and MySpace. Online social networks tend to be more private in nature, but the trend is toward increasing "publicness" and connectivity. This embrace should be considered a tool not just for expanding marketing strategies globally but also to engage in more participatory, democratic interaction through the promotion of conversation. Such conversation can be identified as consummatory—that is, self-fulfilling—communication that offers an immediate enhancement of life (i.e., which can be enjoyed for its own sake) as opposed to instrumental, or practical, communication that historically has been the mainstay of public relations communication. Although a 2009 survey by the networking corporation Communispace suggested that only 6% of the 64% of people who had heard of Twitter were in fact using it (Klaassen, 2009), the "Twitter revolution" that surrounded the 2009 Iranian election crisis shows that, in a globally networked society, information cannot be controlled, and, once it is circulating, it is both powerful and unstoppable (Subervi, 2009).

The primary public relations goal of an organization should be to encourage and to promote an understanding of its organizational goals through an interaction with citizens, whose sense of active contribution should be recognized by the organization through implementation and innovation resulting from citizens' contributions, including the organization's acts of social responsibility. New social media provide tremendous opportunities for an "organic" interaction between members of the public and organizations, as well as with governments on all levels. Some organizations, such as MTV and Coca-Cola, have already engaged in social networking, with the intent to create communities that they can observe—moving toward a more anthropological approach rather than a strictly quantitative approach (that has dominated public relations scholarship and practice) to measure the outcomes of public relations. However, the question remains whether these communities created by using social media make a truly virtual public space (i.e., the so-called Habermasian public sphere) or whether these media are just another means to obtain feedback on the organization's behavior by creating semicontrolled "private spheres."

If a conclusion remains premature, it is certain that management was and is one of the main functions of public relations practice and that managing public relations in a global context is becoming more complex. Global communication influences organizations and their publics, and communication innovations make understanding global publics more urgent. Professionals and organizations that want to succeed in the global environment must recognize the strengths of the new social media that allow for building local awareness and local communities, linking them to the wider global context. The unpredictability of how and why humans organize allows organizations to influence and, to some degree, manage messages as well as to be more watchful about what is said. In a global virtual social space, messages can spread from their origins to a global arena, and mistakes will be even more costly for organizations to make. New social media, hence, are the point of intersection between global and local, and the very idea that they are social will hopefully push organizations toward bridging participatory gaps and building communities, while maintaining good communication strategies.

References

Baker, S. (2009, March 25). Following the luxury chocolate lover. *BusinessWeek*. Retrieved from http://www.businessweek.com/technology/content/mar2009/tc20090325_892605.htm

Culbertson, H. M., & Chen, N. (Eds.). (1996). *International public relations: A comparative analysi*s. Mahwah, NJ: Erlbaum.

Cutlip, S. M., & Center, A. H. (1971). *Effective public relations*. Englewood Cliffs, NJ: Prentice Hall.

Deuze, M. (2007). *Media work*. Cambridge, England: Polity Press.

Dewey, J. (1927). *The public and its problems*. New York, NY: Holt.

Dozier, D. M. (with Grunig, L. A., & Grunig, J. E.). (1995). *Manager's guide to excellence in public relations and communication management*. Mahwah, NJ: Erlbaum.

Epley, J. S. (1992). Public relations in the global village: An American perspective. *Public Relations Review, 18*(2), 109–116.

Freeman, R. E. (1984). *Strategic management: A stakeholder approach*. Boston, MA: Pitman.

Friedman, T. L. (1999, March 28). A manifesto for the fast world. *The New York Times Magazine*. Retrieved from http://www.globalpolicy.org/component/content/article/172/29945.html

Friedman, T. L. (1999). *The Lexus and the olive tree*. New York, NY: Farrar, Straus Giroux.

Grunig, J. E., & Hunt, T. (1984). *Managing public relations*. Boston, MA: Wadsworth.

Grunig, J. E., & Repper, F. C. (1992). Strategic management, publics, and issues. In J. E. Grunig (Ed.), *Excellence in public relations and communication management* (pp. 117–157). Hillsdale, NJ: Erlbaum.

Ihlen, Ø. (2008). Mapping the environment for corporate social responsibility: Stakeholders, publics and the public sphere. *Corporate Communications: An International Journal, 13*(2), 135–146.

Jenkins, H. (2006). *Convergence culture: Where old and new media collide*. New York: New York University Press.

Klaassen, A. (2009, March 30). Using social media to listen to consumers: A vocal few don't represent the majority but could signify a larger issue. *Advertising Age*. Retrieved from http://findarticles.com/p/articles/mi_hb6398/is_200903/ai_n31533082

Kruckeberg, D., Starck, K., & Vujnovic, M. (2006). The role and ethics of community-building for consumer products and services: With some recommendations for new-marketplace economies in emerging democracies. In C. H. Botan & V. Hazleton (Eds.), *Public relations II* (pp. 485–497). Mahwah, NJ: Erlbaum.

Kruckeberg, D., & Tsetsura, K. (2004). International journalism ethics. In A. S. de Beer & J. C. Merrill (Eds.), *Global journalism* (4th ed., pp. 84–92). Boston, MA: Pearson Allyn & Bacon.

Kruckeberg, D., & Tsetsura, K. (2008, March). The "Chicago School" in the global community: Concept explication for communication theories and practices. *Asian Communication Research, 3*, 9–30.

L'Etang, J. (2008). *Public relations: Concepts, practice and critique*. Thousand Oaks, CA: Sage.

Moreley, M. (2009). How to manage your global reputation: The public relations agency. In K. Sriramesh & D. Vercic (Eds.), *The global public relations handbook* (pp. 851–870). New York, NY: Routledge.

Newsom, D., Turk, J. V., & Kruckeberg, D. (2010). *This is PR: The realities of public relations* (10th ed.). Boston, MA: Wadsworth Cengage Learning.

Skinner, D., Compton, J. R., & Gasher, M. (Eds.). (2005). *Converging media, diverging politics: A political economy of news media in the United States and Canada*. Lanham, MD: Lexington Books.

Sriramesh, K., & Vercic, D. (2009). A theoretical framework for global public relations research and practice. In K. Sriramesh & D. Vercic (Eds.), *The global public relations handbook* (pp. 3–22). New York, NY: Routledge.

Subervi, A. (2009, June 17). Iranians twitter as government burns: Ahmadinejad's public relations nightmare. *The Ethical Optimist*. Retrieved from http://ethical optimist.com/2009/06/17/iranians-twitter-as-government-burns-ahmadinejad's-public-relations-nightmare/

Vercic, D., Grunig, L. A., & Grunig, J. E. (1996). Global and specific principles of public relations: Evidence from Slovenia. In H. M. Culbertson & N. Chen (Eds.), *International public relations: A comparative analysis* (pp. 31–65). Mahwah, NJ: Erlbaum.

Werther, W. B., & Chandler, D. (2006). *Strategic corporate social responsibility: Stakeholders in a global environment*. London, England: Sage.

Wolcott R. B., Jr. (1990). New technology, global market influence future of counseling. *Public Relations Journal, 46*(11), 38–40.

20

The Culture of Gamework

Aphra Kerr

While the digital games industry has become increasingly marketized and professionalized in its 40 years of commercial existence, at the same time it has maintained some of its DIY roots and is somewhat ahead of other media industries in its attempts to facilitate and appropriate amateur productions. The increasingly globalized nature of digital game development gives rise to challenges and tensions related to managing development projects across transnational networks of companies, managing inputs of amateur producers, and managing communities of players. The digital game industry is used today in media and communication studies as an example both of cocreative culture (Jenkins, 2006; Raessens, 2005) and of precarious labor (Kline, Dyer-Witheford, & De Peuter, 2003; Kücklich, 2005; Postigo, 2003, 2007; Terranova, 2004; see also Annet Aris, and Toby Miller, in this volume). These concepts are not necessarily exclusive, and both can be usefully employed to understand work in game production networks in particular (Kerr, 2006) and media work more generally (Deuze, 2007).

To understand the culture of gamework we need to pay attention to the range of actors (human and nonhuman) in game production networks, the differences in power between these actors, and the experiences of workers within the development companies and those external actors they engage with. Increasingly, game production networks flow beyond firm boundaries, and certain functions are outsourced (e.g., human resources, middleware, testing, marketing, community support, content creation). Little is known about the relationships generated and how they are managed. Most of our information on gamework is based on game "postmortems" and interviews with professional developers (Cassell & Jenkins, 1998; Deuze, Martin, & Allen, 2007; Kline et al., 2003) with relatively little based on ethnographic work. These interviews tend to perpetuate the myths of individual/designer-driven projects. The reality is much more market driven and subject to much negotiation among actors.

Why so little actual ethnographic work in companies? Partly this relates to some of the issues examined in this chapter (i.e., the desire to protect intellectual property rights and working conditions within companies). The digital games industry shares many characteristics with other cultural industries including its youthful age profile, its flexible working hours, the erasure of boundaries between work and play, the need for constant re- and up-skilling, and a high degree of mobility among industry workers. However, while the industry tries to cultivate an image of a creative industry that maintains links to its anarchic or hacker origins, academics in Canada and North America have written about a culture of "militarised masculinity" and of "net-slaves" (Kline et al., 2003). Further, despite a decade of entrepreneurial feminism, the representation of women in the U.S. and U.K. games industry has remained very low compared to that in other creative industries, and experienced older staff tend to leave the industry. What research we have points to significant project and workplace management issues that impact negatively the culture and experience of gamework.

This chapter adopts a sociological approach to analyzing how the digital games industry operates and how the culture of gamework is socially constructed through the practices of a range of human and nonhuman actors. In the next section we examine the influence that globalization, industry consolidation, and technology are having on the industry. We then examine how these three trends impact professional transnational production networks and the opportunities and challenges posed by technology, different occupational communities, modders, and gameplayers. The data that exist would suggest that while the digital games industry is becoming increasingly professionalized, it is still an industry that is struggling with professionalism, where practices are often less formalized than in other media sectors and where employment for many workers is precarious (Gill & Pratt, 2008). These issues have serious implications for the diversity and retention of staff in the industry.

Overview of the Sector and Key Trends

The digital games sector can be conceived as a creative industry and displays many similarities with more traditional media industries in terms of relations of production, the role of publishers, and the importance of distribution (Kerr, 2006). However, digital games are based on the commodification of play and the development of new technologies to mediate how players interact. Further, and in common with many traditional media sectors, digital games have embraced digital networks to develop new transnational networks of production, new types of games, new distribution channels, and new and more productive relationships with their players. In order to understand the digital games sector we have to identify key actors in the production network including developers (amateur or professional), publishers, distributors, service companies, retailers, and players. These actors are increasingly employing new technologies (another actor) to coconstruct one-off, persistent, and serialized forms of content.

The idea for a new game can come from an individual, but the most common practice is for it to come from an internal group within a development company or from a publisher, conforming to what Williams (1981) calls "market professional" and "corporate professional" (p. 52) market relations, respectively. In both scenarios the idea is funded via an advance from a publisher, and the level of royalties depends very much on the reputation and track record of the developer. Thus a new game concept is developed by a development team in collaboration with a publisher and, if it is on a console platform, with the platform manufacturer as well. At each stage during development there are milestones that must be met, and on completion a quality approval process is usually conducted by the hardware manufacturer and/or publisher.

While development teams have internal managers these are usually overseen by a producer from a publishing company. Thus innovation and the creative process in the games industry can involve negotiation between different companies, and although the core creative work is usually done by a single team within a development studio the ideas and concept must be negotiated with the funder. Artisanal productions still occur where individuals or small companies develop their own ideas and self-publish or deal with an aggregator (e.g., Kongregate). However, corporate relations with a publisher are still more common, and such funding is supplemented with income from advertising and product placement. The widespread use of market research and analysis of player data indicates that production is increasingly shaped by market data rather than purely by development teams or companies.

While some development companies create games for multiple platforms, many specialize in games for particular platforms, and this is related to the fact that each subsector or segment of the industry is structured differently (Kerr, 2006). Developing for different markets—such as the console, massively multiplayer online, or casual—requires different internal skill sets and competences and different external networks and relationships. For example, developing a game for a console platform requires one to deal with the hardware manufacturers and enter into their quality control system. Developing a game for the PC means dealing with a greater number of competitors but fewer intermediaries. Developing a game, or porting (i.e., translating) your game to a mobile platform, introduces major engineering and distribution issues as one must contend with different telecommunications companies and hundreds of handsets. However, developing a mobile, social, or casual game for the Web involves a much smaller team and amount of time as compared to the much longer console development process or the process to develop a retail PC game. Meanwhile, developing a massively multiplayer online game (MMOG, such as *World of Warcraft*) involves large teams of developers but also a large team of technical and community support to service the ongoing (i.e., persistent) game.

One trend that is clear is that the digital games industry is becoming more globalized in terms of the geographical spread of its production networks. This does not mean that ownership or control over production networks is becoming more diversified. In order to understand the spatial distribution of digital games production one needs to differentiate between where the production is geographically located and where the ownership or control of production and publishing is located. Traditionally the key centers of publishing and development of games globally were in Japan, the United States, and the United Kingdom, followed by France, Germany, and the Nordic countries. While publishing has continued to operate out of the United States, Japan, and France, development has now diversified, and the top five (in terms of total numbers employed) include the United States, Japan, Canada, South Korea, and the United Kingdom (Skillset, 2006). Emerging centers include China and Eastern Europe. Increasingly, as in the film business, the production of digital games hardware and disks occurs in offshore low-cost locations like China, Taiwan, and Hungary while certain stages of software production are still occurring in high-cost Western industrial countries. Not quite so low-cost locations, like Canada and South Korea, have benefited from substantial institutional and government support to grow their industrial base. Localization and customer support functions are also moving to lower-cost locations near to market. Interestingly, development companies tend to be more regionally distributed within countries than many other creative industries. As production becomes more complex and companies require more specialized services this trend may change. Jennifer Johns (2006) argues that game "software production tends to operate within three supra-regional contexts" (p. 153). These regions are the United States, Europe, and Japan, and they are demarcated by some arbitrary and some not-so-arbitrary technological, economic, social, and cultural barriers. Thus even as the industry has moved toward a transnational production model, including offshoring and outsourcing, the distribution of these products is regionally demarcated and controlled by a small number of privately owned multinational companies.

A second trend is the increasing growth of a small number of multinational companies through mergers and acquisitions and a focus on vertical integration. This is particularly occurring in relation to the hardware manufacturers and some publishing companies. The total number of independent game development companies in the United Kingdom fell from 295 in 2000 to 166 in 2008 (Oxford Economics, 2008). While employment numbers remained largely static, independent companies were merging—growing into "superdevelopers" with multiple production teams—or were bought out by publishing companies. From the late 1990s the industry has become increasingly concentrated, with a smaller number of companies controlling or effectively acting as gatekeepers in the console part of the industry in particular. Given that this is the largest part of the industry in value terms, particularly in the United States, this concentration of power in a small number of American and Japanese companies is significant. One consequence of such concentration is the creation of barriers to entry, making it very difficult for many first-time independent developers to reach certain markets. Another result of vertical integration is that publishers have greater control over the creative process and workers. This can involve indirect or direct project management, aesthetic input, market testing, and in some cases the removal of intellectual properties from production teams. Control of the main console hardware platforms means control of the pace of technological change in these platforms and the quality of all content that gets published on the system.

According to publicly available data on the earnings and profitability of publishers, the top three have significantly more earnings than the rest and are companies registered in the United States and Japan.[1] Only Ubisoft and Atari/Infogrames (both French) are challenging the dominance of American and Japanese companies in the top ten software publishers in digital games. At the same time, competition between the big three console companies is strong, and there are disincentives to cooperating. While there are a small number of very large companies in the sector there are also many small companies that are largely dependent on these large multinationals for access to capital and distribution networks.

A final issue that is crucial to any understanding of the digital games industry is the role of technology. Each new console does not simply mean an incremental increase in platform power and speed but can mean a complete reappraisal of production networks, worker skills, budgets, and management structures. With three competing platform systems each replacing its platforms almost twice a decade this results in particularly short cycles of creativity and innovation and places huge demands on education programs and workers to reskill. Meanwhile all of these platforms are now adding online capabilities and a variety of services including content downloads. This is to compete with a range of new competitors offering online game services via the PC (Jöckel, Will, & Schwarzer, 2008) and mobile phones. For example, Telltale Games in the United States offers short episodic games for download and/or preorder DVDs including games like *Sam & Max* and *Wallace & Gromit*.[2] Thus gaming platforms influence all elements of the games production process, and companies and workers can become locked into the sets of competences and relationships that develop around particular platforms that can stifle their ability to innovate.

Working for the Digital Games Industry

How do globalization, consolidation, and technological change affect work and managing work in the digital games industry? For current-generation console developers there is a need to scale up development team sizes, and this is having an impact on the management of production and workers' conditions. Today's development teams and budgets have grown, and team sizes not unlike those for a small film are common so that managing the development process and streamlining the development pipeline have become major issues. Not all companies can make this transition. This is an industry with its origins in DIY noncommercial popular culture, and many of its top managers are artists or programmers. Innovation scholars have highlighted the relative lack of process maturity in game companies in the United States (Tschang, 2005) and the "low self-reflective capacity" of game firms in the United Kingdom (Grantham & Kaplinsky, 2005, p. 192) where "few firms embody structured and/or specialized management processes" (ibid., p. 196). Some companies are turning to management techniques from the mainstream software industry (such as "agile" and "scrum" iterative approaches, emphasizing teamwork, self-organization, and accountability), to using middleware instead of developing all the code in-house, and to out-sourcing to third-party companies. They are also increasingly looking to get amateur players involved in playtesting, moderating online forums, and con-tent creation (Humphreys, Fitzgerald, Banks, & Suzor, 2005). By contrast, a U.K. trade mission to Japan was impressed with their management systems and ability to deliver projects within 18 months regardless of complexity (TerKeurst, 2002).

In the United States, Canada, and the United Kingdom prevailing man-agement structures and poor project planning often lead to poor working conditions. These include very high weekly working hours, particularly com-ing up to a deadline, which is called "crunch time" in the industry; a lack of remuneration for overtime; and a lack of proper accreditation. Anecdotal stories and interview data have been backed up by quality-of-life surveys con-ducted by the International Game Developers Association (IGDA; Hyman, 2008), which suggest that poor working conditions are relatively widespread. They also point to a high expectation by workers that they will leave the industry within 10 years. Workers in quality assurance departments where games are tested are particularly critical of working time and remuneration issues. Interviews in Canada have highlighted high levels of stress, long hours, and an almost "mercenary" expectation of employee loyalty (Dyer-Witheford & Sharman, 2005, p. 203).

The development of quality-of-life managers in some companies points to attempts to address working conditions (Deuze et al., 2007). But stories of poor working conditions still surface in the United States and the United Kingdom, and attempts by professional associations to tackle them have had limited success. In Europe professional games associations and some gov-ernments have lobbied against a Working Time Directive, which attempts to limit the maximum number of working hours to 60 hours a week, saying such legislation would make it impossible for European game developers to compete with companies elsewhere.[3] And while conditions in large studios have been the subject of press coverage, conditions in small startups and independent development studios, which have little power to negotiate with their funders and fewer resources, remain underexamined.[4] The fact that some committee members of the IGDA explicitly support crunch time has led to little effective action by the IGDA. In addition, little is known about conditions in Eastern European and Asian development companies that are working for hire.

Working conditions may account in part for the fact that in the United Kingdom the age profile of the industry is younger than the creative media workforce as a whole: Three quarters are aged under 35 years compared with more than two fifths (43%) in this age group across the whole creative media workforce (Skillset, 2006). Working conditions may also influence the representation of women in the industry, which is very low at 12%, compared with 42% of the wider creative media industries' workforce and the fact that people from a Black, Asian, and Minority Ethnic (BAME) background make up just (4%) of the workforce. De Peuter and Dyer-Witheford (2005) found a similar demographic in Canada where the workforce was "relatively young, generally well paid but unevenly precarious, and overwhelmingly male." The lack of age, gender, and ethnic diversity in the workforce is an issue that is only starting to raise its head at industry conferences, although gender diversity has been an issue for over a decade (Cassell & Jenkins, 1998). The IGDA has a "Women in Games" special interest group, and in both the United States and Europe separate organizations exist to promote greater representation of women in the industry.[5] These organizations would appear to have had little impact on the industry in the United States and the United Kingdom to date.

Working conditions in the games industry are seldom critically examined in industry publications, and recruitment articles can be particularly deceptive. A 2005 supplement with a games industry magazine in the United Kingdom stated, "It is the most exciting industry in existence. . . . Few people ever seem to leave. . . . You just need skill, enthusiasm and determination." One interviewee when asked directly about work conditions stated they had "generally improved, though it's a long-term process and many studios are still trying to find the magic formula. Many larger and more global companies have the financial reserves and organisational infrastructure to incorporate policies such as holidays 'in lieu,' flexitime, [and] overtime payments."[6] The supplement went on to say that in a highly creative and demanding industry "a certain element of crunch" should be expected. In an industry with a high percentage of degree-level or qualified workers (two thirds in the United Kingdom) it is interesting to read that few game courses are seen as worthy of industry accreditation in the United Kingdom, companies have problems recruiting, and there are skill gaps and shortages (Grantham & Kaplinsky, 2005). Representative bodies like TIGA in the United Kingdom cite the lack of relevance of some university game courses and the attractiveness of jobs overseas.[7] Companies that cannot find the appropriate "talent" run their own training programs or become involved in running university competitions. One European example is the *Dare to be Digital* competition run out of Abertay in Scotland, which gives student teams 10 weeks to develop a game prototype with industry mentoring.[8]

Encouraging game modding and hobbyist competitions is part of the industry's relentless search for adequately trained talent, but the rules governing these practices demand more attention. Modding is largely made possible because publishers bundle tools and give support to the modding community. While modders work for free, the end-user licensing agreements governing the software involved make it clear that ownership of the content produced remains with the developer or publisher of the game (Taylor, 2006), and the tools create certain techno-aesthetic conventions that modders must operate within. Nieborg and van der Graaf (2008) explored Counterstrike modification teams that, though consisting of amateurs, conformed to the typical proprietary practice of professional development companies. While many of these teams iterate on existing games, they can also generate incremental innovations whose ownership and value remain the property of the publisher of the game. Kücklich (2005) argues that the games industry tries to maintain the perception of modding as play, but in reality this "is the basis of the exploitative relationship between modders and the games industry." Indeed many academics have suggested that modders are a source of financial value to companies (Kücklich, 2005; Nieborg & van der Graaf, 2008; Postigo, 2007; Søtamaa, 2007). Others have pointed out that "unruly modders" may actually require new management methods (Humphreys et al., 2005). Certainly modders generate value for the professional industry either directly, if their outputs are commercialized, or indirectly through extending the life cycle and marketing of the original work (de Peuter & Dyer-Witheford, 2005).

The digital games industry shares many characteristics with other cultural industries including its youthful age demographics, flexible working hours, the erasure of boundaries between work and play, and the need for constant re- and up-skilling (Deuze, 2007; Gill & Pratt, 2008). One interesting difference that emerged from research in the United Kingdom suggests that the industry has a relatively low percentage of freelancers, just 8%, compared to 29% across the wider creative media industries. This does not necessarily reduce the insecurity felt by workers, however. There appears to be a high degree of mobility among industry workers (both among game companies and into other media industries), and much of this is involuntary and due to what Vinodrai (2006) would call "disruptions" (i.e., takeovers, companies going out of business, projects getting shelved, or companies moving projects or certain functions to low-cost locations). The need to build up a portfolio combined with the industry structure, pace of technological change, and production practices often acts to undermine long-term relationships with particular firms and the industry. Combined with the high degree of burnout in the industry these features militate against experienced designers and programmers staying in the industry and potentially impact the quality of management available.

With such uncertainty and mobility one might presume that workers would look to institutional communities beyond the firm for support. However, the occupational and professional communities available to workers in this industry are fragmented. The project team for most commercial and some amateur productions draws on two rather distinct occupational groups: programmers and artists or designers. Each has its allegiances to different communities of practice, and while they must communicate with each other this is often not addressed in their primary qualification and is a skill that must be learned on the job (Preston, Kerr, & Cawley, 2009). While each has its own occupational knowledge communities there is rather weak professional representation for these groups as game developers, and in the North American and European contexts there are separate representational bodies for developers and for publishers. Quite often these bodies adopt opposing stances on issues of relevance to the industry, particularly on working conditions. The formation of a European Games Developer Federation (EGDF) signals an attempt to unify, but so far the focus has been on organizing events and lobbying for financial support from public bodies. This lack of unity within the industry is a barrier when it comes to addressing key issues facing the industry, particularly relating to working conditions (see also Geert Lovink and Ned Rossiter, in this volume).

Academics and game companies are increasingly realizing that gameplayers also contribute to the culture of gamework. For some, "it is through the labour of the players . . . that culture and community come to grow" (Taylor, 2006, p. 133). In a very real sense players are involved in cocreation of the game through their interaction in the game and their contributions to a range of related artifacts such as Web sites. The contribution of a player through gameplay and the unseen use of player data to tailor in-game advertising and services certainly indirectly generate value (Andrejevic, 2009; Humphreys, 2008). Some players have turned their social and cultural capital into economic capital through real trading of items or through disruptive activities such as farming and cheating. Such disruptive practices stimulate game development companies to innovate to overcome such practices. Some companies, like CCP, the company behind EVE Online, have introduced elected player councils to represent players and communicate directly with developers.[9] Thus professional developers, modders, and players operate in a dynamic relationship that is mediated by capital and unequal power relationships. The networks, communities, and relationships created through gamework and gameplay are in clear tension with very individualized careers and legal restrictions on play.

Conclusion

The digital games industry operates on a global scale, but ownership and revenue within the industry are increasingly concentrated in a small number of multinational companies headquartered in a small number of countries. Existing in a dynamic and contested relationship with these large corporations are many small development and service companies, modders, and players. Increasingly, production is driven by the market and by consumers who are players and in some cases modders. As digital games production has become corporatized and ideas for games increasingly are owned by, and come from, publishers, the myth of the creative auteur recedes into the background. While bedroom modders still exist and indie teams toil to develop original ideas, they often modify these ideas in accordance with capitalist logic and the demands of multinational publishers. There are examples of cocreation in what could be conceived of as "open innovation" networks, but more common are examples of multinational firms appropriating and in some cases exploiting the work of unsalaried gameplayers.

This chapter has focused on the culture of gamework in the United States, Canada, and the United Kingdom. While certain characteristics are shared with other media industries, including the sense that work can be fun, other characteristics, like the longer-term contracts, acceptance of crunch time, lack of workforce diversity, and ongoing loss of experienced staff may be more specific or at the very least more pronounced in this sector. The skills mismatches and shortages faced by the industry indicate that educational institutions, companies, and workers have trouble keeping up with the pace of innovation in the industry. For all workers, however, the actions of a small number of multinationals and the rapid pace of technological change offer both opportunities and threats. Workers are not well equipped to deal with the threats. Many small to medium-sized companies do not have proper human resource personnel and programs. Worker representation at a collective level beyond the firm is poor and far from unified, particularly across borders. Similarly, players and modders are dispersed and far from realizing their direct or indirect value and power. In this context both professional and amateur game workers increasingly rely on informal and often virtually mediated networks and associations for support, information, and knowledge in order to deal with the corporate and market needs of gamework.

References

Andrejevic, M. (2009). Productive Play 2.0: The logic of in-game advertising. *Media International Australia, 130,* 66–76.

Cassell, J., & Jenkins, H. (Eds.). (1998). *From Barbie to Mortal Kombat: Gender and computer games.* Cambridge, MA: MIT Press.

de Peuter, G., & Dyer-Witheford, N. (2005). A playful multitude? Mobilising and counter-mobilising immaterial game labour. *Fibreculture, 5.* Retrieved from http://journal.fibreculture.org/issue5/depeuter_dyerwitheford.html

Deuze, M. (2007). *Media work.* Cambridge, England: Polity Press.

Deuze, M., Martin, C. B., & Allen, C. (2007). The professional identity of Gameworkers. *Convergence, 13*(4), 335–353.

Dyer-Witheford, N., & Sharman, Z. (2005). The political economy of Canada's video and computer game industry. *Canadian Journal of Communication, 30,* 187–210.

Gill, R., & Pratt, A. (2008). In the social factory? Immaterial labour, precariousness and cultural work. *Theory, Culture, Society, 25*(7–8), 1–30.

Grantham, A., & Kaplinsky, R. (2005). Getting the measure of the electronic games industry: Developers and the management of innovation. *International Journal of Innovation Management, 9*(2), 183–213.

Humphreys, S. (2008). Ruling the virtual world: Governance in massively multiplayer online games. *European Journal of Cultural Studies, 11*(2), 149–171.

Humphreys, S., Fitzgerald, B., Banks, J., & Suzor, N. (2005). Fan-based production for computer games: User-led innovation, the "drift of value" and intellectual property rights. *Media International Australia, 114*, 16–29.

Hyman, P. (2008, May 13). Quality of life? Does anyone still give a damn? *Gamasutra.* Retrieved from http://www.gamasutra.com/view/feature/3656/quality_of_life_does_anyone_still_.php

Jenkins, H. (2006). *Convergence culture: When old and new media collide.* New York: New York University Press.

Jöckel, S., Will, A., & Schwarzer, F. (2008). Participatory media culture and digital online distribution—Reconfiguring the value chain in the computer game industry. *International Journal of Media Management, 10*(3), 102–111.

Johns, J. (2006). Video games production networks: Value capture, power relations and embeddedness. *Journal of Economic Geography, 6*(2), 151–180.

Kerr, A. (2006). *The business and culture of digital games: Gamework/gameplay.* London, England: Sage.

Kline, S., Dyer-Witheford, N., & De Peuter, G. (2003). *Digital play: The interaction of technology, culture and marketing.* Montreal, QC, Canada: McGill-Queen's University Press.

Kücklich, J. (2005). Precarious playbour: Modders and the digital games industry. *Fibreculture, 5.* Retrieved from http://journal.fibreculture.org/issue5/kucklich.html

Martin, C. B., & Deuze, M. (2009). The independent production of culture: A digital games case study. *Games and Culture, 4*(3), 276–295.

Nieborg, D., & van der Graaf, S. (2008). The mod industries? The industrial logic of non-market game production. *European Journal of Cultural Studies, 11*(2), 177–195.

Oxford Economics. (2008). *The economic contribution of the UK games development industry.* Oxford, England: Oxford Economics. Retrieved from http://www.oxfordeconomics.com/free/pdfs/gamesimpact.pdf

Postigo, H. (2003). From Pong to Planet Quake: Post-industrial transitions from leisure to work. *Information, Communication and Society, 6*(4), 593–607.

Postigo, H. (2007). Of mods and modders: Chasing down the value of fan based digital game modifications. *Games and Culture, 2*(4), 300–313.

Preston, P., Kerr, A., & Cawley, A. (2009). Digital media sector innovation in the knowledge economy: Rethinking knowledge inputs and policies. *Information, Communication and Society, 12*(7), 994–1014.

Raessens, J. (2005). Computer games as participatory media culture. In J. Raessens & H. Goldstein (Eds.), *Handbook of computer game studies* (pp. 373–388). Cambridge, MA: MIT Press.

Skillset. (2006). *Computer games sector—Labour market intelligence digest.* Retrieved from http://www.skillset.org/uploads/pdf/asset_13239.pdf?2

Søtamaa, O. (2007). On modder labour, commodification of play and mod competitions. *First Monday, 12*(9). Retrieved from http://firstmonday.org/htbin/cgiwrap/bin/ojs/index.php/fm/article/view/2006

Taylor, T. L. (2006). *Play between worlds: Exploring online game culture.* Cambridge, MA: MIT Press.

Teipen, C. (2008). Work and employment in creative industries: The video games industry in Germany, Sweden and Poland. *Economic and Industrial Democracy, 29*(3), 309–335.

TerKeurst, J. (2002). *Games are like fruit: Japanese best practice in digital game development.* Dundee, Scotland: University of Abertay Press.

Terranova, T. (2004). *Network culture: Politics for the information age.* London, England: Pluto Press.

Tschang, F. T. (2005). Videogames as interactive experiential products and their manner of development. *International Journal of Innovation Management, 9*(1), 103–131.

Vinodrai, T. (2006). Reproducing Toronto's design ecology: Career paths, intermediaries and local labour markets. *Economic Geography, 82*(3), 237–263.

Williams, R. (1981). *The sociology of culture.* Chicago, IL: University of Chicago Press.

Notes

1. http://kotaku.com/5030320/here-are-the-top-20-publishers-in-the-business-ranked-according-to-cash-money-intake

2. http://www.telltalegames.com

3. http://www.europarl.europa.eu/news/public/documents_par_theme/908/default_en.htm

4. http://www.gamewatch.org

5. http://www.womeningames.com/, http://www.igda.org/women, and http://womeningames.wordpress.com

6. http://www.edge-online.com/magazine/how-break-games-industry

7. http://www.skillset.org/games/accreditation; only five practice-based courses have been accredited so far. See http://www.edge-online.com/features/interview-tiga%E2%80%99s-richard-wilson for an interview with the new TIGA CEO regarding skills and courses. TIGA is the developers association in the U.K.

8. http://www.daretobedigital.com

9. "CCP encourages respect, dialog, interaction and cooperation on a deeper level between its employees and customers than is common in online games" (see http://www.ccpgames.com/en/company/about-us.aspx).

21

Same as the Old Boss? Changes, Continuities, and Careers in the Digital Music Era

Eric Harvey

After an all-time peak in 1999 fueled by teen pop purchased on compact disc at record stores, electronics chains, and select online retailers, the financial fortunes of the major label–controlled recording industry[1] have been in steady decline. Throughout the 1990s, MP3s—digital music files ripped from those CDs and compressed to roughly 10% of their original size—were floating around the Internet, though not in enough numbers, or with enough speed, to bother the labels. The rapid rise of peer-to-peer networking put an end to that ignorance, however. Peer-to-peer—and its younger sibling BitTorrent—was a revolutionary new distribution system for digital music developed by globally dispersed code writers with no connections to any aspect of the music industry, and with little desire to continue feeding profits into it. In response, the recording industry—which, as Williamson and Cloonan (2007) remind us, is the one music industry most affected by illicit downloading—opted to sue them. Furthermore, instead of overhauling an approach to selling recorded music that seemed more ancient by the day, the labels stubbornly stuck to their guns, making some superficial adjustments but refusing to consider any approach that did not involve acquiring maximum profits at every turn, on their terms. As a result, a rash of major music stars, from Madonna to Radiohead, jumped ship for new, experimental methods of selling their music, and themselves.

Yet digital music technologies have been far from detrimental to the fortunes of the smaller independent labels. In fact, indie labels and artists have proven adept at navigating digital music culture—expanding, professionalizing, and aggregating their more flexible operations while working with fans and curating highly individualized, oft idiosyncratic, and frequently astonishing musician rosters. Over the past decade or so, indies have expanded as dramatically as their major label counterparts have contracted, which makes sense: Indie labels and musicians operate in a culture governed by flexible and nonhierarchical relationships and ad hoc partnerships, with low financial overhead and small workforces, all while emphasizing autonomous artist-label relations and a desire to experiment. In many respects, indie labels are perfectly suited for a networked, collaborative music world.

Keith Negus's (1999) influential assertion that "production does not take place simply 'within' a corporate environment . . . but in relation to broader culture formations and practices that are within neither the control nor the understanding of the company" (p. 19) is truer than ever after a decade of such continuous change in music culture. As such, it will provide the framework for the following essay, in which I pose the following questions: How have the major labels and indies adapted to the changing landscape of digital music over the past decade? How have their strategies come from similar templates and goals? How new are these strategies? What are the possibilities and/or pitfalls for someone seeking to start a career in music right now? It is certainly true that artists may more easily and efficiently produce, record, and distribute their music digitally, and fans have myriad new options through which to discover new music. Yet at the same time, the older ways of doing things have not simply disappeared, and it thus becomes important to address new media technologies by assessing the ways in which they rupture with, and build upon, their predecessors.

Though the Recording Industry Association of America (RIAA) employs some notoriously fuzzy math to assign the recording industry's financial woes to illicit downloading (Lessig, 2004), much of the blame can be attributed to its own myopic business practices in the face of significant change. Three examples will show that the recording industry opted to sue its competitors and customers as piracy facilitators instead of working with them or taking the initiative to innovate itself. In September 1998, Diamond Multimedia released the first portable MP3 player—the Rio PMP300—and was subsequently hit with a lawsuit by the RIAA, under a dubious interpretation of the 1992 Audio Home Recording Act (AHRA).[2] Diamond would emerge victorious in that suit, but the recording industry still did not act quickly enough. In October 2001, Apple Computer reenergized its fledgling position in the PC market by introducing the iPod—a sleekly packaged, sturdy hard drive as MP3 Walkman. Steve Knopper (2009) argues that by April 2003, after the labels were forced to opt in to the iTunes Music Store at the steep expense of ceding pricing control to a technology manufacturer, Apple had basically taken over the business model of the music industry.

The recording industry's reaction to peer-to-peer file sharing was equally Draconian, more widely covered in the press, and just as self-destructive. Instead of working to transform Napster's extensive illicit client base—which numbered in the tens of millions by 2002—into a legal MP3 market, the recording industry not only sued the service into submission but also publicly defamed downloaders as pirates. The RIAA's litigious approach to down-loading culture—which Lessig (2008) likened to America's failed "drug war"—has not stifled file-sharing activity in the slightest. Yet perhaps more crucially, the strategy has also led to a decadelong hemorrhaging of consumer goodwill toward the music industry. Goodwill can be seen as a useful capi-talist fiction describing the affective connections between consumers and commodities, which corporations can productively exploit by engendering positive associations with their products and brands. After a decade of pub-licly antagonistic relations with music fans, it could well be argued that, to the degree the average fan is aware of the industry, his or her regard for it—and desire to connect with it—is lower than ever. In a recent interview, one music technology and industry journalist explained the situation succinctly: "The anger towards the major labels is well-deserved. They are the only industry I can think of that openly scorns, disrespects and tries to fleece their audience at every turn. People see this theft as tit for tat" (Brownstein, 2009).

A third factor in this testy relationship emanated from the recording indus-try's insistence on crippling its legally purchased MP3s with digital rights man-agement (DRM), a set of technological and commercial constraints backed by the legal and commercial guarantees of 1998's Digital Millennium Copyright Act (DMCA). According to Jessica Litman (2001), the DMCA has facilitated a new paradigm in which "copyright is now seen as a tool for copyright own-ers to use to extract all the potential commercial value from works of author-ship, even if that means that uses that have long been deemed legal are now brought within the copyright owner's control" (p. 14). When embedded into MP3 files, DRM technologies disallow legally purchased MP3s to circulate beyond a preset number of computers or portable devices, regardless of the intention of the listener, an unprecedented limitation of freedom that Lessig (2004) contextualizes succinctly: "Technology becomes a means by which fair use can be erased; the law of the DMCA backs up that erasing" (p. 160). A consistent firestorm of negative press about DRM, as well as Amazon.com's late-2007 DRM-free entry into the digital music market, eventually led to an agreement between the labels and Apple to sell DRM-free copies of music.

Because they dragged their feet adapting to new technologies, the major labels have had to try and adapt their old business models to a new digital reality, in which sales of physical media (CDs) are declining steadily and prof-its from digital have not yet been able to recoup the losses. Traditionally, as Negus (1999) reminds us, labels relied on a diversified portfolio of artists, organized into genres and managed by different departments within the orga-nization, to help negotiate the ever-uncertain music market.

With financial fortunes plummeting, the major labels have expanded on this notion in a manner unique to the current moment. Initiated in 2002 by an agreement between British pop star Robbie Williams and EMI, the "360" deal gives labels a financial stake not only in the sales of albums and singles but in merchandising and live performance as well, in the hope that ancillary profits will help offset the ever-shrinking physical music market. In exchange, the artists get larger up-front advances, ostensible advantages in cross-market promotion, and other benefits. This management transformation, which has become pervasive throughout the industry, means artists are treated more than ever as brands, and what we have typically come to know as the recording industry is gaining interest in much more than simple recordings. Moreover, it is not just record companies getting into the 360 game. By the latter half of the decade, Madonna, U2, and Jay-Z—three of the biggest artists of all time—had struck 360 deals with Live Nation, a concert promoter that had broken off from Clear Channel in 2006. Through its Artist Nation initiative, Live Nation was able to use its significant live venue holdings, and the promise of eight-figure advances, as leverage to wrench these artists away from their label contracts.

These contracts are not limited to established artists, either. For up-and-coming musicians, executives assert that 360 deals lessen the pressure on cutting a hit record or single immediately and allow for a more holistic, gradual growing process through touring, merchandising, and fan interaction—a clear move away from the "blockbuster" teen-pop moment that started the decade. The fact remains, however, that while these deals are novel, they are also incredibly risky—not only for the investors, who still must deal with an unpredictable music market, but particularly for young artists who risk losing control over the nonrecorded aspects of their career, which can often be very lucrative. Though the style of doing business has changed, the bottom line for the major labels remains the same: managing a diversified portfolio by monopolizing revenue streams.

Until relatively recently, artists have had few options to market and distribute their music widely and efficiently other than through labels. In 2007 and 2008, however, two noted acts inventively translated the goodwill of their extensive fan bases to independent success on the Web, by choosing to work from within downloading culture, rather than against it. Having recently fulfilled its EMI contract, the critically and popularly acclaimed U.K. band Radiohead chose to release *In Rainbows* on its own in October 2007, with no advance press. Explaining the gambit, bandleader Thom Yorke quipped, "Every record for the last four—including my solo record—has been leaked. So the idea was like, we'll leak it, then" (Byrne, 2007). A week after a cryptic mention of the new album on the band's Web site sent the music Web into a flurry of excitement, eager fans were informed of another novelty: They could pay whatever they chose for a low-quality MP3 (160 kbps) version of the album—including nothing at all.

Though many commenters rushed to praise Radiohead for embracing the same sort of experimental spirit in selling its albums that the band had long done with the music itself, the *In Rainbows* method still relied heavily on physical media and long-established marketing techniques. The album for download was encoded at a low bit rate (160 kbps), ostensibly to drive consumers to stores for physical copies of the album. Indeed, alongside the download link were options to preorder the CD and record, as well as an expensive "discbox" for die-hard fans. In other words, the MP3s worked as a newfangled loss leader for the physical media—a carrot on a stick to whet appetites enough to buy the hard copy. It worked, too: *In Rainbows* would reach the top spot on the Billboard chart that next January, sponsored by the independent label ATO Records (yet with distribution by RED, owned by Sony Music), and the discbox would sell 100,000 copies.

That next May, Trent Reznor, who had led the equally popular industrial metal band Nine Inch Nails since the late 1980s, decided on a similar approach. Accompanied only by the words *This one's on me*, Reznor gave away *The Slip* as a free download. Reznor, long a proponent of artist-fan interaction, parted from Radiohead's model by giving his album away in a variety of high-quality digital formats, all covered by a Creative Commons license, which allowed fans to remix and recirculate the music for noncommercial purposes, with attribution. Like Radiohead, however, Reznor also profited from the physical release of the album: *The Slip* would reach the #12 spot on Billboard's U.S. chart. Undeniably, these new independent-minded strategies were successful for Radiohead and Nine Inch Nails, inasmuch as they shed their labels and used the Web to build incredible buzz and goodwill for the eventual physical release of their new albums. Yet at the same time, much of these artists' success in these ventures came from the extensive media coverage that typically attends the news of any new release by internationally famous artists, especially innovative and generous offerings like these. There exists little evidence to suggest that this sort of model would work for lesser-known acts.

This sort of "going it alone" strategy has been embraced in a different, less inspiring way by the major labels and artists releasing hip-hop music, still one of the driving artistic forces in popular music today. Over the last decade, as hip-hop's musical influence permeated all corners of popular music, rappers themselves were ingeniously using the Web's nonmarket capacities to promote themselves with an updated version of an old-school technology. The mixtape, which emerged along with hip-hop culture in the late 1970s, retained the name even when it moved to the CD format and started being sold at local record stores. With the Internet, peer-to-peer, MP3s, and cheap digital production, however, mixtapes have been expanded and reimagined again—occasionally called "ziptapes," due to the file extension of archived MP3s—by up-and-coming rappers as a necessary component of a self-made marketing strategy, or by more established artists as a way to maintain the attention of a fickle public inundated with new artists every day. Million-selling rappers 50 Cent and Lil' Wayne are just two of the most noteworthy artists to rely on the unregulated mixtape market, which *The New York Times* referred to as "a cornerstone of the hip-hop industry" (Sanneh, 2007), to bolster their careers. Yet once they became a lucrative quasi-independent industry with its own stars such as DJ Drama, the major labels once again cited piracy concerns to call in the RIAA for a massive drug-style bust, like the early 2007 raid on Drama's studio (Sanneh, 2007).

These instances are rare, however, because the major labels realize that mixtapes, even those with significant uncleared samples of copyrighted material, work well as completely free promotion for official releases. Many have become art in their own right, as well: Lil' Wayne's *Da Drought 3*, The Clipse's *We Got It 4 Cheap, Vol. 2*, and M.I.A. and Diplo's *Piracy Funds Terrorism*, among many others, are regarded among these artists' best work. Yet this does not excuse the fact that mixtape culture is an individually funded grassroots promotional system in which rappers are more or less left to teach themselves the ropes, without the benefit of a label and industry veterans to help them choose a wise career path. The labels are more than willing to let rappers build a career for themselves on the independent circuit, however, before scooping them up and attempting to capitalize on their self-made hype.

While the major labels have spent the last decade resisting the digital turn at all stops, independent labels and artists, part of a movement that originally emerged in the wake of punk, have flourished by embracing the Internet and MP3s. Ed Droste, the singer-songwriter for the revered and popular indie quartet Grizzly Bear, explained:

> If we were putting out music in the early 90s . . . I don't think we'd have the fanbase that we have . . . were not for our songs being able to spread around the internet and gain attention. I think it'd be harder, if not impossible, for a band like us to have gotten where we've gotten. (Breihan, 2009)

Benkler (2006) has remarked that the hub-and-spoke structure of the 20th-century mass media model has given way to an Internet-supported distributed network model, which allows for many smaller clusters to take shape around particular sites, projects, ideas, and so forth. Through the affordances of blogs, social network platforms, and sites like Flickr and YouTube, the people within these clusters can not only interact with each other but also share ideas, opinions, and works with like-minded others in ways unimaginable a decade ago. For smaller indie artists and labels who would be ecstatic to sell in the five-figure range, this transformation means more audiences for more artists than ever before. Thus, what was formerly a struggle by indie artists and labels to break out of a local market has exponentially expanded into a patchwork global network of collaborators, consumers, and fans and a more potent impact on popular culture that renders terms like *subculture* and *underground* quaint.

The existing literature on postpunk indie locates the origins and ideologies of the term as a quasi-Puritanical ideology in danger of assimilation. Some (Hibbett, 2005; Thornton, 1996) have framed indie music and culture through a Bourdieuian lens of social exclusiveness gained through the possession of rare knowledge and cultural artifacts, while others (Hesmondhalgh, 1999; Lee, 1995) have questioned how indie's stark DIY precepts can survive in a music culture in which dealing with the major labels eventually becomes a necessity. Yet over the past decade, as U.S. indie has appended a global network of online collaborators and fans to its rickety network of campus bars, dusty record stores, and broken-down vans (Azerrad, 2001; Kruse, 2003), it has shed many of its attendant preoccupations with punk's spartan authenticity as quickly as it dropped the rock qualifier. Largely due to the heterogeneous clusters through which it circulates and transforms itself, the term *indie* today can incorporate electronic and dance music as easily as rock and punk, and the most successful labels—Sub Pop, Warp, Beggars, and Merge, for example—have developed business strategies that employ both new and old media and major label affiliations and techniques that have made them more stable and profitable than ever before, while retaining, and even bolstering, their capacity to curate and distribute idiosyncratic music.

A large part of indie's stabilization began in the 1990s, in the realm of physical distribution. In 1993, with the major labels still profiting from their fabrication of grunge and alternative from the fertile ranks of late-1980s American indie culture, Warner Music Group started the Alternative Distribution Alliance (ADA), which ensured that beloved indie labels could gain easier entry into previously untapped retail markets and "big box" chain stores. At the same time, ADA's work with indies allowed Warner not only to take a healthy cut of the profits at little cost but also to develop longer-term relationships with small independent record stores—a small but crucial commercial network with a fervent customer base. Though ADA has always focused its energies on physical music, it remains a force in distribution despite a dwindling market today and still retains a large roster of noteworthy indie labels that use its services.

While ADA is a crucial part of many indies' distribution plans, other labels have taken another step, by diversifying their brands and managing their own distribution arms. The sort of professionalization, industrialization, and brand management practiced by Bloomington, Indiana's small label Secretly Canadian or New York– and London-centered Beggars Group—both of which rely on ADA for distribution—would be a strange sight to the strictly principled but fledgling outfits Rough Trade and Wax Trax chronicled respectively by Hesmondhalgh (1999) and Lee (1995). Since starting in 1996, Secretly Canadian has expanded to operate aside two other labels, Jagjaguwar and Dead Oceans, and started its own distribution and manufacturing outfits—SC Distribution and Bellwether Manufacturing. For its part, Beggars is older and larger—starting in 1973 as a small London record shop called Beggars Banquet and spawning a successful indie label in 1977—and has expanded since then into a label group, encompassing legendary indie labels such as Rough Trade, 4AD, Matador, and XL, while maintaining offices in Canada, Germany, Japan, and New York.

Though the Internet has mostly been kind to indie artists and labels, many of the power relationships remain, particularly in the realm of licensing. To compete with the major labels for a share of the digital music, the Beggars

Group formed the American Association of Independent Music (A2IM) in 2005, which works by aggregating small labels into a larger collective bargaining force, allowing them much more leverage in negotiations with retail outlets such as MySpace Music, which recently relaunched as a competitor to iTunes and Amazon. More recently, the digital music distribution service TuneCore, which had already represented indie artists in negotiations with iTunes and Amazon's MP3 services, struck a deal with MySpace Music to allow *any* artist, whether represented by an aggregator, a label, or nothing at all, to distribute his or her songs through MySpace Music for a flat fee and share in part of the site's ad revenue.

Much coverage in the popular music press over the past half-decade has championed those bands that have seemingly mastered the Internet completely on their own. Indeed, a bevy of startup options exist for those artists who seek to go it alone—CD Baby, Amie Street, and SellaBand, among dozens of others, offer cheap ways for artists to distribute their music and profit from it—or, with SellaBand, to raise money to record in the first place. Yet by and large, these sites alone do not get indie artists coverage in *The New York Times*, on NPR, or in *Rolling Stone*—in these cases, again, many of the old rules still apply. Robert Strachan (2007) reveals that the much-buzzed-about artists Clap Your Hands Say Yeah and Arctic Monkeys—both of which were framed in the press as grassroots, DIY success stories—were represented behind the scenes by powerful PR concerns with lengthy track records of breaking successful artists.

Indie labels and artists have indeed succeeded in negotiating the rough corporate waters of online music distribution, promotion, and licensing, yet the issue of music's online circulation *before* its official release remains a thorny issue with which many indies are ill equipped to deal. As Radiohead was well aware of by the time of its *In Rainbows* stunt, all albums leak in advance of release—sometimes via a pressing plant employee ripping a master copy and uploading it to the Internet and other times due to an absent-minded critic losing track of an advance promotional copy, among other reasons. While it has yet to be proven if leaked albums negatively affect sales—most indications at this point are that they do not, at least in any significant capacity—indie labels and artists still understandably want to control their own promotional schedules and try to guarantee that their music is heard only through approved channels. Major labels have sent the RIAA after infringing Web sites and bloggers, but indies most often work with leaks instead of expressly against them. Most labels have success e-mailing infringing Web sites asking for files to be removed, but that tactic only temporarily bandages the situation—the music is still circulating and will continue to do so. Some labels have taken more experimental steps and altered their business models as a result. On a few of its releases from some of its more well-known and beloved acts such as Yo La Tengo and the New Pornographers, the Beggars Group, in a strategy similar to Radiohead's, initiated a plan called "Buy Early, Get Now," in which fans were rewarded with immediate MP3 downloads of albums and bonus tracks in exchange for preordering the physical copy of the record.

Of course, music fans are not simply pirates seeking free and early access to their favorite tunes. Henry Jenkins (2006) and a few others (Gray, Sandvoss, & Harrington, 2007; Hills, 2002) have situated the fan vis-à-vis the cultural industries, noting the ways in which affective labor is actively considered as part of marketing plans. While the major labels pay lip service to fans, indies have led the way in this regard, working with bloggers, message board participants, and other online denizens to help spread the word about smaller artists who otherwise might go unnoticed. This sort of publicity and critical work is especially crucial during a decade in which the writeable Web and a declining economy have eliminated the venues for music critics (the print arms of *Paste*, *Blender*, and *Vibe* all folded in recent years). Though some would argue that this sort of unpaid labor is exploitative, Nancy Baym and Robert Burnett (2009) find otherwise in their study of Swedish indie music fans. The fans interviewed by Baym and Burnett report that they receive many rewarding, though nonmonetary, benefits for their time and effort, including relationships with artists, promotional items, and the knowledge that they are contributing to the success of musicians they love.

Music bloggers in particular have emerged as the primary promotional targets for online indie success. Many indie labels, as well as a new crop of small PR firms, have developed mutually beneficial relationships with bloggers, servicing them with advance copies of albums and singles—a privilege formerly exclusively enjoyed by professional critics. Though blogs are mainly run by individuals, like the indie labels themselves, their labor is most productive when viewed cumulatively. In this regard, one of the most important innovations in music promotion, discovery, and tracking over the past 10 years is the MP3 blog aggregator Hype Machine. In a way, the Hype Machine has emerged as the SoundScan chart of the indie MP3 Web and stands as close as exists to a comprehensive statement of the most popular indie tracks on the Internet at any given time.

Though most music bloggers happily do so out of the desire for a productive and rewarding public pastime, a handful have used blogging as a springboard to other venues and opportunities. A few bloggers who started building their audiences early—around 2004, when the "boom" in blogging hit after coverage of the phenomenon in *Rolling Stone* and *The New York Times*— such as Gorilla vs. Bear and My Old Kentucky Blog, have parlayed their popularity into ancillary income by selling ads on their sites. Stereogum—which emerged in 2004 out of a VH1 employee's ample free time and quickly became the most popular music blog—acquired its first round of investment capital in late 2006, which the three investors, including the blogger himself, then exchanged in 2008 for a multimillion-dollar ownership stake in social media empire Buzznet. Music bloggers have found work in the shrinking critical sector as well as professional employment elsewhere, writing for sites such as Pitchfork.com, Spin.com, Wired.com, and Guardian.co.uk. A few other bloggers with a more promotional and curatorial bent have launched indie record labels and concert booking outfits. Recently, a few enterprising and creative individuals have launched sites that focus on live performance. Daytrotter catches touring musicians passing through northern Illinois, records live sessions with them, and posts MP3s and commentary for each. La Blogotheque is a Parisian blog that videotapes artists playing in nontraditional settings throughout the city.

Conclusion

At the start of the 21st century, musicians seeking to form a band and entrepreneurs trying to start a label find seemingly endless new technologies designed to help them do so. Yet the fact that those same technologies are available to everyone else has led to a glut of music competing for a limited amount of attention—leading some critics to coin the cynical neologism *landfill indie*. From the other end of the spectrum, though these same technologies—Twitter and MySpace in particular—have proven useful as a way for existing stars to maintain some form of contact with their fans and followers, they have proven far less useful as star-making mechanisms. It is useful to keep in mind that, though it appears that online superstars are born overnight, in fact even the most independent-seeming organization is often backed by behind-the-scenes promotions workers and significant capital investment, not to mention associations with retail outlets. Indeed, the reverse situation might seem to be the case: As digital technologies have allowed more entrants into music culture—artists making and labels releasing music, and fans downloading it, often freely—the major label system has not adapted but has moved in the opposite direction, shedding employees and cutting promotions and artist and repertoire budgets as profits for recorded music elude them.

Yet as I have tried to emphasize in the preceding remarks, gaining a foothold in digital music culture is far from dire for aspiring participants, though it does require a shift in paradigm and the establishment of some very reachable goals. Music stardom may be as out of reach as it has ever been, and alternately, Benkler (2006) warns us not to give in to the utopian discourses surrounding the networked information economy, which offer unreachable benchmarks. Instead, he continues, it is most important to realize that digital music exists in something of a liminal zone, a networked public sphere that "allows hundreds of millions of people to publish whatever and whenever they please without disintegrating into an unusable cacophony . . . and . . . filters and focuses attention without re-creating the highly concentrated model of the mass media" (Benkler, 2006, p. 253; see also Marina Vujnovic and Dean Kruckeberg, in this volume). Starting any sort of career in the music industries—whether performing and recording, managing, critiquing, distributing, or promoting—remains as dicey a proposition as ever. Yet though many of the models, power relationships, and rituals might be the same, the emergent, ever-shifting infrastructure of digital music culture, if reckoned with, can very well help sustain a career that would not have existed a decade ago.

References

Azerrad, M. (2001). *Our band could be your life: Scenes from the American indie underground, 1981–1991*. Boston, MA: Little, Brown.

Baym, N., & Burnett, R. (2009). Amateur experts: Amateur fan labor in Swedish independent music. *International Journal of Cultural Studies, 12*(5), 433–449.

Benkler, Y. (2006). *The wealth of networks: How social production transforms markets and freedom*. New Haven, CT: Yale University Press.

Bourdieu, P. (1984). *Distinction: A social critique of the judgment of taste*. Cambridge, MA: Harvard University Press.

Breihan, T. (2009, February 18). Grizzly Bear's Ed Droste tells all about *Veckatimest. Pitchfork*. Retrieved from http://pitchfork.com/news/34640-grizzly bears-ed-droste-tells-all-about-iveckatimesti/

Brownstein, C. (2009, November 10). To pay or not to pay? Q+A with Eliot Van Buskirk and Jay Sweet. *NPR's Monitor Mix with Carrie Brownstein*. Retrieved from http://www.npr.org/blogs/monitormix/2009/11/to_pay_or_not_to_pay_q_a_with.html

Byrne, D. (2007, December 18). David Byrne and Thom Yorke on the real value of music. *Wired*. Retrieved from http://www.wired.com/entertainment/music/magazine/16-01/ff_yorke

Gillespie, T. (2007). *Wired shut: Copyright and the shape of digital culture*. Cambridge, MA: MIT Press.

Gray, J., Sandvoss, C., & Harrington, C. L. (2007). Introduction: Why study fans? In J. Gray, C. Sandvoss, & C. L. Harrington (Eds.), *From fandom: Identities and communities in a mediated world* (pp. 1–16). New York: New York University Press.

Hesmondhalgh, D. (1997). Post-punk's attempt to democratise the music industry: The success and failure of rough trade. *Popular Music, 16*(3), 255–274.

Hesmondhalgh, D. (1999). Indie: The institutional politics and aesthetics of a popular music genre. *Cultural Studies, 13*(1), 34–61.

Hibbett, R. (2005). What is indie rock? *Popular Music and Society, 28*(1), 55–77.

Hills, M. (2002). *Fan cultures*. London, England: Routledge.

Jenkins, H. (2006). *Convergence culture: Where old and new media collide*. New York: New York University Press.

Jones, S. (2002). Music that moves: Popular music, distribution and network technologies. *Cultural Studies, 16*(2), 213–232.

Knopper, S. (2009). *Appetite for self-destruction: The spectacular crash of the record industry in the digital age*. New York, NY: Simon & Schuster/Free Press.

Kruse, H. (2003). *Site and sound: Understanding independent music scenes*. New York, NY: Peter Lang.

Lee, S. (1995). Re-examining the concept of the "independent" record company: The case of Wax Trax! Records. *Popular Music, 14*(1), 13–31.

Lessig, L. (2004). *Free culture: The nature and future of creativity*. New York, NY: Penguin Press.

Lessig, L. (2008). *Remix: Making art and commerce thrive in the hybrid economy.* New York, NY: Penguin Press.

Litman, J. (2001). *Digital copyright.* New York, NY: Prometheus Books.

Negus, K. (1999). *Music genres and corporate cultures.* London, England: Routledge.

Sanneh, K. (2007, January 19). With arrest of DJ Drama, the law takes aim at mixtapes. *The New York Times.* Retrieved from http://www.nytimes.com/2007/01/19/technology/19iht-web.0119mixtapes.html

Strachan, R. (2007). Micro-independent record labels in the UK: Discourse, DIY cultural production and the music industry. *European Journal of Cultural Studies, 10*(2), 245–265.

Thornton, S. (1996). *Club cultures: Music, media and subcultural capital.* Middletown, CT: Wesleyan University Press.

Williamson, J., & Cloonan, M. (2007). Rethinking the music industry. *Popular Music, 26*(2), 305–322.

Notes

1. I use "major labels" to refer to the music interests of the multinational corporations that control the vast majority of the U.S. music market. At the time of writing, those are Universal Music Group, Sony Music Entertainment, Warner Music Group, and EMI.

2. The RIAA attempted to define the MP3 player as a "recording device" and then suggested that it did not employ the proper copy protection standards laid out by the AHRA.

22

"Life Is a Pitch"

MANAGING THE SELF IN NEW MEDIA WORK

Rosalind Gill

In this chapter I pull together the findings of a number of studies of new media work—including my own research in the United Kingdom, the United States, and The Netherlands—to explore what it means to "manage" lives in new media. I use *management* here not in its conventional or "business school" sense but with a more critical inflection that comes from Marxist, feminist, and poststructuralist thinking. I'm interested in how workers themselves manage lives that are characterized by processes of speeding up, intensification, and contingency. Using a Foucauldian optic, I will suggest that working in new media involves multiple practices of *managing the self in conditions of radical uncertainty.*

The chapter is divided into three—unequal—sections. In the first, I briefly locate new media in the context of rapid transformations of work in capitalism and introduce the studies on which this paper is based. In the second—and by far the longest—section I highlight 10 key features of contemporary new media work including precariousness, new inequalities, and relentless pressures to keep up and stay abreast of changing technologies. Finally, in the conclusion I pull together the threads to argue that new media work calls forth or incites into being a new ideal worker-subject whose entire existence is built around work. She must be flexible, adaptable, sociable, self-directing, and able to work for days and nights at a time without encumbrances or needs and must commodify herself and others and recognize that—as one of my interviewees put it—every interaction is an opportunity for work. In short, for this modernized worker-subject, "life is a pitch."

Precarious Work

Transformations in advanced capitalism under the impact of globalization, rapidly developing information and communication technologies, and changing modes of political and economic governance are producing a situation in which increasing numbers of workers in affluent societies are in insecure casual or intermittent employment. Of course, this has long been the experience of most workers, for most of the time throughout the history of capitalism, but what is new is the way in which this is now extending even to professional workers in the affluent North and West. The last decades have seen a variety of attempts to make sense of the broad changes in contemporary capitalism that have given rise to this—through discussion of shifts relating to post-Fordism, postindustrial society, network society, liquid modernity, information society, new capitalism, and risk society (see also Toby Miller, and Mark Deuze and Leopoldina Fortunati, in this volume). While accounts vary significantly in their readings of the causes of transformations, there is some consensus that this "runaway world" (Giddens, 2002) or "brave new world of work" (Beck, 2000) is characterized by risk, insecurity, and contingency in which more and more of the costs of work are borne by the workers themselves. As Deuze (2007) puts it, "This is a time when most people experience their lives as a perpetual white water, living in a state of constant flux and uncertainty" (p. x).

In these accounts creative workers—and new media workers in particular—occupy a special place. They are seen by critics and celebrants alike as the forerunners of the future of work—exemplars of the move away from traditional notions of career to more informal precarious and intermittent employment; poster girls and boys for a future in which the need to constantly train and retrain, updating skills and knowledge, will be an ongoing requirement; immaterial laborers in informational capitalism and iconic members of "the precarious generation," potential subjects in a new "precariat" that may yet pose a threat to capitalism (see Gill & Pratt, 2008, for a useful summary of these debates).

At the same time, these workers have been endowed a leading role in policy discourses—part of the creative class (Florida, 2002) charged with providing a panacea for all social ills: regenerating urban areas, fostering community and social cohesion, and improving health, well-being, and quality of life. Above all, they are hailed by governments around the world as "new model workers" of the future: self-sacrificing, self-directed, entrepreneurial, accustomed to precarious employment, and motivated to produce big hits—ideally ones that will merge creativity with the financial possibilities of information-technology (IT) startups, generating a rapprochement between art and commerce (Caves, 2000; see also Chris Bilton, in this volume). Icons of new economy thinking, small entrepreneurial creative businesses are hailed as flexible and "risk tolerant." In this neoliberal rhetoric in which securities and benefits are seen as smothering enterprise and creativity, poor pay and profound insecurity are discursively sweetened (Beck, 2000), made palatable by talk of free agency (Pink, 2001) as if "an existential test of character" invites people to be exhilarated by the "thrill of proving themselves by finding out if they have what it takes to prevail in the heady swim of self-employment" (Ross, 2009, p. 5; see also Terry Flew, in this volume). If the buzz of risk taking does not appeal there are also the pleasures of the work itself—points repeatedly emphasized in policy documents: "Just imagine how good it feels to wake up every morning and really look forward to work. Imagine how good it feels to use your creativity, your skills, [or] your talent to produce a film or edit a magazine. Are you there? Does it feel good?" (from *Your Creative Future,* quoted in Nixon & Crewe, 2004, p. 141). At times these ideas can be mobilized with an almost breathtaking cynicism. In the United Kingdom, a Work Foundation report titled *Staying Ahead,* published late in 2007, asserts:

> The creative industries are peopled by creative talents who themselves get pleasure and utility from what they do. They are "called to their art." One upside from a business perspective (although it attracts complaints of exploitation) is that the "reservation" wages—the lowest they are prepared to work for—are lower than the marginal value of what they produce, making labour particularly cheap. The downside is that the "talent" care deeply about how creative work is organised, which may discourage concessions or compromises to management.

Discussing this report, Mark Banks and David Hesmondhalgh (2009) suggest that employers be warned: The creative is cheap, and potentially a source of trouble.

Do You Believe the Hype?

So far, we have seen little evidence of that "trouble" (e.g., resistance or refusal)—outside a few celebrated or notorious examples, mostly in the computer games industry (see, for example, de Peuter & Dyer-Witheford, 2006; Terranova, 2004). On the contrary, accounts of work in new media (and other creative industries) have sometimes borne a striking similarity to the policy hyperbole (e.g., Leadbeater & Oakley, 1999).

Excitement, buzz, pleasure, and autonomy are accorded a central place. Moreover, as I argued some years ago (Gill, 2002), new media work has had a good press. It is popularly regarded as exciting and cutting-edge work, and its practitioners are seen as artistic, young, and cool—especially when compared with the previous generation of technologically literate IT workers (e.g., programmers and software designers) who had a distinctly more nerdy or geeky image. The work itself is seen as creative and autonomous, and working environments and relationships are viewed as relaxed and nonhierarchical. When new media businesses are shown on television, the now standard tropes of representation include a trendy warehouse setting in the cultural quarter of a city, a group of young people coded as diverse (male, female, Black, White, gay, straight) and as creative (untidy, chaotic, obsessive), who work long and unusual hours (e.g., getting up at lunchtime and then working through the night) and relate to each other in a casual and informal manner. This view of new media work is not limited to television producers but is widely shared among the general public, academics, policymakers, and even new media workers themselves—who cite the youth, dynamism, and informality of new media work as some of the main reasons it was attractive to them (Gill & Dodd, 2000).

However, in the last few years, a number of studies have offered a different picture of working lives in new media—one that recognizes the pleasures but also looks at some of the costs of this kind of working life—attending to what Angela McRobbie (2006) calls "the pleasure-pain axis." Taken together, these studies offer a remarkably consistent portrait of new media work. In what follows, I highlight 10 key features of these working lives, drawing on my own research over the last decade, conducted in seven European countries and the United States, which has featured cross-national surveys, as well as more than 250 in-depth interviews (see Gill, 2007; Gill & Dodd, 2000; Pratt, Gill, & Spelthann, 2007).

The interviews from which I quote in this paper were conducted among new media workers in Amsterdam (see Gill, 2007, for full report). The term *new media work* covers an extraordinary diversity of different occupations. Rather than imposing our own definitions, interviewees were invited to tell us how they described their own work, and among the job titles we heard there was barely a single overlap. Self-descriptions included programmer, interaction designer, editor, copywriter, business manager, artist, illustrator, researcher, content manager, freelance concept maker, software document writer, consultant, project manager, Web site developer, and entrepreneur. Participants in the study also fell into many different categories of employment—freelancers, company owners, or employees—frequently moving between these on a regular basis or even combining different statuses at the same time (e.g., working freelance in their own time but also being in paid employment to "pay the bills" or "learn more skills").

It quickly became clear that work biographies in new media are extremely rich and complex and bear little resemblance to traditional notions of the "career" with their expectations of linear development and progression of the hierarchy. They are what Lisa Adkins (2008) has called "DIY biographies"—working lives lived with a sense of needing to be adaptable and ready to have a go at anything.

New Media Lives: 10 Key Features

1. Love of the Work

A consistent finding of research on new media workers is the passion it inspires and the profound affective ties people develop to their work

(Neff, Wissinger, & Zukin, 2005; Ross, 2003). The sheer enjoyment of the work was mentioned by many of my interviewees who said, for example, "It's like being paid for your hobby." For some, this derived from the sensuous experience of creative work itself; for others it was the buzz of the working environment. As Bas, a man in his 30s, put it, "The atmosphere at work is relaxed, jovial. There is music on in the office and people have lively conversations. No dull factory humanoids here." Still others were inspired by "the chance to communicate in new ways" and the opportunities to work in a new medium that "does not have a tradition like other art forms have" and is therefore "open to people to develop it."

2. Entrepreneurialism

A certain entrepreneurialism defines many working in new media (Neff et al., 2005). This can be seen in both the economic organization—the proliferation of microbusinesses or independents—and the habits and dispositions and mentalities of the workers, with their aspirations to innovate, create, and be pioneers (Adkins, 2008; see also Eric Harvey, in this volume). As one of my respondents put it, "The only limit is our imagination. We are learning, making it up, creating it."

Unlike studies in the United States, in which financial reward was often mentioned (Batt, Christopherson, & Rightor, 1999), research in Europe has not highlighted money as a particular motivation for new media workers (see also Susan Christopherson, in this volume). Nevertheless, an entrepreneurial thrill was central to involvement in new media work—particularly the autonomy to direct one's own work when and where one likes without being answerable to a boss.

3. Short-Term, Precarious, Insecure Work

Precarious and intermittent work seems to be endemic to life in new media, as with much other cultural work (Banks, 2007; Deuze, 2007; McRobbie, 2002, 2007; Ursell, 2000). This is clearly the case for freelancers, who often combine several different jobs in order to survive. These might be multiple new media jobs or, more commonly, jobs in teaching or the service sector to pay the bills. In my studies, insecurity was a defining feature of freelancers' lives. As Harry put it, "It's insecure. Maybe I will look for jobs two days a week to pay the rent. But really I'm too busy for that." Worrying about the next piece of work was a major preoccupation: "I was wondering, shit where is the next assignment. Two or three months now without assignments. Gee!"

The insecure conditions experienced by freelancers translated into concerns about lack of access to benefits, insurance, and pension schemes and attendant worries about becoming ill, having an accident, or having to work into old age. Not surprisingly these concerns were experienced most acutely by the older age groups in our research. Moreover, many people could not bridge downtimes over periods like Christmas, and few were able to take holidays. Regulating the flow of work also produced anxiety: "In an ideal situation I have two or three assignments at the same time. Lower than that is scary and higher than that is too busy. But two or three assignments is good." Yet most people shared the view that it was always too risky to turn down work—and this in itself could produce problems, not in the least exhaustion:

> It's very intensive and I don't have enough time to rest. Because it's always going on. And if you don't plan something for yourself, someone will call and say you have to be there, and there. You can't say no to a job. Because you don't know when the next job is going to be.

But those in contracted employment were not necessarily faring much better. A steady contract might only be for 3 months, and some people were in the seemingly paradoxical position of having stock options in the company yet being on a zero-hours contract, which meant that they could lose their job without any notice at all.

4. Low Pay

Contrary to the myths and to examples of companies that were able to develop a single big hit, breakthrough project (McRobbie, 2007), or concept, thus attracting major financial rewards, most people in new media work for very low pay. Again, freelancers or microbusinesses are disproportionately affected by this, and "second jobbing" is common. Superficially, hourly rates might appear reasonably high, but these rates were rarely an accurate reflection of real pay—not least because of the pressures to pitch low in order to get a piece of work or because of a marked tendency to underestimate how long an assignment would take. Respondents repeatedly told us that "it always takes me three times longer than I think it will" with the effect that all the excess hours are unpaid. Time budgeting and other business or self-management skills were occasionally mentioned in interviews as desirable to learn, yet it is not clear that such training would actually help freelancers, given the competitive pressures on prices that most feel constrained by—that is, "to win the contract, you sometimes have to quote it for less than it will actually cost you." Without interventions such as fixed union rates for the job, it might be expected that freelancers who pitched at the appropriate level would simply not get the job. Interviewees were painfully aware of this.

Another factor was the desire to do good work for organizations to whom one was sympathetic or with whom workers were connected through a web of friendship and business contacts. Connected to this, too, was the sacrificial ethos described by Andrew Ross (2000), in which commitment to values of a higher nature—for example the idea of art for art's sake or of creativity as a calling—feeds into a mentality in which workers are prepared to accept appalling pay and conditions that would, in other sectors, be regarded as nakedly exploitative.

5. Long-Hours Cultures

Creative work in new media is marked by very long hours—particularly among those who freelance or work in their own microenterprises. In my study, participants reported regularly working between 60 and 80 hours per week.

One respondent explained exactly how he settled on the length of his working week: He learned from others about the maximum number of hours it was possible to work over a long and sustained period without burning out, and he tried to keep to this number: 65 hours each week. Many people regularly had to "pull all-nighters" in order to finish projects but then found themselves in periods without any work at all—the classic example of what Andy Pratt (2002) has called a "bulimic" style of working. But work was not just *intensive*; it was also marked by *extensification* (Jarvis & Pratt, 2006) across different spaces of the workers' lives—not just in a workplace but also at home, on the train, on the beach. For some this was experienced as pleasurable, a matter of "putting everything into my own company" and "doing something I like" that "gives me energy." For others it was almost a badge of commitment. In response to a question about how her work fit with the rest of her life one young woman answered, "I don't do anything else. Well, some things. But it is creative and I put everything in that. And if you don't love what you do, you better stop." Even this interviewee, however, did acknowledge that she might want to work for fewer hours as she grew older and to "have some time for myself."

6. Keeping Up

Compared to other creative fields (e.g., fine art, performance), new media work is an industry in which knowledge changes at an extraordinarily rapid pace, new software packages and standards proliferate, and people experience intense pressure to keep up and stay abreast of current developments. The time needed to stay up-to-date and reskill was often experienced as an additional requirement on top of already long working hours:

> Well I think the hours that we make . . . it is sometimes really incredible. Working through the night happens regularly, and if you have kids as well . . . well I don't know. Plus you have to keep up and that takes time and energy as well.

Constantly keeping up with new knowledge in the field sometimes produces anxiety and fears of being left behind or becoming ill through overwork:

> I do find the speed of change intimidating at times, I admit that. I find it difficult to keep my work in check. I used to take work home with me, in order to be able to read. And that has become a habit. . . . It's a privilege to have a job which is also your hobby, but it shouldn't make you ill.

Even the thought of having relentlessly to check, monitor, and update one's skills could sometimes be experienced as oppressive.

7. DIY Learning

New media workers are generally highly educated, often to degree level and beyond. However, they are also likely to have been disappointed by their experiences of formal education, critiquing the dominance of theory over practice in university education, the failure of courses and teachers to keep pace with change, and the lack of preparation for working in business environments or, crucially, for managing portfolio careers or other nonstandard forms of employment. The vast majority favored learning informally from the Net, from other people, or through trial and error—"learning by doing," as one interviewee put it.

8. Informality

The informality of work in new media has many aspects. On the one hand are the legendary workplaces of Apple, Microsoft, Google, and other huge corporations with their 24/7 cultures and promises that all needs can be met within the organization (see Bronson, 1999). Features of these much mythologized work environments have filtered down into medium-sized enterprises with table football, TV packages, freely available food and drink, and a general bohemian "work as play" ethos (de Peuter & Dyer-Witheford, 2006; Ross, 2003). This too can be seen in the "club to company" (McRobbie, 2003) atmosphere of many microbusinesses and startup companies—a "friends' club that got out of hand" as one of the interviewees put it. But more than this, informality is the structuring principle on which many small and medium-sized new media companies seem to operate: Finding work, recruiting staff, and getting clients are all seemingly removed from the formal sphere governed by established procedures, equal opportunities legislation, or union agreements and located in an arena based on informality, sociality, and "who you know."

Fundamentally, finding work in new media—in whatever capacity or contractual status—is based on an amalgam between two commonplaces that circulated through the interviews. These were the phrases *It's all down to who you know* and *You are only as good as your last job* (Blair, 2001). The two could sometimes be in tension but often worked in concert—particularly in the absence of official accounts of workers' achievements, such as employer references, formal qualifications, or accreditation (in a context in which, as we have seen, much learning is done informally or on the job). The entire economy of (new) media work opportunities operates through contacts—people you meet at conferences, parties, drinks evenings, friends of friends, ex-colleagues, and so on.

Informality propels networking to center stage in the lives of new media workers. As one interviewee said, "It never hurts to network. That is true. I am friends with a lot of companies who do the same and I have established that the more people I know who do the same as I do, the more work I have." Others told us that networking had become a necessity or obligation: "Monday night is the only night I don't have networking drinks." The requirement to network and build contacts also brings other pressures, named by Melissa Gregg (in press) as the "compulsory sociality" of the neoliberal workplace, in which one can never really switch off or relax and one is never totally away from work. Indeed, in this sense, the entire self is a work project that must be presented in all the right ways on all the right occasions. This "work on the self" will be returned to later in this chapter as a key part of managing (new) media work.

9. Exclusions and Inequalities

As noted earlier, one of the potent myths of new media work beloved by TV producers, policymakers, and new media workers themselves is that the field is cool, creative, and egalitarian. However, new media workplaces have turned out to be characterized by a number of entrenched and all-too-old-fashioned patterns of inequality relating to gender, age, class, race and ethnicity, and disability.

In addition to rather familiar patterns of inequality relating to access to work within the field, rates of pay, and so on, there seem to be a number of new forms of inequality emerging relating it to precisely the features of work that are most highly valued—autonomy, flexibility, and informality (Mayerhofer & Mokre, 2007; Perrons, 2003). As I have argued elsewhere (Gill, 2002), the increasing prevalence of informal practices for hiring staff or issuing contracts raises grave concerns for equal opportunities—concerns that are extremely difficult to contest or even discuss because of the lack of transparency in the process. Similarly the flexibility of new media work does not necessarily serve equality well. As Diane Perrons (1999) has noted, there is a flexible discourse of flexibility, and invariably this is not determined in the workers' interest.

Round-the-clock working in order to finish a project did not suit all workers, and this was perceived as a particular problem for those with—or contemplating having—children. Disproportionately this impacted women (though some men were also aware of it), as one female interviewee mentioned:

> We are trying to have a baby, so then we will see. I definitely want to keep on working and have my own income. I hope it won't get less. So I think I'll bring the baby to the creche. But frankly I have no idea. I am a bit afraid and I think nothing is arranged to women like me who have their own companies.

Meanwhile, another study participant reflected on the worries he and his female partner—also involved in new media work—have about having a family:

> I have a relationship with somebody. She is also involved in this work. I don't know if we are going to have kids. It scares the living hell out of me, the whole idea. Because overwork is just the reality of what I am doing, like all people in new media. Horrifying overwork is the reality. Like how many hours a week? Oh man, the amount of hours I have to put in in a week on this job—it amounts to 2 full-time jobs easily. And I mean I am working with a very good planner and I'm having a hell of a time keeping the hours. That is what I'm most scared of in my personal life. The impact of having no time for a kid or . . . that is what I'm most scared of. If I had some kids, boy it would be a tough life.

Perhaps not surprisingly, studies have indicated the very small proportion of women in new media who have children (Batt et al., 1999; Gill & Dodd, 2000), and this was also the case in my own research—a finding that resonates with discussions of the emergence of more complex inequalities in other creative industries (including journalism and academia).

A further distinctive contribution to inequality in new media work is what I call a postfeminist problem, namely the increasing unspeakability of structural inequalities. This unspeakability of inequality could be seen in relation to race and ethnic minorities too. In my research it was clear that interviewees had a deep attachment to the notion of the field as "diverse" and "egalitarian" with success based solely on merit. This led to a reluctance, even a refusal, to see or speak of inequalities. It was striking, for example, that only 3 interviewees (out of 34) mentioned the overall dominance of White people in the new media scene in Amsterdam—despite direct invitations to reflect on this. But a Black respondent, Stefan, told us how potential clients could "hear" his non-Whiteness, and how he then had to expend a great deal of time and energy elaborating on his background—only to frequently not get a callback:

Well I am Surinami and people who call me hear that I am Surinami.
Then I usually have to explain that even though my name is Stefan
I am not Dutch. If need be I will tell them my life story. People try to
put you in categories but they can't put me in a category. It's simply
impossible. I want to be able to work with everybody, Dutch and
Surinami. Not for one specific target group.

Another relatively recent arrival to Amsterdam commented, "At [the
major new media company] where I worked before, all the cleaners, waiters
and security guards had brown skin and brown faces, and all the web designers had blond hair and blue eyes." It is striking that two of the three people
who commented on this issue were themselves immigrants to The
Netherlands; it simply did not seem to be visible or worthy of comment to
others among our participants—a tendency that tells us a great deal about
the normalization and power of Whiteness.

10. No Future

Finally, one striking finding from my research has been the inability of
workers to imagine—realistically—their futures. Toward the end of the interviews, I asked a seemingly innocuous question: "What do you think you'll be
doing in 5 years' time?" Anyone who has ever been interviewed for a position
in a large company or public sector organization will recognize this as one of
a number of standard inquiries. In occupations like law or teaching or sales the
preferred response is clear: You must express ambition, a desire to move up the
hierarchy, a wish to be successful. Asking the same question of new media
workers, however, produced perplexing answers. Respondents would either
point to imagined futures characterized by lifestyles of wealth and glamour
("sipping champagne on my yacht") or, alternately, depict no future at all
("I really have no clue. I can't see myself continuing"). Occasionally, a single
individual offered both kinds of response.

These polarized responses on the one hand fantasize a life of extreme success with all its trappings and on the other express complete failure or even a
void as new media workers could seemingly not articulate any sense of their
future. I argue that for these workers material conditions of radical uncertainty lead to an inability to project ahead into the future in a realistic or
meaningful way, and suggest that this constitutes one of the new but hidden
injuries of precarious work.

Managing the Self: When "Life Is a Pitch"

In their book *Managing Creativity*, Howard Davis and Richard Scase (2000)
ask an important question: "What should replace the management principles
and practices inherited from industrial society in the organisations which

predominate in post-industrial society?" (p ix). Research on new media work suggests that older, established management practices have little role in contemporary precarious working lives. In their place, a different form of management has taken hold—a management of the self, in which power operates not through formal, top-down structures or bureaucratic rationalities but through *technologies of selfhood* in which a novel form of worker-subjectivity is incited into being.

In this new neoliberal form of governmentality new media workers are constituted as autonomous, self-regulating, responsibilized subjects. If the superficial bohemian chic of new media workplaces suggests relaxed informality, this is only part of the story; beyond the significations of play an intense self-discipline is required. However, this is not self-discipline as it is traditionally understood (early mornings, cold showers, and highly polished shoes are not required!) but a much more thoroughgoing, wholesale *management of the self,* which requires the radical remaking of subjectivity. It may not even be experienced as such—indeed, it's much more likely to be understood as simply "the way things are."

In new media work there is a great deal to take care of—particularly, but not exclusively, for those freelancing or setting up microbusinesses. You are required to train yourself; keep up-to-date; find or create your own work; monitor your progress; compare yourself with others; anticipate what will come next; maintain your distinct reputation; meet deadlines whatever costs they exert on your body or relationships; prepare for contingencies such as illness, injury, or old age; make contacts; network; and socialize—and to do all of this in an atmosphere in which your success or failure is understood in entirely individualistic terms.

There is no time when you can switch off, because all of life has become a "social factory" (Tronti, 1966), an opportunity for work. Whoever you meet, wherever you go—a friend's wedding, a high school reunion, a cycling holiday with friends—represents a possible opportunity. There is no outside to work, as one of our interviewees put it: "Life itself is a pitch."

References

Adkins, L. (2008). *Creativity, biography and the time of individualisation.* Paper presented at Creative Biographies Seminar, Open University, May.

Banks, M. (2007). *The politics of cultural work.* Basingstoke, England: Palgrave Macmillan.

Banks, M., & Hesmondhalgh, D. (2009). Looking for work in creative industries policy. *International Journal of Cultural Policy, 15,* 415–430.

Batt, R., Christopherson, S., & Rightor, N. (1999). *Net-working: Working life in a project based industry: A collaborative study of people working in new media in New York.* Ithaca, NY: Cornell University Press.

Beck, U. (2000). *The brave new world of work.* Cambridge, England: Polity Press.

Blair, H. (2001). "You're only as good as your last job": The labour process and labour market in the British film industry. *Work, Employment and Society, 15*(1), 149–169.

Bronson, P. (1999). *The nudist on the late shift*. London, England: Secker & Warburg.

Caves, R. E. (2000). *Creative industries: Contracts between art and commerce*. Cambridge, MA: Harvard University Press.

Davis, H. H., & Scase, R. (2000). *Managing creativity: The dynamics of work and organization*. Buckingham, England: Open University Press.

de Peuter, G., & Dyer-Witheford, N. (2006). A playful multitude? Mobilising and counter-mobilising immaterial game labour. *Fibreculture, 5*. Retrieved from http://journal.fibreculture.org/issue5/depeuter_dyerwitheford.html

Deuze, M. (2007). *Media work*. Cambridge, England: Polity Press.

Florida, R. L. (2002). *The rise of the creative class*. New York, NY: Basic Books.

Giddens, A. (2002). *Runaway world*. London, England: Profile.

Gill, R. (2002). Cool creative and egalitarian? Exploring gender in project-based new media work in Europe. *Information, Communication and Society, 5*(1), 70–89.

Gill, R. (2007). Technobohemians or the new cybertariat? New media work in Amsterdam a decade after the web. *Network Notebooks*. Amsterdam, The Netherlands: Institute of Network Cultures.

Gill, R., & Dodd, D. (2000). *New media: Working practices in the electronic arts*. Final report submitted to Directorale General V, European Commission, Brussels, Belgium.

Gill, R., & Pratt, A. (2008). In the social factory? Immaterial labour, precariousness and cultural work. *Theory Culture Society, 25*(1), 1–30.

Gregg, M. (in press). On Friday night drinks: Workplace affect in the age of the cubicle. In M. Gregg & G. J. Seigworth (Eds.), *The affect theory reader*. Durham, NC: Duke University Press.

Jarvis, H., & Pratt, A. C. (2006). Bringing it all back home: The extensification and "overflowing" of work. The case of San Francisco's new media households. *Geoforum, 37*(3), 331–339.

Leadbeater, C., & Oakley, K. (1999). *The new independents—Britain's new cultural entrepreneurs*. London, England: Demos.

Mayerhofer, E., & Mokre, M. (2007). The creative industries in Austria: The glories of the past vs. the uncertainties of the present. In G. Lovink & N. Rossiter (Eds.), *My creativity reader: A critique of the creative industries* (pp. 141–150). Amsterdam, The Netherlands: Institute of Network Cultures.

McRobbie, A. (2002). From Holloway to Hollywood: Happiness at work in the new cultural economy. In P. du Gay & M. Pryke (Eds.), *Cultural economy* (pp. 97–114). London, England: Sage.

McRobbie, A. (2003). Club to company. *Cultural studies, 16*(4), 516–531.

McRobbie, A. (2006). *Creative London—Creative Berlin*. Retrieved from http://www.ateliereuropa.com/2.3_essay.php

McRobbie, A. (2007). *The Los Angelisation of London: Three short-waves of young people's micro-economies of culture and creativity in the UK*. EIPCP paper. Retrieved from http://eipcp.net/transversal/0207/mcrobbie/en

Neff, G., Wissinger, E., & Zukin, S. (2005). Entrepreneurial labour among cultural producers: "Cool" jobs in "hot" industries. *Social Semiotics, 15*(3), 307–334.

Nixon, S., & Crewe, B. (2004). Pleasure at work? Gender consumption and work based identities in the creative industries. *Consumption, Markets and Culture, 7*(2), 129–147.

Perrons, D. (1999). Flexible working patterns and equal opportunities in the European Union: Conflict or compatibility? *European Journal of Women's Studies, 6*(4), 391–418.

Perrons, D. (2003). The new economy and the work life balance: A case study of the new media sector in Brighton and Hove. *Gender Work and Organisation, 10*(1), 65–93.

Pink, D. H. (2001). *Free agent nation: How America's new independent workers are transforming the way we live.* New York, NY: Warner Books.

Pratt, A. C. (2002). Hot jobs in cool places. The material cultures of new media product spaces: The case of the South of Market, San Francisco. *Information, Communication and Society, 5*(1), 27–50.

Pratt, A. C., Gill, R. C., & Spelthann, V. (2007). Work and the city in the e-society: A critical investigation of the socio-spatially situated character of economic production in the digital content industries, UK. *Information, Communication & Society, 10*(6), 921–941.

Rose, N. S. (1996). *Inventing our selves: Psychology, power and personhood.* Cambridge, England: Cambridge University Press.

Ross, A. (2000). The mental labour problem. *Social Text, 18*(2), 7–34.

Ross, A. (2003). *No-collar: The humane workplace and its hidden costs.* New York, NY: Basic Books.

Ross, A. (2009). *Nice work if you can get it: Life and labor in precarious times.* New York: New York University Press.

Terranova, T. (2004). *Network culture: Politics for the information age.* London, England: Pluto Press.

Tronti, M. (1966). *Operai e capitale.* Turin, Italy: Einaudi.

Ursell, G. (2000). Television production: Issues of exploitation, commodification and subjectivity in UK television markets. *Media Culture & Society, 22*(6), 805–825.

Walkerdine, V., Lucey, H., & Melody, J. (2001). *Growing up girl: Psychosocial explorations of gender and class.* Basingstoke, England: Palgrave Macmillan.

Work Foundation. (2007). *Staying ahead: The economic performance of the UK's creative industries.* London, England: Author.

SECTION IV

Future Perspectives

23 Managing Media Companies Through the Digital Transition

Annet Aris

In the Western world, digital media are more and more dominating the media landscape. New media companies have become powerful players, which increasingly compete for the share of mind of consumers and advertising revenue. Traditional media companies are starting to be affected in their core and are forced to rethink their business models fundamentally. This has major implications for the way these companies are managed, and some long-held beliefs are put into question. This chapter will assess the impact of these developments on the organization of "traditional" media companies in the Western world by addressing the following questions:

1. What will be the key effects of digitization on the business models of "traditional" media companies?

2. How will this affect the future skills needed?

3. What can media companies do to acquire these new skills fast and constructively (i.e., without destroying the "old" skills)?

Digitization Changes the Fundamentals of the Media Organization

In almost all Western countries broadband has reached more than half of the households, and interactive digital TV and mobile data platforms are being rolled out at high speed. Consumer, but increasingly also advertiser, behavior is adapting fast, and there are clear signs that long-predicted trends are now becoming reality. Amplified by the financial crisis, many traditional media companies have seen their revenue collapsing and are realizing that this revenue will only partly return as the economy recovers. Digitization enables the fulfillment of numerous latent consumer needs, to which traditional analog media could not cater. This is also partly why the new offerings are adopted so quickly by end consumers. Advertisers have been slower to adapt due to system inertia; however, they are now following suit. What are these needs, and how do they affect the business models of traditional media companies?

1. Content à la Carte

One of the key value propositions of traditional media companies—TV channels, music majors, newspapers, magazine and book publishers—was their ability to create and/or select content that would please their audience and expand its horizons by introducing new, unexpected experiences and insights. The burden of selection and exploration was taken away from the end consumer, and at the same time the experience could be shared with many others who were exposed to the same content at the same time. Already with the early rise of the Internet and the explosion of legal and illegal music downloads it became clear that consumers were disgruntled by the fact that they were forced to consume (and pay for) the "whole" package and that mass media were often not able to cater to their individual taste. With the emergence of sophisticated search engines on-demand consumption quickly spilled over to other types of content like news (e.g., often over 50% of online news articles are currently accessed through search engines rather than through the home page of the newspaper). As high-speed broadband gains market share, on-demand consumption of video content is also increasing fast. In the United Kingdom, one of the most advanced countries in the digital arena, over 50% of all Britons used video on demand in 2009, and ITV, the leading U.K. commercial broadcaster, expects that in 2013 20% of TV viewing time in fully digital households in the United Kingdom will be on demand.

Traditional media companies have always claimed that the "couch potato," which lingers inside all of us, will not disappear overnight and the social importance of joined media consumption will remain high, as highly successful reality shows and TV series show. Consumers will not want to go through the trouble of scouting their own content. Google, on the other hand, with its mission "to organize the world's information and make it accessible and useful to all," is a staunch believer in the initiative of the individual.

The truth, however, is, as always, in the middle. There are indeed only a few consumers who are willing to actively discover their own content. For example, in the music industry it is estimated that only 10% of all consumers have a clear personal music taste; others are mostly influenced by recommendations by friends and by the frequency with which they hear a song. However, there are many other ways for consumers to get to content they like. In the music industry, which involuntarily became the front-runner in this field, smart music portals such as Last.fm, Pandora, and Spotify have developed various techniques to preselect music for their users; TiVo is investing heavily in techniques to proactively record TV content based on the historic viewing behavior of its customers; search engines are investing big-time in developing more refined behavioral and contextual search approaches; and many smart electronic program guides (EPGs) are being developed to improve the access to video content. Last but not least social networks such as MySpace and Facebook also play an important role in selecting and recommending content to peer groups.

In summary, traditional media companies will have to embrace the fact that a significant share of content will be consumed on demand ("nonlinear") and a large number of (specialized) parties will try to own the access interface to this nonlinear content and get a share of the pie.

2. Content Everywhere

For many years it has been predicted that consumers will access their content independent of where they are and the appliance they use. However, difficulties in adapting the content to the various formats, rights issues, and cumbersome user interfaces of mobile data devices have prevented this prediction from coming true. The recent rise of high-speed broadband is changing this, as more and more viewers can access high-quality video on their PCs; TV manufacturers such as Philips and Samsung are launching Internet protocol television (IPTV)–enabled TVs, which offer access to YouTube and other portals the moment the TV is switched on, and appliances such as common interface (CI) cards are allowing people in a simple way to access the Internet through their TV without cumbersome set-top boxes.

Also the launch of the iPhone was a breakthrough in the use of mobile data devices because of its intuitive, easy-to-use interface; low costs for data (the iPhone switches automatically to the local Wi-Fi network); and open interface, which stimulated an avalanche of attractive data applications. In Norway shortly after the launch of the iPhone, 50% of mobile data traffic was through the iPhone, although it had a market share of only 1%. Other mobile phone manufacturers are following suit quickly.

In addition e-reader devices, which for a long time were not taken seriously as they were cumbersome and expensive and content was lacking, are now seriously pushed by powerful players such as Amazon and Google and are gaining momentum. With the expected launch of tablet PCs in summer 2010 a next generation of readers will come on the market, which is an alternative not only to books but also to magazines and newspapers.

Rights are still an issue, but rights owners are realizing they have to follow suit in order not to be outdone by piracy. For media companies this means that they will have to start to take the multiscreen approach seriously, also including mobile.

3. Content for Free

One of the most worrisome developments in the digital media world is the trend toward "free content." As the marginal cost of distributing digitized content is very low and in many cases tending to zero and piracy is rampant, more and more media companies are switching to free digital content models that are financed by advertising. The problem they are facing, however, is that so far they have managed to capture only 5%–10% of the online advertising markets, and the rates are significantly below the offline rates. Many media companies complain that they are "exchanging analog dollars for digital cents."

Even the analog world is affected by the trend to free content: To stay competitive, traditional media companies have also started to offer their offline content increasingly for free as the rise of free commuter newspapers shows. This has caused an overall shift away from paid content to advertising-financed content. In The Netherlands, for example, in 2002, 60% of media content (box office; video or DVD; newspapers; magazines; books; TV, excluding public license fees; radio; Internet, excluding access and e-commerce and games; and outdoor advertising) was paid for by the consumer and 40% by advertisers, but in 2007 this number had shifted to respectively 48% and 52%.

It is clear that in the midterm advertising revenue will not be able to compensate for the loss in paid content fully and media companies will have to look to other sources of revenue as well as try to regain income from paid content. Many media companies are experimenting with "third-party income" (i.e., deals with platform operators such as cable and telecom companies such as Orange in France, and mobile device manufacturers like Nokia, where consumers get access to content for free if they subscribe to the platform and/or buy the device). Several others are trying to enter the field of e-commerce.

A major challenge for media companies is thus not only to increase their income from advertising revenues but also to find creative new ways to generate revenue, like making revenue-sharing deals with platform operators and/or e-commerce players and enticing consumers to pay for digital content through innovative subscription and/or micropayment offerings. At the same time media companies will have to face the reality that most likely overall revenue in the industry will decline and significant cost reductions will be needed in all functions.

4. Vocal Consumers

In the analog world consumers were passive receivers of content, their taste strongly guided by a few "expert" opinion makers, like radio DJs, movie critics, TV programmers, or retail chains.

With the rise of the Internet, consumers now have the chance to express themselves and be heard directly. For some consumers this means that they actively contribute content themselves (e.g., video clips or blogs). For media companies this is both a threat and an opportunity. The threat is that the Internet is flooded by free content that can be quite successful and takes away eyeballs from professional content. On the upside, the Internet offers a unique opportunity to scout for new talent.

Although the group that actively creates content is small (it is estimated that about 1% of consumers contribute around 90% of all user-generated content, or UGC), a much larger group contributes by rating content, either actively by posting comments, recommendations, and classifications or passively as its surfing behavior is used as input for recommendation machines. Social networks play an increasingly important role in shaping tastes, and often a few key opinion leaders in these networks can wield a significant influence. Consumers' true likes and dislikes become transparent, and not only "professional experts" but also influential "amateur" opinion makers can influence the success of media content greatly.

In a world where the end user not only consumes but also actively contributes to content generation and selection, media companies will have to be able to actively engage with consumers, incorporate their contributions, and understand who are the key opinion makers at the nodes of social networks.

5. Global Reach

With the exception of some (U.S.) blockbusters, media content used to be local. A deep understanding of local taste and customs was the key to success. Even international TV formats and magazine titles had to be adapted carefully to local taste to become successful. Rights were sold on a country-by-country basis. Also advertisers followed a strong local approach and only talked to local sales forces. For this reason most European companies have followed a decentralized approach, where each country had its own organization, which mostly could operate as an independent profit center.

With the rise of digital platforms these rules of the game are changing. Content can spread around the world without limitations; when not legal, it is pirated. Niche products can become attractive as they can reach global audiences. The major players in the new media world such as Google, Amazon, Microsoft, and eBay are global players, which, although they still have country organization, have centralized several of the most strategic functions, such as product development. There are significant international scale effects in the development of platforms and applications, and also advertisers are slowly moving to more international campaigns.

For traditional media companies this means that they will have to rethink their staunchly decentralized country-by-country approach and start to carefully think through which functions and activities need a more international approach in order to create the critical mass and speed needed to compete with the new media giants.

6. Targeted and Performance-Based Advertising

Traditionally advertisers and media agencies have been slow to adopt the new media, and even now the proportion of advertising money spent on digital media is in most Western countries way below the proportion of time spent with these new media. Traditional media companies have long felt relatively safe, as they claimed that they were the only ones who could guarantee reach and frequency to mass advertisers and offer a superior (emotional) quality of their advertising offerings. In addition the rules of the game in the advertising ecosystem (i.e., the roles of the various players), payment rules, and measurement practices are resistant to change, which makes it difficult and costly to introduce new cross-media advertising approaches.

The initial growth of Internet advertising was mostly driven by the growth in search advertising, which was simple to use, accessible to all, and low risk due to the pay-per-click (or cost-per-click) payment model. This offer also has clear limitations due to its format, and the traditional mass advertisers have not significantly shifted their budgets. However, the tipping point seems to be nearing. With the rise of video on demand, advertisers can create attractive clips and attach them to professional video content. More important, digital platform operators will be able to target advertisements much more precisely to individual households, both through the Internet and through TV broadcasting platforms, thus ensuring that the number of relevant viewers per advertisement slot goes up significantly. New measurement methods are being developed, which can measure much more precisely whether an advertisement has been viewed (e.g., with help from the set-top box) and what its impact was (e.g., through online consumer panels, measurement of page visits and clicking behavior, or even links with databases of retailers). Emerging online advertising sales networks can guarantee reach and frequencies similar to or larger than traditional media channels. Last but not least more and more digital media companies are offering performance-based payment models, which take the risk away from the advertiser.

It seems that the digital advertising ecosystem is finally getting organized and will be able to offer advertising opportunities that can guarantee a higher marketing return on investment than traditional media.

In order to defend their share of the advertising pie, traditional companies will have to find ways to offer not only reach but also better targeting and effect measurement. They will have to develop analytical skills to be able to place advertisements optimally across their media and develop performance-based pricing models.

New Digital Media Skills Will Have to Be Built

The developments described above have major implications for the way media companies are organized and the skills that are required in each department.

Traditionally most media companies, especially those in Europe, have been organized in a highly decentralized way. Profit centers were mostly organized per medium (TV, magazines, books, etc.) and within those divided per country. Each organization was fully self-sufficient and would often compete with its neighboring profit centers. This model worked very well in a market where little overlap between media existed and intimate local knowledge and networks were key to success. However, in the digital world these premises are challenged. On the one hand the benefits of individual profit centers are declining as demand becomes more cross-media and international, and on the other hand there is the strong need to significantly reduce cost. It becomes more and more ineffective to keep a large number of individual back offices and sales forces, and many media companies are already considering or are in the process of centralizing their back office functions and sales forces. Also the roles of the individual functions will have to change fundamentally.

Changing Role of the Content Creator: From Soloist to Director

In the analog world, the role of the content creators (journalists, authors, producers, etc.) had many similarities with that of a star musician—that is, their skills were centered on producing ("performing") pieces of content for one specific medium ("the instrument"). In the digital world their role is changing fundamentally and is becoming more one of a director of an orchestra or even of a "digital DJ" (see also Chris Bilton, in this volume). The content has to be produced in such a way it can be cascaded across different media ("multiple instruments"), and also the scope of content has to be redefined to include besides pictures, sounds, and words digital applications ("synthesizing"). Instead of producing just their own content or managing a few artists their role will increasingly become to find their way in an avalanche of content available, both professional and user generated, and select the right offering for the right audiences ("directing"). Also, instead of a one-way street, content creators will have to open up to their audiences and be willing to moderate two-way communication and thus create a new value-added product ("DJ-ing?").

The interesting question is whether these new roles can be performed by the same content creators from the old world or whether a new group of "digital creators" will emerge. Will the traditional "soloists" become more and more independent suppliers looking for places where there is demand for their individual pieces of content, be it through blogs or freelance contributions? The latest developments in the newspaper industry in the United States point to this direction; however, examples in Europe, for instance with Axel Springer AG in Germany (Aris & Bughin, 2009), show that it is also possible to transform many of the soloists into effective digital creators.

The Creation of the Ultimate Marketing Machine

Marketing will become the key to success for future media companies. With a much larger supply of content and no limitations on distribution, the name of the game will be to get the right content to the right consumer at the right time and when possible to create the critical mass to launch a blockbuster in a fragmenting world.

In traditional media companies marketing had a strong business-to-business (BtB) or mass-market focus. In the music industry the key influencers were the radio DJs and the large retailers, and shelf space and store promotions were also of key importance for books and magazines as was the channel position on cable networks for TV channels.

In a digital world where on-demand, interactivity, and universal access play a much more important role, media companies need to become highly sophisticated business-to-consumer (BtC) marketers. Their marketing task will be significantly more complex than that of even the most advanced fast-moving consumer goods companies, as media companies have many more products and many more channels to manage. They will have to identify segments along multiple dimensions (i.e., the type of content people like, how and when they would like to consume this content, and the willingness to pay) and also be able to match these segments to segments of advertisers, which will most likely become much more refined than the broad demographic segments currently used.

In addition media companies will need to become masters at customer relationship management as they no longer will be able to sell packages but only individual pieces of content. Getting the consumer to subscribe and cross- or up-selling pieces of content will become key to turn digital cents into digital dollars again. Music companies, which were hit first by the digitization, are already investing significantly in these skills, but increasingly other mass media companies like TV broadcasters are realizing the importance of consumer knowledge. An example of this is the "Canvas" initiative by ITV, the BBC, and British Telecom (BT), where ITV and the BBC plan to deliver linear and on-demand content to BT's IPTV offering for free in return for access to consumer data and the ability to target individual consumers with both their content and advertisements.

Without a doubt there will be significant overlaps between what the marketers do and the activities of the "digital creators" described above, and very close cooperation is needed.

Advertising Sales: From Relationships to Analytics _____

As advertising campaigns move to be more targeted, performance based, and cross-media, the role of the advertising sales force will change drastically. So far media companies have found it very hard to sell cross-media offerings, mostly due to organizational barriers (see Figure 23.1).

The risk media companies run when they do not address these barriers actively is that they will be bypassed by new entrants that offer simple performance-based "self-service" advertising solutions (as Google, for example, is offering not only with its AdSense model for Web sites but also in its joint venture with NBC Universal cable networks, in which advertisers can use an

Figure 23.1 The Main Problems in Selling Cross-Media Campaigns Effectively Seen by Industry Experts Are Related to Organizational and Cultural Issues as Well as Experience

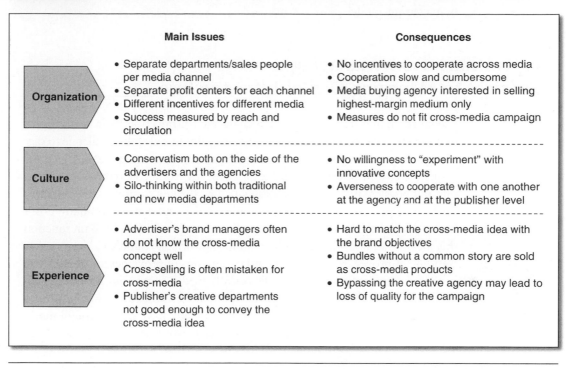

	Main Issues	Consequences
Organization	• Separate departments/sales people per media channel • Separate profit centers for each channel • Different incentives for different media • Success measured by reach and circulation	• No incentives to cooperate across media • Cooperation slow and cumbersome • Media buying agency interested in selling highest-margin medium only • Measures do not fit cross-media campaign
Culture	• Conservatism both on the side of the advertisers and the agencies • Silo-thinking within both traditional and new media departments	• No willingness to "experiment" with innovative concepts • Averseness to cooperate with one another at the agency and at the publisher level
Experience	• Advertiser's brand managers often do not know the cross-media concept well • Cross-selling is often mistaken for cross-media • Publisher's creative departments not good enough to convey the cross-media idea	• Hard to match the cross-media idea with the brand objectives • Bundles without a common story are sold as cross-media products • Bypassing the creative agency may lead to loss of quality for the campaign

Source: McBroom (2009, Exhibit 5). Used with permission.

online interface to bid for TV time directly). Media companies face the choice to become the supplier of pieces of commodity inventory to intermediaries (ad agencies, platform operators that directly interact with the consumer), or they can try to stay in the driver's seat by offering integrated solutions themselves. For this to work, they will have to let go of traditional per-medium measurement as well as "viewership"-based payment models and move to payment models that are based on overall impact of the campaign independent of the medium, whereby impact can vary based on the marketing goals of the advertiser (brand awareness, sympathy, sales, etc.). Several media companies are already actively experimenting with more performance-based payment models also for traditional media.

For this approach to work, the companies need to have a deep understanding of the effectiveness of their media—that is, how to combine media in order to get an optimal engagement, which target groups of advertisers are being reached by what content (beyond the usual demographics), how to measure the impact efficiently (e.g., Internet panels), and the right pricing models. For this sophisticated econometric an analytical model is needed, supported by the right information-technology (IT) infrastructure. The transition needed has similarities to the change process that took place in the airline industry as it transitioned from "selling seats" to sophisticated yield management models.

Operations: From Managing Physical to Managing Digital Infrastructure

Media companies face not only the challenge to transition their current production processes to fully digitized process chains but also the challenge to digitize their archives, which can be a costly and cumbersome process. Given the enormous cost pressure on media companies, structural cost reductions by cutting out physical production processes will be the key to success. At the same time, most processes will require a fundamental redesign to optimally profit from the potential benefits digitization can offer. For the supply chain function this means that not only technology and IT knowledge but also a deep understanding of process reengineering and continuous improvement processes will become increasingly important. Historically media companies have not been very focused on these types of activities, and media companies might have to hire managers from other industries, which already have gone through major restructuring, in order to bring in the necessary expertise.

Overall Organizational Structure: From Decentralized Profit Centers to Open Networks

In a fully digitized media world an integrated approach will be needed across media, functions, and countries (see also Mark Deuze and Leopoldina Fortunati, in this volume). New skills have to be built across the whole organization such as use of digital media, customer relationship management, and customer insights. Within the individual profit centers there will not be enough critical mass to build these skills, and coordination between profit centers will be time-consuming and most likely ineffective. For this reason media companies will have to look for new organizational designs. History has learned that a top-down centralized approach with forced synergies does not work well, as too many things are happening at the front line. More likely a mix of solutions will have to be found, in which some functions will be centralized, some will remain fully decentralized, others will be coordinated in a matrix-like structure, and quite a few activities will be connected through open networks, where not only employees from the companies but also many "outside experts" work together. This "messy" approach will feel uncomfortable at first, as the contrast with tightly run, independent profit centers will be large; however, when the revolution does not come from the inside, it will come from the outside, and slow movers are most likely to be overtaken by new players who know how to play according to the new rules.

When and How to Create the "Digital" Media Organization

For many of the developments described above, the timing is still highly uncertain. Some events might occur at a much faster pace than currently expected; others will happen only the day after tomorrow. The big challenge for traditional media companies is thus to know when and how they should prepare their organizations for the new roles and skills needed in the digital world. This is not a new question for media companies; already since the "first" Internet wave, which started in the late '90s, they have been experimenting with ways to best change their organizations. So far three phases can be distinguished—a top-down conglomeration approach, a fragmented online versus offline approach, and a more or less integrationist approach— which I will discuss below.

Phase 1: The Top-Down Approach: Creating the World's Leading "Multimedia Content Machines"

This period lasted from the late '90s until the collapse of the first Internet hype in the early 2000s. Key protagonists were major media conglomerates such as Time Warner, Bertelsmann, and Vivendi. Inspired by the fast growth of the first-wave Internet giants, such as AOL, Yahoo!, and Amazon, the leaders of these companies decided to force-speed their companies into the digital era by investing heavily in promising Internet players as well as launching a multitude of individual Web sites. At the same time they strongly believed that they could create a competitive advantage over the pure Internet players by creating cross-media synergies between their various content divisions and their Internet activities. The organizations were shaken up as a large number of "new economy" people were brought in and profit centers were told to work closely together (e.g., by forming synergy committees) and chief content officers were appointed. In addition, major acquisitions were made, such as the takeover of Time Warner by AOL and the acquisition spree of Vivendi around the world, all for the belief that this would lead to additional synergies.

As the Internet bubble collapsed, so did these strategies. The cause was not only the financial overextension due to overpriced acquisitions and unrealistic expectations with regard to the development of Internet advertising markets but also significant internal resistance against radical changes in a world where traditional media still brought over 90% of revenue. In addition, the top-down synergy expectations turned out to be highly unrealistic; in many cases there was little overlap between the audiences of the individual media properties, and thus there were very limited true synergies. Although directionally right, these strategies failed because they were implemented too early (many of the developments on which they were built are only taking place now) and too fast for the organizations to be able to absorb. As a result, around 2002 these strategies were discontinued, management was exchanged, many Internet activities stopped, and companies reverted back to their previous ways.

Phase 2: Separation of Online and Offline Activities

The second phase, which lasted from 2002 until approximately 2004–2005, was mostly characterized by retrenchment; most media companies had burned their fingers badly and discontinued most of their Internet activities with the exception of a few modest Web sites that accompanied their print titles or TV channels. The group of people managing these Web sites was a separate entity from the main media as was the online advertising sales force. Primacy was clearly with the traditional media. On the consumer side, however, Internet usage kept growing at a faster pace as predicted, in spite of the economic collapse. During this period several Internet startups built online positions that would make them the winners later on. A clear example of this is the online classified market: Most newspapers missed out on this market as they were hesitant to cannibalize their print classifieds, which gave companies like Monster and the Scout24 Group in Germany the opportunity to build leading and highly profitable positions. To the extent that media companies still dared to invest in the digital world, this was mostly done through a careful venture capital approach, in which a separate entity would invest in promising startups, albeit keeping the amount of funds limited. The startups would be kept separate from the organization so that they would not be squashed by the much more powerful traditional media.

Phase 3: Careful Buildup of Integrated Functions

As broadband penetration proceeded at a much higher speed than expected and companies like Google showed tremendous success, also in the advertising world, traditional media companies started to realize that they could no longer afford to keep their traditional businesses separate from the digital world and that more substantial digital investments were needed. This change in attitude started around 2004–2005.

Besides a few large digital acquisitions, such as MySpace by News Corporation and Bebo by AOL, media companies also started to change their internal structures: More and more newspaper companies launched so-called integrated newsrooms where journalists would produce both offline and online and increasingly also video content. Advertising sales forces were kept separate for a longer time, but by 2008–2009 several media companies, such as Axel Springer in Germany, had started to integrate their on- and offline sales forces across media, in order to be able to offer attractive cross-media packages and new types of offerings (see Figure 23.2).

Figure 23.2	Axel Springer's Cross-Media Products Create Additional Value Through a Second Branding

Axel Springer's Cross-Media Innovations

- The **"Volks-Produkt"** initiative of Bild
  - Every other week promotion of another mass product that fits to the audience of Bild
  - Additional branding as "Volks-Produkt" generates a lot of value
  - So far very successful campaign with huge impact on sales
- The **"Welt-Klasse"** and **"Welt-Premiere"** initiatives of the Welt Group
  - Only done for premium products fitting to the Welt
  - Again additional value created through branding of the products as "Welt-Klasse" or "Welt-Premiere"
- All three initiatives only involve Springer's own media channels plus in-store promotions
- Directly driven by Axel Springer without much involvement of media agencies

Examples of the Campaigns

Dieminger, May 2009, Axel Springer

Source: McBroom (2009, Exhibit 28). Used with permission.

Accelerated by the economic crises, more and more media companies are also starting to centralize many of their back-office functions, partly to save on costs but also to cater to the larger need for integration in the digital world.

The Next Phase: Skill-Based Networks?

Although media companies are edging toward a digital organization, the focus so far has been mostly on adaptations of the organizational structure, and few have started to invest seriously in the skill building needed to address the digital challenges (and opportunities).

A few companies, such as EMI under the ownership of Terra Firma, are trying more radical approaches by centralizing key functions such as marketing, production, distribution, and back office and bringing in experienced management from outside the industry to manage these functions and bring in new skills. Whether this approach will be successful is still to be seen, as of course organizational resistance is also significant.

What, then, can media companies do to ensure that a critical mass of new skills is built in time for the "digital wave"? The answer will unfortunately be messy. Parts of the organization, especially those related to development of digital businesses and sophisticated marketing and advertising effectiveness modeling, will have to be concentrated more so that top talent can be attracted and good ideas can be rolled out quickly. New talent will have to be brought in from other industries, which are ahead in terms of the skills described above, and will have to be given enough leverage to function effectively within the organization. Win-win alliances will have to be built with other players in the industry, such as cable and telecom operators and mobile manufacturers, which have complementary skills, and traditional animosities will have to be buried. Part of the innovations will still be coming from the outside, and media companies will have to learn to function in open networks where outside talent can contribute easily and get rewarded fairly.

Developing a creative strategy around which skills to build when and how will be key for media companies to survive the transition to the digital world. In an environment as uncertain as the current one, the main driver of success will be to have the right skills in-house to react quickly as circumstances change. History has shown that top-down approaches do not work, and the key constituencies of the organization will have to be involved in this process. Involving the creatives too will be key, as they are not only essential to the success of any media company but, as experience has shown, they will also be able to come up with creative solutions for the skill-building process, which can be much more effective than those from the business side.

A rocky but exciting journey lies ahead, and media companies will have to be prepared to rethink their basic premises without at the same time destroying their creative strengths.

References

Aris, A., & Bughin, J. (2009). The Welt Group, creating new business models for news provision. In A. Aris & J. Bughin (Eds.), *Managing media companies: Harnessing creative value* (2nd ed., pp. 38–56). Hoboken, NJ: Wiley.

McBroom, N. (2009, June.). *Improving the success of cross media campaigns.* INSEAD MBA project. Berlin, Germany: Axel Springer.

24 Urgent Aphorisms

NOTES ON ORGANIZED NETWORKS FOR THE CONNECTED MULTITUDES

Geert Lovink and Ned Rossiter

Four Stages of Web 2.0 Culture: Use. Modify. Distribute. Ignore.

—Johan Sjerpstra

In between the blog posting and the tweet there is the aphorism, a centuries-old literary form that should do well among creative media workers. Zipped knowledge of the 21st century.

Already for 18th-century German experimental physicist and man of letters Georg Christoph Lichtenberg (1853/2000), there was an impossibility for knowledge to capture the totality of things: "It is a question in arts and sciences whether a *best* is possible beyond which our understanding cannot go" (p. 3). The answer to Twittermania is not the thousand-page magnum opus. Today, in a techno-culture where the link never ends, there is a need to give pause to thought. This is the work of the aphorism. As Karl Kraus (1986) states, "An aphorism doesn't have to be true. The aphorism should outstrip the truth, surpassing it in one sentence." This text is dedicated to the creative workers, migrants, vagabonds, activists, and intellectuals of this world: Abandon the state, create multiple expressive forms, engage in transborder relations (affective, intellectual, social, political), and invent new institutional forms!

Where to situate the study of network cultures? It hovers between a public form of mass informality and hard-core techno-determinism. The social noise we see scrolling down our screens is a waste product of techno-settings in which our sweet entries are situated. Interface is king, with the consequence that real techno-aesthetic intervention increasingly becomes a lost archive in the history of network cultures.

In retrospect the techno-determinism proposed by Friedrich Kittler (1999) remained an unfinished project. Kittler's post-1968 German media theory has not gone through many alterations since the early 1990s. The once bold statement "media determine our situation" does not shock anyone these days and has become an empty phrase. The media a priori are so obvious that they seem to have drifted into the realm of the collective unconscious. Henceforth no Kittler school. The grown-up Kittler-Jugend are dedicated to scattered projects on the margins of academia. People once again obsess over their small careers and seem to have forgotten the primal energy that collective imagination can unleash. New generations read German media theory with interest but simply no longer have the time to read the necessary libraries to fully enjoy the details. Kittler himself abandoned contemporary techno-analysis and retired in imaginary Old Greece. How can there be a critique when such a position itself is still obscure and on the brink of disappearing? One starts to sympathize with the programmer geeks when techno-determinism is sublimated by the highly attractive commercial sheen of Web 2.0.

Why network? We ought to ask this question. Why is the network, this empty signifier, the emerging-becoming-dominant paradigm of our age? Most of us will grow into network(ing) like children grow in and out of clothes. It takes some time to realize that we dedicate fixed periods of the day to the social-technical networks that are out there without factoring it in. Networking and communicating through e-mail, chats, Twitter, and social networking sites are technological forms of daydreaming, a sphere we enter into and then come out of. The dreamtime in the techno-cloud could be compared to the siesta at the village square or chats in the local bar. It is time dedicated to the social. What we get out of it is diffuse and impossible to quantify.

Why organize(d) networks? Ever since we launched this concept in 2005 we have seen organized networks (or orgnets) as just one of many possibilities (Lovink, 2007; Rossiter, 2006). But if the tendency is that networks, over time, will simply have to become more structured, then why bother? Long live techno-social determinism. The orgnet question should be precluded with why we still talk about organization in an era that seems to celebrate looseness and noncommitment. The Organization Man as originally proposed by William H. Whyte (1956) is alive and well to this day. He did not disappear with the so-called end of industrialism. In fact, his powers have multiplied even if his mind and soul are no longer exclusively beholden to the demands of The Organization. Today, The Organization Man has moved beyond that institutional terrain and penetrated the life of networks. Everyone is Organizing. Such was the great master plan of the "organizational complex" (Martin, 2003). Cooked up as a Cold War dream to extend the military-industrial complex into the realms of aesthetics and technology, the organizational complex fused the modulation of patterns from the Bauhaus School with the cybernetic programming of control. "Media organize." This Marshall McLuhan–inspired maxim by Reinhold Martin truncates even further Friedrich Kittler's (1999) earlier synthesis that "media determine our situation," the key difference being the organizing capacity of communications media, which carry with them The Organization Man Updated. This leaves us with the question: Are we The Organization Men? Wouldn't it be great to deconstruct the very .org concept to pieces in order to get rid of it, once and for all? Is not there behind any call to organize a desire to restore the über-organism once called tribe, church, society, or nation-state?

Not all online group initiatives work. Many fail. So can orgnets. The failure of a network is, however, not entirely without some work. There is a labor involved with failure. So we are using the notion of work in a different sense. We wish to invoke the idea of sustainability as a core feature of the work of networks. Failure is all too often the common result of fragile conditions and the fragments of demands placed on those involved in building and guiding the network. Social dust is a necessary precondition of the will to scale.

We are here to stay. The sustainability issue is a highly political one. Once a network becomes sustainable it addresses the problem of time, which tends not to be the default of networks. More often networks are about the dimension of space—quite frequently, they are transnational in orientation. The material property of spatially distributed social-technical relations that are forever being remade through the logic of connection and speed provides sufficient grounds for distraction from the problem of time understood as the experiential condition of duration. This was the analysis of Canadian communications theorist and political economist Harold Innis (1951, 1986), whose writings in the late 1940s and early '50s sought to address how it was that ancient civilizations rise and fall due to the spatial or temporal bias of their communications media and transport systems. The biases of our time are known to all but ignored by even more.

There ain't no time, only overtime. The political aspect of networks is closely associated with the sustainability of time. The annoying network is the one that lasts the test of time and refuses to disappear. Networks as technoversity are connected to develop a diverse range of standards, practices, modes of governance, and techno-social relations. They collectively produce their own idioms of knowledge, one platform or system distinct from the next, all predicated on the will to communicate. The technoversity of networks is not simply about distribution across space but about maintaining lines of differentiation over time.

The realization of the social is no longer possible outside an understanding of the constitutive power of technologies. There is no pure social realm. The social is inseparable from the technology. We speak of healthy bodies and populations, but what is the healthy techno-social body? Why are fluidity and transformation such celebrated values these days? How can we design the care of the self for a social-technical network?

With so much real concern around ecological futures, how come there is so little concern within networks of techno-social futures? The net-cultural preoccupation with immediacy works against both the histories of the present and the present conditions of the future. Network cultures have their own distinct apparatus of capture: Respond, now! To cleave out time from the work of networks requires a certain act of refusal through the practice of delay, or, if you happen to be a member of the techno-economic elite, you simply log off. But these are not options for the networked masses. How, then, to reinvent a politics of autonomy in the time of networks? Such work requires new modalities of organization whose ambition is singular: conspire to invent new institutional forms.

Networks are not renowned for their managerial efficiency. Indeed, the very term *management* is one that makes many within networks actively hostile, and they recoil with deep distaste. Networks are more inclined toward antiauthoritarian tendencies. They "unmanage" their cultural formation with little interest in purpose-driven performance indicators and procedural guidelines. And it is no wonder they do this. Such practices are embedded in the highly dysfunctional audit cultures of dominant institutions. Networks are not goal driven. They are galvanized around shared issues and the production of passions and the cultivation of clouds. The network blurs all purpose. That is why we wish to raise the question of management in terms of organization. There can be no successful managerial science for networks. Please listen, once and for all, you brothers and sisters in consultancy land. Shy away from top-down decisions and impulses driven by regulatory *ressentiment*. Information-technology administrators belong in that category—their burning ambition is to ensure that networks never work.

Organized networks are best understood as new institutional forms whose social-technical dynamics are immanent to the culture of networks. Orgnets are partly conditioned by the crisis and, in many instances, failure of primary institutions of modernity (unions, firms, universities, the state) to address contemporary social, political, and economic problems in a postbroadcast era of digital culture and society. In this sense, organized networks belong to the era and prevailing conditions associated with postmodernity. Organized networks emphasize horizontal, mobile, distributed, and decentralized modes of relation. A culture of openness, sharing, and project-based forms of activity is a key characteristic of organized networks. In this respect, organized networks are informed by the rise of open-source software movements. Relationships among the majority of participants in organized networks are frequently experienced as fragmented and ephemeral. Often without formal rules, membership fees, or stable sources of income, many participants have loose ties with a range of networks.

The above characteristics inevitably lead to the challenge of governance and sustainability for networks. It is at this point that networks start to become organized. With a focus on the strategic dimension of governance, organized networks signal a point of departure from the short-termism and temporary political interventions of tactical media. At first glance orgnets are a natural, almost inevitable development of the network society as described by Manuel Castells (1996). Yet nothing is "natural" in virtual environments. Everything needs to be constructed. And if so, under whose guidance? Who sets the very terms under which networks will cultivate their roots into society? Will this process of institutionalization have a (built-in) financial component?

As a political concept, organized networks provide what urban theorist Saskia Sassen (2006) calls an analytical tool with which to describe "the political" as it manifests within network societies and information economies. The social-technical antagonisms that underscore the political of organized networks are instantiated in the conflicts network cultures have with vertical systems of control: intellectual property regimes, system administrators, alpha males, a tendency toward nontransparency, and a general lack of accountability.

How to rebuild labor organizations in the network society? This was one of the many unrealized ambitions of the anti- and later alter-globalization movements. And, for the most part, the unions never quite realized that life and labor within a digital paradigm had become the norm. Let us sketch out some of the current conditions challenging political organization within network societies. First, we need to problematize the concept of labor when understood as some kind of coherent, distinct entity. We know well that labor in fact is internally contradictory and holds multiple, differential registers that refuse easy connection (gender, class, ethnicity, age, mode of work, etc.). This is the problem of organization. How to "organize the unorganizables" (to borrow from the title of Florian Schneider's 2002 documentary film)? Second, we need to question the border between labor and life—contemporary biopolitics has rendered this border indistinct. Techniques of governance now interpenetrate all aspects of life as it is put to work and made productive. The result? No longer can we separate public from private, and this has massive implications for how we consider political organization today. What, in other words, is the space of political organization? Paolo Virno (2004), for instance, speaks of a "non-state public sphere." But where, precisely is this sphere? All too often it seems networked, and nowhere. This is the trap of virtuality, understood in its general sense. Of course there can be fantastic instances of political organization that remain exclusively at the level of the virtual, which is the territory of today's "infowars." Here, we find the continued fight over the society of the spectacle. Yet the problem of materiality nonetheless persists and indeed becomes more urgent, as the ecological crisis makes all too clear (although this too is a contest of political agendas played out within the symbolic sphere).

Slogans 'R' Us * T-shirt label: Made for Asia * Today Your Friend, Tomorrow the World * Book title: "Stimulus and Indifference" * Praise Exodus—Blast Decay * Support My Exit * "Children of the Deconstruction" * The Institution is the Message * Project: Deleting Europe * I Joined the barcamp on anticyclic resistance and all I got is this lousy USB stick * ethics is moral punk * Romantic Mobility * Silicon Friends™ * The Art of Attack (3 days intensive) * Post-Exotic: The Boring Other as Kulturideal * Buy More Consume Less * 'Networking is Great to Waste Time Before Dying' * Rejected EU proposal: "Dialectics of Innovation—Creative Warfare in the Age of the Relaxed Crisis"

There are benefits in adopting a combinatory analytical and methodological approach that brings the virtual dimension of organization together with a material situation. This may take the form of an event or a meeting, workshops, publishing activities, field research, urban experiments, migrant support centers, or media laboratories—there are many possibilities. In Italy, Uninomade and the media-activist network and social center ESC are good examples of what we are talking about here. Sarai Media Lab in Delhi, India, would be another. In the instance of bringing many capacities together around a common problem or field of interest we begin to see the development of a new institutional form. These institutions are networked, certainly, and far from the static culture and normative regimes of the brick-and-mortar institutions of the modern era—unions, firms, universities, states. Their mobile, ephemeral nature is both a strength and a weakness. The invention of new institutional forms that emerge within the process of organizing networks is absolutely central to the rebuilding of labor organizations within contemporary settings. Such developments should not be seen as a burden or something that closes down the spontaneity, freedom, and culture of sharing and participation that we enjoy so much within social networks. As translation devices, these new institutions facilitate trans-institutional connections. In this connection we find multiple antagonisms; indeed such connections make visible new territories of the political.

Reading Russell Jacoby's *The Last Intellectuals: American Culture in the Age of Academe* (1987) two decades after it was written makes you wonder how such an independent study would look like, post–Cold War, post-9/11, in the age of the Internet and globalization. Jacoby's description of the "impoverishment of public culture" (p. ix) has not come to a halt. No dialectical turn here. As predicted, the figure of the public intellectual has disappeared. As Jacoby stated, "intellectuals no longer need or want a larger audience; they are almost exclusively professors who situate themselves within fields and disciplines" (p. 6). The nonacademic intellectuals, an endangered species in the 1980s, have vanished for good. The academics who replaced the general intellectuals created "insular societies." There is a widespread fear here of the "single-minded men." But are we really living in the Age of the Expert? It is not the expert knowledge that has become the dominant voice in the media age. Instead, we have witnessed the rise of the celebrity, and the "celebrification" of all spheres of (mediated) life. The professional is hiding inside the walls of the office culture. Instead of a Triumph of the Professional we witness the *Cult of the Amateur* (Keen, 2007), neither of them claiming any of the virtues of the General Intellectual. Nothing in Jacoby's study points at the appearance of citizen journalism, convergence culture (Henry Jenkins), and the decline of professional work due to the rise of free content found in free newspapers and through the Internet. Yesterday's public intellectuals of mass media were not exactly unpaid fellow travelers. What would Jacoby's strategy be after the "de-monetarization" of the media markets?

Communication conditions the possibility of new political organizations. We could say that "the political" of network societies comprises the tension between horizontal modes of communication and vertical regimes of control. Just think of the ongoing battles between Internet and intellectual property regulators such as WIPO (the World Intellectual Property Organization) and pirate networks of software, music, or film distribution. Collaborative constitution emerges precisely in the instance of confrontation. In this sense, the horizontal and vertical axes of communication are not separate or opposed but mutually constitutive. How to manage or deal with these two axes of communication is often a source of tension within networks. Here, we are talking about models of governance, without universal ideals to draw on. More often than not, networks adopt a trial-and-error approach to governance. It is better to recognize that governance is not a dirty word but one that is internal to the logic and protocols of self-organization.

The "participation economy" of Web 2.0 is underscored by a great tension between the "free labor" (Terranova, 2004) of cooperation that defines social networks and its appropriation by firms and companies. How is the "wealth of networks" (Benkler, 2006) to be protected from exploitation? Unions, in their industrial form, functioned to protect workers against exploitation and represent their right to fair and decent working conditions. But what happens when leisure activity becomes a form of profit generation for companies? Popular social networking sites such as Facebook, MySpace, Bebo, Delicious, and the data trails we leave with Google function as informational gold mines for the owners of these sites. Advertising space and, more important, the sale of aggregated data are the staples of the participation economy. No longer can the union appeal to the subjugated, oppressed experience of workers when users voluntarily submit information and make no demands for a share of profits. Nonetheless, we are starting to see some changes on this front as users become increasingly aware of their productive capacities and can quickly abandon a social networking site in the same manner in which they initially swarmed toward it. Companies, then, are vulnerable to the roaming tastes of the networked masses whose cooperative labor determines their wealth. This cooperative labor constitutes a form of power that has the potential to be mobilized in political ways yet so rarely is. Perhaps that will change before too long. Certainly, the production of this type of political subjectivity is preferable to the pretty revolting culture of "shareholder democracy" that has come to define political expression for the neoliberal citizen.

The precarity debate was, correctly, about the material conditions of labor and life (see also Rosalind Gill, Keith Randle, Susan Christopherson, and Aphra Kerr, in this volume). Mistakenly, the precarity discourse remained fixated on the rearview mirror of Fordist production and the welfare state. But there is more to precarity than this. Judith Butler wished to extend the term to include emotional states and affective relations. Yet somehow precarity doesn't satisfactorily capture the intensity—and dullness—of the contemporary soul. What comes closer is the image of the nervous, electric body in the late 19th and early 20th centuries as diagnosed in sociological accounts of urban transformation. The image of digital disembodiment was perhaps a 1990s attempt to update the electric body, but nowadays such a notion just looks sadly comical and misplaced, which brings us back to the materiality of communication vis-à-vis Kittler (1999). Today we have not so much digital disembodiment but the violence of code that penetrates the brain and the body. It is the normality of difference, sending out constant semiotic vibrations, that numbs us. What the precarity meme doesn't catch is the cool frenzy. There is an aesthetics of uncertainty at work. An impulse to *Just Do It!* Extreme Sports. Risk Societies. Financial Derivatives. Creative Classes. Porn Stars. Game Cultures. Today, it seems impossible to escape the network paradigm that is always economically productive, even if it never returns the user a buck. The nonremunerated body remains a body in labor. And it is increasingly exhausted. The brain encounters the limits of the day and everything that is left uncompleted. The endless task of chores ticked off slide over from one day to the next. One becomes tired by looking at the "to-do" list, which reproduces like a nasty virus. Bring on the remix.

The shift from Fordist modes of assembly production to post-Fordist modes of flexibilization cannot be accounted for by reference alone to capital's demands for enhanced efficiency through restructuring and rescaling. The 1970s in Italy saw the rise of *operaismo* (autonomist workerism), where workers refused the erosion of life by the demands of wage labor. Importantly, their unique refusal of labor demonstrates, in theory, a clear capacity of workers to change the practices of capital, for better and worse. The Italian collective strike is a one-off concept workshop, blending the radical with the general. It is in this power of transformation that the common is created (unlike so many other struggles and forms of dissent in Europe). The ongoing challenge remains how to organize that potentiality in ways that produce subjectivities that can open a better life—in Italy and beyond.

Workfare, flexicurity, or "commonfare"—all of these options are variations on the theme of state intervention that is able to supply a relative security to the otherwise uncertainty of labor and life. Such calls are misguided. They presuppose that somehow the state resides outside of market fluctuations and the precarity of capital. The state is coextensive with capital. The 2008 credit crisis has shown the state has little command over the uncertainties of finance capital. How, then, can the state guarantee stability? Furthermore, to whom does the state offer security? Certainly not to undocumented migrants. The call for flexicurity is a regressive, nostalgic move that holds dangerous implications vis-à-vis the formation of zones of exclusion. There is no pleasure principle in being underpaid. The price of freedom is a high one, and it is only a handful of lucky outsiders in the Rest of the West who can afford to work for free, enjoying unemployment while living off a small income. It is a secret lifestyle choice for a diminishing elite of cultural conceptualists and their outsourced army of semiotic producers. This is not what the dreams of the multitudes aspire to realize. There is much political value in targeting not the state but the companies—especially those engaged in the Web 2.0 economy—and insisting on a distribution of income commensurate with the collective labor that defines the participation economy. This may be a more effective strategy for broadening the constitutive range of labor organizations.

If social movements were serious about addressing the economic conditions of workers and engaging the complexities of the political, they would put an end to the mistaken faith in the state as the source of guarantees. Moreover, the logic of the state as a provider of welfare is special to Europe—it does not translate to the situations of workers in many Asian countries, for example. So what are the borders of connection among workers? Does the movement simply reproduce the borders of the European Union? Or does it engage in the much harder but no less necessary work of transnational connection? If so, then targeting the state does not especially help facilitate a common territory of organization. The global circuits of capital are where radical politics should focus their attention. But global capital is in no way uniform in its effects, techniques of management, or accumulative regimes. Political intervention, in other words, must always be situated while traversing a range of scales: social-subjective, institutional, geocultural. The movement of relations (social, political, economic) across and within this complex field of forces comprises the practical work of translation. Translation is the art of differential connection and constitutes the common from which new institutional forms may arise.

Practices of collaborative constitution are defined by struggle. There is no escape from struggle and the tensions that accompany collaborative relations. This is the territory of the political—a space of antagonism that in our view is much more complicated than just a friend-enemy distinction. Again, it is the work of translation that reveals the multiplicity of tensions. As Naoki Sakai (1997, 2006) and Jon Solomon (2007) have written, translation is not about linguistic equivalence or cofiguration but rather about the production of singularities through relational encounters. But let's get more concrete here. What is a relational encounter? It occurs through the instance of working or being with others—of sharing, producing, creating, or listening. Sustaining a range of idioms of experience is a struggle in itself—one that is rarely continuous but rather continually remade and reassembled. This in turn is the recombinatory space and time of new institutions.

Let us unpack the idea of new institutions and their relation to precarity. If we say that precarity and flexibility are the common condition—one that traverses class and geocultural scales—then we can ask what the situation is within which precarity expresses itself. The situation (concept + problem) will define the emergence of a new institution. Situation, here, consists of virtual or networked, material, affective, linguistic, and social registers. We are of course always in a situation, but how to connect with others? The point of connection brings about tensions—the space of the political—and the ensemble of relations furnishes expression with its contours. Real power lies not in the spectacle of the event but rather subsists within the resonance of experience and the minor connections and practices that occur before and after the event. That is the time and space of institution formation. The rest is a public declaration of existence.

The question of organization persists: Who does it? How is organization organized? For Keller Easterling (2005), this is the role of the orgman, the one who—without a "frontier enthusiasm"—"designs the software for new games of spatial production. . . . The coordinates of this software are measured not in latitude and longitude but in the orgman argot of acronyms and stats—in annual days of sunshine, ocean temperatures, flight distances, runway noise restrictions, the time needed for a round of golf, time needed for a shopping spree, TEUs [20-foot-equivalent units], layovers, number of passengers, bandwidth, time zones, and labor costs" (p. 1).

The orgmen of networks, then, share something with the alpha males and sysops (system operators). Both administer behaviors in symbolic or technical ways, shaping patterns of relation. Indeed, the software architecture used by any network is its own orgman. Organized networks would do well to diversify their platforms of communication, adopting a range of software options to enable the multiplication of expression and distribute as much as possible the delegation of network governance. If one platform starts to fall flat—say a mailing list—then perhaps the collective blog is going to appeal to more. Whenever the collective labor of a network can be galvanized around forms of coproduction (making an online journal, organizing an event, setting up a file-distribution system, producing a documentary, identifying future directions, staging a hack, designing slogans), then the life of the network finds that it has a life. Such techniques of collaborative constitution keep in check the proto-fascistic tendencies of the orgman that lurks within every network. The tension between these two registers of network sociality is a necessary dynamic. The challenge is to keep the game in play, gradually shifting the limits of the network disposition.

If we were to reinvent cybernetics (as an organizing logic of recombination, feedback, noise, etc.), outside the military-industrial context of the Cold War, what would it be? First of all, it would no longer be obsessed with biology and bio-metaphors. The aim of computer networks is not to mimic the human by copying or improving human features such as the brain, memory, senses, and extensions. The question of agency and the relation between humans and nonhumans, as thematized by, for example, Bruno Latour and the actor-network theory crowd, is a typical remainder of the cybernetics 1.0 era (see also Liz McFall, in this volume). In the past cybernetics tried to figure out how to connect the individual (human) body to the machine. It presumes we still have an issue with "intelligent machines." The cybernetic 1.0 age was both worried and drawn to the idea that the human can(not) be replaced by thinking machines. The result of this was a decades-long irrelevant debate over artificial intelligence (AI). These days no one is concerned if and when the machines take over. Have you ever been scared by the idea that a computer can and will beat you at chess? Sure it can, but so what? We know Big Brother is storing all the information in the world. AI is here to stay but is no longer a key project in technology research. Whereas cybernetics 1.0 tried to schematize human behavior in order to simulate it through models, cybernetics 2.0 is concerned with the truly messy, all too human, social complexity. We are not ants. We are more and behave as less. Our understanding has to go beyond the boring mirror dynamic of man and machine. Computer science will have to make the leap into interhuman relations in the same way as humans are adapting to the limits set by computer interfaces and architectures. Stop the mimicry procedures and restart computer science itself.

According to Martin (2003),

> What counts is not the size of the basic components (such as neurons, which are similar in humans and ants) but their organization, which determines the "absolute size" of the organization's nervous system—its upper limit of growth and index of social advancement. An organism's social potential, conceived in terms of its ability to organize into complex communication networks, is thus measured as a function of the size of its internal circulatory and communications system, which is a function, in turn, of their own organizational complexity. The original analogy between the social and biological organism is thus collapsed, as the two become directly linked as part of the same network. . . . A relational logic of flexible connection replaces a mechanical logic of rigid compartmentalization, and the decisive organizational factor is no longer the vertical subordination of parts to the whole but rather the degree to which the connections permit, regulate, and respond to the informational flows in all directions. (p. 23)

What are the limits of potentiality for the organized network? While impossible to answer in terms of content (every network has its own special attributes), we can say something here about form. Form furnishes the contours of expression as it subsists within the social-technical dynamics of digital media. How these relations coalesce as distinct networks situated within and against broader geopolitical forces becomes a primary challenge for networks desiring scalar transformation—a movement that also consists of trans-institutional, disciplinary, subjective, and corporeal relations whose antagonisms define the multiple registers of the political. The question of limits takes us to the transcalar practice of transversality—the production of multiple connections that move across a range of social, geocultural, and institutional settings. There are also strategic questions: Who do you collaborate with? How local are you? Are you willing to deal with the cynical professionals of traditional media? Do you believe in meme power, viral marketing, and subliminal dissemination with the chance of hitting the zeitgeist lottery, or in the hard work of political campaigning?

Collaboration is always accompanied by conflict and struggle. This is a matter of degree. And there'll be plenty of exhilaration that keeps the momentum going. But tensions will always be present. Better to work out an approach to deal with this; otherwise you'll find your projects go kaput!

References

Benkler, Y. (2006). *The wealth of networks: How social production transforms markets and freedom.* New Haven, CT: Yale University Press.

Castells, M. (1996). *The rise of the network society.* Cambridge, MA: Blackwell.

Easterling, K. (2005). *Enduring innocence: Global architecture and its political masquerades.* Cambridge, MA: MIT Press.

Innis, H. A. (1951). *The bias of communication.* Toronto, ON, Canada: University of Toronto Press.

Innis, H. A. (1986). *Empire and communications.* Victoria, BC, Canada: Press Porcépic.

Jacoby, R. (1987). *The last intellectual: American culture in the age of academe.* New York, NY: Basic Books.

Keen, A. (2007). *The cult of the amateur: How today's Internet is killing our culture.* New York, NY: Doubleday.

Kittler, F. (1999). *Gramophone, film, typewriter* (G. Winthrop-Young & M. Wutz, Trans.). Palo Alto, CA: Stanford University Press.

Kraus, K. (1986). *Aphorismen. Sprüche und widersprüche. Pro domo et mundo. Nachts.* Frankfurt, Germany: Suhrkamp.

Lichtenberg, G. C. (2000). *The waste books* (R. J. Hollingdale, Trans.). New York: New York Review of Books. (Original work published in 1853)

Lovink, G. (2007). *Zero comments: Blogging and critical Internet culture.* London, England: Routledge.

Martin, R. (2003). *The organizational complex: Architecture, media and corporate space.* Cambridge, MA: MIT Press.

Neilson, B., & Rossiter, N. (2008). Precarity as a political concept, or, Fordism as exception. *Theory, Culture & Society, 25*(7/8), 51–72.

Rossiter, N. (2006). *Organized networks: Media theory, creative labour, new institutions.* Rotterdam, The Netherlands: NAi Publishers.

Sakai, N. (1997). *Translation and subjectivity: On "Japan" and cultural nationalism.* Minneapolis: University of Minnesota Press.

Sakai, N. (2006). Translation. *Theory, Culture & Society, 23*(2/3), 71–86.

Sassen, S. (2006). *Territory, authority, rights: From medieval to global assemblages.* Princeton, NJ: Princeton University Press.

Schneider, F. (2002). Organizing the unorganizables. *WASTUN 2.0.* Retrieved from http://wastun.org/v2v/Organizing_the_Unorganizable

Solomon, J. (2007). *Translation, violence and the heterolingual intimacy.* EIPCP paper. Retrieved from http://translate.eipcp.net/transversal/1107/solomon/en

Terranova, T. (2004). *Network culture: Politics for the information age.* London, England: Pluto Press.

Virno, P. (2004). *A grammar of the multitude* (J. Cascaito, I. Bertoletti, & A. Casson, Trans.). New York, NY: Semiotext(e). Retrieved from http://www.generation-online.org/c/fcmultitude3.htm

Whyte, W. H. (1956). *The organization man.* New York, NY: Simon & Schuster.

Index _____

About the Editor _____

Mark Deuze (Weblog: http://deuze.blogspot.com; e-mail: mdeuze@indiana .edu) holds a joint appointment at Indiana University's Department of Telecommunications in Bloomington (United States) and as a professor of journalism and new media at Leiden University in The Netherlands. His published work comprises seven books—including *Media Work* (Polity Press, 2007) and *Media Life* (Polity Press, 2011)—and articles in journals such as the *International Journal of Cultural Studies*, *New Media & Society*, and the *Journal of Media Sociology*.

About the
Contributors _____

Annet Aris is an adjunct professor of strategy at INSEAD in Fontainebleau, France, where she developed and teaches the MBA course Managing Media Companies. She is also a guest professor at, among other schools, the Rotterdam School of Management. She is a board member of OPTA, the Dutch regulatory authorities for telecom, cable, and postal services, and of the Sanoma Group in Helsinki, Finland, a leading European magazine and educational publisher. She worked for McKinsey from 1985 until 2003 and led McKinsey's German Media Practice from 1999 to 2003. Together with Jacques Bughin, she wrote the book *Managing Media Companies, Harnessing Creative Value* (2nd ed., Wiley, 2009).

Chris Bilton is director of the Centre for Cultural Policy Studies at the University of Warwick in the United Kingdom. His attempt to bridge the gap between management and creativity developed out of teaching master's students Creative and Media Enterprises, a course he set up in 1999. He also lectures at Warwick Business School. His latest book, *Creative Strategy: Reconnecting Business and Innovation* (Wiley, 2010), coauthored with Steve Cummings, argues that strategy is (or should be) a creative process and sets out a framework for applying creative thinking to innovation, entrepreneurship, leadership, and organization.

Pablo J. Boczkowski (PhD, Science and Technology Studies, Cornell University, 2001) is an associate professor in the Department of Communication Studies at Northwestern University (United States). His research program interrogates core concepts in social theory by examining cultural processes and formations made particularly visible in the transition from print to digital media. His publications include the award-winning *Digitizing the News: Innovation in Online Newspapers* (MIT Press, 2004), *News at Work: Imitation in an Age of Information Abundance* (University of Chicago Press, 2010), and articles in journals and edited volumes. His current book project, tentatively titled *After the News,* is an account of how institutions decay.

Susan Christopherson is the J. Thomas Clark Professor in the Department of City and Regional Planning at Cornell University (United States). She is an economic geographer whose research focuses on (a) economic development, (b) labor flexibility, and (c) service industries, particularly the media industries. Her recent book, *Remaking Regional Economies: Power, Labor, and Firm Strategies in the Knowledge Economy*, was awarded the 2009 Best Book Award by the Regional Studies Association. She has written over 50 articles and 25 policy reports on topics in economic geography and economic development and media studies.

Charles H. Davis holds the Edward S. Rogers Sr. Chair in Media Management and Entrepreneurship and is a professor in the School of Radio and Television Arts (Faculty of Communication & Design) and in the Entrepreneurship and Strategy Department of the Ted Rogers School of Management at Ryerson University in Toronto, Canada, where he teaches courses in media management and political economy. He works in the area of innovation management and policy, and his current research interests have to do with innovation and entrepreneurship in the media and experience industries.

Terry Flew is a professor of media and communications in the Creative Industries Faculty at the Queensland University of Technology in Brisbane, Australia. He is the author of *New Media: An Introduction* (3rd ed., Oxford, 2008), *Understanding Global Media* (Palgrave, 2007), and *The Creative Industries, Culture and Policy* (Sage, 2011). He has a wide range of research interests and research experience; has been an author of eight research monographs, 28 book chapters, and 48 refereed academic journal articles; and has been an editor of nine special issues of academic journals and refereed conference proceedings. He has been a chief investigator in the Australian Research Council (ARC) Centre of Excellence for Creative Industries and Innovation, the ARC Cultural Research Network, and the Smart Services Cooperative Research Centre. He has led research projects on citizen journalism and "creative suburbia" and was part of a team researching the rise of creative industries in China. In 2009–2010, he was president of the Australian and New Zealand Communication Association (ANZCA).

Leopoldina Fortunati is a professor of sociology of communication at the Faculty of Education of Italy's University of Udine. She is the author and editor of many books, including (with Jane Vincent) *Electronic Emotion: The Mediation of Emotion via Information and Communication Technologies* (Peter Lang, 2009). She is very active at the European level and is the Italian representative in the COST (European Cooperation in Science and Technology) Domain Committee ISCH (Individuals, Societies, Cultures and Health). She is associate editor of the journal *The Information Society*. She is the cochair with Richard Ling of the international association Society for the Social Study of Mobile Communication (SSSMC). Her works have been published in 11 languages: Bulgarian, Chinese, English, French, German, Italian, Japanese, Korean, Russian, Slovenian, and Spanish.

Rosalind Gill is a professor of social and cultural analysis in the Centre for Culture, Media and Creative Industries at King's College London (United Kingdom). She is author of *Gender and the Media* (Polity Press, 2007) and coeditor (with Keith Grint) of *The Gender-Technology Relation* (Taylor & Francis, 1995) and (with Róisín Ryan-Flood) of *Secrecy and Silence in the Research Process* (Sage, 2009). She is continuing to do research in two main fields: cultural and creative labor and mediated intimacy.

Chris Hackley is a professor of marketing in the School of Management at Royal Holloway University of London (United Kingdom). His recent work includes *Marketing—A Critical Introduction* (Sage, 2009); *Advertising* (Sage, 2009), a three-volume edited collection of key papers; and the second edition of his text *Advertising and Promotion: An Integrated Marketing Communications Approach* (Sage, 2010).

Eric Harvey is a PhD candidate at Indiana University (United States) in the departments of Communication & Culture and Ethnomusicology. His dissertation explores the impact of new media networks on indie music rituals. He is also an author and reviewer for the online music magazine *Pitchfork*.

Aphra Kerr is a lecturer in the Department of Sociology at the National University of Ireland, Maynooth. She has been researching the regulation, production, and consumption of digital games for the past 10 years. Her recent book publications include *The Business and Culture of Digital Games* (Sage, 2006), and she has authored a number of journal articles related to digital media, innovation, cultural diversity, and gender. Kerr is a committee member of Women in Games (Europe), and she runs the community and industry Web site http://www.gamedevelopers.ie. Further information can be found at http://sociology.nuim.ie/AphraKerr.shtml.

Dean Kruckeberg, APR, Fellow PRSA (Public Relations Society of America), is director of the Center for Global Public Relations and a professor at the University of North Carolina at Charlotte. He is coauthor (with Kenneth Starck) of *Public Relations and Community: A Reconstructed Theory* (Praeger, 1988) and is coauthor (with Doug Newsom and Judy Turk) of *This Is PR: The Realities of Public Relations* (10th ed., Wadsworth, 2010). He was the 1995 national "Outstanding Educator" of PRSA, was awarded the Jackson Jackson & Wagner Behavioral Research Prize in 2006, and was the 1997 recipient of the Pathfinder Award. Kruckeberg is cochair of the Commission on Public Relations Education. He is a frequent lecturer worldwide.

Lucy Küng is an associate professor at the Media Management and Transformation Centre at the University of Jönköping in Sweden, a senior research fellow at Ashridge Business School in the United Kingdom, and an adjunct faculty member at the University of St. Gallen in Switzerland. She is a member of the supervisory board of the Swiss public service broadcasting corporation, SRG SSR idée suisse, and president of the European Media

Management Association. In addition to many articles and cases, Küng is the author of *Strategic Management in the Media: Theory to Practice* (Sage, 2008), *The Internet and the Mass Media* (Sage, 2008), and *Inside the BBC and CNN: Managing Media Organisations* (Routledge, 2000). Küng holds a habilitation and PhD from the University of St. Gallen.

Geert Lovink is a Dutch-Australian media theorist and critic. He is a research professor at the Hogeschool van Amsterdam (The Netherlands), where he is founding director of the Institute of Network Cultures, and associate professor in media studies (new media) at the University of Amsterdam. Lovink is author of numerous books, including *Dark Fiber* (MIT Press, 2002), *My First Recession* (NAi Publishers, 2003), and *Zero Comments* (Routledge, 2007). His new book, *The Will to Network* (2010), investigates the rise of "popular hermeneutics" inside Web 2.0, large-scale (yet invisible) comment cultures, and the shifting position of new media (studies) inside the humanities. For more information see http://www.networkcultures.org.

Tim Marjoribanks is the T. R. Ashworth Senior Lecturer in Sociology in the School of Social and Political Sciences at the University of Melbourne in Australia. His media research focuses on issues relating to organizational management, journalism practice, and media representations of race and nation. His work has been published in journals including *Journalism Practice*, *Journal of Sociology*, and *Australian Journalism Review*. He coedited a special issue of *Journalism* in 2009 with Mark Deuze on newswork, and Cambridge University Press published his book *News Corporation, Technology and the Workplace: Global Strategies, Local Change* (2000).

Liz McFall is a senior lecturer in sociology at the Open University (United Kingdom). Her interests center on economic life with particular emphasis on the historical formation of markets especially through advertising and other promotional practices. She is the author of *Advertising: A Cultural Economy* (Sage, 2004), is the coeditor with Paul du Gay and Simon Carter of *Conduct: Sociology and Social Worlds* (Manchester University Press, 2008), and has written a number of articles exploring 19th- and early-20th-century life assurance, promotional, and market devices.

Bozena I. Mierzejewska is a postdoc researcher at the Institute for Media and Communications Management at the University of St. Gallen in Switzerland. Her research and teaching interests focus on media management and issues of digitalization within media sectors. Currently she serves as coeditor of JMM—*The International Journal on Media Management*—one of the leading journals of the field.

Toby Miller is a professor of media and cultural studies at the University of California at Riverside. His teaching and research cover the media, sports, labor, gender, race, citizenship, politics, and cultural policy. Miller is the author and editor of over 30 volumes and has published essays in well over 100 journals and books. His current research covers the success of Hollywood overseas, the links between culture and citizenship, anti-Americanism, and electronic waste. His latest books are *Makeover Nation: The United States of Reinvention* (Ohio State University Press, 2008), *The Contemporary Hollywood Reader* (Routledge, 2009), and *Television Studies: The Basics* (Routledge, 2010).

Philip M. Napoli (PhD, Northwestern University) is a professor of communications and media management in the Graduate School of Business at Fordham University in New York City, as well as director of Fordham's Donald McGannon Communication Research Center. His research focuses on media institutions and media policy. He is the author of the books *Audience Economics: Media Institutions and the Audience Marketplace* (Columbia University Press, 2003), *Foundations of Communications Policy: Principles and Process in the Regulation of Electronic Media* (Hampton Press, 2001), and *Audience Evolution: New Technologies and the Transformation of Media Audiences* (Columbia University Press, in press). He has testified before Congress and the Federal Communications Commission on media policy issues. His work has been supported by organizations such as the Ford Foundation, the National Association of Broadcasters, and the Social Science Research Council.

Sean Nixon is a senior lecturer in the Department of Sociology at the University of Essex (United Kingdom) and author of *Hard Looks: Masculinities, Spectatorship and Contemporary Consumption* (UCL Press and St. Martin's Press, 1996) and *Advertising Cultures: Gender, Commerce, Creativity* (Sage, 2003). He is currently completing a study of advertising and postwar social change titled *Ad Men: Advertising, Affluence and Social Change.*

Alisa Perren is an assistant professor in the Department of Communication at Georgia State University (United States). She is coeditor of *Media Industries: History, Theory, and Method* (Blackwell, 2009), and her work has appeared in a range of publications, including *Film Quarterly*, *Journal of Film and Video*, and *The Sage Handbook of Media Studies*.

Keith Randle is a Professor of Work and Organization and Director of Research and Consultancy at the University of Hertfordshire Business School in the United Kingdom, where he also leads the Centre for Research on Management, Economy and Society (CRoMES). In 1988 he established the Film Industry Research Group (FIRG) in the School jointly with Nigel Culkin and subsequently the Creative Industries Research and Consultancy Unit (CIRCU). His research interests are predominantly in the management and the employment experience of knowledge workers, especially those in the creative industries.

Ned Rossiter is an Australian media theorist and an associate professor of network cultures at the University of Nottingham in Ningbo, China, and an adjunct senior research fellow at the Centre for Cultural Research at the University of Western Sydney in Australia. He is author of *Organized Networks: Media Theory, Creative Labour, New Institutions* (NAi